The Complete Idiot's Re

Handy Telephone Directory of Resources for Making Money After You Retire

Administration on Aging	202-245-0742
American Association of Home-Based Businesses	800-447-9710
American Association of Retired Persons (AARP)	202-434-2277
American Bar Association	312-988-5000
American Institute of Certified Public Accountants (AICPA)	201-938-6000
Association of Part-Time Professionals	703-734-7975
Choice in Dying Inc.	800-989-WILL
Continental Airlines (Freedom Certificate booklets for seniors)	800-441-1135
Department of Housing and Urban Development, Housing Counseling Clearinghouse (listing of reverse mortgage lenders)	800-217-6970
DISCOVER (cash back credit card)	800-DISCOVER
Dun & Bradstreet	800-234-3867
Equal Employment Opportunity Commission (EEOC)	800-USA-EEOC
Federal Trade Commission, Division of Marketing Practices	202-326-3128
Gartner Group Learning (senior discounts for CDs and videos on computers)	800-925-2665
Gateway Mastercard (credit toward Gateway purchases)	800-847-7378
Home Business Institute (insurance for home businesses)	914-946-6600
Home Office Association of America	800-809-4622
Hostelling International-American Youth Hostels	202-783-6161
Hulbert Financial Digest (rating service of financial newsletters)	888-HULBERT
Independent Business Alliance (insurance for home businesses)	800-450-2422
Independent Computer Consultants Association	800-774-4222
Institute of Certified Financial Planners	800-282-7526
Internal Revenue Service (IRS)	800-829-1040
International Association of Financial Planners	404-395-1605
International Franchise Association	202-628-8000
Job Training Partnership Act programs	202-393-6226
Macmillan (senior discounts for books)	800-882-8583
National Academy of Elder Law Attorneys	602-881-4005
National Association for the Self-Employed (NASE)	800-232-NASE
National Association of Computer Consultant Businesses (NACCB)	800-313-1920
National Association of Personal Financial Advisors	888-333-6659
National Council on the Aging	202-479-1200
National Fraud Information Center	800-876-7060
QuickBooks	800-4INTUIT
Quotesmith (phone quotes on life insurance)	800-431-1147
Senior Community Service Employment Programs (SCSEPs)	Call your state office on aging
Shell MasterCard (cash back credit card)	800-993-8111
Small Business Administration	800-827-5722
Small Office Home Office Association	800-SOHOA11
Social Security Administration	800-772-1213
Veterans Administration	800-827-8954
Wealthy & Wise (portfolio review by phone)	800-275-2272
Wholesale Insurance Network	800-808-5810

alpha
books

Handy Telephone Directory of Resources for Making Money After You Retire

4 Work	http://www.4work.com
Administration on Aging	http://www.aoa.hdhs.gov
American Association of Retired Persons (AARP)	http://www.aarp.org
America's Job Bank	http://www.ajb.dni.us
Best Jobs USA	http://www.bestjobsusa.com
Career City	http://www.careercity.com
Career magazine	http://www.careermag.com
Career Mosaic	http://www.careermosaic.com
Career Path	http://www.careerpath.com
Careers OnLine	http://www.careersonline.com
CNBC (financial news)	http://www.cnbc.com
E-Span	http://www.espan.com
Fidelity Mutual Funds (information about funds, news, and commentary)	http://www.fidelity.com
Hot Jobs	http://www.hotjobs.com
IEEE Employment	http://www.ieee.org/jobs.html
Intellimatch	http://www.intellimatch.com
Internal Revenue Service (IRS)	http://www.irs.ustreas.gov
International Home Based Business	http://www.getbuzy.com
InterNetWork Marketing	http://www.he.net/~image/nwm/
Job Bank USA	http://www.jobbankusa.com
Job Trak	http://www.jobtrak.com
Job Web	http://www.jobweb.com
MedSearch America	http://www.medsearch.com
Merrill Lynch (on-line investment information)	http://www.merrillynch.com
Monster Board	http://www.monster.com
Morningstar (information about mutual funds)	http://www.morningstar.com
Multi Level Marketing Yellow Pages	http://www.bestmall.com/mall
Nation Job Network	http://www.nationjob.com
National Business Exchange	http://www.director.net/nexis-lexis/sba
Network Marketing Mall	http://www.network-marketing.com/ nmm/nmm.htm
Network Marketing Yellow Pages	http://www.network-marketing.com/ nmyp.htm
Online Career Center	http://www.occ.com
Profit$ Online magazine	http://www.profitsonline.com
Quicken Cash Finder (business loans)	http://www.cashfinder.com
Quotesmith (on-line quotes on life insurance	http://www.quotesmith.com
SeniorNet (articles and info for seniors)	http://www.seniornet.com
Small Business Administration	http://www.sbaonline.sba.gov
Social Security Administration	http://www.ssa.gov
T. Rowe Price Mutual Funds (information about retirement planning, and so on)	http://www.troweprice.com
The Street (mutual fund information)	http://www.thestreet.com
Third Age (senior information)	http://www.thirdage.com
TOPjobs USA	http://www.topjob.com
Trade shows nationwide	http://www.tscentral.com

COMPLETE IDIOT'S GUIDE® TO

Making Money After You Retire

by Barbara Weltman

alpha
books

A Division of Macmillan General Reference
A Simon & Schuster Macmillan Company
1633 Broadway, New York, NY 10019-6785

To my colleagues who make working a joy: Sidney Kess, Elliott Eiss, David Ellis, and Sherry Eisner

©1998 by Barbara Weltman

THE COMPLETE IDIOT'S GUIDE name and design are trademarks of Prentice Hall, Inc.

Macmillan Publishing books may be purchased for business or sales promotional use. For information please write: Special Markets Department, Macmillan Publishing USA, 1633 Broadway, New York, NY 10019.

International Standard Book Number: 0-02-862410-6
Library of Congress Catalog Card Number: 98-85130

00 99 98   8 7 6 5 4 3 2 1

Interpretation of the printing code: the rightmost number of the first series of numbers is the year of the book's printing; the rightmost number of the second series of numbers is the number of the book's printing. For example, a printing code of 98-1 shows that the first printing occurred in 1998.

Printed in the United States of America

Alpha Development Team

Publisher
Kathy Nebenhaus

Editorial Director
Gary M. Krebs

Managing Editor
Bob Shuman

Marketing Brand Manager
Felice Primeau

Senior Editor
Nancy Mikhail

Development Editors
Phil Kitchel
Jennifer Perillo
Amy Zavatto

Editorial Assistant
Maureen Horn

Production Team

Development Editor
Nancy Warner

Production Editor
Kristi Hart

Copy Editor
Anne Owen

Cover Designer
Mike Freeland

Photo Editor
Richard H. Fox

Illustrator
Jody P. Schaeffer

Designer
Glenn Larsen

Indexer
Chris Barrick

Layout/Proofreading
Angela Calvert
Pamela Woolf

Contents at a Glance

Contents

Foreword

At a recent dinner party in Hollywood, comedienne Phyllis Diller asked me a startling, irreverent question: "Art, would you like to know how to make God laugh?" I replied in some confusion, "Not really, I'm a Baptist and we take Him very seriously." She giggled and said, "On the off chance that you'll meet him, here's the answer: *Tell him your plans for the future!*" That's funny. And, of course, very true.

Because life *is* what happens to you while you're making *other* plans. And that's especially true before you're 50.

After 50, life is what will happen to you if you *didn't* make plans for your postretirement years. That can be scary.

When I appeared in 1912, the average child born that year could expect to live to be 46 or 47. So the "later" years were brief. Today, on average, we have been given an extra *30* years, and we had better realize that it is imperative to plan for them. How do we live between, let's say 60 and 80?

First, of course, comes planning for healthy years, which involves not smoking, moderate drinking, a low-fat diet, regular exercise, a good night's sleep, a good breakfast, and positive thinking.

And a close second is *financial* good health.

I discovered this while doing research for my national bestseller, *Old Age Is Not For Sissies*. My extensive interviews with seniors revealed to my surprise that "Independence" is the number one concern about life in general after retirement. No one wants to be a burden on their children. No one wants to be scraping along on charity, or government hand-outs. And, of course, most of us realize now that you can't live on Social Security alone.

That's why this book is a *must* read. It answers nagging questions about how much we've prepared for postretirement.

Get it. Read it. And then *do something* about it.

—Art Linkletter

Introduction

When the Social Security Act was created in the mid-1930s, the retirement age when benefits would be paid was pegged at 65 (the same age as today). Yet, believe it or not, the average life expectancy at that time was just 63! Yep, the government thought that most workers wouldn't live long enough to collect a penny on their retirement contributions. In fact, the very idea of retirement was a concept for the fortunate few. Most people simply died before they could retire.

Well, advances in health and science have changed all of that. People as a rule don't die at 65 anymore. Many retire at or around that age. Others continue to work well past that age.

Today, 65 isn't old; in fact, it's practically middle age. Many people today spend as many years in retirement as they did while working.

If you're like most of us, you probably worked for your entire adult life. You've put in long hours and can remember those days when you felt sick as a dog but dragged yourself to work anyway. At those times, you looked longingly to the time when you'd be able to retire. Maybe you pictured yourself sitting on a beach reading a book or just lying back on the couch doing nothing more exciting than putting your feet up, clasping your hands behind your head, and staring into space. Well, that time of retirement is here at last.

But your expectations for retirement may have fallen short of those daydreams in several ways. After a lifetime of activity, you may have found out that you're not the kind who can just sit around doing nothing. You long to get back in the thick of things. Or maybe the financial demands of your life—paying the mortgage; sending your kids to college; paying for their weddings; taking vacations; or meeting unexpected fiscal crunches from job layoffs, uninsured property damage, investments gone bad, or high medical bills—have left you a little short on retirement income. That pile of money you planned on setting aside for retirement just never materialized.

There's no time like now to size up where you stand and get started on making some money in your retirement. Maybe it's time to start a second (or third) career to utilize your talents. Or perhaps you need to examine your finances to squeeze some extra cash from your resources. Or it might just be that you want to do a little of both: work *and* maximize your investment and pension income.

Well, I'm here to help you achieve your objectives. There are many ways to approach your goal of having enough retirement income so that you don't have to worry. Only you can decide, after reading through this book, which way or ways is best for you.

How to Use This Book

There are currently almost 44 million people receiving Social Security benefits. If you're one of them, or about to become one of them, maybe you've already accepted the fact that the monthly Social Security check is not enough to live on. If you're not a Rockefeller with a trust fund or an inheritance to live on, you need more than Social Security benefits to make your retirement a financially comfortable one. Okay, maybe you have a pension coming in as well. It, too, may not be enough to live on, at least in the style you're used to. What are you going to do? You've got several choices: Keep working in some way, shape, or form; get some extra dollars from your retirement savings; or find other ways to make it on the pot you've put together thus far.

This book will guide you, step by step, in mapping out a game plan for making money in your retirement. The information in this book will help you decide whether you want to return to work— full-time or part-time—start a business, or simply extract the most dollars from the resources you've already accumulated. It will also show you how to make your retirement dollars go further than you thought possible.

This book contains seven separate parts. Each part covers a different way in which you can make money in retirement and even have something left over to pass to your family when you die.

Part 1: Rating Your Postretirement Revenues lets you assess where you stand. You need to know what you've got before you can begin to build on that base. You'll gain an understanding of how much you'll need for the rest of your retirement years by factoring in your life expectancy and lifestyle. You'll get to total up all of your resources, from savings, pensions, Social Security benefits, and more. And you'll see how long your money can be expected to last.

Part 2: Remaining in the Rat Race…at Least a Little Longer gives you ideas on working after retirement. How can you be retired and work? It's easy. You can get a new job, or work part-time, or start your own business. The opportunities in the job market are there if you know your rights in the workplace. Or you may find you now have the time to launch a business idea you've been hatching for years. Either way, you'll want to know how to avoid losing even one dollar of your Social Security benefits.

Part 3: Making Your Investments Work for You shows you how to take what you've got and make it go further. Maybe the portfolio you put together when you were working isn't right for you now that you've retired. By re-arranging your investments, you can get more income. Perhaps you've got some nonproductive assets you can turn into money-makers. It's not as hard as it sounds if you know where to look.

Part 4: Pensions Plus tells you all about company retirement plans and IRAs and how to make the most of them in retirement. After all, you've put your money into them for years. Now it's time to reap what you've sowed. Make sure it'll go far enough to cover you comfortably throughout your retirement years. If you've just been given early retirement, know what to do *before* you take your pension. If you're married and about to retire, you need to be careful about the type of pension option you select. If you've got an IRA and haven't begun to tap into it, you'll want to understand the rules on taking distributions to avoid penalty, continue to build up your savings, and make your nest egg last as long as you do.

Part 5: Avoiding Catastrophe shows you how to avoid financial disaster. Many people in retirement are on fixed incomes. If you're one of them, you need to budget your spending so you don't get into a spending frenzy. You also want to avoid scams targeted at seniors so you don't lose your nest egg to fraud. And nothing can wipe you out financially more quickly than an accident, a chronic illness, or a serious disease. There's not much you can do to prevent these things from happening, but you can take steps now so that you won't lose your life savings should they befall you. You'll learn about long-term care insurance to protect you if your health fails. You'll find out about life insurance to protect your loved ones who may be relying on you. And you'll see how you can take legal steps so that it won't be necessary to involve the courts in your financial affairs should you become incapacitated.

Part 6: It Pays to Be Old gives you many ideas for saving money. A dollar saved means one less dollar you need to earn or receive in retirement benefits. Fortunately, you may be entitled to a number of different breaks just because of your age. See what discounts you may be eligible for. Understand how to get property tax reductions. And learn about special income tax breaks for seniors.

Part 7: Leaving Something to Your Heirs tells you what you need to know to pass your property on to your family or friends in the most effective way. You want things to go smoothly, and you want to keep the tax man's take to a minimum. You've got to know how to put your affairs in order. It's important to know why you need a will and what it should say. And there are many ways you can leave your property to others without costly and time-consuming probate. Or you might want to start passing on your property now, while you're alive, instead of waiting until you die.

Road Signs

As you travel through the pages of this book, you'll see special bits of information signified by little pictures to guide you. They'll give you a little extra help in navigating your way through the strategies for making money after you've retired.

Senior Info

This box is a catchall: It gives you interesting facts and figures on retirement and on making money at this point in your life.

Word to the Wise
Contains words and expressions on money matters that may be new or confusing to you.

Cash Crash
Warnings about things you should avoid if you want to stay out of money trouble.

Golden Years Ideas
Extra information that you can use—a phone number, Web site, or tip— that can help you do something better or easier.

Special Thanks From the Publisher to the Technical Reviewer

The Complete Idiot's Guide to Making Money After You Retire was reviewed by an expert who not only checked the technical accuracy of what you'll learn in this book, but also provided invaluable insight and suggestions. Our special thanks are extended to Dana Shilling.

Dana Shilling, a Brooklyn native who now lives in Jersey City, is a 1975 graduate of the Harvard Law School and a writer and speaker on topics of law and personal finance. She is the author or coauthor of about two dozen books, including *The 60-Minute Financial Planner*, published by Prentice-Hall, which is Macmillan's corporate sibling.

Acknowledgments

Thanks are due to many people, most of whom don't even know they've helped me. I'm talking about my clients, friends, and other people I've met throughout the years who've shared their retirement stories with me and given me ideas on how to make more retirement income. Special thanks go to my husband, Malcolm Katt, a stockbroker, who's read the financial chapters in this book and has offered some valuable suggestions to improve them. Thanks also to my friend, Elliott Eiss, editor of the *J.K. Lasser Tax Institute*, for reviewing the pension material in this book. And, finally, I'm grateful to my editor, Nancy Warner, who worked with me to fine-tune this book.

Part 1
Rating Your Postretirement Revenues

If your retirement years are stretching out before you in an endless sea, but you're afraid your financial boat may take on water, now is the time to do something. You can plug those holes, take on more supplies, or change your course so you won't sink.

In order to make any plans, you have to know where you stand. You need a good idea of what retirement means: how long it may last for you and how much income you'll need for that time. You need to take stock of what you have and don't have so you can see if you can meet those retirement income needs.

Retirement income is the key to a secure retirement. There are three main sources of retirement income: your personal savings, your pensions, and Social Security benefits. Adding up these sources will give you a good idea of where you stand and whether you need to make new plans.

Chapter 1

What's Enough?

In This Chapter

➤ Living long and prospering

➤ Knowing your expectations

➤ Adjusting expenses after retirement

➤ Calculating how long your money will last

So you've packed it in, quit the rat race, propped your feet up on the sofa, and are ready to begin retirement. There's just one thing nagging at you. Will your money last as long as you do? We're not fortune-tellers who can predict with any certainty how long you'll live. We can, however, make almost sure that however long that is, your money will still be there for you.

In this chapter, you'll learn how to make an estimate of how long you can expect to live (barring a car accident, avalanche, or other catastrophe no one can guess at). You need this estimate to make certain financial choices. You'll also explore your lifestyle and its impact on your life's savings. Finally, you'll find out how long money can be expected to last by using different "what ifs." In the next chapter, you'll find out how to total up your retirement income to know if it's enough to cover what you've decided you need.

How Long Will You Live?

If you could talk to the man upstairs and ask when you're going to die, would you want to know? Probably not. But in order to plan out your retirement finances and make sure you don't outlive your money, it's helpful to have some idea about your life expectancy.

Life expectancy is the first variable you'll need before you can decide if you've got enough money or if you need to make some more in order to have a secure retirement.

Playing the Odds

Life expectancy is something that has changed considerably over the years. The changes are due primarily to improvements in health care and medicine. For example, a child born in 1996 (the last year for which statistics exist) has a life expectancy of 76.1 years. This is 29 years *longer* than a child who was born in 1900.

But you weren't born yesterday. What's your life expectancy? It's different for men and women. A man who is 65 today can expect to live an additional 15.5 years. A women who is 65 can expect to live even longer, an additional 19.2 years. So if you're male and play the averages, you'd better plan to have your money last until you're over 80 years old. And, according to U.S. Census Bureau figures, a person who reached 65 in 1995 had a 41% probability of living to 90 or over!

The funny thing about life expectancy is that the longer you live, the longer your life expectancy becomes. No matter how old you are, you continue to have *some* life expectancy; centenarians (people at least 100 years old) have a life expectancy of 2.7 years. Every time you beat the odds (and live past your original life expectancy), the odds go up.

Life expectancy tables are based on insurance actuarial tables that are compiled over many years. But tables don't necessarily take into account your lifestyle. If you exercise regularly and eat a healthy diet, your life expectancy can extend. If you're a smoker, don't exercise, and eat fried foods and rich desserts, your life expectancy diminishes.

In determining your life expectancy, play it safe. Don't rely on the averages. Be conservative and add on a few years as a cushion for planning purposes. After all, a significant percentage of people now live into their 90s and beyond, and you might just be one of them.

> ### Senior Info
>
> The fastest growing segment of our population is the 85+ group. Today that age group makes up about 1.4% of the population. It's 31 times larger than it was at the start of this century. By the middle of the next century, the Census Bureau expects this age group to be nearly 5% of the population. The Social Security Administration lists about 66,000 people who are at least 100 years old. The White House sends out more than 50 birthday cards each day to those reaching their century milestone.

What's Up Your Family Tree?

Life expectancy statistics are based on averages. But you may not be average at all. Maybe your father, his father, and his grandfather all died of heart disease in their 60s. You can hope you take after your mother's side, medically speaking, but you can realistically assume that your life expectancy may be shorter than the average.

By the same token, if you're a woman and the women in your family have lived into their 90s, you too may yet become a nonagenarian (someone in her 90s).

Of course, just because my grandmother died of colon cancer doesn't mean I will, too. There's no certainty I'll get the disease even though there's a genetic propensity for it. But even if I do, advances in medicine, including early detection, mean that I stand a good chance of living longer than my grandmother did.

Do You Have Champagne or Ginger Ale Tastes?

How much retirement income is enough? The answer is not the same for everyone. It depends in part on your lifestyle. If you're used to living lavishly, you'd better be sure that your retirement money will continue to support that lifestyle. If you're content with living modestly, you also need to make sure that your funds will be enough.

To know if your money will be enough, you'd better find out how much you need and compare it with what you have.

What Did You Expect?

You've probably dreamt about retirement for a long time. Well now it's here. What did those dreams include? Were you out golfing at your country club? Were you traveling around the world?

Maybe these expectations are realistic, but maybe they're not. It depends on the money you've put aside until now (and how long that money needs to last).

Maybe your expectations were more modest. You simply want to have time to do what you didn't before, such as gardening, taking walks, spending time with your family. Money may not be an important factor in achieving your dreams.

Cash Crash

If you're married, make sure your dreams aren't a nightmare for your spouse. Maybe you always thought you'd move to a warm climate and a slower pace of life, but your spouse still plans to cross country ski from her backyard. The failure to consider your spouse's plans for retirement could become a costly mistake.

Now is the time to fine-tune your expectations so they coincide with your pocketbook. Make a budget of what you think you'll be spending each month in retirement and list this information in the following worksheet. If you're already retired, you know exactly what you're spending in retirement. Some items, of course, are paid once a year, so you'll have to break them down into a monthly amount for purposes of this budget (simply divide the annual cost by 12 to find your monthly amount). Even if you've never used a budget and don't think you could live with one, it's helpful to complete this exercise to know what income you'll need each month.

The "other" category is as broad as you need it to be. Maybe you have to continue providing some income to your children or grandchildren. Maybe you've gone back to school. Whatever your expenses, just make sure you're reasonably accurate in including them in this list.

Your anticipated retirement budget

Monthly Expenses	Cost
Housing (rent or mortgage, property taxes, utilities, homeowners' insurance, repairs)	$
Food and personal items	$
Medical expenses (including Medicare, supplemental Medicare insurance, long-term care insurance)	$
Clothing	$
Car and other transportation	$
Entertainment	$
Income taxes	$
Other	$
Total	$

Expenses You Can Kiss Goodbye

So now you know what it's costing you each month to live in retirement. Maybe you've noticed that something's missing. Now that you're retired, you're *not* spending certain money. You're not commuting to work. You're not paying Social Security and Medicare taxes on wages. You're not spending other money related to a job. This means you need less income because you no longer have to pay for these expenses.

Make a list of the expenses you no longer have to get an idea of the additional monthly funds you can spend in other ways (only some of the expenses in the chart may apply to you). In making your list, be sure to figure the expenses on a monthly basis and fill in the following worksheet.

Work-Related Expenses	Amount You're Saving
Commuting costs (train or bus fare; gas and tolls for car)	$
Lunches out	$
Social Security and Medicare taxes on earnings	$
Clothing for work	$
Dry cleaning of work clothes	$
House cleaner	$
Other	$
Total	$

What you can save by not *working*

(Of course, if you continue to work in your retirement years, even part-time, you'll continue to have some or all of these expenses.)

Another expense you need to take into account when you're no longer working is income taxes. Once you stop earning a wage, you'll save income tax on the earnings you used to pay taxes on. Yes, you'll probably still have income taxes to pay—on your pension and investment income. But you won't be paying income tax on your paycheck.

How Long Will Your Money Last?

Social Security benefits continue until you die. Certain company pensions also continue until you die. But

Golden Years Ideas
Some experts use this rule of thumb for deciding how much income you should expect to need in retirement compared with income during your working years: 75% of preretirement income. Of course, personal lifestyle can alter this figure considerably.

other sources of income may be less certain. They last as long as you let them. For example, if you take your company pension in a lump sum, then you control when and to the extent you'll receive benefits. You want to know how long you can expect your nest egg to last, given certain variables that we're about to discuss.

Word to the Wise
The *CPI (Consumer Price Index)* is a measurement figured by the federal government of an increase in the price of certain items. This CPI number is used by the government to figure the increase in Social Security benefits and to adjust the federal income tax brackets and other items each year.

The Certainty of Inflation and Taxes

There are two primary factors that affect how long your money will last. One is inflation, and the other is taxes. Both of these factors are a certainty you can't ignore.

Inflation means your retirement dollars will buy less, so you'll need more retirement dollars just to stay even. For example, let's say you've got a fixed retirement income of $25,000 a year. Inflation will eat into the buying power of that money in short order. Fixed income leaves you in a fix when it comes to inflation. You'll need to grow your retirement income just to keep pace with the ravages of inflation.

Senior Info
The historical rate of inflation measured by an increase in the CPI has averaged just over 3% a year since 1926. This means that the buying power of a dollar is cut in half after 12 years. It takes $2 to buy the same $1 loaf of bread that it did 12 years earlier. And should double-digit inflation like we had in the late '70s and early '80s ever return, buying power is cut even more rapidly.

Table 1.1 shows annual inflation for the past 25 years.

Table 1.1 Annual Inflation Rate Over the Past 25 Years

Year	Rate	Year	Rate	Year	Rate
1972	3.4%	1981	8.9%	1990	6.1%
1973	8.7%	1982	3.6%	1991	3.1%
1974	12.3%	1983	3.8%	1992	2.9%
1975	6.9%	1984	3.9%	1993	2.7%
1976	4.9%	1985	3.6%	1994	2.7%
1977	6.7%	1986	1.1%	1995	2.5%

Year	Rate	Year	Rate	Year	Rate
1978	9.0%	1987	4.4%	1996	3.3%
1979	13.3%	1988	4.4%	1997	1.7%
1980	12.5%	1989	4.6%		

Source: U.S. Bureau of Labor Statistics

Taxes affect what retirement money you have to spend. Depending on your sources of retirement income, some may be tax free (fully available for spending), while some may be taxable (you have only what's left after you've paid taxes on the income). For example, the $1,000 of interest you earn on municipal bonds is not subject to federal income tax, but the $1,000 of interest on Treasury bonds is federally taxable. If you're in the 28% federal income tax bracket, you'll have $1,000 of interest to spend from your municipal bond interest but only $720 ($1,000 interest less $280 taxes) of your Treasury bond interest. Of course, there may be state income tax on municipal bonds. In figuring the impact of federal income taxes on your retirement income, don't ignore the alternative minimum tax (AMT). AMT is designed to ensure that even high income taxpayers will pay at least some income tax. In actuality, the AMT can affect even middle-class people who claim certain deductions or credits or have certain types of income (such as private activity municipal bonds which are free from regular income tax but potentially subject to AMT).

To complicate matters, tax rates are not static. The rates have risen and fallen over the years. Currently, there are five regular income tax brackets: 15%, 28%, 31%, 36%, and 39.6%. (Different tax rates apply to capital gains, which are gains on the sale of stocks, bonds, and other property.) In the past, the top rate on ordinary income has been as high as 70% (in 1982) and as low as 28% (in 1988). Even the Commissioner of the Internal Revenue Service can't tell you where rates will be 5 or 10 years from now.

Arranging your investments to lower your taxes and boost your retirement income is discussed in Part 3.

Cash Crash
The government's CPI may not be a good indicator of your personal inflation index. The CPI, for example, may not mirror increases in the cost of your prescription drugs. Medical costs have increased more rapidly than the CPI. Therefore, your personal inflation index may be even higher, meaning that you want your income to keep up with your needs.

Cash Crash
In looking at the impact of taxes on your retirement income, don't ignore state income taxes. If you live in a state with an income tax, that cuts into your retirement income. You may even consider relocating to an income-tax-free state to avoid this incursion into your retirement income.

Senior Info

There is no state income tax in Alaska, Florida, Nevada, South Dakota, Texas, Washington, and Wyoming. However, Florida has an intangibles state tax that applies to your investment holdings. The intangibles tax doesn't apply to Florida municipal bonds (only to out-of-state municipal bonds).

Emptying Your Nest Egg

Suppose that you've saved up a chunk of money you plan to live off of in retirement. How long can you expect that fund to be there for you? It depends on three items:

➤ The size of your nest egg. How much money are we talking about? A few thousand dollars? A few million dollars? The larger the nest egg, the longer it's going to last because the more income it can produce (reducing the amount of the nest egg you need to deplete in addition to income).

➤ Your rate of return. How much will your savings fund earn each year? This may not be static. Some years you may earn 6%; other years you may earn 10%. It depends on where you have your funds invested. But to get some idea of how long your funds will last, you can *assume* a rate of return that will represent what you expect to average year in and year out. If you're very conservative, assume a modest return. If you're more comfortable with risk, assume a higher return.

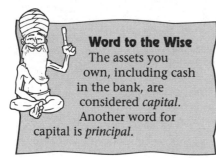

Word to the Wise
The assets you own, including cash in the bank, are considered *capital*. Another word for capital is *principal*.

➤ Your rate of withdrawal. How much of your capital do you need to spend each year, in addition to the income your capital produces? Obviously, this depends on what you've determined earlier in this chapter—your lifestyle. It also depends on your other sources of income (which we'll talk about in the next two chapters). It also depends on how long you'll live. And, finally, it depends on inflation: The higher the rate of inflation, the greater your need for income.

You can use Table 1.2 to see how long your nest egg will last as you empty it for your income needs.

Table 1.2   How Long Your Nest Egg Will Last

% of Capital Spent Each Yr	Rate of Return on Your Nest Egg				
	5%	6%	7%	8%	9%
5%	Forever	Forever	Forever	Forever	Forever
6%	35 yrs	Forever	Forever	Forever	Forever
7%	24 yrs	32 yrs	Forever	Forever	Forever
8%	19 yrs	22 yrs	30 yrs	Forever	Forever
9%	15 yrs	18 yrs	21 yrs	27 yrs	Forever
10%	13 yrs	14 yrs	16 yrs	20 yrs	25 yrs
11%	11 yrs	12 yrs	14 yrs	16 yrs	19 yrs
12%	10 yrs	11 yrs	12 yrs	13 yrs	15 yrs

So, for example, if you've saved $250,000 and it's earning 8%, you can take out $25,000 (10%), and your savings will last for 20 years. If you're 65, this is more than your life expectancy. In other words, you can take $25,000 each year for the rest of your life and not run out of money.

Of course, you can't count on dying in 20 years. You might live longer—considerably longer. In this case, you'd be out of luck if you'd spent all of your life's savings within 20 years. So you need to take a more conservative approach to spending. Some experts suggest adding at least five years to your life expectancy. You might even want to add more just to be safe.

And you might want to factor in the potential costs of needing to spend some time before you die in specialized housing, in a nursing home, or receiving special in-home care. All of these are costly. (Planning for long-term care is discussed in Chapter 19, "Planning for Long-term Health Care Needs.")

Golden Years Ideas
If you take only the interest and dividends you earn on your savings fund, you'll *never* touch a penny of your capital; it'll all be there for your spouse or children when you die (net of any estate or inheritance taxes on your savings fund).

Putting It All Together

The bottom line on deciding what's enough for your retirement depends on your personal profile: How long you can reasonably expect to live, how much do you spend, and how much money do you have (which you'll figure out in the next two chapters)?

If you're like most people, you've come up short. You don't have all the money you need to live in the way you'd like to now and for the rest of your life. Or maybe you're afraid that things you can't predict (bad health, natural disasters, changes in your family) may upset your best laid plans.

That's why you bought this book. It will help you figure out how to make money in retirement to supplement what you already have.

The Least You Need to Know

➤ Your life expectancy affects how much money you'll need to support you until you die.

➤ You may have to adjust the type of lifestyle you planned to have in retirement to match your budget.

➤ Inflation and taxes cut into your retirement income.

➤ If you touch only your interest and dividends on your investments, you'll *never* run out of money.

Chapter 2

Richer Than You Think?

In This Chapter

➤ Finding retirement income from many sources

➤ Turning a rainy day savings account into retirement income

➤ Receiving pensions monthly or taking payments at your discretion

➤ Getting Social Security benefits

➤ Figuring out what your monthly retirement income will be by charting your different sources of retirement income

Remember when you used to get a paycheck every Friday or on the 15th and 30th of each month? That was income you could count on. That was security. Well, the days of a steady paycheck are largely behind you. Now that you're retired, you have to arrange your own income. It may come from more than one source. It may be paid at irregular intervals. It may be larger some months than others. But if you set things up correctly, you'll have a stream of income you can count on to pay your bills and meet your needs.

In this chapter, you'll learn about the different sources of income you may have coming to you in retirement. You'll find out how to tally what you've got. You'll also see how you can organize your incoming cash so you can plan to pay your expenses.

Income, Income Everywhere

Now that you've retired, your income may come in several different forms. You may get returns on your personal savings. You may receive a pension or be able to take withdrawals from retirement accounts. You may be receiving (or entitled to receive) Social Security benefits. Each source, standing alone, may not seem like a whole lot of income. But put them together, and you may be surprised at how large your monthly income really is.

Retirement's Your Rainy Day

All those years you saved and saved, and for what? A rainy day. Well, here's that rainy day. Now you can begin to use your savings to give you retirement income. Instead of putting money *into* these investments, you can begin to take money *out* of these investments.

Table 2.1 lists some of the types of retirement income you may receive from your savings.

Table 2.1 Types of Retirement Income You May Receive

Type of Savings	Nature of Income
Bond mutual funds	Interest
Certificates of deposit (CDs)	Interest
Commercial annuities	Income
Common stock	Dividends
Corporate bonds	Interest
EE bonds	Interest (free from state tax)
401(k) plans	Income
Money market funds	Dividends
Municipal bonds	Interest (tax free)
Pensions	Income
Preferred stock	Dividends
Real estate investment trusts (REITs)	Dividends and/or capital gains
Regular IRAs	Income
Roth IRAs	Tax free if withdrawals taken 5 years after initial contribution and on account of being $59^1/_2$ or meeting other conditions
Savings accounts	Interest
Stock mutual funds	Dividends and/or capital gains

You don't get any income (or capital gains) when you're only getting back what you put in (called your basis or investment). So, for example, when you buy a commercial annuity, the only part that's income is over and above what you put in. Each annuity payment, then, represents a return of your own investment and income earned on the investment; you're taxed only on the income, not on your own investment.

In terms of what you have to spend, it doesn't really matter whether the income is labeled interest, dividends, or something else. However, it's important to know the label because this affects the tax treatment of the income. In the end, it's after-tax income (what you have left to spend after you've paid your taxes on the income) that matters.

For example, you live in New York and receive $1,000 interest from a GM bond and $1,000 interest from a NYS Triboro Bridge and Tunnel Authority. Are both payments equal? The answer is probably no. Let's say you're in the 28% federal income tax bracket. After paying tax on the GM bond, you'll have $720; however, there's no federal income tax on the NYS bond, so you'll have the entire $1,000 to keep. But don't also forget the impact of state taxes. States with an income tax typically levy it on out-of-state bonds but not on in-state bonds (in the preceding example, the NYS Triboro Bridge and Tunnel Authority bond was an in-state bond for a person living in New York). But state income tax applies to both in-state and out-of-state bonds in Colorado, Illinois, Iowa, Kansas, Oklahoma, and Wisconsin. No state income tax applies to in-state and out-of-state bonds in Indiana, North Dakota (if the state's short form is used), and Utah.

In addition to income on your savings, you can generate payments by using up your capital. For example, suppose that you've saved $50,000 that you've invested in CDs. As they become due, you can use some of the cash rather than buy new CDs (you can always tap into your CD before it matures, but you'll pay a bank penalty). You can spend this cash as retirement income. In Chapter 1, "What's Enough?" you saw how long your capital would last, depending on how much of it you used each year and what it was earning.

> **Golden Years Ideas**
> When you spend part of your savings account or CDs, you're not taxed on the amount of savings you use up. You've already paid tax on the money you used for your initial investment and the interest you've earned. So if you spend $10,000 when your CD comes due instead of buying a Treasury bill, new CD, or another type of investment, you aren't taxed on this amount. It's simply your own capital.

Pensions and IRAs

If you've worked for any length of time, you may have some type of pension or retirement money owed to you from your former company. In addition, you may also have saved on your own by contributing to an IRA. Now is the time you can tap into your retirement accounts to produce retirement income.

You're not *required* to begin taking money out of your retirement funds before age 70$\frac{1}{2}$, even if you're retired. (You don't have to take withdrawals from a Roth IRA at *any* time during your lifetime; unless you own more than 5% of the company, you don't have to take withdrawals from company retirement plans at any particular age if you're still working.) Money left in a retirement plan continues to earn money on a tax-deferred basis. You don't pay any tax on the earnings until you begin to take distributions. If you don't have an immediate need for money from your pension or IRA, leave it alone and let it continue to grow.

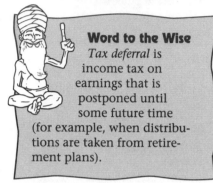

Word to the Wise
Tax deferral is income tax on earnings that is postponed until some future time (for example, when distributions are taken from retirement plans).

Cash Crash
You can't postpone distributions from your regular IRA beyond 70$\frac{1}{2}$ even if you're still working. You'll have to take minimum distributions from your IRA to avoid penalty. This is true even if the money in your IRA is a rollover of company pension plan benefits.

If you continue to work past retirement age, you can continue deferral of your pension. Your employer doesn't have to pay out your retirement plan account when you turn age 70$\frac{1}{2}$ (assuming you don't own more than 5% of the company). But this option for continued deferral applies only to retirement plans with your current employer. So, for example, if you used to work for Company X and earned a pension there, it will begin to be paid out when you reach 70$\frac{1}{2}$ even though you're still working for Company Y.

Starting in 1998, there's a new type of retirement savings plan, called a Roth IRA. While contributions aren't deductible, Roth IRAs offer the opportunity to earn tax-free income. You're not taxed on earnings if funds stay in the account at least 5 years after the contributions are made. If you make contributions to a Roth IRA, you don't have to take funds out at any particular time, regardless of your age or whether or not you've retired. So, for example, if you contribute to a Roth IRA in 1998, 1999, and 2000 when you're working, you don't have to take distributions even though you retire in 2001.

While 70$\frac{1}{2}$ generally means the end of tax deferral and the time when retirement plan distributions must begin, you can certainly take money out earlier. The only drawback is a 10% penalty if you begin withdrawals before age 59$\frac{1}{2}$ and you're not eligible for an exception to the penalty. You can tap your IRA penalty-free for the following reasons:

➤ You're disabled.

➤ You take the money out in a series of payments that are figured under one of several annuity-like methods.

➤ You use the funds to pay medical expenses exceeding 7.5% of your adjusted gross income (even if you don't itemize your deductions).

➤ You use the funds to pay health insurance, and you're unemployed for at least 12 consecutive weeks.

➤ You use the funds for first-time home buying expenses for yourself, your spouse, your child, your grandchild, or even your parent. There's a $10,000 lifetime cap for this exception.

➤ You use the funds to pay for higher education costs for yourself, your spouse, your child, or your grandchild.

If you're owed a company pension, it may automatically be paid to you in the form of a monthly check. Alternatively, you may be given the right to take your pension in a lump sum. You can then roll it over to an IRA or have it transferred directly to an IRA, and begin to take benefits in amounts and on dates most convenient to you.

If you have a regular IRA (and/or rolled over company pension benefits to an IRA), you can set up any withdrawal schedule you wish. You have full flexibility here. Take benefits out weekly, monthly, quarterly, or annually as you desire. The only restriction is the type of investment vehicle you've chosen. For example, funds in a one-year CD can't be withdrawn until the end of the CD's year term (some banks are willing to break CDs before maturity without penalty for IRAs, but they won't do it routinely). Mutual funds may also have restrictions on when they will pay out amounts. Generally, you can arrange for monthly checks from mutual funds holding retirement money.

The point to note about company pensions is the fact that they're generally *not* adjusted for inflation. They're fixed according to your salary or some other measure. Once the pension becomes fixed, it remains at the same level throughout your retirement. As a volunteer firefighter, I'm entitled to $20 per month for each month of service, with benefits payable beginning at age 65. After seven years in the plan, I'm now entitled to a pension of $140 per month. Of course, I won't get that benefit for another 17 years. I wonder what $140 a month will be worth at that time?

How to get the most from your pensions and IRAs is covered in Part 4.

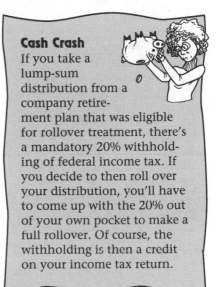

Cash Crash

If you take a lump-sum distribution from a company retirement plan that was eligible for rollover treatment, there's a mandatory 20% withholding of federal income tax. If you decide to then roll over your distribution, you'll have to come up with the 20% out of your own pocket to make a full rollover. Of course, the withholding is then a credit on your income tax return.

Cash Crash

If you were a federal government employee hired before 1984, an employee of a charity before 1984 that didn't arrange for Social Security coverage, or a railroad worker, you're not entitled to Social Security benefits. You may, however, be entitled to similar coverage through your former employer.

Social Security

Social Security is a payment you receive from the federal government because you have worked for at least 10 years and contributed to the Social Security system. Even if you never worked (or didn't work enough to get benefits based on your own earnings), you may still be entitled to benefits because your spouse or former spouse worked. There are many ins and outs to Social Security, and these are discussed in detail in the next chapter. Here you'll get an overview

Golden Years Ideas

You can opt to have your check deposited directly in your bank account by calling the Social Security Administration at 800-772-1213. This will save you the time of having to go to the bank and deposit it, which could, depending on weather and other things that might slow you down, delay your having the money to spend. It also avoids the possibility that your check is lost or stolen from your mailbox. Beginning in 1999, *all* benefits will be direct deposited (you'll no longer have a choice of receiving a check).

Cash Crash

If you're in a stock mutual fund, you may want only the dividends paid to you when earned (and leave your capital alone). Be careful how you arrange for the treatment of dividends. You may have dividends re-invested automatically. Re-investment can apply to ordinary dividends and to capital gains dividends, or you can re-invest only ordinary dividends. Make sure you know how your dividends are being handled and make any changes as you require them.

of Social Security so that you can dovetail it into your other retirement income.

If you worked your whole adult life, there's no question that you're eligible for benefits. In fact, you're eligible if you worked for at least 10 years earning 40 quarters of credit. You're "fully insured" for life. You're a "covered worker."

Your benefits are based on your earnings as an employee or as a self-employed person.

So you're entitled to get benefits. But how much will that be? If you begin to collect at age 65, you get your PIA (your primary insurance amount, which is your full benefits). (Baby boomers beware: After the year 2000, the normal retirement age is going up gradually to 66 and, after 2017, gradually to 67.) If you begin to collect early (between age 62 and 65), you receive a percentage of your PIA.

Figuring out exactly what your benefits could be is very complicated. Luckily, the Social Security Administration makes it easy; it does it for you.

If you've never worked (or your earnings are less than the benefit you collect because of your spouse or former spouse), but your spouse or former spouse is eligible for benefits, you too may be entitled to benefits. The Social Security Administration will figure benefits you may be entitled to because of your own earnings and those you may be entitled to because of your marital status. Whichever way it works out, you'll get the higher benefits. Eligibility to benefits based on your spouse's or former spouse's earnings is explained more fully in the next chapter.

Every year, Social Security recipients get a raise. Their monthly benefit is increased for a cost-of-living adjustment. Don't get carried away and spend your raise all in one place. The increases have been rather modest, especially in recent years. So, the average monthly benefit amount for all retired workers increased from $749 in 1997 to $765 in 1998. Table 2.2 will give you an idea of just how modest the annual increases to Social Security benefits have been since 1985.

Benefits don't begin automatically; you must apply for them. But the application process is simple. You don't have to fill out any lengthy forms. You just give certain information to a Social Security claims representative over the phone or at a local Social Security office. Then you may be required to submit proof of eligibility (copies of a birth certificate, marriage license, decree of divorce, or death certificate of a spouse). To find your local office, just call the central Social Security Administration number at 800-772-1213.

If you're not already collecting benefits, you can file in the month when you become eligible. Even better, file within the three months before your birthday so that benefits will begin promptly. You're not penalized if you file late.

Deciding when to take benefits and other ideas for getting the most from your Social Security benefits are discussed in the next chapter.

Table 2.2   Annual Increases in Social Security Benefits

Year	Cost-of-Living Increase
1985	3.5%
1986	3.1%
1987	1.3%
1988	4.2%
1989	4.0%
1990	4.7%
1991	5.4%
1992	3.7%
1993	3.0%
1994	2.6%
1995	2.8%
1996	2.6%
1997	2.9%
1998	2.1%

Source: Social Security Administration

Putting Your Income Together

Maybe some or many of the income sources we've talked about apply to you. How many? How much? Now is the time to put numbers down on paper to see where you stand. Without this information, you can't decide whether you should continue to work or whether you need to increase your retirement income in some other way.

It's important to understand that some sources of income may be monthly, some twice a year, and some just once a year. You have to know when it's coming in to know how much income you have to spend each month.

Income on Demand

You can arrange to have income paid to you from certain sources when you want it. You just have to know how. The following are some scenarios you can use to arrange for income payments:

Cash Crash
Generally, there's a premature withdrawal penalty if you take money out of a CD before maturity. However, for CDs held in your IRA, the bank may waive penalties if you're over 59$^1/_2$ and you want the money before the CD's maturity. Ask the bank about possible penalties.

Golden Years Ideas
If you want tax-free income and also want the certainty of a monthly income, consider buying a municipal bond fund that can send you interest monthly (though the amount of interest can vary). Even better, consider a unit investment trust because interest each month is fixed. Nuveen's unit investment trust even pays you slightly more if you take the money less frequently (quarterly or semiannually). You can also work with a stockbroker to structure a municipal bond portfolio so that you'll get interest when you want it.

➤ If you have money in mutual funds, contact the fund to ask how to arrange for monthly checks. You'll find the fund's toll-free number on your monthly statements from the fund. Usually you must send them some paperwork to arrange for monthly checks.

➤ If you have an IRA, you can arrange investments so that you can then set up monthly payments. Again, if the IRA is invested in mutual funds, contact the fund to arrange for monthly payments. If the IRA is in a bank CD, you can't arrange for monthly payments.

➤ If you have money in savings accounts, payments to you will not be automatic. You simply withdraw an amount that you require for income each month. You may be able to arrange for automatic transfers to a checking account so it's more convenient to pay your bills.

If you're not happy with how your monthly income plays out, you might want to reposition your holdings. For example, you can use your CDs and Treasury bonds, which don't necessarily pay you monthly income, in order to buy a commercial annuity. The annuity can then be tailored to begin paying you monthly benefits. This is called an immediate annuity because you start to get benefits from the time you pay for the contract. You'll continue to earn income on your investment and can be guaranteed a monthly income for life. You can even arrange for the annuity to continue paying income to your spouse if you die first.

In choosing a commercial annuity, be sure to check the rating of the insurance company selling you the contract. There are several independent rating systems (though A.M. Best Co. is the best known). You can find a list of these rating systems at your local library.

When buying a commercial annuity, understand that you're paying a price (a commission). This eats into what's being invested for your return.

Schedule of Income

One source of retirement income can come from interest on municipal bonds bought over a period of years. The trouble with municipal bonds is that they pay interest just twice a year (six months apart), and the months of payment may be different for different bonds. To know when to expect income (some months are better than others), create a chart like Table 2.3, showing expected interest from each of your bonds.

Table 2.3 Sample Schedule of Municipal Bond Interest Payments

Jan	Feb	Mar	Apr	May	Jun	Jul	Aug	Sep	Oct	Nov	Dec
500		280	1350	380	650	500		280	1350	380	650
1200			1500	170		1200			1500	170	
220						220					
1920		280	2850	550	650	1920		280	2850	550	650

In this example, a total of $12,500 of tax-free interest is earned each year. However, as you can also see, two months of the year (February and August) don't pay any interest.

Now put your income together to see what's coming in each month. Use the following worksheet to record your income from different sources. In the Social Security benefits column, you'll be able to enter a fixed amount. In the Pensions and IRAs column, you may or may not be able to enter a fixed amount. In the Personal savings column, the amounts may vary from month to month. You may have particular flexibility in this column to adjust your income needs. Then add the columns across to find your total monthly income.

As you review your monthly income, you may notice that it varies. Income in some months may be larger than in others. You need to adjust your budget to account for these variations. For example, you may need to *save* some income from one month to cover large expenses in the next month. (Budgeting to avoid catastrophe is explained in Chapter 18, "Keeping Spending in Line.") Or you may need to withdraw more of your savings in a low-income month. In retirement, you can't rely on a stable paycheck for monthly income. Your monthly income is, to a large extent, up to you to determine.

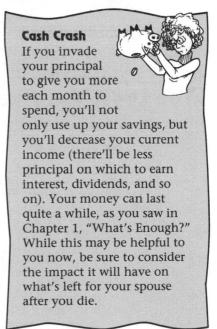

Cash Crash

If you invade your principal to give you more each month to spend, you'll not only use up your savings, but you'll decrease your current income (there'll be less principal on which to earn interest, dividends, and so on). Your money can last quite a while, as you saw in Chapter 1, "What's Enough?" While this may be helpful to you now, be sure to consider the impact it will have on what's left for your spouse after you die.

Schedule of monthly income payments

Month	Personal Savings	Pensions and IRAs	Social Security Benefits	Total Monthly Income
January	$	$	$	$
February	$	$	$	$
March	$	$	$	$
April	$	$	$	$
May	$	$	$	$
June	$	$	$	$
July	$	$	$	$
August	$	$	$	$
September	$	$	$	$
October	$	$	$	$
November	$	$	$	$
December	$	$	$	$

*Personal savings are your investments, such as stocks, bonds, savings accounts, and commercial annuities outside your retirement plans. It may include not only your current income on savings (interest, dividends, capital gains), but also withdrawals from your principal.

The Least You Need to Know

➤ Retirement income is made up of payments from different sources.

➤ Your personal savings are a major source of retirement income.

➤ Commercial annuities can be used to provide for fixed monthly income.

➤ Pensions and IRAs may be paid to you on a monthly basis or at your discretion.

➤ Social Security benefits are paid monthly and are adjusted annually for inflation.

➤ Retirement income may vary from month to month.

Chapter 3

Social Security Benefits: Now or Later?

In This Chapter

➤ Starting your monthly benefit checks

➤ Getting benefits as soon as you can

➤ Waiting past 65 to collect

➤ Collecting benefits on your spouse's or former spouse's earnings

➤ Figuring what you'll keep in benefits after paying federal income taxes

Remember all those years of working and having money withheld from your paycheck? Part of the withholding was federal income taxes. Another part was the employee share of the Medicare tax. But the part that's going to give you income in retirement relates to your share of FICA (Federal Insurance Contribution Act), which is the Social Security tax. And if you owned an unincorporated business, you paid your share of the Social Security tax through self-employment tax that you included along with your federal income tax payments each year. Well now is the time to collect. Right? Not so fast. Maybe it's better to wait awhile. Or maybe it's better to start as early as possible. The one thing for sure is that you'd better know the ins and outs of Social Security so you'll be able to collect all that you're entitled to.

Most of what's in this chapter is designed for those of you who haven't yet begun to receive monthly Social Security checks. But even if you've already started to get your benefits, you'll want to know how your benefits are affected if you work even part-time. And even if you aren't still working and don't plan to work, you may want to look over the information in this chapter, which may be of interest to your spouse or a friend.

In this chapter, you'll learn the basics of claiming your Social Security benefits. You'll see when it's better to delay your application and when it's better to start collecting as early as you can.

ABCs of Social Security

Social Security is a federal benefits program that entitles you to benefits because you've worked long enough and paid into the system. But unlike a retirement plan, there's no Social Security account in some bank with your name on it. Your contributions over the years were not saved up by the government and invested just for you. The system works by having the contributions of current workers pay the benefits for retired workers.

Senior Info

The number of current workers for each retiree has been declining dramatically in recent years due to the increase in the number of retirees. In 1940, there were 159.1 workers for each retiree. This so-called "dependency ratio" dropped to 16.5 in 1950, and to 5.1 in 1960. By 1990, the number of workers for each retiree was only 3.4. It's expected that the dependency ratio will be 2 to 1 by the year 2030.

If you've worked for at least 10 years (or 40 quarters), you're considered "fully insured." You're entitled to Social Security benefits. The *amount* of benefits you'll collect depends on what you earned during your working years. Earnings include your wages and any net self-employment income from being a sole proprietor (such as a consultant or independent contractor) or a partner in a business.

You may have heard about problems with the Social Security system and expectations that it will collapse. Don't panic. That doomsday prediction is years off (not until after 2029, according to Shirley Chater, Commissioner of Social Security). Before then, it's probable that there'll be some changes made in the current system. If you're already collecting Social Security benefits or expect to collect soon, your benefits are secure.

What's Coming to You

If you haven't started to collect Social Security benefits, it's a good idea to check with the Social Security Administration to see what's coming to you. This will ensure that all your earnings (your wages and self-employment income) have been properly credited to you. If you wait too long to correct a mistake (generally more than about three years), you're out of luck.

The Social Security Administration can also give you an idea of what you can expect in the way of a monthly check after you retire (and what your spouse will be entitled to). The formula, which is based on what you earned and how long you worked, used to figure your benefits is very complicated. You're better off letting the government work it out for you.

Senior Info

If you're at least 58 years old (and you're not already collecting benefits on disability), you should receive an annual earnings statement showing the earnings you have been credited with for Social Security. If you haven't received the statement, call the Social Security Administration (SSA) at 800-772-1213. Beginning in 2000, earnings statements will be sent to all workers age 25 and older.

At any age, you can receive a free benefit estimate statement showing what you've contributed over the years and what your anticipated benefit will be at retirement. To get your benefit estimate statement, file Form SSA-7004. You can receive Form SSA-7004 at your local Social Security office or by calling the Social Security Administration at 800-SSA-1213.

The only information you need to provide is:

➤ Your name (and all other names you may have worked under, such as a maiden name)

➤ Your Social Security number (and any other Social Security numbers you may have used)

➤ Your date of birth

➤ Your sex

➤ Your actual earnings for last year (wages and/or net earnings from self-employment income)

➤ Your estimated earnings for this year

Golden Years Ideas

The Social Security Administration expects to be able to provide a benefit estimate (but not a listing of your contributions) through the Internet once it works out a way to safeguard your privacy. Check the Social Security Administration's Web site at http://www.ssa.gov. If you don't own a computer with access to the Internet (or know someone else who does), you may be able to use one at your local library.

Golden Years Ideas

At the time this book was prepared, there was a measure afoot to permit withholding of federal income tax from Social Security benefit checks. If this rule is enacted, you'll be able to elect to have withholding at the rate of 7%, 15%, 28%, or 31%. Depending on your benefit and other income, withholding could eliminate the need to make quarterly estimated tax payments.

➤ The age at which you plan to stop working and begin to collect benefits

➤ The average yearly amount that you expect to earn between now and retirement. Do not give the total earnings you expect to receive during this period— only the annual earnings. In making an estimate, factor in cost-of-living, performance or scheduled pay increases, or bonuses.

➤ The address where you want the statement sent (probably your home address)

Sign and date the form in the space provided and enter your daytime telephone number (including the area code). Send the form to:

Social Security Administration
Wilkes Barre Data Operations Center
P.O. Box 7004
Wilkes Barre, PA 18767-7004

It usually takes several weeks to receive your statement.

Your monthly benefits are based on your primary insurance amount (PIA), which is the full Social Security benefit payable at age 65. Your PIA depends on how much you earned over your working years. There's a maximum PIA, which is based on the wage base limit in effect each year. If you worked in 1997, the maximum earnings that would be taken into account were $65,400, the wage base limit for the year (in 1998 the wage base is $68,400). However, you may have earned less than the limit in some or all years. In this case, your PIA is below the maximum PIA. Again, don't try to figure exactly what your PIA is; let the Social Security Administration do it for you.

Keep in mind that the monthly check you receive from Social Security may be *smaller* than the benefit amount you expect. If you're 65 and receiving Medicare, the premium for Medicare Part B is automatically withheld each month from your Social Security benefit check. If you retire *after* 65, you'll have to arrange to have the premium deducted from your benefit check.

Retirement Age

Collection of benefits doesn't depend only on what you've paid into the system. You also have to meet an age requirement. There are three critical ages:

➤ Normal retirement age is the age at which full retirement benefits (your PIA) can first be paid.

➤ Early retirement age is the age when reduced retirement benefit payment can begin. For people who are disabled, "early retirement" means retirement after 62 and before normal retirement age.

➤ Late retirement age is any age after normal retirement age. Late retirement age, such as at age 69, means you'll receive an increased retirement benefit because you delayed the receipt of benefits beyond the date when you could have taken them.

Currently, the normal retirement age is 65. If you were born before 1938, you can begin to receive benefits for the first month in which you reach 65. If you turn 65 on October 15, 1998, your first Social Security check will cover the month of October.

Senior Info

When the Social Security system went into effect in 1935, the life expectancy of a man who actually reached 65 was just two more years. Most men did not even reach retirement age because their life expectancy was just 63 years. A male born today has a life expectancy of well into his 70s, and those actually reaching retirement age can expect to live more than 18 additional years.

Looking ahead, baby boomers will see that the system is stacked against them. Beginning in the year 2000, the normal retirement age will begin to increase gradually (see Table 3.1).

Table 3.1   Normal Retirement Age for Social Security

If you were born in:	Your normal retirement age is:
1938	65 years, 2 months
1939	65 years, 4 months
1940	65 years, 6 months
1941	65 years, 8 months
1942	65 years, 10 months
1943–1954	66 years

continues

Table 3.1   Continued

If you were born in:	Your normal retirement age is:
1955	66 years, 2 months
1956	66 years, 4 months
1957	66 years, 6 months
1958	66 years, 8 months
1959	66 years, 10 months
1960 or later	67 years

Cash Crash
Making false statements (including leaving out pertinent information) can result in civil or criminal penalties. For example, the fine for making a false statement can run as high as $5,000. The fine can be collected through the courts or withheld from your Social Security benefits or any federal tax refunds you may be owed.

Golden Years Ideas
You can apply for both Social Security benefits *and* Medicare coverage at the same time because you're treated as enrolled in Medicare after you prove entitlement to Social Security benefits.

So, by 2005, the normal retirement age will be 66. Because I was born in 1950, I'll have to wait until I'm 66 to reach the normal retirement age. By 2022, the normal retirement age will be 67. It's not scheduled to go any higher at this time.

Applying for Benefits

Just because you're eligible for benefits, don't look for checks to arrive automatically or to be credited to your bank account. You have to apply for benefits, and you have to apply at the right time.

You don't have to fill out any lengthy forms or questionnaires. You simply call or stop into your local Social Security office. A representative will take your information, feed it into the computer, and print out a form for you to sign.

In addition to your signed application form, you need certain supporting documents as proof of age and marital status. These might include:

➤ Birth certificate

➤ Religious birth record

➤ Marriage license

➤ Decree of divorce

➤ Death certificate for a spouse

You need originals or certified copies. Documents in foreign languages are okay and will be translated by the Social Security Administration. If you're not sure which documents you need or whether the ones you have will be acceptable, just call your local Social Security Administration office and ask a representative.

You should start the application process *before* you're eligible to collect benefits. Don't wait until your 65th birthday passes to call the Social Security Administration. It's generally a good idea to call *three* months before your 65th birthday if you want benefits to start on your normal retirement age.

The Sooner the Better for Benefits

Today, you can start to collect Social Security benefits as early as age 62. You don't have to wait until you're 65 to receive benefits.

Senior Info

According to the Social Security Administration, about half of all men and 60% of women start to collect their Social Security benefits at age 62. Nearly one-third of men between the ages of 55 and 64 are not employed (which means that two-thirds are still working).

If you've already retired from your job or your business and need the funds, then by all means start your benefits as soon as you can. But if you have other money to pay your bills, the question you have to ask yourself is whether it's a good idea to collect benefits as early as possible. The answer depends on something you can't know for certain: how long you'll live.

If you begin to collect benefits at 62, you'll receive a reduced benefit (smaller than you would if you'd waited until 65). The reduced benefit is the monthly amount you would have received at age 65 reduced by $5/9$ of 1% (0.5555%) for each month that your retirement is before your 65th birthday. So, for example, if you decided to retire from your job at age 64 (one year before your 65th birthday), your benefits would be reduced by 6.666% (0.5555% × 12 months). If you begin to receive benefits at age 62, which is the earliest possible date, the reduction would be 20%.

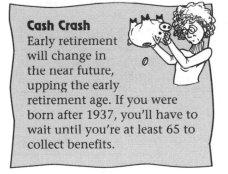

Cash Crash
Early retirement will change in the near future, upping the early retirement age. If you were born after 1937, you'll have to wait until you're at least 65 to collect benefits.

Before you decide to take early retirement benefits, think hard about it. The reduction is permanent; when you reach 65, you won't be able to then collect the normal benefit amount that you would have received if you had waited until 65 to begin taking benefits. Decide whether you think you'll get more benefits over your lifetime by applying early instead of waiting until normal retirement age.

As a rule of thumb, if you were to take benefits as early as possible, you would come out ahead unless you lived past age 84. But if you live past 84, the total benefits you collect from Social Security will be smaller than if you had waited until 65 to begin collecting. This assumes that there'll be an annual 3% cost-of-living adjustment to benefits and that there is an 8% investment return. (Even without taking cost-of-living and investment return into account, the break-even point—the point when you would have collected the same benefits taking early retirement as waiting until 65—is 77 years old.)

If you decide to apply for early retirement benefits, understand that you won't collect for the month you turn age 62 (as you would for the month you reach 65 for normal retirement benefits). You'll collect beginning in the *next* month. If you turn 62 in November 1998 and apply for benefits, they'll begin in December. And you can't start your Medicare coverage until you're 65, even though you're already receiving Social Security benefits.

Delayed Gratification Has Its Reward

Suppose that you have a company pension or you're still working. You have enough money to live on. You don't have to take your benefits at age 65. You're not required to begin at this time. In fact, there's some incentive to waiting a little longer. If you delay the receipt of benefits past age 65, you're rewarded by receiving a larger benefit when you actually begin to receive them.

In 1998, the DRC is 0.4583% for each month that benefits are postponed (5.5% annually). The DRC increases as in Table 3.2.

Table 3.2 Delayed Retirement Credits

In this year:	DRC per month is:	DRC per year is:
1999	0.4583%	5.5%
2000 and 2001	0.5%	6.0%
2002 and 2003	0.5417%	6.5%
2004 and 2005	0.583%	7.0%
2006 and 2007	0.625%	7.5%
2008 and later years	0.67%	8.0%

As you can see, things get even better if you were born in 1943 or later. You'll get the top DRC of 0.67% per month increase in benefits (8% annually) if you postpone retirement until 70. But there's a downside, too. As the normal retirement age increases, the time in which you can earn DRCs decreases because the maximum age for earning DRCs remains at 70. So I'll earn DRCs of 8% annually if I wait until 70 to collect benefits, but I'll earn them for only four years because my normal retirement age is 66, not 65. I'll get as much as a 32% increase in benefits.

Does waiting pay off in the long run? The answer depends in part on how long you'll live. Again, I'm not a fortune-teller, and neither are you. If you live into your 80s, you'll get more money in the long run than if you started your benefits at 65.

Another factor to take into account is whether you're still working, even part-time, or have a business. This is because earning over a set amount before you turn 70 can cause a reduction in your benefits. In 1998, if you earn more than $14,500 (which is $1,209 monthly) and you're at least 65 but under 70, you'll lose one dollar in benefits for each three dollars of earnings over this limit. So why collect benefits only to have them taken away?

Golden Years Ideas
Postponing the receipt of your Social Security benefits doesn't mean you can't begin Medicare coverage at 65. In fact, you should apply for Medicare at 65; don't wait even if you delay Social Security benefits. You need to apply for Medicare within three months before or seven months after your 65th birthday for Medicare benefits to begin when you turn 65. If you don't act within this 10-month window, you'll have to wait until an enrollment period, which is the January, February, and March of each year.

The earnings ceiling for full benefits is scheduled to increase as shown in Table 3.3.

Table 3.3 Earnings Limit for Those Age 65–69 for Receiving Full Benefits

Year	Earnings limit if you're 65–69
1999	$15,500
2000	17,000
2001	25,000
2002 and later	30,000

There's a special rule for the first year of retirement. You can receive your full benefits in any month you earn $1/12$ or less of the earnings limit. So if you begin to collect Social Security in 1998, you'll get your full check as long as your monthly income is below $1,208 ($1/12$ of $14,500). In 1999, however, you can't rely on this rule. Your annual earnings will determine any reduction in benefits.

Golden Years Ideas
Once you're 70 years old, you can collect your enhanced benefits and, even if you work, there's no penalty. Benefits are not reduced after your 70th birthday no matter how much you earn.

Cash Crash
If you're working as a consultant to your former employer or are otherwise self-employed, be sure your fees (less your expenses) don't exceed the limit. Social Security looks closely at self-employed individuals collecting benefits to make sure that the income they're reporting is correct. If you're at the company every day, full-time, Social Security won't believe that you're getting only a small fee. You could lose your benefits!

Those age 62 up to 65 have a lower earnings limit. The limit for 1998 is $9,120 (which is $760 a month). For each $2 of earnings over this limit, $1 in benefits is lost. The earnings limit can be adjusted annually for inflation.

Your investment income doesn't affect your Social Security benefits. Even if you're a millionaire clipping coupons on your muni bonds from the deck of your yacht, your benefits won't be reduced.

For Better or For Worse, In Sickness and In Health

Everyone is entitled to collect on his or her own earnings. If you've worked enough, the benefits on your own earnings may provide you with the maximum benefits. But you may not have worked enough or earned enough to get top benefits. If you're married, or were married, you may be able to collect on your spouse's (or former spouse's) earnings. You'll collect on your own earnings, or as a spouse (former spouse, or widow[er]), whichever gives you the greater benefits. By the same token, your spouse can collect on his or her own earnings, or based on your earnings, whichever provides the greater benefit. This means that more than one person can collect on a single worker's earnings: The worker him- or herself, a spouse (or ex-spouse), and, after the worker dies, a surviving spouse (or a surviving divorced spouse).

Spousal Benefits

Let's consider a fictional example to illustrate spousal benefits. Harriet was an executive secretary when she married her boss in the early 1950s. They agreed that she would stay at home and raise the kids. Once they were grown, he was doing so well that she never returned to the workplace. He's retired now, collecting a benefit based on his earnings, and she's in her early 60s. Harriet will be able to collect on her own earnings, or on her husband's, depending on which method gives her the larger benefit. More specifically, she'll get benefits based on her earnings provided she worked at least 10 years, or a spouse's benefit, set at 50% of the benefits that her husband collects, whichever is more. As a family, he'll get 100% of his benefits, Harriet will get 50% of his benefits, or 100% of her own benefits, whichever is greater, up to a family maximum.

At what age can she begin to collect benefits? The answer depends on which benefits she'll receive.

➤ If she collects on her own earnings, she can get reduced benefits at age 62 or normal retirement benefits at 65.

➤ If she collects a spousal share, benefits can begin at 62.

You can't collect a spousal share until your spouse begins to collect benefits. So if your spouse is younger than you and your own earnings are not enough to get you benefits, you'll just have to wait. However, you can start out with your own smaller benefits and begin to receive the spousal share once your spouse retires.

The Social Security Administration will figure the benefits both ways and pay the larger benefit. It's a good idea, if you're in Harriet's situation, to request an estimate of benefits, as suggested earlier in this chapter, to know whether your own earnings will give you a larger benefit than the 50% spousal share. This will let you plan for the age you expect to retire.

Widows and Widowers

If your spouse has died, you can, of course, collect benefits based on your own earnings. But if your earnings were small, or if you didn't work long enough, you may be entitled to survivor benefits based on your spouse's earnings.

You can receive survivor benefits if you fall into *any* one of the following three categories:

➤ You're a surviving spouse without any dependent children, and you're at least 60.

➤ You're a surviving spouse who is disabled, and you're at least 50.

➤ You're a surviving spouse with a child under age 16, or a child of any age who is disabled. You can be any age. There's no minimum age to collect in this category.

To be a qualified widow(er), you must have been married at least nine months before your spouse's death (unless the death was an accident or some other unforeseeable event).

If you start taking benefits at 60, you receive 71.5% of your deceased spouse's benefits. If you wait until 65, you'll get 100% of those benefits. Or, when you reach 62, you can start to collect on your own benefits if they're larger than your widow's benefits. If you re-marry after you're 60, you won't lose your benefits. If you're over 50 and disabled, remarriage won't affect your benefits.

Those Who Are Divorced

If you're divorced, you can, of course, collect benefits based on your own earnings. But if your earnings were small, or you didn't work long enough, you may be entitled to

Golden Years Ideas
You can collect benefits as a divorced former spouse even though your ex hasn't started to collect benefits.

benefits based on your former spouse's earnings. You're entitled to the same benefits as a surviving spouse if:

➤ You were married at least 10 years.

➤ You are at least 62 years old.

➤ You've been divorced for at least two years.

Take your marriage certificate and divorce decree to the Social Security office (or call them on the phone) and ask what benefits you're entitled to.

Things get a little complicated if you're collecting Social Security benefits based on your former spouse's earnings and you decide to remarry. If you remarry before you're 60, you can't collect benefits based on your ex's earnings unless your ex has died. But if your new marriage ends in divorce or death, benefits can resume (you'll probably collect on the basis of your first marriage, but if the benefits you'd receive as a widow of your second marriage are more than those as a divorced spouse from your first marriage, you'll get the greater benefit).

Golden Years Ideas
If you remarry someone who's collecting widow(er)'s benefits, there's no loss of benefits.

What Does the Government Take Back in Taxes?

For 50 years, Social Security benefits were tax free. Then, when the federal government needed revenue, these benefits became fair game. Now, depending on your income and the size of your benefits, you may still be able to receive benefits tax free. But for many, a large chunk of benefits—50% in some cases, 85% in others—are treated as income and subject to tax. It's important to know whether your benefits are taxed so you'll know how much you'll be able to keep (and spend as you wish) after paying the government. The following are the guidelines for taxation of benefits:

Word to the Wise
For purposes of figuring the taxable portion of your Social Security benefits, *income* means all of your regular taxable income (wages, dividends, gains from stock sales, and so on), plus interest on municipal bonds and one-half of your Social Security benefits. Add these items together to see whether you've crossed the tax-free limit.

➤ Your benefits are completely tax free if your income is below $25,000 if you're single (you're single if you're a widow or widower), or below $34,000 if you're married and file a joint return with your spouse.

➤ Your benefits are 50% included in income if your income is between $25,000 and $34,000 if you're single, or $34,000 and $44,000 if you're married and file a joint return.

➤ Your benefits are 85% included in income if your income is over $34,000 if you're single, or $44,000 if you're married and file a joint return, or any amount of income if you're married and file a separate return but did not live apart from your spouse for the entire year.

You don't have to keep track of your Social Security benefits throughout the year (though you should know how much you're getting). The Social Security Administration will send you an annual statement on Form SSA-1099 showing your annual benefits. Remember that you figure your tax on benefits without regard to any Medicare premiums that were withheld.

Cash Crash
These percentages may change at any time. While the Social Security system is supposedly on sound footing now, should concerns arise, these percentages could increase. There have been suggestions that wealthy individuals *not* be entitled to benefits at all. Short of this drastic change in the system, benefits for such individuals could become 100% taxable in the future.

The Least You Need to Know

➤ If you've worked for at least 10 years, you can assume you're entitled to Social Security benefits.

➤ Benefits are not paid automatically; you must apply for them.

➤ You can retire as early as 62, but you'll get smaller monthly benefits than if you waited until 65.

➤ You can receive larger monthly benefits by delaying retirement past 65.

➤ A spouse can collect on his or her own earnings or receive a spousal benefit, whichever is larger.

➤ Divorced spouses may be able to collect benefits based on their ex's earnings.

➤ Depending on your income from all sources, including your Social Security benefits, you may pay no tax on benefits, or tax on 50% or 85% of your benefits.

Part 2
Remaining in the Rat Race...at Least a Little Longer

Retirement for many people is only the end to a first career. It doesn't mean sitting at home and waiting for their death knell. It's a brand new start to the rest of their lives. It's an opportunity to slow down in their current job, begin a new career, or even start their own business.

No matter how old you are (except in very limited cases), you're never too old to work in a job or run a business. That's what the law says. You should know the law and your rights so you're armed with information when you're seeking a postretirement job. You should also know what benefits, particularly medical benefits, may be available to you on and off the job to help you through retirement.

If you decide to start up your own business, there's a lot to learn about. You may want to buy a franchise or turn your hobby into a full-time occupation. Getting the right information will help you make informed decisions.

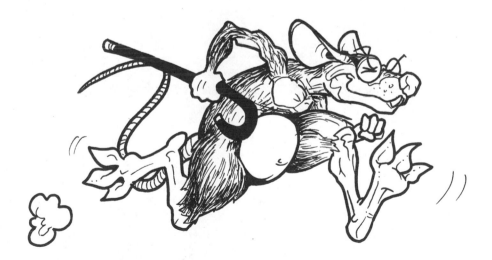

Working...
The Second
Time Around

Retirement for you may be a state of mind, a time of life, or living in a new community. It doesn't have to mean you aren't working. You may want to use your retirement as an opportunity to begin a new career, start up your own business, or just slow down from your previously breakneck pace.

In this chapter, you'll learn about your rights in the workplace. Just because you're in your golden years doesn't mean you're too old to work. You'll decide whether it really pays to work, or whether it would cost you more to work than to stay at home. You'll also find out about health care issues in connection with working and how you can build up additional pension benefits by continuing to work. And you'll see what other benefits you may be entitled to if you work.

In the chapters that follow in this part of the book, you'll learn about different working options: working part-time, starting a new career, starting your own business at home, franchising and turnkey operations, and turning a hobby into a business.

It's Your Right to Work

Maybe you need to keep active, and you love what you do for a living. Maybe you just need the money. Maybe your spouse can't stand to have you around the house all day, and 18 holes of golf just won't fill up your time. Whatever your motivation for working, be assured that the law protects you. If you're over 40, the law makes sure you don't suffer from any age discrimination in the workplace. This means that your rights to being hired, promoted, and receiving job benefits are protected.

Senior Info

According to the U.S. Department of Labor, many seniors are still in the workplace after age 65. The Bureau of Labor Statistics shows that in 1994, 17.2% of people past their 65th birthday were still employed.

The federal law that gives you protection from discrimination in the workplace is called the *Age Discrimination in Employment Act* (or *ADEA* for short). It covers employees, and potential employees, over the age of 40 who work for employers that regularly have 20 or more workers. If you're an independent contractor, this law won't protect you from age discrimination that may have occurred.

Word to the Wise

An *independent contractor* is a self-employed person who contracts to provide work according to his or her own methods. This person isn't under the control of the person or business for whom the work is being performed. An independent contractor is *not* an employee and doesn't receive a Form W-2 but instead receives a Form 1099-MISC.

The ADEA means that an employer can't fail or refuse to hire you on the basis of your age, or discriminate in the terms or conditions of employment. An employment agency can't decline to refer you for employment on the basis of your age. A labor union can't decline to give you job assignments because of your age.

However, there's an important exception in ADEA protection. If for the past two years before retirement, you served in a high policy-making position and were entitled to a large pension that couldn't be lost, then compulsory retirement at age 70 isn't treated as discriminatory.

Most, but not all, states also have anti-age discrimination laws like the ADEA. The District of Columbia also has anti-age discrimination laws.

If You've Been Discriminated Against

Your company's official policy is *not* to discriminate on the basis of age. But unofficially it may do so. If you suspect that you've been discriminated against because of your age (you didn't get that raise you'd been expecting, you've been terminated, or you've been passed over for promotion in favor of a younger worker) and the only reason you were targeted by your company was because of your age, then you may have a case.

First, check out your situation with the Equal Employment Opportunity Commission (EEOC) at 800-USA-EEOC. Then, if you're ready to press your claim, get a lawyer to represent you. Don't try to be your own attorney. Make sure the lawyer you hire has handled these types of cases. If you don't know any lawyer who specializes in this area of the law, call your state or county bar association and ask for a referral.

Be sure to interview any lawyer you're considering to represent you. Ask about his or her experience in age discrimination cases. Ask about fees. Many lawyers are willing to work on a contingency basis. This means that the lawyer will receive a percentage of anything you collect (be sure to agree in writing on what that percentage will be). If you don't win, you don't owe the lawyer anything other than perhaps his or her expenses.

Be prepared for a lengthy process. Your case may wind its way through state administrative actions and then federal administrative actions before you ever get to a court room. You may, in fact, never see the inside of a court room (if your employer is found to be in the wrong and settles up with you at that point). Many employees are also subject to arbitration requirements, so they can go to an arbitrator but *can't* sue their employers for age discrimination.

Protection for Your Disability

Employers can't discriminate on the basis of age, or they'll violate the ADEA. But if they regularly employee at least 15 workers, they're also prohibited from discriminating on the basis of a person's physical or mental disability. The Americans with Disabilities Act

Cash Crash
Just because you've been replaced with a younger worker doesn't automatically mean there's been any discrimination by your employer. Usually employers aren't guilty of age discrimination where they simply hire less highly paid workers (who typically are younger). You may *feel* like you've been discriminated against because you've been successful in climbing the corporate ladder, but you probably won't succeed in pushing your claim of age discrimination.

Cash Crash
If you think you've been discriminated against, don't delay your action. Would-be plaintiffs must satisfy strict timing requirements and may have only six months from the date of the illegal discrimination to start the charge process (although the allotted time might be longer). If you wait too long, you may be out of luck, even if you were in the right and your employer was in the wrong.

(ADA) provides protection against discriminating against a person qualified to do the job on the basis of that person's disabilities. The law requires employers to reasonably accommodate a disability, such as providing wheelchair access to the building and bathrooms, or help for those with hearing impairment.

The ADA protects people who suffer a physical or mental impairment that substantially limits one or more of their major life activities. Advanced age, by itself, isn't considered an impairment. However, medical conditions associated with age, such as hearing loss, osteoporosis, or arthritis, would be an impairment.

If you believe you are the victim of discrimination in the workplace because of your disability, you can try to remedy the situation. The amount of damages you can recover is limited by federal law (based in part on the size of the company).

Does It Pay to Work?

Okay, so it's your right to work. But does it make sense to do it? Before you rush out and take a part-time or even a full-time job, be sure you know what it's going to *cost* you to work. Yes, there are expenses to working that you don't have if you stay home.

In Chapter 1 you listed the expenses you could kiss goodbye by *not* working. Well, if you're planning to work, even part-time, you'll have to take the expenses back into account. Here's a list of some expenses you may have if you work (outside of a home-based business):

➤ Commuting costs. (Don't forget the *time* factor of commuting since the national average is 3.7 hours each week.)

➤ Lunches out

➤ Clothing for work

➤ Dry cleaning for work clothes

➤ Other expenses (such as someone to clean your home)

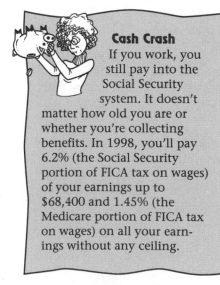

Cash Crash
If you work, you still pay into the Social Security system. It doesn't matter how old you are or whether you're collecting benefits. In 1998, you'll pay 6.2% (the Social Security portion of FICA tax on wages) of your earnings up to $68,400 and 1.45% (the Medicare portion of FICA tax on wages) on all your earnings without any ceiling.

If you're collecting Social Security benefits and you're under age 70, remember that you're limited in what you can earn before you begin to have those benefits reduced. In 1998, your earnings limit is $9,120 if you're under 65; your earnings limit is $14,500 if you're between 65 and 70. If you go over these limits, which is something you're probably trying to avoid by taking a part-time job, you'll lose $1 in benefits for each $2 of excess earnings if you're under 65, and $1 in benefits for each $3 of excess earnings if you're between 65 and 70. There's no benefit reduction, regardless of earnings, once you turn 70.

Medical Coverage at 65

Employers aren't *required* to provide medical coverage for their workers. But the fact that they do provide coverage is a chief reason for many individuals to continue to work. This is because the cost of individual medical coverage runs so high.

The nature of medical coverage changes at age 65. This is the age at which private coverage ends, and Medicare begins. If an employer *does* have a group health plan, it must continue to cover working seniors and their spouses (even if the spouse is over 65). (The only exception is small employers...those with less than 20 employees.) Medicare is treated as a "secondary payor." While the employer *must* offer the same coverage to seniors that it does to younger workers, those 65 and over can *reject* the employer's coverage and choose Medicare instead. If your employer pays for your coverage, then you probably won't reject it. But if you have to pay for employer coverage, it may be cheaper to reject it and pay only for Medicare. If you've already retired and are still receiving health coverage from your old company, Medicare is your primary payor in this case.

Even though medical expenses are covered primarily by Medicare for those 65 and older, medical expenses are a significant cost factor. People this age spend about 14% of their income on medical costs. Even just the cost of medical insurance (Medicare and supplementary policies) can be a heavy burden for some of you. It's important to know where you stand, medically speaking, if you continue to work.

Word to the Wise
Medicare is a comprehensive federal health insurance program primarily for those age 65 and older.

Medicare Means Minimum Protection

If you're 65 and "insured," you're entitled to Medicare coverage whether or not you're working. You're fully insured if you've worked for at least 10 years. You get Medicare coverage, Part A (Hospital Insurance) without any extra cost to you (that's why your called "insured"). Even if you're not insured and aren't automatically entitled to Part A coverage, you can get it by paying for it. The cost in 1998 is $309 a month (the monthly premium can change annually).

You get Medicare coverage, Part B (Supplemental Medical Insurance, which is like a major medical policy that covers doctor's charges, prescription drugs, and certain other expenses) by paying a monthly premium. You get to pick which doctors you'll see and what services you'll receive. The monthly premium in 1998 is $43.80 (the monthly premium is set each year, and is expected to reach $105.40 by 2007). This amount is subtracted from your monthly Social Security benefits. If you're not yet collecting benefits because you're still working, or your benefits are suspended because your earnings exceed a certain amount, then you must pay the Part B premium directly to the Social Security Administration. You're billed for the monthly premiums on a quarterly basis (but you're allowed to pay monthly if you're financially unable to do it quarterly). You send your check to the Social Security Administration at the address indicated on your bill.

Just because you're entitled to Medicare doesn't mean your spouse is. Each spouse's Medicare eligibility is determined separately. There's no such thing as "spousal" coverage like there is under company health plans or for Social Security benefits. Someone who's 65 and who worked long enough to be insured can collect as well as someone who's uninsured, like a nonworking spouse (provided that person pays for coverage).

There are three payments systems under Medicare:

➤ Traditional fee for service (although doctors are limited in what they can charge...usually no more than 15% over the Medicare schedule amount). Here, the doctor is reimbursed by Medicare for 80% of the approved charge for the service under Part B; you generally pay the balance. Hospital bills are covered, with you picking up the co-payments and deductibles.

➤ Medicare managed care (HMOs and Medicare+Choice). You can choose to use managed care instead of traditional fee for service. In this case, your HMO decides what care is reasonable and necessary and whom you should get it from (you may have some range of choice here). Medicare+Choice begins on January 1, 1999 (within initial enrollment during November 1998). You'll find more information on Medicare+Choice later in this chapter.

➤ Private-payment option. Beginning on January 1, 1998, you're allowed to contract with a doctor to go outside of Medicare. By private contract, you can agree to pay for charges, and your doctor agrees not to submit any charges to Medicare. This contract must be signed *before* any services are provided and can't be signed if you're lying in a pool of blood or are in some other health care crisis. If you make this contract, your supplemental health policy (which you'll learn about in just a moment) won't cover any costs because Medicare isn't covering any costs. What's more, the Medicare limits on doctor's fees don't apply if you make this private contract. But if you have a special heart condition and there's a cardiologist whom you absolutely must use and who has opted out of Medicare, this private contract route may be for you. It doesn't mean you're out of Medicare entirely—only for this one doctor.

> **Word to the Wise**
> *COBRA coverage* is continued medical insurance through your employer's group plan that must be offered when a person retires or terminates for reasons other than gross misconduct. You pay 102% of the premium that the company would otherwise pay.

If you leave your job and you're over 65, your employer doesn't have to offer you any health insurance (you already have Medicare). COBRA coverage ends where Medicare begins.

But even if you're not entitled to COBRA, your spouse may be protected. If your spouse isn't yet eligible for Medicare when you leave your job, your spouse can continue his or her company coverage for 36 months (or until eligible for Medicare).

Close the Gap With a "Medigap" Policy

Medicare goes only so far. Under Part A, there are all kinds of deductibles. In 1998, for example, your Part A deductible is $764 for each hospitalization. There are no co-payment responsibilities until your hospitalization has lasted 60 days. Then your co-insurance for hospital stays between 61 and 90 days is $191 a day; for stays over 90 days, it's $382 a day. Under Part B, in 1998 there's a yearly deductible of $100, and then most expenses are covered only up to 80%. You must pay these deductibles and other co-payments from your pocket, unless you carry special insurance. The type of coverage that picks up where Medicare leaves off is called *Supplemental Health Coverage*, or *Medigap*.

Senior Info

After you leave the job, you may be without medical coverage other than Medicare or personal coverage you pay for. Only a third of retirees continued to receive employer-paid health insurance as of 1994 (the latest year there were statistics on this topic). This number is continually dropping. The U.S. Supreme Court has decided that companies can, under certain circumstances, end their promise to pay health coverage for retired workers. More and more retirees must finance their own coverage.

Your employer probably *won't* offer this coverage to you; you'll have to shop for it and buy it yourself. But shopping has been made easy by a federal law that standardized Medigap policies. As a result, you have 12 different types of supplemental insurance plans to choose from. The more comprehensive the coverage, the higher the cost.

Ten plans, labeled A through J, must offer a core of benefits, and then offer additional benefits, like the cost of preventative medical care, foreign travel emergency, and at-home recovery. There are also two additional plans that coordinate with high-deductible plans for Medicare-Medical Savings Accounts (MSAs). The best time to buy a Medigap policy is three months before or four months after your 65th birthday (or six months after you apply for Medicare Part B). The reason for this is that it's open enrollment time for insurers. They can't turn you down, regardless of your medical condition. After this window of opportunity has passed, you'll have to wait for special enrollment periods.

Golden Years Ideas

If you switch to a Medicare HMO, don't drop your exiting Medigap coverage just yet. Make sure you like the new plan before you terminate your supplemental health insurance. If you drop your Medigap and then drop out of the HMO, you'll have to wait for a special enrollment period and may have a certain waiting period for coverage to begin for pre-existing conditions.

Cash Crash

Before you rush to enroll in these alternative plans, make sure you understand that with private fee-for-service plans and Medicare MSAs, you're paying the *full* cost of medical service and not a reduced price or partial fee amount. Medicare MSAs are only an experimental plan limited to the first 390,000 enrollees.

Medicare-HMOs

Instead of buying insurance to supplement Medicare, consider another option: Medicare-sponsored HMOs. Like regular HMOs, these managed care plans limit your choice of doctors and services to those within the HMO but reduce or even eliminate your out-of-pocket expenses. This means you don't have to buy a Medigap policy.

Medicare HMOs are rather new, and only about 12% of Medicare beneficiaries have opted for this route. They're especially attractive to seniors with good health histories who aren't concerned with the HMO's limitations.

Medicare+Choice

Beginning in 1999, there are other alternatives for managed care in addition to traditional Medicare HMOs. (Enrollment in November 1998 starts coverage in 1999.) These alternatives are called Medicare Part C, or Medicare+Choice. If you're entitled to Part A and enrolled in Part B, you can elect to receive Part C from a Medicare+Choice organization. This is an alternative to traditional fee-for-service Medicare (which you need to supplement with a Medigap policy).

Medicare+Choice plans may be:

➤ Preferred provider organizations (PPOs) and provide reimbursment for doctors, hospitals, and other health care providers at a fixed rate for the type of service provided.

➤ Private fee-for-service plans. These plans provide reimbursement to doctors, hospitals, and other health care providers at a fixed rate for the type of service provided.

➤ Medicare MSAs. These are special medical savings accounts designed to let healthy seniors reduce their medical costs. You opt out of Medicare and, if you stay healthy, will be able to *earn* tax-free money. Your Medical Savings Account will receive from the government a voucher good for medical care equal to the average Medicare payment per individual (that number for 1999 hasn't been determined yet). You then use part of the voucher to buy a catastrophic medical policy (one with a high deductible). The deductible for 1999 is set at $6,000 and will be indexed annually for inflation in later years. The balance of the voucher is invested tax free. If you need coverage, you're on the hook for the deductible and co-payments, and the plan picks up the rest. If you're healthy and don't use the funds in the MSA for medical costs, amounts over the deductible become yours, tax free. You can't, by law, buy a Medigap policy to cover your deductible.

If you choose a Medicare+Choice plan, you can disenroll (drop out of the managed care plan and go back to regular Medicare coverage) on a monthly basis through 2001. In 2002, disenrollment means re-enrollment once during a six-month period; after 2002, there's a three-month period. There's also an annual period each November in which you can disenroll and re-enroll in regular Medicare. However, there may be a problem in picking up Medigap insurance which, in most states, may have a waiting period for a pre-existing condition, or charge a higher fee for immediate coverage.

Getting What's Yours

Medical coverage isn't the only benefit you may receive from your employer. If you're working, you may be entitled to any number of job-related benefits. Because your employer pays for the benefit, you have that much more in your pocket to spend on other things.

Some employers offer benefits under a cafeteria plan. It's not an eating room, but like any cafeteria, the plan allows you to choose from a menu of benefits. You take the ones of interest to you and decline the rest. For example, employees without children would have no need for child-care coverage.

Build Up Your Pension

Next to medical coverage, one of the most valued benefits is a pension. If you work, you may be able to increase your pension benefits. For many women, this is a key factor in deciding to continue working, because they may have been out of the job market while their children were young and didn't build up pension credits.

How much you can build up benefits depends on whether your employer has a qualified retirement plan.

If your employer has a qualified retirement plan, you can't be kept out of the plan, regardless of how old you

> **Word to the Wise**
> A *cafeteria plan* is a plan in which an employee can choose between cash or other taxable benefit and at least one tax-free fringe benefit. Tax-free benefits include, for example, health coverage, dependent care assistance, adoption assistance, and group-term life insurance. You're not taxed on the tax-free benefit choice even though you *could* have taken the taxable one.

> **Golden Years Ideas**
> You can earn pension credits on your current job even if you're collecting a pension through a former employer. The receipt of pension benefits doesn't even affect the amount of credits you can earn on your current job.

Golden Years Ideas
While retirement plans generally are required to make distributions when a person turns 70$\frac{1}{2}$, a person (other than someone who owns more than 5% of the business) who's still employed can postpone distributions until retirement. Waiting to take distributions until then means pension benefits will continue to build up tax free. This delayed payout option applies only to your current employer. You'll have to take distributions from plans of prior employers even though you're still working elsewhere.

are. So if your employer has a 401(k) plan, you'll be able to make contributions for yourself and receive matching employer contributions to the extent provided in your plan. In the past, you didn't have to be included in certain types of retirement plans if you were hired within five years of the plan's normal retirement age (typically 65), but that is no longer the case.

If your employer doesn't have a plan, you're eligible to contribute up to $2,000 a year to an IRA. You'll have to decide what kind of IRA you contribute to: a deductible IRA, a regular nondeductible IRA, or a nondeductible Roth IRA. Even if your employer has a qualified plan, you can still increase your retirement fund through IRA contributions. Your choices are a deductible IRA (assuming your adjusted gross income is below a set dollar amount that increases each year) or a Roth IRA (assuming your adjusted gross income is below an even higher set dollar amount).

If you're treated as an active participant in your employer's qualified retirement plan, you can deduct full IRA contributions only if your adjusted gross income is below the limits in Table 4.1.

Table 4.1 AGI Limits for Making Deductible IRA Contributions by Active Participants

Year	Single	Married Filing Jointly
1998	$30,000	$50,000
1999	31,000	51,000
2000	32,000	52,000
2001	33,000	53,000
2002	34,000	54,000
2003	40,000	60,000
2004	45,000	65,000
2005	50,000	70,000
2006	50,000	75,000
2007	50,000	80,000

The IRA deduction phases out for adjusted gross income above these limits.

If you're married and your spouse is an active participant, and you're working and don't have a pension plan at work, you can deduct your own IRA contributions if adjusted gross income reported on your joint return is below $150,000 (a partial deduction for adjusted gross income between $150,000 and $160,000).

The top Roth IRA contribution can be made only if adjusted gross income for singles is below $95,000, or $150,000 on a joint return.

Whichever type of IRA is selected, the total annual contribution per person is still only $2,000.

If you're self-employed, you have a wide range of pension plan options to choose from. Besides an IRA, you can use a Keogh plan, a SEP (simplified employee pension), or SIMPLE plan (savings incentive match plan for employees). Each of these pension options has different contribution limits and other rules. If you adopt any of these plans, you're treated as an active participant for purposes of figuring whether your IRA contributions are deductible.

Plenty of Perks

Besides medical coverage and a retirement plan, employers may offer other fringe benefits. The following are some benefits that may come with the job that are of particular interest to seniors:

➤ Long-term care insurance. You may be able to get special medical coverage for yourself and your spouse called long-term care insurance. This covers the cost of a nursing home or in-home care for Alzheimer's, Parkinson's, or other chronic illness or disability not covered by Medicare. This insurance generally provides a fixed dollar amount per day (such as $100 per day or $150 per day). Many policies pay only *half* the daily amount for each day of home care. The cost of coverage becomes steeper as you age, so if it's offered as an employer-paid benefit, it's a good deal for you.

Golden Years Ideas

If your spouse has retired and you're still working, you can contribute to your spouse's deductible IRA as long as your spouse is under age 70$\frac{1}{2}$ by the end of the year. This is so even though you're over this age and barred from making deductible IRA contributions.

Golden Years Ideas

Assuming you're eligible, a Roth IRA may make sense if you don't expect to need the money right away. The funds can stay in the account indefinitely; there's no requirement that you start to take distributions at age 70$\frac{1}{2}$ as there is with a regular IRA. What's more, if you leave the money in the account for at least five years, then everything comes out tax free; you're never taxed on the earnings.

Cash Crash

Medicare covers only acute illnesses and recuperation from acute illnesses, not long-stay, custodial care. And if Medicare doesn't cover it, then your supplemental Medicare policies (called Medigap policies) also won't cover it. You need special insurance called long-term care insurance.

➤ Life insurance. Your employer may have a group-term life insurance plan to provide you with term life insurance. The coverage may be modest. Senior executives might get greater coverage, but at the possible cost of paying income tax on the value of the benefit.

➤ Disability coverage. Usually you can't get disability coverage once you're past 65. But check with the carrier if your employer offers this type of coverage and you're dependent on your job for income.

➤ Education assistance. You're never too old to learn. If your employer is willing to pick up the tab, you may want to broaden your horizons. Maybe you'll learn to handle a new computer program. Maybe you'll take a management course. If the opportunity is there, why not take advantage of it?

➤ Transportation assistance. Getting to and from work may be a hassle. The chore can be eased somewhat if your employer helps you out financially. You may get to use a company car, receive free parking at work, or be given a monthly transit pass.

➤ Outplacement services. If you've been given early retirement, you may also have received an invitation to outplacement services. Your company may pay another company to give you help with your résumé, interview skills, and even provide you with space to conduct your job search in.

Tax Cost or Savings From Employer-Paid Perks

Some benefits are entirely tax free, some may be partially tax free, and others may be taxable. As a practical matter, you don't have to figure what's taxable and what's not. Your employer does it for you and gives you this information on your annual W-2 form.

But you may want to know ahead of time whether you're getting something for nothing. Table 4.2 gives you a rundown of how your benefits stack up for the tax collector.

Table 4.2   Taxation of Employee Benefits

Benefit	Tax Treatment
Health insurance	Tax free (unless the plan flunks tax requirements)
Qualified retirement plans	Tax free when contributions are made; taxable when distributions are taken
Nonqualified retirement plans	Generally tax-deferred (but ask your tax adviser about your plan)

Benefit	Tax Treatment
Long-term care insurance	Tax free
Group-term life insurance	Tax free up to $50,000 coverage; excess taxable at $2.10 monthly premium per $1,000 excess if age 65 to 69; $3.76 monthly premium per $1,000 excess if 70+; up to $2,000 coverage for spouse and dependents tax free
Education assistance	Non-job-related undergraduate courses are tax free up to $5,250*; job-related wholly tax free
Company car	Taxed on your personal use
Free parking	Tax free (up to $175** a month in 1998)
Monthly transit passes	Tax free (up to $65** a month in 1998)
Van pooling	Tax free (up to $65** a month in 1998)
Outplacement services	Tax free

*Through June 30, 2000.

**Amounts adjusted annually for inflation.

It's important to remember that even if the benefit is taxable to you, you're probably still ahead of the game by getting it than if you had to pay for it yourself. For example, if you were given free parking in a downtown garage next door to your office building and the value of the monthly parking was $200 ($25 a month over the tax free limit), you would be taxed on $300 ($25 monthly excess times 12 months). Assuming you're in the 28% tax bracket, your cost for the benefit for the entire year would be only $84 ($300 benefit × 28% tax bracket). That means you would have received a $2,400 benefit (the value of parking for the year) at a modest cost of $84.

The Least You Need to Know

➤ Employers generally can't discriminate against you on the basis of your age.

➤ Employers may have to make reasonable accommodations for your physical or mental impairment.

➤ You're entitled to Medicare coverage even if you're still working, but employer health coverage is your primary payor unless you reject it.

➤ Medigap insurance picks up where Medicare leaves off.

➤ Pension credits can be earned even if you're collecting a pension from a former job.

➤ As long as you work, you may be able to continue tax-favored IRA contributions.

➤ If you continue to work, you may be eligible for a number of employer-provided fringe benefits.

Chapter 5

Part-Time Work for Full-Time Rewards

In This Chapter

➤ Working part-time at your old company or a new one

➤ Temping to your own beat

➤ Consulting to use your skills and experience

When Irving was 68, he sold his dental practice and retired, or so he thought. Within six months, he was working two and a half days a week providing dental services for prisoners at the county jail. For Irving, retirement meant giving up the headaches of running his own business but still doing the kind of work he loved, only at a slower pace. You, too, may be able to capitalize on your life's experiences to find part-time work after you retire from your full-time job.

In this chapter, you'll learn about your options for part-time work. Maybe you can just reduce your workload, or maybe you have to look for a new job that's part time. You'll find out about becoming a temporary employee, and you'll learn about turning your expertise into a consulting arrangement.

Old Gray Mare Ain't What She Used to Be

After a lifetime of working long and regular hours, you may want to slow down a bit. That doesn't mean you want to put your feet up on the couch as a full-time occupation. You'd prefer to stay in the work force, at least some of the time. Luckily, the timing couldn't be better. Employment is at an all-time high. This means there's a demand for good workers in many different fields. Mandatory retirement is a thing of the past. Older workers who have knowledge and experience are growing more prized as the demand for good workers increases.

And employers are growing more accepting of different types of work schedules. Large companies are particularly amenable to various alternatives to full-time work. Here are some of the new work schedules that may fit into your retirement plans:

➤ Flex time is setting your own hours as long as you work a minimum number each week. So if you're an early riser and like to get started before everyone else comes into the office, you may be out of the office and on the tennis courts by 3 o'clock.

➤ Seasonal work is working on a full-time basis but at only certain times of the year when the employer's needs are the greatest, such as a department store's needs at Christmas time.

➤ Job sharing is two workers splitting the responsibilities of one job. You may work the afternoon shift if a young mother prefers to work the first part of the day so she's home when the kids get back from school.

➤ Part time, in most cases, is working less than 35 hours a week. Part time may mean reduced hours for five days a week, or working full hours but for just a few days a week.

➤ Telecommuting is working full-time but working from home on the schedule you set. Telecommuting saves you the time (and expense) you'd otherwise spend in getting to and from work.

➤ Temporary work is like seasonal work except you don't work for the company; you are an employee of the temporary agency and provide services to the company.

Even smaller companies may be receptive to your request to cut back on your hours or share your job responsibilities with someone else. If the company doesn't already have a policy regarding alternate work schedules, it can't hurt to ask.

Senior Info

According to the American Association of Retired People (AARP), about 18% of those between the ages of 65 and 69 work part-time. That percentage drops to 11% for those age 70 to 74, and 14% of those 75 and older are still working part-time.

Set Your Own Hours

If you haven't yet retired and like where you're at, you may be able to stay put and become "semi-retired." This means simply reducing the number of hours you work.

The benefits to staying on the job are many:

➤ You're familiar with the work and the people (and presumably like what you're doing, where you're doing it, and with whom you're doing it).

➤ You may be able to continue to enjoy company benefits, such as retirement plan contributions and employer-paid health insurance (even if you're already 65).

➤ You don't have to look around for other work.

From the employer's perspective, your years of experience and training are retained.

Finding Part-Time Work

Part-time work may make good sense for you, but it's not always easy to find it. If your old employer doesn't want or need you, here are some ideas to help you locate a part-time job to meet your needs:

➤ Networking. Ask friends, family, and the corner grocer who's looking for help. Word-of-mouth can be a powerful thing when it comes to finding a part-time job. Employers may not bother to advertise the position but may be in need of the help.

➤ Classifieds. The newspapers may list part-time work separately from the usual employment opportunities. Check for headings on the columns of the classified ads for "part-time."

➤ Business and professional organizations. If you belong to an organization, you may learn, by word-of-mouth or through the organization's publication, about part-time job opportunities.

➤ State employment office. Check with your state employment office for job listings. Employers may tell the state about an opening (there's no cost to the employer, nor to you, for getting a job in this way).

Golden Years Ideas
The Association of Part-Time Professionals is a nonprofit organization to help you in working or planning to work part-time. They're at 703-734-7975.

Temping

Permanent part-time work isn't the only way to work fewer hours in retirement. Sherri wanted to work for the winter months but also wanted her summers free to play a round of golf or two and travel to see her grandchildren in different parts of the country. Getting a permanent job would have limited her to just two weeks of annual vacation (maybe more after she'd been on the job for many years). Even working part-time may not be a solution for her because she'd still be limited to just a few weeks off each year; the rest of the time she'd be stuck with her part-time schedule. Fortunately, she didn't despair. There was an employment answer for her (and may be it's an answer for you, too): temporary work.

It used to be that clerical help and laborers were able to find day jobs by working for temporary employment agencies. But now, temping is no longer limited to these types of jobs. Everyone's doing it—accountants, lawyers, nurses, even rocket scientists! Yes, Kelly, the nation's largest temporary employment company, now has a division just for science and technology experts. If you've got a skill, there's probably a temporary job waiting for you.

Senior Info

There are more than 7,000 temporary employment agencies in this country, double the number of just a few years ago. The U.S. Department of Labor, Bureau of Labor Statistics, says that the number of temporary and leased employees increased 300% from 1982 through 1993, compared with gains of only 23% in employment in general. Gains in temporary employment are expected to be even greater in the coming years.

To find a temporary employment agency near you, check you local Yellow Pages, or contact the National Association of Temporary and Staffing Services, 119 S. Asaph Street, Alexandria, VA 22314; phone 703-549-6287.

Do You Have the Temperament to Temp?

Golden Years Ideas

It's not uncommon for temporary assignments to turn into full-time employment. It's a win-win situation for all involved. You're already familiar with the company, so you should have a good idea about whether it's right for you. And the company already knows who you are and obviously is pleased with your work. Of course, it's not a good idea to accept a permanent job unless you're prepared to give up the flexibility of temporary work.

It takes a certain personality to be able to walk into a company or new situation cold and catch on to the work (and meld with the other workers) without missing a beat. Before you put yourself into temporary work, make sure you understand what you're getting into.

Here's how temping operates. You apply to a temporary agency and, if they like and need your skills, you'll be sent to a business on a temporary assignment. You don't do the job search; the agency does it. You'll be told what the job involves, where it's located, the hours you're expected to work, and how long the job's expected to last. You can, of course, accept or decline an assignment.

Once you get to the assignment, you'll be told what the company wants you to do. When you're working at the company, you're really the employee of the temporary agency, not the company whose office you're sitting in. The company may want you to stay on longer, or the job may be completed earlier than expected. Be sure to let the agency know the status of your assignment.

If things work out, you may be asked back if and when needed. Or you may just move on to a new assignment at a different company.

Benefits and Burdens of Temping

There are pluses and minuses to temporary employment. Here are some of the good points:

➤ Time flexibility. You get to work when you want (by accepting or declining assignments). Of course, most assignments are full-day commitments; don't expect to find too many part-day temporary jobs. But, depending on what type of work you do, there may not be a steady stream of assignments unless you're willing and able to do other types of work. And, if you continually decline assignments, the agency may stop offering you new ones.

➤ Variety. You'll probably never get bored with the same old office routine. Quite the contrary. You'll go from company to company and get to see how they operate. You'll meet new people all the time.

➤ Pay. You'll receive a competitive wage for the work you do. However, the amount you're paid depends on the skills involved. Basic clerical work may pay only minimum wage; providing experienced legal assistance on a corporate lawsuit may pay handsomely.

All is not perfect with temporary work. There's a downside to consider:

➤ Income uncertainty. Because you're not earning a regular salary, there's no guarantee you'll earn what you need from working. Your weekly check may be larger or smaller than you expected, depending on the assignment you've accepted.

➤ Lack of benefits. You may be sent to do word processing at IBM, a company known for its generous employee benefits. Don't expect to enjoy them, even if your assignment lasts for months on end. You're the employee of the temporary agency and only entitled to any benefits they may offer. Typically, there are none. In most cases, you won't get medical benefits. You won't get pension benefits. Some agencies give "vacation pay" if you work a certain number of hours during the year.

If, after comparing the pros and cons to temping, you decide it's for you, then jump right in. After all, there's very little commitment here. All you have to do is complete an assignment if you accept it. If, after working temporary, you decide it's *not* for you, then you can look into other work options.

To find a temporary employment agency in your area, look in your local phone directory. If the first agency fails to get you jobs, move on to the next agency.

Join the Ranks of Consultants

As the number of middle managers laid off in corporate downsizing of the '80s and '90s increased, so did the number of consultants. Instead of returning to another company in the same rat race, many choose to become their own bosses and offer their skills to whomever is interested.

What are you consulting about? Most consultants use the very skills they learned on the job in their consulting business. A senior programmer given early retirement from IBM may become a consultant on programming. Someone who had been in management becomes a management consultant. Businesses like to use consultants to provide added expertise without having to hire a new employee. This saves the company from having to provide benefits or make a long-term commitment beyond the length of a particular project.

Successful consultants love their status. They can often command high fees for their services. They may work for several different businesses at the same time. And they can accept or decline jobs when it's best for them. Consultants are self-employed individuals who are really in their own business. They generally have all the same problems and concerns as anyone starting their own business. These problems and concerns, and how to address them, are explained in Chapter 7, "Starting Your Own Business at Home."

Senior Info

It takes time to build up a consulting business. The National Bureau of Professional Management Consultants says that it generally takes more than three years to make enough from consulting to cover expenses and their own compensation. The Bureau says to be prepared to subsidize yourself (cover your expenses and what you need in the way of salary) 100% the first year, 70% the second year, and 20% the third year. Of course, you could get lucky and be in the black from the start.

Keeping Consulting to a Limit

Because consulting usually isn't 9 to 5, it's included in this chapter on part-time work. Many who go into consulting have a vision of working when they want to and having plenty of time off. However, many consultants wind up working *more* than 9 to 5 and would hardly call what they're doing "part-time."

That's what happened to Martin, a physics professor at an Ivy League school, when he retired. He didn't want to just sit around collecting his pension, so he set up a consulting business to provide information to corporations on his area of expertise (which is too complicated to explain here!). His wife became his assistant, scheduling his appointments and keeping his books. Within a few months, Martin was flying all over the country at the expense of his clients, and he had more work than he knew what to do with. He never did get that time off to read the books he'd been putting on a reading list for 30 years.

Like Martin, the problem for some fortunate consultants is knowing how to limit assignments. They're afraid to turn one down because there's no guarantee that another one will come along. However, if consulting is meant to complement retirement, then limits are a must.

With calendar in hand, plot out the time you want for yourself. Then plot out the assignments you've already accepted. Make sure they don't overlap. If you've already filled in a lot of work time, don't accept any more assignments until there are more free spaces.

Marketing Your Services

When Harry, an engineer, was given early retirement by his company, he jumped at the generous severance package. But after a few months, he was bored, and the company found that it still needed his input. The perfect solution for both of them was for Harry to provide services to his former employer on a consultant basis.

But not everyone has a ready-made outlet to provide consulting services to. Unless you're like Harry, you'll have to look around for a company (or companies) willing to take you on. Marketing your services is not that simple.

First you have to define yourself. Don't try to do it all; carve out a niche or specialty you can offer. The term "computer consultant" is too broad. Are you offering services in setting up computer systems? Teaching computer software? Designing computer software?

> **Cash Crash**
> Don't get into legal hot water in going after your former employer's customers. You may be in violation of a noncompete agreement you signed as part of your employment contract or severance agreement. You may get in trouble for revealing company trade secrets. If you think you're treading on thin ice, talk to an attorney before you fall into the water.

> **Golden Years Ideas**
> Join a trade association to help you market your services. For example, computer consultants might consider the Independent Computer Consultants Association (ICCA) (800-774-4222) or the National Association of Computer Consultant Businesses (NACCB) (800-313-1920). ICCA can be used for networking to find assignments; NACCB helps find assignments for consultants.

As a consultant, you're in your own business and must market yourself as such. You'll have to let potential customers know you're available. A phone call to the right person can be the most effective and efficient way to land a consulting contract. Network with other consultants to find out what's going on in your area.

Drawing Up a Consulting Agreement

For some people, a handshake is ironclad. But today, corporate personnel come and go, so the person you may have shaken hands with could be out the door, and the new guy won't know who you are. The best way to protect yourself is to have a contract that spells out your rights and obligations with respect to the person or company you provide the services to. (The company you do business with probably will insist on it for its own protection.) The type of contract you use for this purpose is called a *consulting agreement.*

Cash Crash
If you write your own consulting agreement, be sure to have a lawyer review it for you to make sure you didn't leave anything out. While you'll pay for the service, you'll be able to deduct it as a business expense.

Cash Crash
A contract is one way to protect yourself. Another is to have errors and omissions insurance to protect yourself from claims of damage resulting from your errors, omissions, or wrongful acts in the performance of your services. The basic cost of an annual policy runs about $1,000 a year. Check with an insurance agent who handles E&O coverage.

The company you're doing the work for may insist on using its own form. But many smaller companies that have either never or rarely used consultants may not have stock agreements. The ball may be in your court to come up with one (or at least have some input into their agreements). You can have an attorney draw one up for you (it shouldn't cost too much because it's a simple legal document), or you can write one yourself. Be sure that you address these key points in your agreement:

➤ Type of work. Spell out what you're expected to do and where you're expected to do it (on company premises or at your own location).

➤ Compensation. Describe how much you'll be paid (by the hour, by the job, and so on) and when you'll be paid (weekly, monthly, upon completion of the job). Also state whether you're to be reimbursed for any expenses, such as your travel, telephone, or postage costs.

➤ Status as an independent contractor. It's important to spell out that your relationship with the company is one of an independent contractor and not as an employee. Of course, the relationship must be genuine; if you're really just an employee under the complete control of the company, the label of independent contractor won't protect the company from IRS claims of liability for employment taxes on compensation paid to you. And you may be entitled to employee benefits as well.

➤ Starting and finishing the job. Put in writing when you're supposed to start the job and when the relationship between you and the company is set to end. Sometimes, the arrangement is a one-time thing. But typically, contractors and the company may extend the relationship indefinitely by renewing the consulting agreement.

Use the following agreement as a starting point for your own agreement. Tailor it any way you like.

THIS AGREEMENT, dated *(add the date you make the agreement)* between *(your name)*, residing at *(your address)* (the "Consultant") and *(name of person or company you're providing services to)*, doing business at *(address of person or company)* (the "Company").

WHEREAS, the Company wishes to retain the Consultant as an independent contractor, and the Consultant wishes to be retained in such capacity and perform certain services for the Company.

NOW THEREFORE, in consideration of the mutual covenants contained herein, the parties agree to the following terms and conditions:

1. Commission of work. The Company retains the Consultant to provide the following services *(describe what type of work is to be done)*.

2. Compensation. The Consultant shall receive the following compensation *(describe the compensation: by the job, hourly, monthly, etc.)*. Said compensation shall be paid *(monthly, quarterly, etc.)* following submission of a bill for services.

The Company also agrees to reimburse the Consultant for *(enter expenses that the company will reimburse, such as all ordinary and necessary business expenses, only travel expenses, insurance, etc.)*. Said reimbursement shall be paid *(monthly, quarterly, etc.)* following submission of a bill for expenses accompanied by corroboration of expenses *(such as receipts, canceled checks, etc.)*.

The Company shall not provide the Consultant with any other compensation or benefits, including but not limited to medical or pension benefits, vacation, holiday or sick time.

3. Contractor's status. The Consultant shall be treated in all respects as an independent contractor, and the Company shall not withhold any taxes on account of services rendered to it by the Consultant. The Consultant represents that he/she is holding himself/herself out as a consultant to others and assumes all the risk of the Consultant's classification as an independent contractor and not an employee.

Consulting agreement—page 1.

4. <u>Commencement and termination</u>. This Agreement shall commence on *(end date that work is to start)* and shall terminate upon the earlier of: (1) the last day of the 12th month following the date of this Agreement unless this agreement is not canceled by the parties, in which event it shall be renewed for one additional year under the same terms set forth herein unless modified in writing, (2) the death or substantial disability of the Consultant, or (3) the cessation of the business of the Company.

5. <u>Entire agreement</u>. This Agreement constitutes the entire agreement between the parties hereto, supersedes all existing agreements between them, and cannot be changed or terminated except by a written agreement signed by the parties and may not be assigned by either party.

6. <u>Severability and waiver</u>. In the event that any term of this Agreement shall be held to be illegal, invalid, or unenforceable, the remaining terms shall not be in any way affected or impaired thereby.

The failure by either party to seek redress for a violation of any term in this Agreement shall not constitute a waiver nor prevent redress for a subsequent violation.

7. <u>Governing law</u>. This Agreement shall be construed in accordance with the laws of the State of *(add your state)*.

Company

By: *(President's signature)*
       (President's name), President

Consultant

By: *(Your signature)*
       (Your name)

Consulting agreement—page 2.

The Least You Need to Know

➤ Part-time employment is a popular work alternative for many retirees.

➤ Instead of leaving your job, you may become "semi-retired" by arranging for part-time work.

➤ Working for a temporary agency gives you the flexibility to work the times of the year you want and have the rest of the time off.

➤ Being a consultant lets you use your skills to work as much, or as little, as you want.

Chapter 6

Starting Over With Second (and Third) Careers

In This Chapter

➤ Planning before it's too late

➤ Deciding on a second career

➤ Retraining yourself

➤ Landing the job you want

Harold owned an ad agency that provided advertising work for Fortune 500 companies. In his mid-60s, after more than 40 years in the business, he retired. That ended his first career. Within a year, however, he was on to his second career: head of a new business providing seminars on coping with death, retirement, and other major life changes. You'd never know he retired. But he looks upon himself as the beneficiary of retirement (the opportunity to try something new).

In this chapter, you'll learn how to start your new career, or as the *Wall Street Journal* calls it, your "postcareer career." You'll see how to decide on what career is best for you and how to break into it. You'll find out where you can go for retraining if you need new skills at your age to stay in the workplace. And you'll get help in making the changeover to your new career.

Preplanning for Your Postretirement Career

If you haven't yet retired, don't wait until you've cleaned out your desk before you start thinking about another career. Begin right away to make career plans so you'll be able to slip into a new job when you retire. Maybe it's just another job doing the same thing you've been doing. Maybe it's an entirely new career. If you've already retired and miss being able to bring home a paycheck or gossip at the water cooler, you can still re-enter the job market in a new career.

The first step in planning is to decide what you're going to do. This may or may not require you to get some job training or go back to school. Then you can begin your job search.

What Do You Want to Do When You Grow Up?

You asked yourself that once before, maybe even more than once, and came up with an answer. Now is the time to do it again. Decide what you want to do with the rest of your life. There's still plenty of time to develop a new game plan for a career and act upon it. Remember that you may have nearly as many years in retirement as during your so-called working years.

Of course, you have to be realistic. Even if you always wanted to be a surgeon or an astronaut, there are some careers that may be out of the question.

Assess Your Strengths and Weaknesses

What are you good at? Where do you fall short? Your strengths and weaknesses may suggest what to do and not to do with your next career.

Take the following test to help you decide what direction you want to take in your second career. Answer the questions as honestly as you can (cheating won't help, and no one but you will see your answers).

Job skills you already have

Skill	Strong	Somewhat	Weak
Sales ability			
Computer literacy			
Financial management know-how			
Personnel experience			
People skills			
Business operations know-how			

In what category did you indicate a strong ability? Look at the following list to see the type of career that might match up with your skills:

➤ Sales ability. This skill can always be used to sell just about anything. Beyond a job in sales, you might also consider advertising, market research, or public relations (PR). These aspects of marketing all involve selling a product, a service, or a person.

➤ Computer literacy. Today, in almost any office job you take, knowledge of how to work a computer is essential. You can use your proficiency to work in just about all companies, organizations, and government offices.

➤ Financial management know-how. If you have bookkeeping and accounting skills, many companies will be interested in having you use those skills for them. But you can also consider such areas as cost control, credit and collections, and even banking.

➤ Personnel experience. Hiring and firing is a skill. Understanding job benefits is a skill. Training and motivating workers is a skill. Use these skills in a personnel department. Or consider employment agencies and outplacement services firms.

➤ People skills. If you can manage people and have experience with doing so, use your skills in almost any line of work. Supervisory positions may be open in industries you have worked in. Or try using your old skill in a new industry.

➤ Business operations. You may be skilled in a particular aspect of business operations, such as quality control, inventory control, or pricing. The knowledge of that operation from one particular industry can be applied to another industry.

Get Help

If, after you've self-assessed your skills, you still have no idea which direction to take, maybe you would benefit from some help. Talk over your options with friends and family. "Brainstorm" with them to narrow down your choices.

Maybe casual help won't do, and you need professional career guidance. When I was just out of college and unsure about what career path to take after being a history and government major, I went for career counseling at Columbia University. After a battery of tests and several one-on-one sessions with a counselor, I decided to go to law school. If you're stuck in a rut, you, too, might consider career counseling to help you get a fix on which way to go. For example, Dial-a-Mentor provides over-the-phone counseling (e-mail at rozrelin@aol.com). The company itself was founded as a second career by someone who found retirement boring. Sources for counseling services include your local community college as well as private career counselors. Look under "Career and vocational counseling" in your local Yellow Pages.

Check out the cost before you sign up. You may pay for a series of sessions at a flat fee, or you may pay by the hour.

If you've been given early retirement by a large corporation, you may receive outplacement assistance at no cost to you. Your former employer may have contracted with a company to provide you with counseling and job placement help. You may be given counseling, a desk, a telephone, and all the time you need to find a new job.

Turn Volunteer Work Into a Paid Job

Take your new career for a test drive. How? Start doing volunteer work for an organization even while you're still working. This will allow you to become familiar with the job itself and with the organization. You may be able to turn your volunteer job into a paid position as Catherine did. For many years, she was active as a volunteer on her community organization's fundraising committee. In this activity, she gained fundraising skills that she was able to translate into a job after retirement from a job as a manager of a plumbing supply business. A small, nonprofit organization hired her as its fundraising director—a paid position doing much the same as she had done for years as a volunteer.

Generally, you don't have to have any special skill to do certain volunteer jobs, such as helping the National Audubon Society restore ecosystems for birds and provide educational programs for the public (212-979-3000). Once you're in the organization, you can see what paid positions become available.

Turning a hobby into a job is explained in Chapter 9, "Turn Your Leisure Time Into Dollars."

Retooling Your Job Skills

Maybe you lack computer know-how or other skills that will allow you to move into a second career. Maybe you just want to do something different. It's not too late to get the skills you need or want.

To paraphrase Thomas Wolfe, "You can't go back to the old job again," especially if that job's been eliminated in corporate downsizing or outmoded by today's technology. Get with it! Learn the skills that are most prized in today's job market.

One highly valued skill these days is computer literacy. Sure, your grandchild is a whiz. But you can be, too. Here are some places to learn WordPerfect, Excel, Netscape, and other new skills that will allow you to work well past your normal retirement age:

➤ Take a course at a community college. The cost is usually modest (especially if the school offers incentives for seniors).

➤ Learn a particular software program in an adult education program. When I switched from using WordPerfect to Microsoft Word, I took a six-week course on Word that met two evenings a week at the Board of Continuing Education, not far from my home. In this brief time, I learned all I needed to know to handle all basic functions and then some. The cost for this course: only $60.

➤ Sign up for special training programs designed for seniors. Your community may offer programs specifically designed for so-called displaced homemakers (women who haven't worked in years or at all but who must now get a job) and for seniors who are low-income people. For example, in my area, the county offers a computer training program for qualified individuals (those who are over 55 and living on very low incomes). While they're in training, the program pays the minimum wage for 20 hours a week for up to 40 weeks. The instruction is given at a community college and is usually completed in four months. Following completion of the course, there's job placement assistance. Check out the programs in Table 6.1.

Table 6.1 Sources of Retraining

Training Program	Contact	Description
Job Training Partnership Act programs	Call National Association of Counties at 202-393-6226 to find a local program	Training disadvantaged persons 55 and over
Senior Community Service Employment Programs (SCSEPs)	Your local telephone number or call your state office on aging	Work-training programs for disadvantaged persons 55 and over

Getting the Job You Want

As you may remember from job searches earlier in your career, the process can be lengthy and discouraging. With that knowledge under your belt, now is the time to begin.

Looking for your postretirement positions is really no different from the job searches you've conducted throughout your working career. There are basically three phases to your job search: locating openings, contacting these openings, and, if you're called for an interview, convincing the company why they should hire you instead of everyone else they've seen.

Locating Openings

There are an infinite number of ways to find a job. There's no single right way; the one that works for you is the right way. You can, of course, go the conventional route and comb through the classifieds each week or use an employment agency. Or you can try a less conventional route, which just may pay off for you.

Networking puts others to work helping you find a job. Remember when you moved to your area and asked your next-door neighbor to recommend an internist? That's networking. You can use the same process to locate a job opening that's right for you. Let people know you're looking and what you're interested in. Use contacts you've made over the years to help you find a job. Don't be shy about calling in favors owed to you. Join a networking group or form your own. In some places, laid-off workers have formed informal job clubs to share leads, information, and be supportive to each other. A key benefit to networking is being able to locate jobs that aren't advertised.

Job councils for seniors can also be helpful in locating job openings. If you're over 50, you may be able to use a special type of employment agency geared for seniors. Many cities and counties throughout the country have set up senior personnel employment councils. These are essentially employment agencies, but they're not commercial; they're either government sponsored or part of a nonprofit organization. To find a senior job council near you, call your local Office for the Aging listing on the Blue Sheets of your Yellow Pages under government listings.

Internet job searches are becoming an effective way to search for a job. If you own a computer that's tied into the Internet or you have access to one (through a friend or at your local library), you can do a job search on-line. You can use your computer to search for openings and/or post your résumé for interested employers to look at. In this way, you can conduct your search 24 hours a day, 365 days a year, and never leave your home.

Senior Info

There are more than 5,000 Web sites with more than a million job openings listed each day. Most major corporations are now using the Internet to post positions. State and federal agencies are also getting on-line. You can circulate your résumé without the postage costs if you go on-line. While there's no data as yet on how many openings are filled through the Internet, there are many success stories to inspire on-line hopefuls.

Of course, there's one negative to posting your résumé on-line that you should keep in mind and that may result in the loss of privacy. People you know may trip across your vital data on-line. If you're still employed, you don't want your current employer to see that you're looking for another job. The following are just some of the many Web sites for job hunters:

America's Job Bank	http://www.ajb.dni.us
Best Jobs USA	http://www.bestjobsusa.com
Career City	http://www.careercity.com
Career Magazine	http://www.careermag.com
Career Mosaic	http://www.careermosaic.com

Career Path	http://www.careerpath.com
Careers OnLine	http://www.careersonline.com
E-Span	http://www.espan.com
4 Work	http://www.4work.com
Hot Jobs	http://www.hotjobs.com
IEEE Employment	http://www.ieee.org/jobs.html
Intellimatch	http://www.intellimatch.com
Job Bank USA	http://www.jobbankusa.com
Job Trak	http://www.jobtrak.com
Job Web	http://www.jobweb.com
MedSearch America	http://www.medsearch.com
Monster Board	http://www.monster.com
Nation Job Network	http://www.nationjob.com
Online Career Center	http://www.occ.com
TOPjobs USA	http://www.topjob.com

Also call your local unemployment office for its Web site. A number of unemployment offices are now posting job openings on the Internet.

A Winning Résumé and Cover Letter

Your résumé and cover letter may be a company's first glimpse of you; unless they're both good, it will be its last. A cover letter should accompany each résumé you send. Here are some guidelines for a résumé that will catch the eye of the reader:

➤ Make it look good. Use quality stationery and a clear typeface.

➤ Include vital information. Tell the reader your work experience. (List your entries in *reverse* chronological order, with the most recent entry first.) In addition to names of prior employers and dates of employment, include how *you* made a difference to the company. If you introduced a new method that saved 20% on costs, shepherded your department through a transition to a new computer system, or increased sales by 30%, highlight that information. Don't include personal information, such as your marital status, your birthday, number of children you have, your weight and height, or information about your health.

➤ Keep it short. Limit your résumé to one to two pages. You don't have to include information about a part-time job you had in college 40 years ago. You don't have to list your clubs and awards from your college days unless your college days were very recent.

Golden Years Ideas

Make it perfect. Don't have *any* typos or spelling errors in your résumé or cover letter. These are an immediate turn-off to the reader. Have someone else read over your résumé and cover letter to check for any errors. Don't rely only on your computer's "spell check" to catch them.

You can get an idea about how a good résumé looks by checking out books in the library. You can also use résumé templates available on certain word processing software. For example, Microsoft Word has three different résumé templates that guide you through making your own résumé. You fill in the information when you're prompted to do so.

Here are some guidelines for a dynamite cover letter that's sure to get read:

➤ Make it look good. Just like your résumé, quality stationery and a clear typeface are a must for your cover letter. Use the same paper and typeface for your résumé and letter.

➤ Keep it short. Your cover letter should be no more than one page.

➤ Make it personal. Address your letter to the right person. Don't use "To Whom It May Concern." You may have to call the company to find out who to address your letter to. If the ad is to a post office box, then use "Dear Employer." Use the correct title of the person, such as Dr. If you're writing to a woman and you don't know how she refers to her marital status, be safe and use Ms.

➤ Get to the point. Use short, clear sentences to get your message across, state what job you're applying for, and why you'd be ideal for it.

An Interview They'll Remember

It's been said that first impressions make lasting impressions. A person may be able to size you up in a matter of minutes. So make the most of the few minutes you have by doing the following:

➤ Arrive on time. Traffic jams, a flat tire, or a broken wrist watch are all plausible reasons for being late, but that won't help you. The impression you've made by arriving late is that you're always late and that you'll be late to work if you're hired. In effect, if you arrive late, the interview is already over.

➤ Dress appropriately. Sure you're retired, but don't wear your tennis shoes to an interview for an office job. Body language is also essential during the interview. Sit up straight, don't fidget, and make eye contact with the interviewer.

➤ Come prepared. Be ready to tell the interviewer why you're the right person for the job. Also ask questions that show you are already familiar with the company. One common note that is sounded on interviews with some retirees changing careers is that they're "overqualified." Will a former high-level manager now be able to take orders from a middle management type? The employer thinks you won't be satisfied with the work and that you'll leave. Convince the employer that you're really interested in this particular job and that you're committed to making it work.

Follow up your interview with a thank-you letter within a couple of days. Make it short: a paragraph or two. Thank the interviewer for the opportunity of speaking with him or her (it will help to remind that person who you are), restate your qualifications for the job opening, and add anything you forgot to tell the interviewer when you met.

Senior Info

A problem that some retirees encounter when job hunting is a negative stereotype of an older worker. Employers may be under the misconception that it costs *more* to hire the elderly. There's no basis in fact for this belief. For example, one research group found that there was no significant difference in health insurance costs for older and younger workers. Also, older workers not only offer employers their experience and skills, but also can *cost* employers less because of a high work ethic and low turnover. If you find resistance to being hired and you think it's because of some prejudice due to your age, be sure to communicate the real facts to the employer.

The Least You Need to Know

➤ Start looking into a second career even before you've left the first one.

➤ Assess your job strengths and weaknesses to help you decide on a second career.

➤ Get retraining to broaden your career paths.

➤ Conduct a job search on-line or through networking.

➤ Make an impression with a dynamite résumé and cover letter.

➤ Convince the interviewer to value your experience and to hire you.

Chapter 7

Starting Your Own Business at Home

It's been estimated that between three and five million home-based businesses will start up this year. Will you be one of them? I've run my business from home for 15 years and have seen the opportunities for home-based businesses swell. Maybe you've thought about starting a business now that you've retired, and your home would be an ideal location to start from. I couldn't agree more, as long as you understand that there are risks and problems associated with this choice.

In this chapter, you'll see the many advantages of starting a business from home (and the drawbacks). You'll learn about the best types of businesses to run from home. And you'll find out about the problems that come with operating from home so you'll be able to avoid them.

It's fair to say that all the information you need on starting and running a home-based business can't fit in this one chapter. After all, I wrote an entire book on the subject, *The Complete Idiot's Guide to Starting a Home-Based Business.* If you think you want to go the home business route, I suggest you read further in other sources after you've digested the material in this chapter.

Is Working From Home for You?

Don't be hasty. Before you answer this question, consider both the good points and bad. Working from home offers many advantages, especially for older individuals. But there are negatives that you shouldn't overlook.

> **Senior Info**
>
> Working at home doesn't mean you're alone. You can join with the millions of other home-based business owners by joining special trade associations, such as the American Association of Home-Based Businesses (800-447-9710); Home Office Association of America (800-809-4622); and Small Office Home Office Association (800-SOHOA11). Another trade association that can help, though not limited to home businesses, is the National Association for the Self-Employed (800-232-NASE).

Good Reasons for Working at Home

Here are some positive reasons for working from home:

➤ Your business operating expenses are low. The reason: You're already paying the rent (or the mortgage). You don't have to pay the added cost of running a business from an office or storefront.

➤ No commute. You don't have to get from home to office; you're already there! This saves you the time you would have spent in commuting that you can use for your leisure activities or to get a few extra winks in the morning. It also saves you money that you'd otherwise spend on gas, tolls, or a train or bus ticket each day. Over the course of a year, this expense can certainly add up.

➤ Flexibility. You can combine your work schedule with any other activities you want or need to pursue. Maybe you have to baby-sit Brian, your grandchild, two afternoons a week. Maybe you want to sit in a weekly afternoon poker game. If you work from home, you can set your own hours (within the limits of the business you're running) and have time for personal pursuits.

Drawbacks to Working From Home

Working from home is not all roses. You need to weigh the disadvantages that come from having your business in the same place where you live. The following are some of the possible drawbacks:

➤ Lack of privacy. You can't shut out the business world as easily as you can when you work outside the home. The phone may ring at any hour of the day. Your inventory may be sitting in your family room. Your spouse may be lounging on the couch in front of you while you're hard at work.

➤ Loss of space. You'll have to cede some living space to your business. Depending on what business you run, this may be a little or a lot.

➤ Isolation. Some people thrive on the social ongoings of an office setting. Market research has shown that friendships on the job are a very important reason why people (women especially) keep working, and operating from home doesn't address this need. Working at home means you're alone, or almost alone, most of the time. Of course, you're not a prisoner of your home office and can arrange to get out even if the business doesn't take you there.

➤ Lifestyle change. Going from working in an office for someone else to working at home for yourself is night and day. In the first instance, you're basically operating 9 to 5 doing one job (the skill you have). In the second instance, you're working an unlimited schedule doing a multitude of jobs. As a business owner, you're not only doing the same skills you did as an employee, but you're also in charge of marketing, finances, ordering supplies, and everything else.

➤ Discipline. When you worked outside the home, the job defined what you did and when you did it. Now you have to set your own boundaries. You have to make sure that you're the type of person who can get down to work when the laundry or other distractions around the house are calling to you.

Businesses You Can Easily Run From Home

You may already have a general, or even a specific, idea about the type of business you'd like to run from home. But maybe you're still fishing. There's an idea out there for you.

With today's technology, more and more businesses can operate successfully from home. Having access to the Internet means that a small business run from someone's living room in White Fish, Montana, can get the same information that General Electric can get. That's why consultants can operate so successfully from home (consulting was explained in Chapter 5, "Part-Time Work for Full-Time Rewards"). However, not every kind of business lends itself to a home-based operation. Here's a listing of just some of the businesses you can easily run from home and their start-up costs:

➤ Antiques dealer. You don't have to have a storefront in your home to be in the antiques business. You can sell your items in several other ways: on the Internet through your own Web page, at an antiques mall by taking a booth, or at antiques shows by being an exhibitor. Many retirees are into the antiques business because they've already spent a lifetime collecting their goodies. Cost: from $0 to $50,000 or more, depending on whether you already have an inventory you can sell. The cost of setting up and maintaining a Web page is modest (about $75 a month). Space in an antiques mall runs about $125 to $150 a month. An area at an antiques show runs about the same.

➤ Bed and breakfast. If your home is a white elephant (or you want to buy one), you may be able to turn it into a profit center. If you're in a tourist area, a bed and breakfast allows you to take in handsome fees for weekend lodgers. You provide a room, breakfast, and local information on what to see and do in the area. Of course, there's a lot of work involved in maintaining your home and meeting the needs of your guests. A handyman's skills are invaluable here. And having adequate insurance to cover potential liability for accidents by guests and other occurrences. Cost: up to $250,000 or more, depending on whether you already own a home and what condition it's in. You may have to make costly improvements to bring it up to code or to make accommodations required by the Americans with Disabilities Act.

➤ Bill collection. With a telephone and persistence, you can make a business out of helping local businesses collect on their unpaid bills. You earn a percentage of the amount you collect (ranging from 25% to as high as 50%). But just make sure you know the rules of debt collection under the Fair Debt Collection Practices Act and the Fair Credit Reporting Act so you won't get into trouble. Cost: virtually nothing (just your phone).

➤ Catering and food services. If you've spent a lifetime of baking fancy birthday cakes for your family, you may be able to use that skill for profit. You can charge $15, $25, or more for custom designed cakes. You may be able to supply baked goods to local restaurants that advertise "home made" or take orders from individuals who need a three-tiered mocha wedding cake or a Power Ranger birthday cake for their 8-year-old. A neighbor of mine paid for all her Christmas shopping and then some by making chocolate candies that she sold at Christmas time, Valentine's Day, and Easter. You may also be able to cater parties and dinners by preparing food in your home if local health codes allow it. Cost: a few hundred dollars to get the pots and pans you don't already own and to advertise your business.

➤ Cleaning and handyman services. If you're adept in these areas, you can work from your home to provide these services. Louis, a retired cop from Newark, took to appliance repairs to supplement his pension. He worked on refrigerators, dishwashers, washing machines, and other appliances. Cost: up to a few hundred dollars to get the right tools and supplies.

➤ Freelance writer. All you need is a personal computer and expertise on a particular subject, and you're in business. You can sell your services to newspapers, magazines, or even write books as I do. Cost: $0 to $3,000 (depending on whether you already own a computer and printer).

➤ Mail order. Catalogs abound. L.L. Bean and Victoria Secret catalogs bring in millions in sales. But there are dozens of small specialty catalogs that are making a living for their owners. You can certainly run a catalog business from home. Talk to manufacturers to get the rights to distribute their products through your catalog. Cost: a few hundred to several thousand dollars, depending on whether you already own a computer and how much your inventory will cost.

➤ Word processing. If you used to be a secretary in an office, you can use your word processing skills to run a business of typing materials for other people. You can prepare letters, term papers, or manuscripts. Competition in this type of business is high because there are so many people offering this service. Try to specialize, such as typing up doctor's notes. Cost: $0 to $3,000 (depending on whether you already own a computer and printer).

Many of these ideas are discussed in greater detail in Chapter 9, "Turn Your Leisure Time Into Dollars." You can find many other ideas for home-based businesses listed on the Internet (for example: http://www.getbuzy.com).

Do Market Research Before You Begin

Your idea may be great, but does your community really need another house-cleaning service? Take the time before you put in any money to see whether your business has a chance of flying. Do some market research to find out some necessary information:

➤ Identify potential customers or clients. Who are you trying to reach? Get numbers. For example, if you want to provide word processing services to doctors in your area, find out how many doctors there are. This is the *maximum* number of customers if you got 100% response. Now obviously, you won't get this kind of interest, but if you get 5%, how many customers does that mean? You can find demographic information about how many people live in your area and what income brackets they're in by checking local census information at your library.

➤ Find out who the competition is. How many other businesses are offering the same product or service as you in the same area? Maybe there's room for one more, or maybe the market is already saturated. If there's competition, decide how you're going to distinguish yourself from the rest of the pack. Lower prices? A better guarantee? Some free service?

Senior Info

To help you find out the information you're looking for about similar businesses in your area and how they're doing, talk to your neighborhood bankers, Chamber of Commerce, economic development agency, and the local Small Business Administration Office. You can find the location of these contacts in your Yellow Pages (remember that government listings are in the Blue Pages).

➤ Set your price. After you've answered the first two questions about need for your business (customers or clients) and competition, you're ready to figure out what you can charge. If all your competitors are charging $6 a page for word processing, you can't charge $10 unless there's a very good reason for the extra cost (for example, you work overnight). If you want to lowball your competitors, make sure you'll still make a profit (that there's money left over after paying your expenses). There's no point in working for nothing.

What It Costs to Get Started

As you can see from some of the ideas listed earlier for home-based businesses, it may cost almost nothing to get started. But, on the other hand, there may be many costs involved. In fact, many businesses have the highest expenses at the start when income is the lowest. Use the following worksheet to figure what it's going to cost you to open your doors for business.

Start-Up Item*	Estimated Cost
Accounting fees (to set up books and accounts)	$
Advertising and promotion	$
Computer, telephone, copier, fax	$
Insurance: liability, other (separate or add-on to homeowners)	$
Inventory (if the business is product oriented)	$
Legal fees (to incorporate or obtain a special zoning permit)	$
Licenses/permits	$
Miscellaneous and unanticipated expenses	$
Occupancy costs (to make your space usable for business)	$
Office furniture (desk, file cabinet, etc.)	$
Office supplies (stationery, business cards, paper, etc.)	$
Tools and equipment	$
Total Start-Up Costs	$

Worksheet for projecting startup costs

Be sure to include your personal living expenses (which include your rent or mortgage, utilities, food, medical, and other personal expenses).

Tax Savvy for Your Home Business

Once you're in business, Uncle Sam becomes your partner for life, sharing in your profits and monitoring your activities. Taxes for your business—what you'll pay, what return you'll file, and when you'll file it—depend on how you've legally organized your business. If you haven't taken any special steps and you're in business by yourself, you're a sole proprietor and report your business income and expenses on your personal income tax return (using Schedule C or Schedule C-EZ). If you've incorporated or set up your business in some other form, you'll use different forms and schedules to report your business income and expenses.

It's not so much what you earn as how much you can keep after-tax that determines how profitable your business really is. Most expenses you incur for your business will be deductible, but there may be special rules or limits. For example, many of your startup expenses can't be deducted immediately but instead are written off over five years or more.

One of the chief advantages to working from home is the opportunity to deduct some of the expenses you're already paying for, such as your utilities, as a business expense. As long as your home is the principal place of business for you, a portion of your home expenses can be deducted (assuming you have enough business income against which to claim a deduction). To find out more about deducting your home office expenses, refer to IRS Publication 587, Business Use of Your Home, which you can obtain for free by calling 800-829-1040.

If you think taxes are one area you can't handle on your own, get the right kind of help. Tax software, like TurboTax for Business, can guide you through the tax return process. Use a tax professional, such as an accountant, to handle matters for you. If you already use a CPA for your personal returns, don't assume the same person is the best one to handle your business affairs. If you need to locate a CPA in your area, call your state CPA society (listed in your Yellow Pages) for a referral.

Golden Years Ideas

Make sure you do things right to keep out of trouble with the IRS (and your state tax authority if applicable). You usually need an employer identification number (it's like a business's Social Security number), which you can get by completing IRS Form SS-4 (you'll find a copy of it in Chapter 9). Make sure you meet all business tax filing deadlines. Call the IRS at 800-829-1040 to get Form SS-4 and other tax reporting information for your business.

Getting Your Business Started

Having an idea about the type of business you're going to run and what it's going to cost you is step one in the start-up process. Next, you need to make a plan about how you're going to run the business. You may also need to raise cash to get started.

Make a Business Plan

Word to the Wise

A *business plan* is a report stating what your business is all about, how you intend to cover your expenses and make a profit, where you see the business three or five years from now, and how you expect to get there.

Even if the last time you wrote a report was in school 50 years ago, you now need to make a business plan. You don't have to be a Hemingway to write a business plan. All you need is to write down in straight talk the necessary information about your business.

Having a business plan is essential. It lets you organize your ideas about the business and discover the strengths and weaknesses about your business concept. It's required if you're planning to raise money at a bank or with family and friends. It will also guide you in the future to bring your business along.

Senior Info

You can write the plan yourself by using books on business plan writing to guide you. You can use commercial software if you have a computer (for example, Jian Biz Plan Builder for Windows is about $90). You can pay an expert (which can run up to several thousand dollars). My favorite way: using the guidance you can get from the Small Business Administration's Web site (http://www.sbaonline.sba.gov), which has not only an outline for a business plan, but also blanks of all the financial forms you need to include (projected start-up costs and your personal financial statement). You can even find shareware (software you pay a small fee to use) just for writing business plans.

Even if you don't go the whole nine yards and include every section suggested in business plan guides, and no matter how small you are, you should *at the very least* put down on paper how you're going to make the business work.

What's the business going to be doing? Describe your product or service. Also tell how your business is organized from a legal standpoint. Table 7.1 displays choices.

Table 7.1 Comparison of Business Forms

Type of Entity	What the Owner Is Called	Suitability for One-Person Business	Implications of Form
Sole proprietorship (including independent contractor)	Owner (proprietor)	Yes	You and the business are one and the same. You report business income and expenses on your personal tax return. You are personally liable for the debts of the business.
Partnership	Partner	No	Partnership is not a taxpayer (you report your share of business income and expenses on your personal return). You are jointly and severally liable for the debts of the business.

continues

Table 7.1 Continued

Type of Entity	What the Owner Is Called	Suitability for One-Person Business	Implications of Form
Limited liability company	Member	No*	LLC is not a taxpayer (unless it chooses to be treated like a corporation). You report your share of business income and expenses on your personal return. There is no personal liability.
C corporation	Shareholder	Yes	Corporation is a taxpayer (you report only wages, dividends, and other payments made to you on your personal return). No personal liability.
S corporation	Shareholder	Yes	The S corporation is not a taxpayer. You report your share of business income and expenses on your personal return. No personal liability.

One-member LLCs are permitted in some states.

What are your monthly expenses to run the business, and how will you pay for them? List your expenses. Then list your *expected* revenue each month. If your revenue is more than your expenses, you're probably okay. If your revenue falls short, make a plan for how you expect to cover your expenses until the business grows into being profitable. You can use the following worksheet to figure out what it's going to cost you each month to be in business. Because of space here, the worksheet contains only six months of expenses; you should project out for at least a year. Some expenses are fixed (they're the same each month), while some are variable (they can be higher or lower from month to month).

Cash Crash

There are many implications from how you form your business besides how business income is taxed and whether there's personal liability. Be sure to discuss your options with an attorney before you take any action.

Do you need a loan? If you have savings you can use to get the business going, that's fine. But if you need outside financing, forget the informalities and go the full-blown business plan route. Finding the money you need to get started is discussed in the following section.

Expense	January	February	March	April	May	June
Accounting and legal fees	$	$	$	$	$	$
Advertising	$	$	$	$	$	$
Depreciation	$	$	$	$	$	$
Insurance	$	$	$	$	$	$
Licenses/permits	$	$	$	$	$	$
Loan repayment	$	$	$	$	$	$
Miscellaneous expenses	$	$	$	$	$	$
Office supplies	$	$	$	$	$	$
Payroll costs*	$	$	$	$	$	$
Travel and entertainment	$	$	$	$	$	$

Worksheet for projecting operating expenses

*If you incorporate your business, you're an employee, and the corporation is responsible not only for paying your wages but also for paying certain taxes on those wages.

Finding the Cash to Get Started

The number one reason why businesses fail is undercapitalization—not having enough cash to pay expenses and get up and running before the business is self-supporting. Even though you're working from home, there may still be a need for money to buy equipment, pay for advertising, and more. You may be able to use some savings, but retirees often are reluctant to dip into their capital for a business that isn't guaranteed to succeed (and what business is?).

If your savings won't carry the day, there are two ways to raise money: equity and debt. Equity means bringing in investors who share the ownership of the business with you. Debt means borrowing—from family, friends, or your corner bank. Equity doesn't have to be repaid, but it means you have an ongoing

Golden Years Ideas
Have a business person review your plan before you put any money into the idea. Free help is available from SCORE (the Service Corps of Retired Executives, under the auspices of the SBA) and from your local economic development office. You'll find listings in the Blue Pages of your phone book.

relationship with your co-owner, even if that owner has only a small (minority) interest in your business. The investor may poke his nose into what you're doing and expect the business to achieve certain revenues so he'll see some return on his investment. Debt requires monthly cash outlays to pay off, but once you're paid up, you're done with the lender (unless you take out another loan).

Here are some places to look if you need to borrow money:

➤ Friendly lenders. Ask your relatives or friends to lend you the money. You'll repay them, along with interest. They may be able to get more interest from you than they're earning in a savings account.

➤ Yourself. Instead of cracking open your piggy bank, you may have funds you can borrow from that you never thought about. Your stocks and bonds sitting with your broker may be one loan source to look into. You can go "on margin" by borrowing against the value of your portfolio (up to 50% of most securities; 90% of Treasuries). Repayment is made on your terms when and to the extent you can. Interest varies from month to month as interest rates fluctuate. Your home's equity is another source of borrowing, usually at very favorable interest rates. But the downside is the fact that you're putting your home at risk if your business fails and you can't find another way to pay off the home equity loan. Another personal source for borrowing is your life insurance policy. The loan is made quickly—usually within as little as 24 hours—and you repay the loan when you want to. The chief drawback to these sources is that the money isn't in the place you originally intended. If you borrow against your life insurance policy and die before you've repaid the loan, your beneficiary will get less than you'd planned (the loan is subtracted from the proceeds). A last resort is your personal credit cards. Interest on this source of borrowing is *very* high, but you may want to use it nonetheless to finance the purchase of a computer or other business equipment you need to get started and plan to pay off quickly.

Cash Crash
If you borrow from your Aunt Anna or your neighbor Ned, make sure that they understand the risk that your business may fail and they won't be repaid. Put the loan terms (interest and repayment schedule) in writing for their protection. Then, if you're delinquent, they'll be able to deduct their loss as a bad debt. If you don't, the IRS may say it was a gift to you.

➤ Personal loan. If you have a good credit rating and the bank believes you can repay the loan, you can get a personal loan. Both commercial banks and savings and loan associations make these loans. You don't need a business plan for a personal loan; all the banker asks is the purpose of the loan (not the details about how you're going to plan parties at the local catering hall). The chief drawback: higher interest rates than you'll pay on the following loan sources.

➤ Commercial loan. Commercial banks are in the business of lending money to businesses. But don't let the name fool you. As owner of the business, your credit history and assets are key to getting a loan. As owner, you'll almost always be *required* to guarantee repayment of the loan. This means you're personally liable for the business's debt even if you've incorporated. Most commercial lenders are interested in the big guys (those looking for $50,000, $100,000, or more), but some may now be willing to lend as little as $5,000. Interest rates on commercial loans fluctuate (when this book was being written, rates were at a four-year low). You don't necessarily have to go from bank to bank to find a loan; you can now do it on the Internet. As of April 1998, 10 financial institutions have joined rank to offer one-stop shopping for small business cash needs (line of credit, loan, or even a business credit card) through Quicken Business Cash Finder (http://www.cashfinder.com.

➤ Small Business Administration (SBA) loan. The SBA doesn't lend money. Instead, it provides guarantees to commercial lenders to encourage them to lend money to small business owners.

There are various SBA loan programs, some of which are good for starting up a business and others for expanding one. A home-based business isn't precluded from these programs. Two key programs you might want to ask about are Fa$trak loans that allow commercial lenders to grant loans without SBA approval (saving you considerable time) and LowDoc loans that simplify the loan application process by requiring only a one- or two-page form to be completed. Whichever loan route you take, be prepared to wait up to several months before you see any money. If you get turned down by one bank, don't get discouraged (it may only mean the bank has already lent its quota for the month). Go on to the next bank.

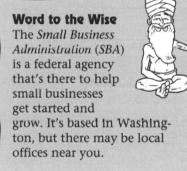

Word to the Wise
The *Small Business Administration* (SBA) is a federal agency that's there to help small businesses get started and grow. It's based in Washington, but there may be local offices near you.

➤ Special resources for women, minorities, and disabled individuals. For example, the SBA's 8(a) program offers financing assistance to minority-owned enterprises (at least 51% of the owners must be socially and economically disadvantaged U.S. citizens, American Indians, or Alaskan natives. The National Organization of Women, along with Wells Fargo Bank, have made about $1 billion available for financing of women-owned businesses. Special SBA loan programs, such as HAL-2, are also geared just for disabled individuals.

Golden Years Ideas
Check out SBA programs by calling the SBA at 800-827-5722. You can also get some loan information on-line at http://www.sbaonline.sba.gov.

Cash Crash
You can deduct the expenses of using part of your home for business (a portion of rent, utilities, maintenance, insurance, and so on) *only* if the home office is your principal place of business *and* you use the space regularly and exclusively for business (use of the kitchen table isn't "exclusive"). "Principal place of business" means the location where you earn your living. For freelancers, it's the office at home; for electricians, it's the clients' homes and offices. But beginning in 1999, a home office is treated as a principal place of business if it's used for substantial administrative activities (ordering supplies, scheduling appointments, keeping the books) and there's no other fixed location for these tasks.

Setting Up Your Business Space

Working from home may be highly desirable. That doesn't mean it's easy to do. There are special obstacles to working from home that you'll need to overcome, such as space and zoning issues.

A Place of Your Own

While Lillian Vernon claims to have started her catalog business from her kitchen table in Mt. Vernon, New York, most people don't find it convenient to work and eat on the same surface. You're better off locating your business in a spare bedroom, den, or corner of a family room if at all possible.

Locating your business in space designated just for this purpose will limit your distractions. It's also essential if you want to claim a home office deduction off your income taxes.

Equip your office with all that's necessary, probably a computer, fax, copier, telephone, answering machine, file cabinet, and supplies (stationery, business cards, and other supplies to run your business). Make sure the space you've set aside is large enough to house your business. You may need to rethink your setup or modify the space. For example, if you're using a spare bedroom, you may want to outfit the closet with shelves to store your books and supplies.

Zoning Restrictions Can Cost You

Just because you want to work from home doesn't mean you can, or at least not without some payment to your town or city. The law may limit the type of businesses that can be run from your home. Check you local zoning regulations to make sure you're not in violation of the law. Penalties and fines can result if you go ahead and run a business when the zoning law says you can't.

If you work alone, as a word processor or freelance writer, there shouldn't be any problem. The same is true for professional offices, such as dentists and lawyers, even if employees and customers are involved. Zoning laws generally allow these types of businesses to be run in residential areas. But if you're planning to restore antique cars in your front yard, the town may have something to say about it. Even if you want to put up a sign, there may be town codes on the size of the sign.

In some places, zoning laws now mean you're allowed to run a business from home, but it's going to cost you. Annual license fees, which are really just a tax, are being imposed by many localities across the country. In Tacoma, for example, there's a $122 annual fee that more than 14,000 home-based businesses have already paid for the privilege of operating a business at home. Fees in most other locations are modest (less than $100 or slightly higher), though some places are eyeing home businesses as a potential source of significant revenue.

Insurance Needs

If you're doing catering at your home and your customer comes to meet you there and falls on your steps, will your homeowner's policy cover the liability? Probably not! A homeowner's policy generally covers only personal visitors, not business visitors (which can include the UPS and FedEx person who delivers your business packages). Or if you're running an antiques dealership and your Ming vase is smashed, will your homeowner's policy cover the loss? Probably not! You have two choices:

➤ Upgrade your homeowner's policy. Review your homeowner's policy with your agent and add a rider to or get an endorsement on your existing policy to cover your needs. For example, because I have only occasional business visitors, I was able to add a rider to cover potential liabilities for less than $50 a year. Add coverage for business equipment (your computer and other machinery), which may not otherwise be covered.

➤ Get special coverage. Take out a separate policy for your home business. For only a few hundred dollars a year, a policy will cover not only liability for injuries by business visitors but also damage to or theft of business property (furniture, computer, inventory, and so on). These policies may even include coverage for data reconstruction if your computer is wiped out. My friend who runs a financial planning business from his basement

Golden Years Ideas
Zoning laws in many localities haven't kept up with changing times and may have blanket bans on just about any home business. Don't let that stop you completely. You may be able to ask for a variance or a special use permit (an exception to the rule in your case). Talk to the right person in your town or city. Try the zoning board planning board and see how far you get. Ask about the procedures for requesting a variance. You may need to work with a lawyer who regularly handles zoning matters if your town seems resistant to your request.

Golden Years Ideas
You can find inexpensive business policies through various trade associations, although you have to pay the modest membership fees to join them. Two examples are Home Business Institute (914-946-6600) and Independent Business Alliance (800-450-2422). If these don't provide coverage in your area, check with your insurance broker.

pays only $320 a year with a $250 deductible to get contents protection up to $15,000, liability up to $500,000, and data reconstruction up to $10,000.

Selling Yourself

Once you've organized your business, you need to sell your service or product. Unless people know you've got something to sell, you may be sitting on the best mousetrap ever invented, but your inventory will gather dust. Marketing savvy is covered in the next chapter.

The Least You Need to Know

➤ There are many personal and financial reasons why it's good to work from home, but there are also drawbacks to consider.

➤ Many types of businesses lend themselves to being run from home.

➤ Market research will help you target your audience and set your prices.

➤ Write a business plan to fine-tune your idea and to help you raise money.

➤ Explore all avenues of cash, from personal resources to SBA loans.

➤ Make sure your business isn't violating zoning laws.

➤ Set up your home office to suit your personal and business needs.

➤ Make sure you carry enough liability and property insurance for all contingencies.

Buying a Packaged Business

Ed, who had worked as an engineer at a Fortune 500 company for his entire career, always dreamed of owning his own business. Once he reached retirement age and left the company with a comfortable pension, he just didn't feel like sitting at home. But he also didn't want to start a business from scratch. Instead, he and his wife decided to open a Mail Boxes Etc. in his neighborhood. The concept for this business was one that had already been thought through by someone else and packaged for him to buy. It was a franchise. But franchises aren't the only way to go if you don't want to think up an idea by yourself and research its viability.

Word to the Wise

Before you rush out to buy a franchise, make sure you understand the business arrangement you're getting into. A *franchise* is a business arrangement that gives you the right to sell a product or service in a fixed area. The company that's selling the concept to you is called the *franchisor*; you, who do the buying, are called the *franchisee*.

Cash Crash

Don't make a big investment in a franchise before you find out how long it's going to take before you can break even and take salary from the business (the very reason you're going into the franchise in the first place). If you'll have to borrow to pay the franchise fee, be sure to factor in the interest you're going to pay to repay the loan.

In this chapter, you'll learn about franchises and other business opportunities you may want to pursue. You'll learn how to find the one that's right for you and how to protect yourself from fraud and other problems. You'll also learn about network marketing and whether there's a future in it for you.

What's Franchising All About?

When you hear the word "franchise," you think instantly of McDonalds and KFC. It's true that many franchises are in the food industry, but that's not the complete story. Franchising started more than 125 years ago by Isaac Singer as a means of selling his new sewing machine. Even though that particular franchise is long dead, the concept is thriving.

Here's how a franchise works: You buy a franchise by paying a *franchise fee*. Depending on what you buy, franchise fees can be as high as several hundred thousand dollars (for major national chains like McDonalds or Burger King) or as little as a few thousand dollars ($5,000 is fairly typical for an inexpensive franchise). Most fees run in the range of $15,000 to $25,000. The fee entitles you to sell the product or service under the name of the franchise. The fee is just the tip of the iceberg. You also have to spend money to set up the business (taking a lease on a storefront; buying equipment and supplies plus inventory; paying legal, accounting, and licensing fees to set you up; and insurance of many kinds).

The up-front fee isn't the end of your relationship with the franchisor. You'll also have to pay a percentage of sales. And, when you see the Subway ads on TV, it's the franchisees who are paying part of the cost through advertising fees (sometimes called a *surcharge*). Where uniformity of product and services is an important issue, franchisees will probably be required to buy their supplies from the franchisor or from the franchisor's list of approved suppliers.

Senior Info

There are about 5,000 different franchise opportunities out there today. Of these, 3% allow franchisees to operate from home. Franchised businesses account for 33% of all retail sales in the country. According to a 1993 study reported in *Business Week* magazine, franchises have a higher failure rate (35%) compared with non-franchise businesses (28%). It may be that the added cost of the up-front franchise fee and annual fees make it more difficult for some franchise businesses to succeed.

What a Franchise Can Do for You

So you know what it's going to cost you. But what do you get out of the bargain? The following items are generally supplied with the purchase of a franchise:

➤ Name recognition

➤ Training and support

➤ Supplies

You get to call yourself Subway and sell Subway's distinctive sandwiches if that's the franchise you've selected. Having the name means the public recognizes immediately what you have to sell. The public knows your product (the different kinds of sandwiches), your price range (though prices for the same sandwich vary across the country), and your quality (the freshness, the quantity). You may have to pay an advertising fee to keep the name in the public's eye. But even more than the name itself, you get a proven business idea.

Golden Years Ideas

Retail and fast-food businesses operated from storefronts and in malls are the most costly franchises. Less expensive are service-type franchises, some of which can even operate from your home.

McDonalds has its Hamburger University; MailBoxes Etc. has its MBE University. Both of these franchises, and many others, offer a comprehensive training program. During a two-week program from Mail Boxes Etc., you'll learn not only how to wrap porcelain so it won't break in shipping, but also how to run the business, from keeping the books to payroll requirements. Some franchises may offer training only by audio or videotapes, which may not be enough to get you going.

Two weeks training, a storefront stocked with supplies, and an idea about how things run is probably not enough to cut it. You need to have ongoing support from the franchisor. This may be scheduled checkups by the company or help on call when you need it.

Sign up as a McDonald's franchisee, and you become a lifetime consumer of the company's french fries, coffee stirrers, and embossed napkins. You might be allowed to buy cooking oil from wherever you want, but then again, maybe not.

Is Franchising for You?

Now that you're retired and you're looking for a second career, there are three big questions you need to answer before you explore a specific franchise company:

➤ Is the franchising arrangement something you can live with? Sure you get the "name." But you give up some freedom on how you're going to operate your business when you agree to become a franchisee. The company tells you how to do what you're doing. You need to have the type of personality that makes you a "company man (or woman)."

Golden Years Ideas

Instead of starting a franchise from scratch, you might want to buy a resale. About 15% of all franchises change ownership each year, and this may be appealing to you. You'll get a business that's already established, but in exchange, you'll pay a premium. This type of purchase may cost you more, but the risk is reduced.

➤ Can you afford to risk your capital? Now that you're retired, you may not want to put your savings on the line even though you're looking to get more income. Even if you borrow to get started, you probably have to give a personal guarantee on the loan, so you're still at risk. Starting a franchise, just like starting any other business, entails risk that you must be prepared to face.

➤ Are you prepared to put in the time? Do you have visions of owning a McDonald's without having to flip hamburgers yourself? Not so fast. Most franchises require the owner to spend a certain number of hours on the job. They don't encourage absentee owners. If you think you're going into a franchise as an investment only and will be able to retain "retirement status," check again. It may be possible down the road to lighten up on the hours you put in, but in the beginning, owning a franchise is a time-consuming activity.

Finding a Perfect Match

If the idea of a franchise sounds appealing, if you're in a financial position to accept the risk, and if you're prepared to put in the time, then it's time to find *the* franchise for you. In narrowing down your choices from the thousands of franchises out there, keep in mind what you like to do (and don't like to do) and the financial commitment required to get into the business.

It's not hard to locate franchises you may be interested in. Just look at your local mall or Main Street for ideas. Hundreds of franchises are listed on the Internet. Most listings describe the business of the franchise, whether it's Computer Doctor that fixes computers, Candleman that sells candles and accessories, or Beverly Hills Weight Loss and Wellness that provides diet plans. Many also list the estimated initial investment, including not only the franchise fee, but also equipment, supplies, insurance, and other costs to get started.

Before You Sign on the Dotted Line

If you've found a franchise that's up your alley, then to paraphrase the advice from the old Christmas song, make a list and check it twice before you put your money down. Here are the points you should be sure about before you ante up:

➤ Your territory. When you become a franchisee, you're limited in where you can sell your stuff. The company may tell you where you have to locate your store, or what neighborhood you can peddle your services in. Sounds restrictive? Not really, because it's really protection for you. After all, you don't want two Subways on the same block if you're one of them. So make sure your agreement spells out what territory protection you have.

Senior Info

You can learn about your rights and the franchise industry by getting free information from the International Franchise Association (202-628-8000). They won't tell you about individual franchises, but they will give you material on what a franchisor is required to do.

➤ Your costs. What's your up-front fee (the initial franchise fee)? What's your ongoing fee? This is usually expressed as a percentage of sales or by some other formula. How often do you have to make this payment (monthly, quarterly, annually)? What other fees do you have to pay (an advertising surcharge, a renewal fee)?

➤ Your obligations. The company is giving you a franchise because it expects you to have a certain amount of sales. Make sure you understand what you have to do, in what time frame you must do it, and most importantly, what happens if you fail to meet these quotas (will your franchise be terminated?).

➤ The company's obligations. What is the company going to do for you in terms of training and support? In addition to the initial training, some companies provide toll-free numbers to answer your questions as they arise. They may also have newsletters to keep you up to date with developments about the company and its product or service.

Cash Crash
Get it in writing. Don't rely on any conversations you've had where promises were made. Put it down on paper and make everybody sign. Have your accountant review the numbers and make sure your lawyer (someone knowledgeable in franchise law) has reviewed the franchise agreement before you sign.

Word to the Wise
Documents that contain financial and other information about the franchise and the franchisor as required by law are called *Uniform Franchise Offering Circulars*.

Golden Years Ideas
Make up your own list of about 10 franchisees in your area. Talk to or visit them and ask what's on your mind. Don't fall for the line of a *singer* (a liar paid by the company to sing its praises).

➤ Termination policy. After getting into the grind of running your franchise, retirement may have been better than you thought and you're looking for an escape clause (though you can try to sell the business). There may be none, unless the franchisor commits fraud or files for bankruptcy. If you're allowed out, there may be penalties to pay. Also check the flip side on what it takes for the franchisor to terminate you. It shouldn't be as easy as 30 days notice without any good reason. Many states limit the franchisor's power to terminate an ongoing franchise, as long as the franchisee continues to meet its obligations.

If you like what you hear but aren't satisfied with the deal you've been offered, don't hesitate to negotiate. You can probably get more favorable terms if you work at it.

You're free to ask the company all these questions, but to be on the safe side, don't just take their word for it. Look at what the company has put in black and white. If you're required to pay at least $500 in the first six months in exchange for goods and services provided to you by the company, then you're entitled to see a *Uniform Franchise Offering Circular*. If the company is reluctant to provide one, or says it's exempt from having to give you one, run, don't walk, to the nearest exit and keep looking for another company to explore.

Easy reading it's not, but the circular should provide you with an audited financial statement about the company. This is a statement prepared by a certified public accountant who is warranting the accuracy of the information about the financial condition of the company. The circular should also provide you with a list of existing franchises.

After you and your advisers (your accountant and attorney) have reviewed the circular, take one more step and check the company out still further. Small business newsgroups and chat rooms on the Internet may have discontented franchisees sounding off. Check with your state attorney general or local Better Business Bureau to see if there have been any complaints lodged against the company. Don't get involved with a problem company.

Turnkey Businesses Aren't Turkeys

Maybe you don't have the cash to invest in a franchise but like the idea of a ready-made business. There are other avenues you can take to find a business you can just slip your key into (turnkey business).

You can buy an existing business if you can wangle the capital to do it (it may be easier than you think). You can buy a business opportunity, which has many of the same features as a franchise but is less costly. You can join the millions of other Americans and jump into network marketing.

Buying an Existing Business

Maybe you're not in a position to do a billion dollar buyout of MCI, but you can probably swing the purchase of a local business…if you know how.

Buying a "pre-owned" business gives you a leg up. You have the concept, the existing customer base, a list of suppliers, and a history of success. Of course, you inherit the burdens and liabilities of the business as well. Maybe the business was late with paying suppliers and has a poor credit rating. That is something you'd have to overcome.

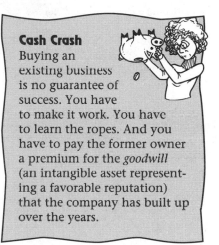

Cash Crash
Buying an existing business is no guarantee of success. You have to make it work. You have to learn the ropes. And you have to pay the former owner a premium for the *goodwill* (an intangible asset representing a favorable reputation) that the company has built up over the years.

There are four stages in buying an existing business:

Stage 1	Finding the business you want to buy
Stage 2	Investigating the business
Stage 3	Negotiating the sale
Stage 4	Getting the keys to the company

Stage 1: Finding the Business You Want to Buy

When Harold, a hardware store owner, decided to retire, there was no son or daughter standing in the wings ready to take over. Harold had two choices: Have a "going out of business sale" and liquidate his inventory, or find a buyer who would take over lock, stock, and wheelbarrow. His retirement may be your opportunity.

But maybe hardware isn't your line. There are plenty of ways to locate businesses for sale:

➤ Word of mouth. You may learn by talking to neighbors, your local banker, or the chamber of commerce which businesses are on the block.

➤ Classifieds. Small businesses may list their sale availability in local newspapers. Check the classifieds under "Business Opportunities."

➤ Internet. Surfing the Web may land you a business.

➤ Business broker. People have made a business out of brokering businesses for sale. A business broker is another name for an agent who can find you a business for the price you want to pay. They don't come cheap and may not handle the modest business you're interested in. Check out the Yellow Pages under "Business Broker."

Golden Years Ideas
You can run a credit check on a business with a Dun & Bradstreet report (800-234-3867). One report costs as little as $79—a small price to pay if the information keeps you from getting into a problem situation.

Cash Crash
Unless you were an accountant in your preretirement career, you'll need one to look over the numbers. The same goes for the legal papers. Get a lawyer to check things out.

Stage 2: Investigating the Business

After your search, you find a gift shop you're interested in. Become Sherlock Holmes. Leave no stone unturned and find out everything there is to know about that shop.

Talk to everyone who'll listen. If they'll talk to you, suppliers, employees, and customers may share important information about what's going on. Maybe the largest customer has just taken his business elsewhere, or a key supplier has gone out of business.

Get the numbers. Look at the company's account books for at least the past three years. The owner won't show them to a tire kicker, but he has to once you sign a *letter of intent* (an agreement that you're serious about buying the business if everything checks out). Also review the company's tax returns to see profit or loss for the past few years. Make sure the company's credit rating is sound.

Check the legal papers. Find out what the business is obligated to do. Look at contracts and leases. Maybe there's only one year left to run on the store's lease. This can mean that you're facing a large rent increase if you buy the business. Or you may be locked into equipment leases for several more years even though the equipment seems outdated to you.

Stage 3: Negotiating the Sale

If the numbers check out and you want to go forward with the purchase of the business, now is the time to negotiate. Price is the main point of contention. You want to pay as little as possible while the seller wants as much as possible. But there are other points to iron out.

You must decide on a payment method. The seller probably wants all the money on closing. You may want to pay the seller in installments (hopefully using profits from the business to pay the purchase price). This may eliminate the need to get outside financing.

There's probably room to negotiate. The seller might go for an installment sale if the purchase price is increased somewhat. Of course, if the business fails, you'll still be obligated to make the remaining installments.

You must also decide on the type of purchase. If you're buying Gift Shop Inc., or any other incorporated business, you can arrange the purchase in two ways: a stock purchase or an asset purchase. If you buy all the stock of the corporation, you own everything it owns: assets plus liabilities. If you buy just the assets, you own only what you buy. Of course, if the Gift Shop isn't incorporated, you're automatically buying the assets. (You can then decide to incorporate the business if you want to.)

As a buyer, you usually prefer an asset purchase. After all, why buy inventory that's been sitting on the shelf for years? But the seller usually wants a stock purchase. It's cleaner because one price fits all; the seller is finished with everything. Obviously, the type of purchase is an important negotiating point.

If you agree on an asset purchase, your negotiating isn't over. Now you have to decide on tax allocations: How the purchase price is broken down among the business's assets. Allocation is important to both you and the seller. It affects what you'll be able to write off through depreciation and amortization. It affects how the seller's gain is reported (what's capital gain and what's ordinary income).

You and the seller agree on an allocation on IRS Form 8594. This allocation is binding on you even though the IRS isn't bound by it. You have to follow it even if the IRS decides to challenge the allocation (for example, disallow some write-offs based on your allocation).

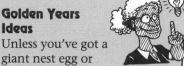

Golden Years Ideas

Unless you've got a giant nest egg or have come into a large inheritance, you'll have to raise the capital to buy the business. Various ways to do this were explained in Chapter 7. If you've decided that your own resources aren't enough to pay the purchase price, check out small business loans through your local bank or the Small Business Administration (http://www.sbaonline.sba.gov).

Word to the Wise

Depreciation means writing off the cost of equipment, buildings and other property over a set number of years specified in the tax law (for equipment, depreciation can be accelerated to permit greater deductions in the earlier years of ownership). *Amortization* means writing off the cost of intangibles (such as good will) ratably over a fixed number of years.

Stage 4: Getting the Keys to the Company

The business isn't yours until you get the keys. To do this, you need to put your agreement in writing and follow through. This means making a contract, paying for the business, and transferring ownership.

A contract for the sale of a business should protect you by spelling out what you're getting and what you have to do for it:

➤ What you're buying. Include a detailed description of the assets, liabilities, and leases and contracts that become yours when you close the deal.

➤ Terms of purchase. Fix the dollar amount of what it's going to cost you to buy. If you're doing an installment purchase to spread payments over several years, then set the interest and payment terms, and any penalties that may result. If you're buying the assets, include the allocation explained earlier. If you're required to pay a percentage of the business's profits (which can be fairly typical), make sure the figure to which the percentage is applied is clearly spelled out, along with the term of this obligation.

Word to the Wise
An arrangement in which a third party (usually a lawyer) holds money until certain conditions are met is referred to as *escrow*. After the conditions are met, the money is turned over to the seller.

➤ Seller warranties. You don't want any surprises after the closing, so put in writing any promises the seller made to you. You might want to put some of the purchase price in *escrow* to be held against the possibility that the seller misrepresented something. When Frank bought a local restaurant, escrow funds were held and used to pay legal fees to clear up problems with the restaurant's liquor license. After a year, the remaining funds were paid to the seller.

➤ Risk of loss. If the Gift Shop burns down before closing, who suffers the consequences? Usually, risk is shared (the buyer and seller each suffer a little). Risk can be minimized, of course, by insurance.

➤ Other things. Maybe the seller is staying on to help with the transition and to show you the ropes. Will he be an employee or work under a consulting agreement? Put it in the contract. Maybe the seller is planning to open another gift shop across the street and take his customers with him. You want to prevent this from happening by having a *covenant not to compete*. The seller promises not to run a competing business in your part of town or some other set area for a limited time (usually a year or two). Put it in the contract.

➤ Closing. We're not talking about shutting down a business, but rather, closing the deal. When is it going to happen? Make sure there's enough time to get the financing you need to pay the purchase price. Where will the papers be signed and the money change hands? (Usually, it's the lawyer's office, but it can be anywhere you agree upon.)

After you sign the contract agreeing to the terms, you follow through. Just like buying a house; once you've closed, the business is yours.

"Business Opportunities" Beckon

Building a better mousetrap is one way to create a business idea. Another is to find someone else who already created the mousetrap. It's called a "business opportunity" and is really just a concept for an idea that's been developed and packaged for you. It's somewhere between a franchise and your own business. To give you some idea of how a business opportunity stakes up against a franchise, look at Table 8.1.

Table 8.1 Business Opportunities Versus Franchises

Factor	Business Opportunities	Franchises
Concept	Yes	Yes
Trade name	No	Yes
Up-front fee	Yes	Yes
Ongoing fees	No	Yes
Restrictions on operations	No	Yes
Protected territory	No	Yes
Extensive training	No	Yes
National advertising	No	Yes

Because you're getting less, you pay less. The up-front cost of a business opportunity can run as little as a few hundred dollars as compared with thousands for a franchise. Of course, you'll still have to pay for equipment and supplies you'll need.

Finding a Business Opportunity

You've seen the ads in magazines such as *Business Opportunity, Home Office Computing, and Entrepreneur*, and in your local newspapers, even if you've never paid attention before. Check out the classifieds in these sources under "Business Opportunities" to find dozens of ideas, some of which may appeal to you. Also, look on the Internet where hundreds of opportunities are listed.

All you have to do is match your talents and skills with the concepts that are out there. Connie was a bookkeeper with a home contractor for many years. When she retired, she wanted something else to do with her time besides watching the soaps. Being good with numbers led her to investigate opportunities not only in bookkeeping (having her own business of doing what she'd always done) but also in claims processing,

Golden Years Ideas
Many business opportunities lend themselves to operating from a home. Review Chapter 7 on home-based businesses to see whether your business opportunity is conducive to working from home.

college scholarship matching, medical and dental billing, and even tax return preparation. Connie's lifelong friend Roz was terrible with numbers. When she retired from her position as personnel director of a midsize manufacturing company, she wanted to "be creative" in her new career. She explored such business opportunities as birth announcement services, button/badge making, gift baskets, and personalized children's books. Whatever you're good at, there's an opportunity for you.

Look Out for Scams

Just because you're not putting in big dollars doesn't mean you can afford to jump in blindly. Do a thorough investigation of the business. Talk to a number of other people who've already gone into the business opportunity you're thinking about.

Even though you're not going into a franchise, if you have to spend at least $500 in the first six months and the seller agrees to provide goods or services, you're entitled to the same protection as a franchisee. You're entitled to see a Uniform Franchise Offering Circular.

Just like franchises, business opportunities fall under the protection of the U.S. Federal Trade Commission. So if a seller says he's exempt from having to give you a circular, check it out with the FTC's Division of Marketing Practices (202-326-3128).

Senior Info

Even if everything seems okay, check the seller out with the National Fraud Information Center (800-876-7060), a nonprofit organization that logs in complaints against business opportunities and franchises. Also, call your state attorney general and your local Better Business Bureau to see if there have been any complaints against the seller.

The Least You Need to Know

➤ Buying a franchise or a business opportunity gives you a pre-packaged business concept.

➤ Franchises cost more than business opportunities to get into.

➤ Buying an existing business requires a lot of investigation.

➤ Network marketing may provide part-time opportunities at a minimum cost.

➤ Check out a purchase carefully before buying.

Chapter 9

Turn Your Leisure Time Into Dollars

In This Chapter

➤ Turning a hobby into a business

➤ Marketing your venture through cyberspace and in other ways

➤ Staying out of trouble with the IRS

Fran always loved dollhouses. She had one as a child. She helped to decorate her daughter's dollhouse, and she couldn't wait until her granddaughter was old enough to begin filling up her own dollhouse. Fran stalked the dollhouse stores and weekend shows to find unique items for herself and others. Soon, she was taking orders from friends who also had dollhouses that needed a Victorian settee or a modern microwave oven. It didn't take her long before she saw the opportunity to turn her hobby into a money-maker. She started her own dollhouse business, selling her wares at shows. If you're like Fran and have a hobby you love, then you, too, may be able to turn it into a business.

In this chapter, you'll learn how you can combine business with pleasure to earn extra income. You'll also see how you can market your concept and find out how to avoid problems with the tax man.

Combining Your Business With Pleasure

The noted book collector A. Edward Newton, who amassed a private library of over 10,000 books by the time of his death in 1940, said "Young man, get a hobby; preferably get two, one for indoors and one for out." For most people, a hobby is a pleasurable distraction from the 9-to-5 grind of work. Maybe they started stamp collecting as children and continued throughout their lives. Maybe they picked up an interest in first editions or cigarette lighters, amassing impressive collections. Maybe they like to square dance or race sailboats.

Those interests can still be pursued in retirement as a hobby. But if you're looking for more retirement income, you may be lucky enough to combine business with pleasure and turn your hobby into a money-maker.

Finding the Business Within Your Hobby

The trick to combining business with pleasure is to see the business potential in your hobby and find out how you can make money at it. That's what George did when he left corporate America after 35 years. He had always loved photography, and people told him he was good at it. Hoping for some extra income to supplement his pension and Social Security, he started a photography business.

He didn't want to compete with the established companies in his area that did weddings and bar mitzvahs. Instead, he aimed for the smaller market, like family reunions, anniversary celebrations, and other events that people want pictures for but don't want to pay top dollar. He advertised his service in the local *Pennysaver* and was able to control how busy he was by declining or accepting jobs as they came his way. His expenses were minimal (only his travel and the costs of the ads in addition to the film he developed in the dark room he'd had for years). Just about every dollar he brought in was profit to him.

The bottom line is to take what you love to do and find a way to make it pay off. Table 9.1 contains some ideas you can use to turn your hobby into a business.

Table 9.1 Correlating Your Hobby With Business Potential

If you're this:	Then you could do this:
A craftsperson	Sell your crafts at shows, church bazaars, or advertise
A gardener	Grow orchids or other exotic plants you can sell to local garden centers or directly to the public (walk-ins or through the mail)
A musician	Perform locally (for example, play piano at a local restaurant) or join with bands or ensemble groups
A sailor	Use your boat to give fishing junkets or tours of the area
A traveler	Become a travel guide (in your town or tour with companies for which you act as a guide)

Setting Up Your Hobby as a Business

If you decide to turn your garage full of '50s and '60s collectibles into a business, think it through. Decide not only how you'll go about selling your stuff, but also how you'll organize your business. Most people start out as sole proprietors because there's nothing special they need to do. If spouses are both retired and start up a business together without taking any formal legal steps, they're automatically a partnership. How to organize your business is explained in Chapter 7, "Starting Your Own Business at Home."

Find out what things you need to do to get started. Here's a rundown of the very first things to do before you can get started:

➤ Register your business. Whether you're a sole proprietor or a partnership, simply file a form with your city or county that you are "doing business as" whatever name you select (Helen Stone, doing business as "Fancy Gift Baskets"). (This is called a DBA.) You need a DBA certificate to open up a bank account in the business's name. Corporations and limited liability companies are organized under state law and, therefore, are registered with the state. (If you incorporate out-of-state, find out what you need to do to operate in-state.)

Cash Crash
Before you open your doors for business, you may want to talk things over with a lawyer. In this way, you'll be sure you set things up right and avoid problems with the government or the public.

➤ Get your tax identification number. This is a number you get from the IRS by filing IRS Form SS-4, which is shown here. You usually need the number to open a business bank account. The form is so simple to file that you can do it yourself even if the idea of a tax form terrifies you. You can even get a number the same day by calling the phone number for your area listed in the instructions to the form and then faxing the IRS a signed, completed form.

➤ Get your sales tax number and the information you need to collect the right tax and to pay it over to the tax authorities (you'll find the information from your state revenue department located in your state capital).

➤ Set up your books. A shoe box to hold receipts doesn't amount to a bookkeeping system for your business. You must have accurate records to know how your business is doing and for legal purposes.

Form **SS-4**

(Rev. December 1995)

Department of the Treasury
Internal Revenue Service

Application for Employer Identification Number

(For use by employers, corporations, partnerships, trusts, estates, churches, government agencies, certain individuals, and others. See instructions.)

▶ Keep a copy for your records.

EIN

OMB No. 1545-0003

Please type or print clearly.

1 Name of applicant (Legal name) (See instructions.)

2 Trade name of business (if different from name on line 1)

3 Executor, trustee, "care of" name

4a Mailing address (street address) (room, apt., or suite no.)

5a Business address (if different from address on lines 4a and 4b)

4b City, state, and ZIP code

5b City, state, and ZIP code

6 County and state where principal business is located

7 Name of principal officer, general partner, grantor, owner, or trustor–SSN required (See instructions.) ▶

8a Type of entity (Check only one box.) (See instructions.)
- ☐ Sole proprietor (SSN) _____
- ☐ Partnership   ☐ Personal service corp.
- ☐ REMIC   ☐ Limited liability co.
- ☐ State/local government   ☐ National Guard
- ☐ Other nonprofit organization (specify) ▶ _____
- ☐ Other (specify) ▶

- ☐ Estate (SSN of decedent) _____
- ☐ Plan administrator-SSN _____
- ☐ Other corporation (specify) ▶ _____
- ☐ Trust   ☐ Farmers' cooperative
- ☐ Federal Government/military   ☐ Church or church-controlled organization
- (enter GEN if applicable) _____

8b If a corporation, name the state or foreign country (if applicable) where incorporated

State

Foreign country

9 Reason for applying (Check only one box.)
- ☐ Started new business (specify) ▶ _____
- ☐ Hired employees
- ☐ Created a pension plan (specify type) ▶

- ☐ Banking purpose (specify) ▶ _____
- ☐ Changed type of organization (specify) ▶ _____
- ☐ Purchased going business
- ☐ Created a trust (specify) ▶ _____
- ☐ Other (specify) ▶

10 Date business started or acquired (Mo., day, year) (See instructions.)

11 Closing month of accounting year (See instructions.)

12 First date wages or annuities were paid or will be paid (Mo., day, year). **Note:** *If applicant is a withholding agent, enter date income will first be paid to nonresident alien. (Mo., day, year)* . . . . ▶

13 Highest number of employees expected in the next 12 months. **Note:** *If the applicant does not expect to have any employees during the period, enter -0-. (See instructions.)* . . . ▶

Nonagricultural	Agricultural	Household

14 Principal activity (See instructions.) ▶

15 Is the principal business activity manufacturing? . . . . ☐ Yes   ☐ No
If "Yes," principal product and raw material used ▶

16 To whom are most of the products or services sold? Please check the appropriate box.   ☐ Business (wholesale)
☐ Public (retail)   ☐ Other (specify) ▶   ☐ N/A

17a Has the applicant ever applied for an identification number for this or any other business? . . . . ☐ Yes   ☐ No
Note: *If "Yes," please complete lines 17b and 17c.*

17b If you checked "Yes" on line 17a, give applicant's legal name and trade name shown on prior application, if different from line 1 or 2 above.
Legal name ▶   Trade name ▶

17c Approximate date when and city and state where the application was filed. Enter previous employer identification number if known.
Approximate date when filed (Mo., day, year) | City and state where filed | Previous EIN

Under penalties of perjury, I declare that I have examined this application, and to the best of my knowledge and belief, it is true, correct, and complete.

Business telephone number (include area code)

Fax telephone number (include area code)

Name and title (Please type or print clearly.) ▶

Signature ▶   Date ▶

Note: *Do not write below this line. For official use only.*

Please leave blank ▶	Geo.	Ind.	Class	Size	Reason for applying

For Paperwork Reduction Act Notice, see page 4.   Cat. No. 16055N   Form **SS-4** (Rev. 12-95)

Source: Internal Revenue Service

Form for Getting Your Tax Identification Number from the IRS

Senior Info

Not good with numbers? Never balanced your checkbook before? Then get help! Use an accountant to set up your business books. You need to keep good records for tax purposes. And it will help you know how your business is doing (and when you're in trouble).

➤ Get insurance. Make sure you're protected in whatever you do. If you're selling collectibles, for example, make sure you carry a policy to cover not only theft but also breakage. The policy should also cover items out on consignment or displayed in shows. Get liability coverage if you need it.

➤ Get any other licenses or permits needed to run your business. You don't want to start a new business with penalties or assessments for failing to get the okays you need. If you're not sure what those licenses or permits are, just call your city, county, or state government offices (you'll find the phone numbers in the Blue Pages of your local phone book).

To Market, To Market

The supermarket isn't the only market around. Any place you can find to sell your afghans, Barbie Doll collectibles, or postage stamps becomes your market. The key is knowing how to tap into the market.

Marketing isn't hit or miss. You need to develop a plan of attack. After all, you have limited dollars to invest in pushing your product, so you want to get the biggest bang for your buck.

If you want your business to succeed, follow the ABCs for your marketing plan.

Word to the Wise
The overall process you use to get people to buy your product is called *marketing*. It includes market research to find out if there's any interest in what you're selling, advertising to inform the public about you, promotions to induce sales, and, finally, clinching the sale.

A. Arrive at a goal. Because you're in business, it's not good enough to just say that you'll sell as much as you can. You need to have some goal in mind in order to make it worthwhile to stay in business. That goal can be a dollar amount of sales, selling a certain number of units, or getting a fixed number of new customers.

B. Be better than your competition. Unless you're selling signed Picassos or other one-of-a-kind items, you're bound to face competition with other people trying to sell the same stuff to the same people. What makes you different? You'd better have an answer to this question so you can distinguish yourself from the rest of the crowd. Maybe you have better pricing. Maybe you have better quality or you're offering a guarantee (for example: you'll buy back the item at the same price with a certain time limit). Find your specialty and exploit it.

C. Capture your marketing forum. There are a great number of ways in which you can advertise and sell your goods. You can't do them all; you have to be selective. Here are some avenues you might explore for advertising:

Billboards

Radio

Catalogs

Samples

Cooperative advertising

Seminars

Direct mail

Signs

Display advertising

Specialty ads (in journals)

Internet

Sponsorship (Little League teams)

Parties (in your home or customers' homes)

Telemarketing

Press release

TV (network/cable)

Print ads (classifieds, magazines, newspaper ads)

Trade shows and flea markets

Promotional contests and prizes

Yellow Pages

Word of mouth

Two main factors determine the forms you'll use: cost and appropriateness. If you're on a limited budget, as most small business owners are, you'll probably forego TV and opt for the less costly (or even free) forms of advertising. You may even be lucky like Linda, a former buyer for Bloomingdale's who now sells her handmade handbags. They're so unique that the local newspaper featured her in an article, calling her the "Bag Lady." This was free publicity that brought in a slew of new customers that turned into big sales.

Some advertising mechanisms are more suited to your product than others. While it's great for the local insurance agent to sponsor the neighborhood Little League team, if you're selling hand knitted sweaters, you won't be sponsoring the neighborhood soccer team. For you, flea markets, word of mouth, or even the Internet may best serve your needs.

Senior Info

Still not sure which way to advertise? Look at what the competition is using. Educate yourself about advertising options. Read, read, read. Don't spend your money until you know what you're doing. Here, we're only going to explore those forums best suited for pushing your hobby-related items.

Trade Shows and Flea Markets

Look in any issue of *Antique News*, a weekly newspaper for the antiques trade, and you'll find dozens of shows and auctions listed each week. If you're a dealer in old Gorham silver patterns or Limoges china, you may want to do shows to sell your goodies. Trade shows generally meet infrequently (once or twice a year) in each location. Flea markets are generally low-brow markets held frequently (like every weekend, or the last Sunday of each month) and offer a variety of merchandise—antiques and collectibles as well as discontinued merchandise, crafts, and even specialty foods.

Trade shows offer you an interested audience (those who attend are usually aficionados of the type of show (antiques, comic books, guns and ammo), though there's no guarantee they're there to buy instead of look. Trade shows are relatively inexpensive to participate in. The cost of a table or booth may be just a few hundred dollars or even less.

Golden Years Ideas

To find trade shows you may want to become a part of, check with the sponsor of the shows you see advertised. You might also find shows listed at http://www.tscentral.com.

While trade shows and flea markets may be an effective way to sell, they're not all roses. You'd better enjoy the gypsy life if you want to stay on the trade show or flea market circuit. One dealer I know from Maine plans his shows according to the climate. With his RV as transportation, he does the trade shows in Florida during the winter months, meandering back to Maine after the winter thaw. Flea-market dealers more typically frequent the same show each week or month (depending on when they're held).

Hang Ten on the Web

Today, even if you're living in a trailer park in Pensacola, you can sell your depression glass to a collector in Amsterdam or Adelaide. The least that you need in order to have a Web site is the *desire* to have one. You can hire others to design, build, and maintain your Web site. At most, you will need a computer, a modem, and some technical skills. If you like to do it yourself, you can do all the work involved in creating and controlling your Web site.

The first step to placing your business on the Web is coming up with a Web-page design. You don't have to be a Michelangelo to work up a home page that's interesting and informative. What you spend on Web page design is up to you. At one extreme, Fortune 500 companies pay millions for their sites. At the other extreme, you can design one for free (as part of your monthly charges, AOL lets you have one free home page per subscriber). You can buy software to help you design your home page, or you can use professional Web page designers (their cost runs from just a few hundred dollars and up, depending on the complexity of your site).

If you have someone else design your Web site, you may also want to hire someone to store and maintain it. For hook-up and storage, there's usually a one-time connection to a storage site (around $100). The storage site is the place that houses your page around the clock. You also pay a monthly storage fee, as modest as $75, so your site is kept in a central computer site to allow access by those on the Web. Depending on how often you need to have your site updated, you may incur additional fees for the updates.

If you want to do some of the work yourself, you're going to need the right equipment. You need a computer and a modem. With prices of hardware dropping, you get state-of-the-art equipment for $2,000 to $3,000. Depending on the sophistication of your site and if you're doing it all yourself (or using a professional for some things), you'll probably need a scanner, so you can feed pictures of your wares into the computer and onto your site (Cost: about $1,000).

Cash Crash

Before signing up to do a show, read the fine print. Some show sponsors require you to agree to a certain number of shows (guaranteeing dealers at the less popular ones). Weigh the added cost of participating in these extra shows before you agree to anything.

Word to the Wise

Your *Web site* is your address on the Internet—where other people can find you. It's also called your *home page* because it's the place you'll soon call home. A Web site isn't just an e-mail address where you can receive messages sent over the Internet; it's a place that people can go to view your wares and find out how to buy them.

You will also need an Internet service provider to have access to the World Wide Web (WWW for short). This is how your Web page can be seen. For this you need a provider (such as America Online or one of the thousands of local providers). Whichever option you use, cost is modest ($10 to $20 per month for unlimited use). Most providers include a limited amount of storage space and monthly traffic allowance with your basic service. If you need more storage space or your Web site is being viewed by a large number of people, you will have to upgrade your service from the provider.

Cash Crash

If you sell on the Net, find out whether you need to collect sales tax. At present, there is a lot of uncertainty about requirements for cross-state sales made over the Internet.

Spread the Word

Standing over the backyard fence and talking about the neighbors is gossiping, a form of communication that's harmful and hurtful to all concerned. But talking about Betty's gorgeous embroidered tablecloths that she's selling is a form of communication your business shouldn't be without. Word-of-mouth is the best (and cheapest) way to advertise your things.

Golden Years Ideas

Go the extra mile to keep your existing customers satisfied. Statistics show that it costs 10 times more to get a new customer than to keep an old one.

Keep your customers satisfied, and they'll satisfy you. They'll be repeat customers. They'll also tell their friends and family about your goods, which is sure to translate into sales, and it doesn't cost you a thing.

Over the years, I've gone to numerous antique shows looking to fill in the missing pieces on a set of flatware in an antique silver pattern. I always leave my name and what I'm in the market for with silver dealers. The good ones follow up by calling me when they have something. You'd be surprised at how few good ones there are. Here I am, a customer ready and eager to buy, and some dealers just don't follow through.

Use your common sense in keeping customer satisfaction. A simple "thank you" (by phone or in a note) for doing business or referring someone else may be all it takes to cement a longtime relationship with a customer.

Keeping Out of Tax Hot Water

When you're in business, Uncle Sam is your partner. You'd prefer that he be a limited partner and keep his take to the minimum. If you've turned a hobby into a business, you'd better understand the special tax rules that apply to you so you won't get into trouble.

Heads, Uncle Sam Wins; Tails, You Lose

Years ago, the federal government decided that it just wasn't right that people should be able to write off the costs of conducting their hobbies and recreational activities. After all, most personal expenses like food and movie tickets generally aren't deductible. So Congress created the "hobby loss rules." If you're running an activity and you don't have a reasonable expectation of making a profit (you're doing it for the fun of it), you still have to report all the income you make from it. But a deduction for your expenses can't be more than the income you take in. So if Edna breeds Yorkies (and can't show a profit motive), she has to report the $2,500 in stud fees she received. But of her $4,000 in expenses (dog food, vet bills, travel to dog shows, and so on), she can deduct only $2,500 (the amount of the income from the activity); the balance of $1,500 is a nondeductible personal expense.

Senior Info

The hobby loss rules apply only if you're unincorporated (you're a sole proprietor or you and your spouse are partners). You can avoid these rules if you incorporate your business. If the business elects S corporation status, which means that you, as the owner, report profit and loss (rather than the corporation itself), you'll be able to deduct business losses on your personal return.

Cash Crash

Being businesslike is no guarantee that the IRS will agree you've got a profit motive. One retired couple who ran an antique glassware business wasn't allowed to deduct their losses even though they kept immaculate books, got a state license to do business, collected sales tax, and advertised in antique newsletters. The reason: Their traveling expenses alone were six times their sales, and they couldn't show there was ever any prospect of turning a profit.

Proving You're in It for the Money

Just because you love what you're doing doesn't automatically mean you don't want to make money. However, if the activity is one that involves some recreational or personal pleasure, be prepared to prove you have a profit motive.

Your actions will speak louder than words. Here's what you need to do to show that you're running a business and not just a hobby:

➤ Be businesslike. It's fine to keep your household finances strewn all over the house, but your business must be run in a businesslike manner. Keep good books and records of your income and expenses.

➤ Put in the time and effort. If you're very casual about your activity, it shows you're not serious about making money. After all, if you spend only a few hours a month at it, there's no realistic way you can expect to make a profit.

Senior Info

If you own a computer, make your record keeping life easy by using software to keep your business info. Even if you don't know anything about accounting, a program called QuickBooks automatically creates books and records from the checks you enter. It also lets you create invoices, maintain inventory records, and make deposits (and Quicken Home and Business let's you track business and personal financial data at the same time) (800-4INTUIT). There are a number of other comparable programs you'll find at your local computer store. And there's plenty of freeware and shareware you can download from the Internet.

➤ Use methods of operation designed to make a profit. No one expects a person starting a business to make money right off the bat. It takes time to build up customers and a business reputation. But if you're losing money year in and year out, you'd better try new ways to improve your operations. Talk to experts. Take a business course at your local community college. Show you're taking action to make the business profitable.

➤ Demonstrate your expertise. If you've never been around horses, how do you expect to make money from breeding them? You'd better be an expert in your own business. Just because you enjoy your activity doesn't make you an expert.

➤ Show profitability when you can. Even major corporations have years in which they lose money. That doesn't mean they didn't want to make a profit. The same goes for the little guy. As long as you can show some profitable years, it bolsters your profit motive.

➤ Hope for appreciation. Some activities may not be profitable from their daily operations, but there's still a chance they'll show a profit from appreciation in their assets that can be sold down the line.

Cash Crash

If you haven't yet retired but run a sideline business that you plan to use as your retirement business some day, don't make the same mistakes that one guy did. He was an engineer who operated a dog care products distributorship. He was unable to put in much time, relying on his wife to see to daily operations, including the business checking account. Despite her best efforts, the business ran at a loss. His *future* hopes didn't allow him to deduct his current losses because he didn't have a realistic profit motive at the present time.

Be Presumptuous

The government recognizes that you can't be expected to make money every year, especially when you're just getting started. So it lets you rely on a presumption of having a profit motive. This delays the time that the IRS can challenge your losses.

If you show a profit in at least three out of five years, you're assumed to have a profit motive. This time frame extends to two out of seven years in the case of breeding, training, showing, or racing horses. To rely on this presumption, you have to file IRS Form 5213 (shown here), Election To Postpone Determination as To Whether the Presumption Applies That an Activity Is Engaged in for Profit.

You must decide to rely on the presumption for the year you start up. However, you have some extra time to make the decision. You can amend that return (you have up to three years from the due date of the return for the first year of the business).

Should you do it? If you do, it's practically a guarantee that the IRS will be at your doorstep at the end of the presumption period to see if you've had enough profit years. (The IRS will be looking only at your business income and deductions, not other items on your returns for those years.) But you don't really have much to lose. Even if you fail the test (for example, you suffer losses in *every* one on those five years), you can always try to show you really did have a profit motive, using the points listed earlier (businesslike conduct, time and effort, expertise, and so on).

If you don't rely on the presumption, you might squeak by the IRS. Then again, you might not, and you'd have to show your profit motive as just described.

The Least You Need to Know

➤ You can turn an activity you love into a business to make extra retirement income.

➤ Set up your hobby to run like a business by getting a sales tax number and required licenses, keeping good books and records, and carrying insurance.

➤ Use the Internet to advertise your business to a worldwide audience.

➤ Avoid the hobby loss rules by running your activity in a business-like manner.

Form **5213**
(Rev. August 1997)
Department of the Treasury
Internal Revenue Service

**Election To Postpone Determination
as To Whether the Presumption Applies That an
Activity Is Engaged in for Profit**
➤ To be filed by individuals, estates, trusts, partnerships, and S corporations.

OMB No. 1545-0195

Name(s) as shown on tax return	Identifying number as shown on tax return

Address (number and street, apt. no., rural route) (or P.O. box number if mail is not delivered to street address)

City, town or post office, state, and ZIP code

The taxpayer named above elects to postpone a determination as to whether the presumption applies that the activity described below is engaged in for profit. The determination is postponed until the close of:
- The 6th tax year, for an activity that consists mainly of breeding, training, showing, or racing horses; or
- The 4th tax year for any other activity,

after the tax year in which the taxpayer first engaged in the activity.

1 Type of taxpayer engaged in the activity (check the box that applies):

☐ Individual ☐ Partnership ☐ S corporation ☐ Estate or trust

2a Description of activity for which you elect to postpone a determination

2b First tax year you engaged in activity described in 2a

Under penalties of perjury, I declare that I have examined this election, including accompanying schedules, and to the best of my knowledge and belief, it is true, correct, and complete.

(Signature of taxpayer or fiduciary)	(Date)
(Signature of taxpayer's spouse, if joint return was filed)	(Date)
(Signature of general partner authorized to sign partnership return)	(Date)
(Signature and title of officer, if an S corporation)	(Date)

For Paperwork Reduction Act Notice, see instructions on back.   Cat. No. 42361U   Form **5213** (Rev. 8-97)

Source: Internal Revenue Service

Form to Use When Relying on a Presumption of Profit Motive

Part 3
Making Your Investments Work for You

Social Security benefits make up an ever-shrinking portion of retirement income for those who enjoy a comfortable retirement. Pensions are important, but they're not everything. To have a truly comfortable and secure retirement, you need to depend on your own resources.

There are many ways to boost your retirement income. You can rearrange your current investments to produce more income. You can turn nonproductive assets, like your home, into money-makers. You can find income in places you never thought to look.

The trick in increasing your retirement income is knowing what to look for. You don't want to take unnecessary risks at this stage in your life. But you also don't want to let opportunities pass you by.

Asset Allocation After Retirement

In This Chapter

➤ Re-arranging your investments

➤ Studying up on investment options

➤ Using investment advisers

During your working years, you were taught to save and save. Americans are notoriously poor savers, but still, some succeed in accumulating an impressive retirement savings pot. The size of that pot at the end of the working years rainbow helps in part to shape how you'll live during your retirement years: in style or just getting by.

In the first part of this book you got some idea about what your retirement income is by adding up your Social Security benefits, pensions, and income from personal savings. That's what your retirement income is if you don't take any steps to improve it. But we're here to improve it. Working full- or part-time is one way to increase your retirement income as you saw in Part 2. Now you're going to see how your current investments can be changed to give you more retirement income. In this chapter, you'll learn how to re-arrange your investments to provide you with optimum retirement income and to ensure that that income continues to be there as long as you need it. In this chapter, you'll be focusing on your stocks and bonds; in the remaining chapters in this part, you'll see how other investments can be used to maximize your retirement income. You'll also learn about doing your own investigations into stocks and bonds and find out about using professionals to help you.

Reworking Your Portfolio

Now that you're retired (or about to become so), the stocks and bonds you own may not be the best investment vehicles for you in retirement. You may need to sell some holdings and replace them with others.

In Chapter 1, "What's Enough?" you learned how to take into account the impact of inflation on your investment holdings. You saw that your income must continue to increase if you want to stay even with your purchasing power given the impact of inflation.

In Chapter 2, "Richer Than You Think?" you looked at the different kinds of investments that produce retirement income. And you learned how to take the impact of income taxes into account when comparing investment options.

Now, in this chapter, it's time to put it all together to learn what to look for in investments *after* retirement to meet your goals. You'll find out about different ways to learn about investments and using brokers for investment advice.

Going for Growth or Income or Both

Maybe you've heard about two different types of investments. One is geared toward *growth*; the other is geared toward *income*. Growth investments aim to provide you with appreciation (turning your $10,000 investment into $15,000, $20,000, or more). You don't receive more cash; it's just that the value of what you own increases. This occurs, for example, because the price of Disney Corporation stock you own on the New York Stock Exchange goes up.

Income investments try to throw off cash in the form of dividends on stock or interest on bonds. So, for example, if you own a stock mutual fund whose investment philosophy is income, you'll receive dividends on your holdings.

There are also investments that try to combine both philosophies (growth and income). For example, stocks in telephone, gas, electric companies and other utilities, and utility mutual funds (those holding utility stocks) generally offer both annual income (possibly paid monthly, quarterly, or otherwise) and the opportunity for price appreciation. There are also "balanced funds" that hold both equity (stock) and income (bonds) in order to provide both growth and income.

By now, you're probably asking yourself which type of investment you should be holding in retirement. There's no single answer. You probably need a mix.

You Need Growth

You need growth to keep your assets growing (after tax) at least as fast as the rate of inflation. If you assume the annual inflation rate is 3% (not too far off from a historic average), then the value of your assets has to grow at least 3%. This isn't much in view of the huge leaps that some stocks on Wall Street have taken in the past three years. There has been an unprecedented return of 20% in the Dow in three consecutive years.

But this isn't the only index. There's the S&P 500, the Russell 2000, and Wilshire 5000 to name a few. Your portfolio may exceed these indexes or fall short, depending on what you own.

Just because Wall Street has had some good years, don't expect this to continue indefinitely. Like Joseph's dream in the Bible, there could well be years of slow growth, or no growth (or even devaluation), following years of plenty.

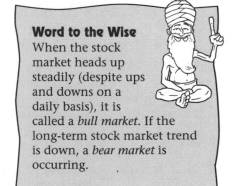

Word to the Wise
The Dow Jones Industrial Average (DJIA) is commonly referred to as the *Dow*. It is a group of 30 stocks that you'll sometimes see referred to as "Blue Chips." The Dow isn't static; stocks are added or dropped from time to time.

You Need Income

In retirement, unless you've embarked on a second full-time career, your Social Security benefits and pension income probably won't be enough to keep you in the lifestyle you've grown accustomed to. You need to get income from your portfolio.

How to split your portfolio between growth and income is highly personal. It depends on these factors:

➤ How much money you have. Obviously, a wealthier person can afford to take more risk (and go for growth) while a person of more modest means may have to put his or her assets to work making income.

➤ How much income you need. This depends not only on the amount of your assets but also on your lifestyle. A wealthy person who lives modestly doesn't need as much income as someone living high on the hog.

➤ Your risk tolerance. The experts can tell you how you *should* be allocating your assets. You're the one who has to live with the consequences of your decisions. You have to be able to sleep at night. Some people can't stand the ups and downs of Wall Street even though they know that in the long run, they'd be better off having some money in it. At the other extreme, there are people who don't have much money but are comfortable risking it all (they have a high risk tolerance). Someone with a high risk tolerance may want to invest in high-tech stocks where the

Word to the Wise
When the stock market heads up steadily (despite ups and downs on a daily basis), it is called a *bull market*. If the long-term stock market trend is down, a *bear market* is occurring.

potential for gain (as well as loss) is great. Someone uncomfortable with risk may want to invest in utility stocks that offer some appreciation potential but feature safety and high dividends.

➤ Current market factors. We've been in a solid bull market since the early 1990s, so many investors don't remember bear markets when stock prices steadily declined or were stalled for years on end. There are many outside factors that can affect the market: conditions overseas, oil shortages, labor shortages, even taxes to name just a few. Some factors favor investing in stocks; others suggest income-oriented investments.

You Need to Consider Taxes

You can't reposition your investments in a vacuum. You have to consider what impact, if any, taxes will have on your investment decisions. If you're looking to increase your retirement income, you'll have to consider what you'll be able to put in your pocket *after* you've paid tax (if any) on that income. Here's a hierarchy of tax results that you should keep in mind when deciding to buy, sell, or hold onto any investments.

➤ Tax-free income. This is the best type of income because it's all yours; there's no sharing it with Uncle Sam by way of taxes. Tax-free income includes the interest you earn on municipal bonds. But when you sell bonds before maturity, you may realize income that's not tax free. You may have a capital gain or loss (which is explained below).

➤ Tax-deferred income. This is the second-best type of income because you don't pay tax immediately; you get to wait. Tax-deferred income is the type you receive on U.S. Savings Bonds, Series EE (unless you elect to report the interest currently) and on commercial annuities (you aren't taxed on the earnings in the annuity until you start to receive annuity payments). Remember that deferral doesn't avoid income, it only delays the payment date.

➤ Capital gains. This is the third-best type of income because it's subject to lower tax rates. Capital gains come in two flavors: short-term and long-term. Short-term gains, which are gains on the sale or exchange of capital assets (like your securities) held for one year or less, are taxed just like ordinary income (explained next). Long-term gains, which are gains on the sale or exchange of capital assets held more than one year, are subject to special rates. A rate of up to 28% applies to assets held more than one year but not more than 18 months; a rate of 20% (10% for those in the 15% tax bracket) applies to assets held more than 18 months. However, collectibles held more than 18 months aren't eligible for the lower rate; they're taxed at 28%. And, when you sell depreciable real property, the unrealized depreciation (what you deducted over the years as straight line depreciation) is taxed at 25% while the rest of the gain is eligible for the 20% rate.

➤ Ordinary income. While any income is always a positive for your pocketbook, ordinary income is the worst kind of income—tax wise—you can receive. Ordinary income includes interest on your savings accounts and corporate bonds and dividends on your stocks and mutual funds (other than capital gains dividends). The tax rate you pay depends on your tax bracket: 15%, 28%, 31%, 36%, or 39.6%.

Mutual funds are becoming more tax-sensitive in view of the differential between the tax on ordinary income (including short-term gains) and long-term capital gains. Be sure to consider the fund's investment philosophy (growth, growth and income, and so on) as well as its tax efficiency (low tax liability for the returns it generates).

Asset Allocation Models

It would be easy to say that *everyone* over the age of 65 should have a certain percentage in stocks (or stock mutual funds), a certain percentage in bonds (or bond funds), and a certain percentage in cash (money market funds and savings accounts) or other investments (real estate, gas and oil, gold). But this can't be done. There are just too many variables, as you've seen. However, there are many different formulas that are in fact used to make asset allocations. You may want to review these formulas and use them as a jumping-off point to make your own allocations:

➤ 80% rule. This asset allocation rule says that you should multiply your age by 80% to find the percentage of your portfolio that should be invested in bonds; the balance can go into stocks or stock mutual funds. So, for example, if you're 65, you should have 52% in bonds and 48% in stocks.

➤ 110 less your age. This asset allocation rule uses the difference between your age and 110 to find the percentage of your portfolio to invest in stocks (or stock mutual funds). So, if you're 65, the difference between your age and 110 is 45. Under this asset allocation formula, you should invest 45% in stocks and 55% in bonds.

➤ 65% equity rule. If you're over 50 but not yet retired, some experts suggest keeping 65% of your money in stocks and stock mutual funds. The other 35% can be divided among bonds and other investments. So, if you're 65 and still working, under this formula you'd have 65% in stocks and 35% in bonds and other investments. Once you retire (it doesn't matter how old you are), you gradually shift more money into bonds and out of stocks.

Senior Info

If you want your holdings reviewed and you don't use a full-service broker, you can use a telephone service called Wealthy & Wise (800-275-2272). They will look at what you're holding in light of your investment goals. They'll give you investment alternatives that may suit you better. The cost: about $125 an hour.

Remember that the asset allocation formulas have to be tailored to your personal needs, so if you want to use any of these formulas, be sure to modify them for your situation.

Relying on Professional Financial Advice

Wall Street is a highly complex thoroughfare. You'll never see all the experts agree on market trends, stock picks, interest rates, and other factors you need to know to arrange your portfolio. So how are you, an investment novice, supposed to make choices? You can do your own research (pick the brains of the experts), or you can rely on what your stockbroker tells you. You can do both: do some research *and* talk to your broker.

Study and Learn

There are plenty of market "experts" out there whose job is to tell you what's going on in the economy, with global economic conditions, and in the stock market. It's easy to tap into this wealth of information if you know how.

Golden Years Ideas

The sole purpose of the *Hulbert Financial Digest* newsletter (888-HULBERT) is to rank financial newsletters according to the advice they've given over time. To see if your newsletters are winners, check out this master newsletter.

There are several daily newspapers dedicated to financial reporting, such as the following:

➤ *The Wall Street Journal*

➤ *Investors Business Daily*

➤ *The Financial Times* (from the UK)

Not only will you find daily price listings, but also articles on trends and other information that can affect your investment decisions. There's also *Barron's*, a weekly newspaper that features stock picks and market analysis.

Financial newsletters abound. Depending on how sophisticated you want to get (and how much you're willing to pay), you can get one or more financial newsletters. These follow selected stocks and mutual funds. Some newsletters have better track records than others do (they've been more successful in finding the winners and predicting the losers).

Financial magazines also abound. You may get lots of general ideas but not necessarily specific recommendations. *Money* magazine, for example, lists only certain mutual funds each month; most individual stocks aren't followed on a regular basis.

If you're trying to be a market timer (someone who looks for the highs and lows of a stock or fund), then magazines just aren't timely enough for you. With today's stock price volatility, by the time information reaches your door, it's old news. As a practical matter, however, you probably shouldn't try to be a market timer, but rather aim for long-term trends. Research has shown that, over significant periods of time, market timers don't achieve higher returns than "buy and hold" investors.

If you have a computer with a modem (or have access to one at your local library or can use your neighbor's), you can log on to key Web sites that will provide you with stock and mutual fund advice, as well as advice on annuities, retirement planning, asset allocation, and more. Table 10.1 lists some sites to explore.

Golden Years Ideas
You don't have to take subscriptions to financial newspapers, newsletters, and magazines. You can find many of them in your local library. But if you do decide you want to buy them, remember that the cost is a tax-deductible investment expense.

Table 10.1 Web Sites for Financial Advice

At this site	You'll find
http://www.morningstar.net	Morningstar's information about mutual funds.
http://www.troweprice.com	T. Rowe Price Mutual Funds give information about retirement planning, their funds, and more.
http://www.fidelity.com	Fidelity Mutual Funds give news and commentary, information about their funds, and daily fund prices (NAVs).
http://www.vanguard.com	Vanguard Mutual Funds' site is packed with useful information and is especially help with investments for IRAs and annuities.
http://www.merrillynch.com	Merrill Lynch provides stock quotes, on-line investment seminars, and research.
http://www.thestreet.com	The Street is a site designed primarily for stock brokers that you can view to find mutual fund information and more.

continues

Table 10.1 Continued

At this site	You'll find
http://www.microsoft.com/msft/	Microsoft offers this site to subscribers, giving access to company reports and a tool to assess stocks and mutual funds.
http://www.cnbc.com	CNBC gives highlights of financial developments and prices.
AOL keyword: fool	The Motley Fool provides investment ideas, model portfolios, and a chat room to exchange ideas.

In addition to "home pages" set up by companies (like the ones listed above), there are also many "chat rooms" and "bulletin boards" on the Internet. These are places for anyone to put his or her two cents in—and they do. Some have ulterior motives for hyping or bad-mouthing a stock (they've taken a position that will benefit from driving the price of the stock up or down). Many people giving advice in chat rooms are not necessarily experts. Some advice in these places may be good, but don't rely on it alone. If you like the sound of some advice from these places, be sure to check it out further before you act.

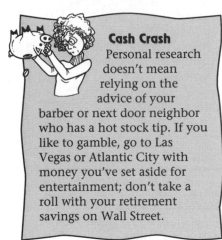

Cash Crash
Personal research doesn't mean relying on the advice of your barber or next door neighbor who has a hot stock tip. If you like to gamble, go to Las Vegas or Atlantic City with money you've set aside for entertainment; don't take a roll with your retirement savings on Wall Street.

Financial Planners Can Serve a Purpose

Financial planners are people who, as their name implies, are there to help you plan your finances. Just about anyone can call himself or herself a financial planner (and many people whose qualifications are dubious do just that). At this time, there are no federal or state licensing requirements for financial planners. You probably want your planner to hold some designation, such as certified financial planner (CFP), a designation given after a course of study has been satisfactorily completed. In addition to people who call themselves financial planners, attorneys, accountants, stockbrokers, and insurance agents may also offer financial planning advice.

What you want a planner to do is take a comprehensive view of your financial picture and help you make decisions on how that picture can be improved. You expect a planner will be knowledgeable in investments, insurance, and other aspects of your finances.

There are two types of planners: fee-only planners, who get paid for their time and advice, regardless of what investment decisions you make, and commission-based planners, who don't charge separately for advice but are paid commissions on investments you make. Both types of planners will give you good advice.

Unless a good financial planner has been recommended to you, you'll be able to find one in your area by calling the Institute of Certified Financial Planners (800-282-7526) or the

National Association of Personal Financial Advisors (888-333-6659) (for fee-only planners). Be sure to ask for referrals before you go forward with any planner.

Stockbrokers Are Not All Created Equal

Most people don't have the time, even in retirement, to devote to researching properly their current and prospective investment holdings. They rely, and rightly so, on the advice of their stockbrokers. But there are different kinds of stockbrokers.

A *stockbroker* is a person licensed by the Securities and Exchange Commission (a federal agency) and state securities regulators to sell securities. A stockbroker at a *full-service* brokerage company (such as Merrill Lynch, Smith Barney, or bank brokerage firm subsidiaries) earns his or her living entirely by commissions. So the advice is free; if you take it, it will cost you something. The rate of commissions depends on what you're buying (stocks, mutual funds, treasuries, and so on). *Discount brokers* (such as Charles Schwab, Fidelity, and Muriel Siebert and Co.) are cheaper on commissions (about 40% less than full-service firms) but offer almost no advice. Then there are *deep discount brokers* (such as Arnold Securities and Wall Street Discount) that offer even greater discounts than the Charles Schwabs and even fewer services.

Table 10.2 has some listings to help you find the firm you're looking for.

> **Golden Years Ideas**
>
> If you do your own research and don't need help in making investment decisions, you can buy your investments through a discount broker and save on commissions. You may trade using a representative (via a telephone automated system), or on the Internet, called e-trading. Costs vary with the mechanism you choose.

Table 10.2 Directory of Brokerage Firms

Firm	Telephone	Web Site
Ameritrade	800-400-3603	http://www.ameritrade.com
Charles Schwab	800-435-4000	http://www.schwab-worldwide.com
DLJ Direct	888-456-4355	http://www.DLJdirect.com
E*Trade	800-ETRADE-1	http://www.etrade.com
Fidelity	800-544-8888	http://www.fidelity.com
Merrill Lynch	800-MERRILL	http://www.merrillynch.com
National Discount Brokers	800-4-1-PRIC	http://www.ndb.com
Quick & Reilly	800-533-8161	http://www.quick-reilly.com
Prudential Securities	800-THE ROCK	http://www.prudential.com
Waterhouse Securities	800-876-7050	http://www.waterhouse.com

Now obviously a broker doesn't have a crystal ball to predict the future of the Dow. (If he did, do you think he'd be working for a living instead of using that crystal ball for his own portfolio?) But you expect that your broker will do a good job by recommending the right mix of investments for you and, hopefully, which investments to fill that mix. If you're happy with the results, you'll stay with the broker. If not, you should find a new one. Review performance on a quarterly or semiannual basis.

Senior Info

For wealthier individuals, a money manager or investment advisor may be the right way to handle investments. You'll see this arrangement called a *wrap account.* For an annual fee (typically 1% to 3% of your portfolio value), someone will manage your assets without consulting you on day-to-day decisions. The management fee includes all transaction costs (commissions), so it costs you the same whether there are frequent or sporadic buying and selling. But if you're holdings are static and you like it that way (you're comfortable with putting most of your money in T-bills and/or mutual funds you don't change too often), don't waste your money on a money manager, no matter how large your holdings may be.

Reading the Fine Print

If you have a brokerage account, you'll get monthly statements listing your holdings and all the transactions that occurred during the month (interest that you earned on your bonds or money market fund, shares you bought or sold). Mutual funds send statements quarterly and every time you buy or redeem shares. You'll also receive confirmation slips from the brokerage firms and mutual funds every time you buy or sell anything.

Golden Years Ideas

You can check on whether your broker has been in any trouble (mismanaging clients' accounts) by calling the NASD (National Association of Securities Dealers, Inc.) Public Disclosure Hotline at 800-289-9999. Your state securities commissioner (or state securities administrator) may also provide its own information.

Review the statements carefully. You're looking for two things: how your assets are doing and whether there are any errors in your statement. Just because you've worked things out with your broker to set up your investment portfolio doesn't mean you're finished for life. You're not! You should regularly monitor your holdings to make sure you're getting what you want. Katherine, a spirited widow in her 80s who was still working as a part-time secretary, had decided several years ago that she wanted to have half her assets in bonds and the other half in equities. In the past three years, her stocks did so well that her portfolio objective was way out of kilter. Her portfolio became more than three quarters equities and only one quarter bonds. By monitoring her statements, she saw the trend but decided to let the new asset allocation remain. Had she wanted to, she could have sold stocks, taken profits, and re-invested in bonds to maintain the 50/50 allocation she originally intended.

Maintaining asset allocation isn't the only reason to review your statements. You'll notice in the fine print at the bottom it says to review the statement carefully to make sure it's correct (that transactions have been reported as you expected and that nothing's been left out). It may also say that you have 10 days to notify the brokerage firm *in writing* about any errors and that the failure to report them within that time means you accept the statement as true and accurate. While the firm may not hold you to the 10-day limit, it certainly will make it difficult to make corrections if you let things drag on for months and months. If you can't figure out what the statement says (each firm's or fund's statement is different), ask your broker for help.

You should also review your confirmation slips promptly to be sure that the transaction was the one you ordered (for example, that the slip shows that you *bought* 100 shares of GM stock and not 200 shares in error). The firms do make mistakes sometimes.

> **Golden Years Ideas**
> If you hate the idea of getting a dozen different statements, you may be able to consolidate. Certain brokerage accounts let you own mutual funds through them (for a small fee). This means, for example, that even though you own a Fidelity Fund, it will show up on your Smith Barney monthly statement.

The Least You Need to Know

➤ Assets need to be allocated between growth and investment vehicles to keep pace with inflation and provide you with retirement income.

➤ Asset allocation formulas are only a jumping-off point for you; these formulas must be adjusted for your personal financial situation.

➤ You can do your own research in financial newspapers, magazines, newsletters, and on the Internet.

➤ You can use a professional—a financial planner or stockbroker—to help you with asset allocation and other investment decisions.

➤ If you do your own market research, you can save money on stock trading by using discount brokers or e-trading.

Turn Your Home Into Retirement Income

Chapter 11

In This Chapter

➤ Figuring what it would cost you to move or to stay where you are

➤ Selling your home to pocket some money for investment purposes

➤ Using reverse mortgages and other financing arrangements to extract cash from your home while staying put

Unless you own a business or have socked away a lot in your retirement accounts, your home (if you own it) is probably your most valuable asset. But it's not doing you much good when it comes to your retirement income. It's *costing* you money, rather than *paying* you money. You can change this situation and turn your home into an important source of retirement income.

In this chapter, you'll learn about what it's costing you to carry your home. This may lead you to a decision to sell and downsize, using the difference in monthly expenses to give you more retirement income. If you decide to stay where you are, you can still benefit from your home ownership. You'll learn about mortgage options you might consider to take the equity out of your home without selling it.

More Than Just a Place to Live

Your home may indeed be your castle, a valuable asset. If you haven't moved around a lot or borrowed against the value of your home, you may be sitting on a mortgage-free home that's worth a great deal. Many people buy their homes when their families are young. By the time they reach retirement age, that 25- or 30-year mortgage has been paid off, and the mortgage burning party has long since past.

That home today may be worth $150,000, $250,000, $500,000, or more. But what good does that value do you now? Not much. It's just a number. True, you have a place to live. But that value isn't giving you any income. If you had that same $150,000 or $500,000 in a mutual fund paying dividends, or in bonds paying interest, or even in a savings account paying interest (although very little), you'd be getting income from your asset. As it is, owning a home is a drain on your income because it costs you to pay taxes, insurance, and maintain it (if you're still paying a mortgage, your monthly cost is even higher).

Downsizing

Do you still need five bedrooms when all your children are grown and have moved away? Maybe you're like my husband who is a big collector and relish the space vacated by college-bound children, so downsizing won't work. But most people can do with less space. Less space can also mean less cost. It also means there's less to take care of (less lawn to care for, floors to vacuum, bathrooms to clean, walls to paint, and so on).

Senior Info

According to the U.S. Census Bureau, 75% of Americans own their own homes by age 50. Of those between the ages of 55 and 64, 80.1% were homeowners; of those 65 and older, 79.2% were homeowners.

When downsizing in retirement, you have several options:

➤ Buy a smaller home

➤ Rent a home

➤ Enter a continuing care facility or assisted living facility

The option you select isn't only a question of money, although that's a big part of it. You also need to take into account your health and lifestyle now...and what you predict it may be in a few years. Of course, your decision isn't permanent. If you buy a smaller home now, and some years down the road you decide you'd prefer to be relieved of the chores of caring for a home and cooking meals, you can always move again (this time to an assisted living facility).

Senior Info

Continuing care facilities are springing up in many communities across the country. Some big corporate names, like Marriott, are getting into the continuing care facility business in response to a growing demand from the increasing "older older" population (those age 85 and over). Today, the average age of a resident in a continuing care facility is 83.

What You'll Save

Owning that large, drafty home may be costing you more money than you need to spend in your retirement years. Getting cozier means your heating and cooling bills will drop (along with other expenses). If you move to a smaller home, relocate to another area where the cost-of-living is not quite so high, or simply decide to rent from now on, you'll save on all or most of your housing-related expenses. So instead of *increasing your retirement income*, you *reduce your retirement expenses*. It comes out to the same thing.

For example, let's say it's now costing you $2,500 a month for your housing costs and, in view of your retirement income, you've budgeted only $2,200 a month for housing costs in retirement. This means you're running at a deficit (like the federal government perennially). You're short $300 each month—money that you're probably taking out of savings rather than from income, or it's income you're using for housing instead of travel or other things you want or need to do. You have two choices: You can either increase your retirement income to cover your $300 a month shortfall ($3,600 more income each year without regard to taxes) or find a way to bring your housing costs down to $2,200.

Use the following chart in Table 11.1 to figure what you're paying now each month to keep your home and what it would cost you if you sold it. (If you're already renting, figure what it would cost you for a less expensive place.) In the columns marked "Your old home" and "Your new home," either enter a figure for rent if you're not a homeowner or a figure in real estate taxes if you are. You'll also have a mortgage payment if you currently have a mortgage and if you don't pay all cash for your new home. If you pay an annual amount (for example, you pay your homeowner's insurance once a year), just divide by 12 to find your monthly amount.

Word to the Wise

A special type of senior retirement community is sometimes referred to as a *continuing care facility* (also called a lifetime care facility). This type of living arrangement provides a housing unit, meals, cleaning, social activities, and, most importantly, some medical services (including long-term care). An assisted living facility is similar but doesn't provide medical or nursing care.

Table 11.1 Monthly Home Costs

Expense	Your Old Home	Your New Home
Mortgage payment	$	$
Real estate taxes	$	$
Rent	$	$
Insurance*	$	$
Repairs	$	$
Heating and cooling	$	$
Water and other utilities	$	$
Other costs	$	$

As a homeowner, you pay homeowner's insurance. If you rent your new home, you'll pay tenant's insurance to protect your possessions.

Of course, when downsizing, if you buy a new home, you'll have to pay closing costs which could run into the thousands of dollars (depending on the cost of your new home and the state you live in). This won't affect your monthly costs but it will have an impact on what cash you'll be able to use from the sale of your old home for retirement income.

If, because of your health condition, you move to a lifetime care facility, your figures for monthly expenses may be a little different than if you simply bought a new home or rented one. You may see your monthly expenses go up. One new facility in my area charges about $3,600 a month for a single person. But this doesn't mean you're out of pocket any more than before (you may even be paying *less* overall than before). This is because the monthly fees you pay for a lifetime care facility cover more than just your housing. You have to take into account the fact that your meals are included. You're also paying for entertainment. And, for some people most importantly, much of your medical expenses are covered. For instance, you don't have to buy a nursing home insurance policy because long-term care is included in part of the lifetime care facility package.

Golden Years Ideas

Did you pay off an FHA mortgage? If your mortgage was insured by the Federal Housing Authority, you may be owed some money. You can get your refund by filing within six years of paying off your mortgage (when you sell your home or refinance the loan). You could be entitled to as much as $4,000 (though the average refund is about $700).

You may or may not be required to pay an entrance fee (sometimes called an accommodation fee or a founder's fee). It can be very high (over $100,000). The fee may be partially refundable to you or your family if you move out or when you die. But the fee isn't like owning your unit (your heirs won't inherit the unit when you die, although they may receive a partial refund of your payment).

In figuring your costs, you should also consider property tax reductions that are available in some places for seniors or veterans. These reductions may make it more cost effective to stay where you are; they're discussed in Chapter 22, "Discounts for Seniors."

Tax Rules Favor Downsizing

What's the use of selling your home at a big profit if Uncle Sam takes a large chunk of it in taxes? None. Fortunately, it doesn't have to be this way. The government may take little or no part of your gain. Here are the basic rules used to figure your profit and what portion, if any, is taxable for federal income tax purposes (state income tax rules vary; some states have no income tax). You need to understand these rules so you'll know what part of the profits you'll get to keep to invest for retirement income and/or in a new home.

You aren't taxed on the first $250,000 of gain on the sale of your principal residence ($500,000 if you file a joint return). The only requirement is that you must have owned and used the home as your principal residence for at least two out of five years before the date of sale (or at least one year if you're forced to move to a nursing home because of a physical or mental condition).

Gain is a tax term meaning *profit*. When you sell your home, the price you agree upon with the buyer isn't all profit. You're allowed to subtract from that price your *basis* in the home (what you paid for it, plus improvements over the years) as well as certain selling expenses (such as the real estate broker's fees). You can best see how these rules mesh together with a simple example.

Let's say you bought your home 26 years ago for $80,000 and have already paid off the mortgage. During those 26 years, you put on a new roof for $5,000 and remodeled the kitchen for $15,000. The home is now worth $200,000. You list it with a broker who charges a 5% commission and, for the sake of this example, let's assume you get what the home is worth. Your basis is $100,000 (the $80,000 you paid plus the $20,000 of improvements). Your gain is $90,000 (the $200,000 selling price less the $10,000 in broker's commissions plus your

> **Cash Crash**
> Paying a refundable entrance fee to a lifetime care facility may result in interest income to you annually even though you don't see a penny of it. The tax law imputes this interest to you (treats you as having received it). However, if the facility is qualified, then no interest is imputed on the first $134,800 in 1998 (this number is adjusted each year for inflation).

> **Word to the Wise**
> The tax term for your main home is *principal residence*. If you have two homes, it's the one you treat as your main home (the place where you vote, have your driver's license, and so on). It can be a condo, co-op apartment (tied to stock ownership), boat, mobile home, or trailer, as long as there are appropriate facilities for cooking, sleeping, and bathing.

$100,000 basis). So, even though you pocket $190,000 (the selling price less commissions), your gain for tax purposes is only $90,000. You have $190,000 to invest for retirement income.

Golden Years Ideas
If you're married, you can claim a $500,000 exclusion even if the home is in just one spouse's name. The only requirement is that the other spouse lived in the home for at least two years before the sale.

If you'd had a mortgage, you would have figured your gain in *exactly* the same way, but you would have had less to invest. You'd have had to use part of the selling price to pay off the mortgage.

But what about taxes? Well, in this example, there are none to worry about. The gain is well protected by the exclusion you're allowed to claim. The exclusion applies as long as you owned and used your home as your main residence for two out of five years before you sold it. It doesn't matter how old you are or whether you (or your spouse) already claimed an exclusion for the sale of a home in an earlier year. You don't have to buy or build a new home to get the benefit of the exclusion, and you don't have to move a certain distance from your old home.

To get an exact number for your profit and whether you'll owe any taxes on it, look at IRS Form 2119, Sale of Your Home, and IRS Publication 523, Selling Your Home. You can get this form by calling the IRS at 800-829-1040 or at the IRS Web site at http://www.irs.ustreas.gov/.

Mortgaging Options to Consider

Maybe you like it where you are. You're comfortable in the home you've lived in for years and couldn't bear the thought of moving away from your garden or your neighbors. You want to stay put, but you also want to increase your retirement income. There are ways you can do this *without* selling out. You do this by tapping into the equity you've built up in your home over the years using a mortgage.

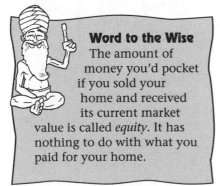

Word to the Wise
The amount of money you'd pocket if you sold your home and received its current market value is called *equity*. It has nothing to do with what you paid for your home.

There are two types of mortgages you can use to get your equity: a traditional mortgage in which you borrow and then begin immediate repayment, and a reverse mortgage or other home equity conversion approach in which repayment is deferred until you die, sell, or permanently move from your home. Because the reverse mortgage approach is geared for seniors, let's look at this option first; then let's see if a traditional mortgage can be of any help to you.

Reverse Mortgages

Remember all those years when you had to make your mortgage payments? Well, now you may be able to have the bank pay you instead of the other way around. It's called a *reverse* mortgage because you're getting a cash advance that doesn't have to be paid back until some time in the future. You get a monthly check, usually for as long as you live or until you sell the home—or when you want payments. In exchange, you give up part of the equity you built up on the house over the years. This is why a reverse mortgage (RM) is a type of *home equity conversion.* You're exchanging your home equity for current income without selling your home.

Cash Crash
RMs are not available in Texas at this time. They're permitted in every other state and in the District of Columbia.

Aside from the opportunity to get your equity out, one of the biggest selling points for RMs is that they're not considered income for purposes of Medicaid qualification. Receiving payments under an RM won't keep you from qualifying for Medicaid if you're otherwise eligible.

If the idea of a reverse mortgage is appealing, look into a federally insured RM program. Under one national pilot program, called the Home Equity Conversion Mortgage (HECM) Insurance Demonstration, insurance is given to the lenders making sure they're covered if homeowner's repayments fall short.

Senior Info

The Home Equity Conversion Mortgage Insurance Demonstration pilot program allows the U.S. Department of Housing and Urban Development (HUD) to back 50,000 reverse mortgages until September 30, 2000 (unless the program is extended as it has been in the past). There have already been 22,000 RMs made under the program by the nearly 150 lenders who participate. You can ask your local bank whether it participates in the program or call HUD's Housing Counseling Clearinghouse at 800-217-6970 to find a lender near you.

Do you qualify for an HECM RM? It depends only on your age and the type of home you have. You must be 62 or older and own and live in a single family (or one-to-four unit home). Condos and manufactured homes *may* qualify; cooperative apartments and mobile homes do not. It doesn't matter whether you have any mortgage left on your home. But if you do, you'll have to pay it off in full with part of the RM. There are no income or asset limitations. In other words, you don't have to show that you have enough income to repay the loan, nor will having too much income disqualify you in any way.

By using an RM, you get income. Here are some of the options on how the income will be paid to you:

➤ Fixed monthly payments for a set number of months (running 10, 15, or even 30 years)

➤ Fixed monthly payments for as long as you live (or until you sell the home)

➤ Cash in amounts you determine (this operates just like a line of credit)

➤ Some combination (monthly payments and a line of credit)

Unlike a traditional mortgage that you start to repay immediately, you don't repay an RM until you die, sell, or permanently move from your home. (If you're married, repayment is postponed until both you and your spouse dies.) In effect, repayment is made all at once from the proceeds of the sale of the home.

Senior Info

When RMs were first introduced in the early 1980s, there was a fatal flaw. After all income was paid out, the entire balance (principal plus interest) was due immediately. This forced homeowners to sell before they wanted to—the very opposite of what they'd planned by using an RM. And often they were left with little or no cash after the sale. These forced-sale RMs have virtually disappeared. Now, lenders use annuities to ensure lifetime income for homeowners, and repayment is deferred until death, a sale, or a move from the home.

The mortgage you can get is figured using a formula. The amount you receive under the RM depends on the value of your home (its appraised value but no more than HUD's

Golden Years Ideas

Federal law now requires lenders of reverse mortgages to disclose the total annual cost of the mortgage (factoring in interest, up-front fees, maintenance fees, and other charges) as an annual percentage rate.

"maximum claim amount") and how old you are when you take the mortgage (the older you are, the more you get). For example, someone who's only 62 would get about 30% of the maximum claim amount; someone who's 95 years old would get about 80% of that amount. This makes sense if you think about it. Because the RM may provide income for the life of the homeowner, the younger the owner, the longer that income stream can be expected to run. So the lender must anticipate there being enough equity in the home at the end of that stream to repay the mortgage. Like a traditional mortgage, you don't get something for nothing. You must pay at closing an RM insurance premium of 2% of the maximum claim amount. In addition, there's a one-half of one percent (0.5%) interest charge on the increasing loan balance. These charges protect both the bank and the borrower. The bank is protected if the loan balance grows to be more than the value of the home. The borrower is protected if the bank should default (income will continue to flow to the home-owner via HUD's guarantee). Then, of course, there's the interest rate on the debt. Rates may be adjusted monthly or annually.

Reverse mortgages aren't for everyone. Understand that you're giving up something valuable to get the income you want. You'll have less (maybe nothing) to leave your children should you live long and your home not appreciate enough to outpace the mortgage obligation.

Other Home Equity Conversion Options

Fannie Mae, a federal agency, offers a variation on the reverse mortgage theme of HUD (discussed earlier). The main difference is that Fannie Mae allows for an equity sharing option. This means that the lender gets the benefit of part of the equity in the home (typically 10% of the value of the home when the mortgage is paid off). In exchange, the borrower gets larger cash payments. Other differences and similarities between the HUD and Fannie Mae options are summarized in Table 11.2.

Table 11.2 HUD Versus Fannie Mae

Characteristic	HUD's RM	Fannie Mae's RM
Eligibility	Age 62	Age 62
Condo qualification	Yes	No
Growing line of credit	Yes	No
Fees	2% origination fee plus 0.5% annual fee on increasing loan balance	2% origination plus 1 point (a fee of 1% of the mortgage) at closing; monthly servicing fee
Maximum home value limit	$160,950	$214,600
How cash is paid out	Fixed, line of credit, or both	Fixed, line of credit, or both
Consumer education programs	No requirements	Borrower *must* attend

You don't have to go to a bank to get the equity out of your home. You can *privately* arrange to translate the equity in your home into cash. Here's how you do it: You sell (yes, it's a sale, but you're still in the house) to someone (usually your child, but it can be any investor). You then *immediately* rent the home from the buyer on a long-term lease. This type of home equity conversion is called a sale-leaseback.

Golden Years Ideas
The favorable home sale rules discussed earlier make it easier to sell a home without any tax cost. In the past, tax experts often advised holding the home until death to wipe out the capital gains. Now, liberal income tax rules do this on a sale, so there's no impetus to hold onto the home for tax reasons.

Golden Years Ideas
The National Center for Home Equity Conversion, a nonprofit organization, can supply you with sample legal documents to be used in a sale-leaseback arrangement for just $39. You can reach them at 612-953-4474.

The advantages of the sale-leaseback for you include:

➤ Immediate cash plus a stream of income. It's just like selling on the open market. You receive a down payment (such as 20% of the current value of the home), plus monthly payments for a fixed period (it's called a purchase money mortgage because you're holding the mortgage paper). In effect, you become a banker for your home, taking in payments in much the same way that your bank took mortgage payments from you. Of course, part of the money you receive will go back to the buyer in the form of monthly rent payments you'll have to make.

➤ Responsibility for upkeep shifted. As a tenant, you no longer have to pay real estate taxes, replace a leaking roof, or carry homeowner's insurance (you'll still insure the contents of the home under a tenant's policy, but this is much less costly).

Of course, there are some negatives to the sale-leaseback that should be considered. You go from being a homeowner to being a tenant. If your child is your landlord, you'd better be comfortable with the arrangement. From your child's (the buyer) perspective, there could be adverse tax consequences to the sale-leaseback arrangement, so talk to a tax advisor before taking any steps. If you're considering a sale-leaseback with a company, make sure they're reputable. You don't want to be thrown out of your house if you're late with one rent payment!

If the idea of a sale-leaseback appeals to you and your child (or if you find an investor who's interested), then find a real estate lawyer who's handled these types of arrangements before. Make sure that the leaseback contract is clear on who is required to pay for what (for example, snow removal). Also, if the leaseback has a term other than your lifetime, make sure it's renewable at your option and that rental increases at renewal are clearly spelled out.

Traditional Mortgages May Be the Ticket

Home equity conversion options are interesting because they allow you to defer repayment. But there's a downside: You can't borrow as much as you can with a traditional mortgage or home equity line of credit. Generally, with a traditional mortgage or a home equity line of credit, you can borrow up to 80% of the equity in your home. So if your home is worth $200,000 and there's no mortgage on it, you'd be able to get a mortgage of up to $160,000. For some people, the traditional route may prove more helpful.

You may be able to earn more on the money than you'd pay in interest. You have to put pencil to paper and figure it out. It's a little complicated, but here's what you need to take into account:

➤ Interest you'd be paying. What interest rate would you be charged? A fixed rate mortgage today is about 7%. If you take out an equity line of credit, the interest rate adjusts periodically (monthly, quarterly, annually).

➤ Interest or other income you'd be able to earn on the money. Now, interest on a passbook savings account won't be higher than you'd have to pay on the mortgage. But many investments run higher. For example, you may be able to find bonds that are paying more than 7%.

➤ Taxes. What would you save in taxes from the interest payments? Remember that mortgage interest is deductible as an itemized deduction on your federal income tax return. What would you pay in taxes from the income you earn? Unless you're holding munis (and you won't find any at this time paying more than 7%), you'll be taxed on the income you earn.

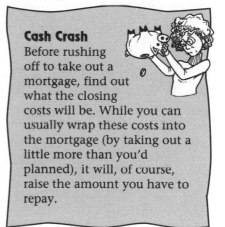

Cash Crash
Before rushing off to take out a mortgage, find out what the closing costs will be. While you can usually wrap these costs into the mortgage (by taking out a little more than you'd planned), it will, of course, raise the amount you have to repay.

➤ Cash flow. Remember that you must make monthly repayments on the mortgage. Your income from the proceeds must be large enough to make these payments and still leave something over. If it's a wash, forget it. If, after your computation, you see that you'll be able to increase your income (after taking into account repayment of the mortgage), then you're ahead of the game.

The Least You Need to Know

➤ Equity you've built up in your home may be a source of income to you.

➤ Downsizing to save money is an alternative to increasing retirement income.

➤ Reverse mortgages don't require repayment until you've died, sold, or permanently moved from the home.

➤ Traditional mortgages may provide retirement income if the numbers are right.

Be a Landlord

In This Chapter

➤ Being a landlord in your own home

➤ Making money from your vacation property

➤ Investing in real estate for rental income

➤ Investing in mortgage-backed securities

Some of the richest people in America got to be that way by owning real estate. Land is a limited commodity (it's something that can't be grown or produced). So the thinking goes, as land is committed for housing developments, malls, industrial parks, and manufacturing facilities and becomes scarcer, it also becomes more valuable. Over the years, this has sometimes been correct, but not always. Still, owning property in retirement not only can be a good way to increase your estate that you can pass on to your heirs but also provide you with retirement income throughout your life.

In this chapter, you'll learn about the advantages to owning a two-family home that you live in. You'll also see how to get income from your vacation home (if you own one). And you'll find out how real estate investments (that you don't live in) can produce retirement income for you.

Owning a Two-Family Home

In many parts of the country, you will find a unique form of housing—the two-family home. Within a single structure, there are two separate units, each with its own living space and cooking facilities. The units may be the same size or of unequal size. Some units may be called "mother-daughter" units because one space is virtually an accessory apartment to a standard size single-family home. Some homes have even added on accessory apartments, called "granny flats," to house a relative under the same roof.

The chief attraction of a two-family home is the rental income you can receive from the second unit (you live in the first unit). That rental income can be used to pay your mortgage and other expenses. Depending on the rental real estate market in your area and the amount of your expenses, becoming a landlord of a two-family home can mean you live for free or almost free (all or some of your housing costs are paid by the tenant). The money you save on your housing can be used for other expenses during your retirement.

Being a Landlord

Sounds great to be a landlord and collect all that rent? Before you rush out to buy a two-family house, make sure you understand what you're getting into and that you have the skills and the temperament for it. Some people find the arrangement works smoothly; others, like me, do not. I once had a tenant who became distraught when his wife left him. He took out his anger and frustration by spilling over the basement floor about a dozen near-full cans of paint. This unpleasant experience put a quick end to my days as a landlord.

As a landlord, you have to work for your money. Here are some of the things you'll have to do if you want to earn that rental income:

➤ Find tenants. You have to find a suitable tenant. This means advertising your space and screening prospective tenants. Be sure to ask for references and check them out thoroughly. You don't want to find the tenant-from-hell as happened in the movies *Single White Female* and *Pacific Heights*.

Cash Crash

When shopping for a two-family home, make sure it's legal. Some people have converted their single-family home into a two-family home in order to get the rental income. The problem: They don't tell the town or city. The area may not be zoned for multi-family dwellings, and if you buy the property, you'd be out of luck to rent it out legally. Mother-daughter homes (or homes with granny flats) may not pose a problem if you live in one unit and your children live in the other (it's all in the one family).

Golden Years Ideas

You can use a preprinted lease that you buy from your local stationery or office supply store. Fill in the blanks and add (in a *rider*) any additional terms you need. You can have a lawyer look your lease over, or you can have a lawyer prepare one for you. Don't skip the step of having a legal review because you can bind yourself to trouble if you don't get professional help.

➤ Negotiate a lease. Once you find the tenant you think will work out, you'll want to put your agreement in writing. Use a *lease* to spell out monthly rent, the period of occupancy (how long the tenant is allowed to stay), security deposit requirements, other terms (obligations to make repairs in addition to or instead of rent), and renewal options, if any.

➤ Make repairs. If the toilet in the rental unit leaks, it's probably your responsibility to fix it. If you're handy around the house, then small repairs shouldn't be a problem for you. If you're all thumbs, it's going to get expensive to bring in plumbers, electricians, and carpenters every time there's a leak, a bad wire, or a crack in the floorboard.

➤ Live with strangers. When you live in a two-family house, you give up some privacy that you used to have living in a single-family house. While you can shut your door, your comings and goings are hard to hide. You hear your neighbors (and they can hear you).

➤ Resolve tenant problems. If you find your tenant doesn't live up to the terms of the lease, you've got big problems. As a landlord, you have to live up to your legal responsibilities even if the tenant doesn't. It's almost impossible to evict a tenant. Even the process of trying is lengthy, expensive, and *very* frustrating. If your tenant is late with the rent, hound him; don't let things slip. Don't agree to renew the lease if you had difficulties with the tenant.

One of the only ways to protect yourself against bad tenants is to get adequate security, such as a two-month deposit. Make sure the tenant understands that the deposit cannot be used to pay the last two months of the lease. The tenant must pay the rent, and the deposit will be returned after you inspect the premises to make sure you don't have to use the deposit to correct problems caused by the tenant. Of course, be prepared for the fact that the tenant may simply stop paying rent a month or two before the lease is up. The security deposit will cover the rent but there may not be any money to make repairs of damages caused by the tenant.

Tax Savings to Pocket

If you're not scared by the prospect of being a landlord, you may reap some financial rewards. You'll be able to deduct repairs on the rental unit. You're also entitled to a depreciation write-off.

You figure your depreciation only on the rental unit (not on the entire structure). The tax law fixes the

> **Word to the Wise**
> Tax deductions that reflect the using up of an asset over time are called *depreciation* (even if the asset isn't used up within that time). Because land generally isn't used up, it can't be depreciated. The deduction relates only to the building. Depreciation is the one deduction you claim that doesn't require you to make a cash outlay each year (after the year of purchase).

period over which you claim depreciation for that unit as 27.5 years. This means that you have to own the rental unit for that length of time to claim all the depreciation you're entitled to. The amount of depreciation you claim each year is figured using a three-step approach. Here's how to do it:

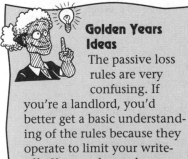

Cash Crash

Being a landlord means being in the business of renting real estate. This requires you to keep businesslike books and records of your income and expenses throughout the year. (See Chapter 7, "Starting Your Own Business at Home," for tips on record keeping.)

1. Take the *lower* of the value of the property at the time you begin to use it for rental or what you paid for the property.

2. Subtract the value of the land.

3. Multiply the results you found in step 2 by a percentage from the following table. Use the number over the column corresponding to the month you first began to rent the unit (for example, if the rental began in July, look under the column marked "7"):

Table 12.1 Depreciation Table*

Year	Jan	Feb	Mar	Apr	May	Jun	Jul	Aug	Sept	Oct	Nov	Dec
1	2.461	2.247	2.033	1.819	1.605	1.319	1.177	0.963	0.749	0.535	0.321	0.107
2–39	2.564	2.564	2.564	2.564	2.564	2.564	2.564	2.564	2.564	2.564	2.564	2.564
40	0.107	0.321	0.535	0.749	0.963	1.177	1.391	1.605	1.819	2.033	2.247	2.461

Source: Internal Revenue Service

You report your rental income and claim expenses on Schedule E of IRS Form 1040. You'll see from the schedule the different types of expenses you can deduct.

Golden Years Ideas

The passive loss rules are very confusing. If you're a landlord, you'd better get a basic understanding of the rules because they operate to limit your write-offs. You can learn about them in IRS Publication 925, Passive Activity and At-Risk Rules, by calling the IRS at 800-829-FORMS.

After subtracting all your expenses from your annual rents, you may find that you show a loss for the year. Your loss is subject to the passive activity loss rules. These rules are *very* complicated. The idea is that you can't write off losses that exceed your income from all passive activities (your rental is a passive activity). However, there's an important exception. You can deduct up to $25,000 of losses from your rental if you actively participate in the rental activity (you set the rents, make rental decisions) *and* your adjusted gross income (AGI) for the year doesn't exceed $100,000, whether you're single or married and file a joint return—you can't claim the allowance if you're married and file a separate return. If your AGI is between $100,000 and $150,000, you claim a part of the $25,000 loss allowance. Your AGI for this purpose doesn't include any taxable Social Security benefits, nor any reduction for IRA contributions.

SCHEDULE E (Form 1040) Department of the Treasury Internal Revenue Service (99)	**Supplemental Income and Loss** (From rental real estate, royalties, partnerships, S corporations, estates, trusts, REMICs, etc.) ➤ **Attach to Form 1040 or Form 1041.** ➤ **See Instructions for Schedule E (Form 1040).**	OMB No. 1545-0074 19**97** Attachment Sequence No. **13**
Name(s) shown on return		Your social security number

Part I   **Income or Loss From Rental Real Estate and Royalties**   Note: *Report income and expenses from your business of renting personal property on Schedule C or C-EZ (see page E-1). Report farm rental income or loss from Form 4835 on page 2, line 39.*

1 Show the kind and location of each **rental real estate property:**	2 For each rental real estate property listed on line 1, did you or your family use it during the tax year for personal purposes for more than the greater of: • 14 days, **or** • 10% of the total days rented at fair rental value? (See page E-1.)	Yes	No
A	A		
B	B		
C	C		

Income:

			Properties			Totals (Add columns A, B, and C.)
			A	B	C	
3	Rents received	3		3		
4	Royalties received	4				4

Expenses:

5	Advertising	5				
6	Auto and travel (see page E-2)	6				
7	Cleaning and maintenance	7				
8	Commissions	8				
9	Insurance	9				
10	Legal and other professional fees	10				
11	Management fees	11				
12	Mortgage interest paid to banks, etc. (see page E-2)	12				12
13	Other interest	13				
14	Repairs	14				
15	Supplies	15				
16	Taxes	16				
17	Utilities	17				
18	Other (list) ➤	18				
19	Add lines 5 through 18	19				19
20	Depreciation expense or depletion (see page E-2)	20				20
21	Total expenses. Add lines 19 and 20	21				
22	Income or (loss) from rental real estate or royalty properties. Subtract line 21 from line 3 (rents) or line 4 (royalties). If the result is a (loss), see page E-3 to find out if you must file **Form 6198**	22				
23	Deductible rental real estate loss. **Caution:** *Your rental real estate loss on line 22 may be limited. See page E-3 to find out if you must file* **Form 8582**. *Real estate professionals must complete line 42 on page 2*	23	(	)(	)( )	
24	**Income.** Add positive amounts shown on line 22. **Do not** include any losses				24	
25	**Losses.** Add royalty losses from line 22 and rental real estate losses from line 23. Enter total losses here				25	( )
26	Total rental real estate and royalty income or (loss). Combine lines 24 and 25. Enter the result here. If Parts II, III, IV, and line 39 on page 2 do not apply to you, also enter this amount on Form 1040, line 17. Otherwise, include this amount in the total on line 40 on page 2				26	

For Paperwork Reduction Act Notice, see Form 1040 instructions.   Cat. No. 11344L   **Schedule E (Form 1040) 1997**

Source: Internal Revenue Service

This is the 1997 schedule. Do not use this schedule to report your rental income; it's included here for illustration purposes only.

Golden Years Ideas

Some people buy a second home with the thought of retiring to it on a full-time basis in the future. They rent out their second home for part of the year until they sell their other home. Rental makes it possible to carry both homes and allows them to acclimate to their new location over a long period of time.

Getting Income From Your Vacation Home

You may own more than one home: one you live in for the greater part of the year and one you use for vacations and brief stays. You can turn your second home into a moneymaker by renting it out. The rental income you receive can be used to offset the cost of carrying the home.

Before you rush out to rent it out, think about what it means to let a stranger rent your home. You have to be comfortable with the idea of someone sleeping in your bed and eating off of your plates. You have to be willing to forego use of your home for the time you set as a rental period. So, for example, if you own lakeside property as a vacation home and decide to rent it out for the months of July and August, make sure that you don't want to use your vacation home at that time. Maybe June and September suit you fine.

Your Down Time Is Up-Rental Time

Decide how long you want to rent out your home. My parents in Florida have a condo in North Carolina that they have up for rental for the entire year. They hardly go there and figure they'll use it when it's not rented out (they're willing to work around the rental schedule). You may not be so flexible. Maybe you routinely use your Arizona home during the winter months to escape your New England winters and don't want to rent it out at that time. You're more than willing to rent it out at any other time of the year. Maybe there's a special event in your area, and you're willing to move out just so you get rental income for that short time. For example, when the Winter Olympics were held in Lake Placid, New York, those who owned summer homes in the area (called "camps") were able to rent them out for a handsome fee.

Renting a vacation home on a limited basis isn't the easiest thing to do. You can, of course, advertise your home's availability (you often see "ski house for rent" with certain weeks listed).

Cash Crash

If you rent out your vacation home, make sure your homeowner's insurance covers you. A tenant can do a lot of damage in a short time. A standard homeowner's policy may not automatically protect you. A call to your insurance agent before you begin to rent out your home can easily adjust your coverage.

You can use a rental agent to help you. Many resort areas have management agents who take charge of not only finding tenants but also make sure that the unit remains in rental shape. Some agents may be attached to a resort development and represent all of the owners in the development who want to rent out their units. Of course, you pay for the service you receive, but it may be worth it. Be sure you understand the arrangement.

Tax Angles to Renting Your Vacation Home

Renting out your vacation home involves the tax man in much the same way as if you rent out a part of your two-family house. However, there are special rules for vacation home rentals. It's helpful to know the rules before you start so you can avoid problems down the road. The rules you use to determine how you report your income and expenses for the home depend on the length of the rental period during the year and your use of the vacation home.

Rule 1: If you rent your home for fewer than 15 days a year, you don't have to report the rental income you get (it's tax free to you). But you can't deduct maintenance costs or depreciation for that time either. So, for example, if you rent out your vacation home (or main home) in Southampton, New York, for the week of July 4 for $1,000, you don't have to report this income. You can't deduct the $100 cleaning bill you paid to get your home ready for the rental (and to put it back in shape after the week it was used).

Rule 2: If you rent your home for 15 days or more within the year *and* your use of the home (including that of your family members) was more than the greater of 14 days or 10% of the number of days the home was rented, you deduct your expenses in a set order to offset rental income. You don't have to count the days you spent getting the home ready for rental, even if you used it for recreational activities during that time. It might sound complicated, but let's walk through it slowly. First you offset the rental income by mortgage interest, real estate taxes, and casualty losses, if any. These deductions aren't limited by the amount of rental income; they can exceed it. But let's say your rental income is more than these deductions. Then you offset the excess rental income by your operating expenses, such as utilities and maintenance. These expenses are limited to the amount of excess rental income. Then, if there's still some excess rental income after offsetting it by operating expenses, you can deduct depreciation (as figured earlier in this chapter).

Because you use the home primarily for personal purposes, you report your expenses as an itemized deduction on Schedule A of your federal income tax return, Form 1040. You also report your income as "other income" on page 1 of Form 1040. You don't report your income and expenses as "rental income" on Schedule E as you normally would.

Rule 3: If you rent your home for 15 days or more *and* you don't use the home for more than the greater of 14 days or 10% of the number of days the home was rented, you report your income and expenses on Schedule E in the same way that you would if you rented part of your two-family home. Again, losses from your rental are subject to the passive loss rules.

Investing in Real Estate

Your home or vacation home isn't the only property around that you can lease out for retirement income. You can own other houses or condos, a strip mall, storefronts, or even garages. As long as there's a market for it, you can get rental income.

Word to the Wise
Paying only a part of the cost of the property to be able to own the whole thing is known as *leveraging*. It usually involves making a down payment and then taking a mortgage to cover the balance of the purchase price.

Cash Crash
Beware of "no money down" opportunities advertised on television and elsewhere. It's not as easy to buy property without any down payment as the sellers of no-money-down sales kits would have you believe. Also beware of the risks of leveraging. If property values decline, foreclosure (and loss of your investment) can becomes a real possibility.

Investing in real estate isn't for everyone. As the old saying goes, it takes money to make money. You need to have enough money to buy the property in order to get the rental income. Fortunately, you can buy property without having every penny of the purchase price. You can use a concept called *leveraging* to become a property owner.

Just to give you an idea of how leveraging gives you a leg up on property ownership, let's take an example. Say there are three condo units for sale in a resort area that you're sure you'll be able to rent out for a big monthly amount. Each unit costs $100,000. You have $60,000 to invest. You put 20% down ($20,000 on each unit) and finance the rest with mortgages. You've leveraged yourself into owning three units for less down than you'd have paid for a single unit outright.

Before you start hunting for properties to buy, make sure you understand how mortgaging affects your rental numbers. In order to make money from your rentals, your monthly rents must be *more* than your expenses. Be sure to figure correctly what those expenses are. In addition to insurance and real estate taxes, your biggest monthly expense will be repayment on the mortgage. But you'll be able to deduct depreciation (which doesn't cost you any part of your cash flow).

Depending on interest rates (which affect the size of your mortgage payments), you may or may not be able to make the numbers work out. The interest rates you pay on commercial property and residential property you don't live in are higher than you'd pay on a mortgage on your main home. The only way to know if a property will produce rental income for you is to push the numbers. Let's see whether the numbers work out on that $100,000 condo that you want to buy by financing $80,000. A 30-year mortgage at 8% costs you $587 a month. Property and liability insurance run $100 a month. You can deduct depreciation of $3,636 a year, or $303 a month. Assuming you make the tenant responsible for utilities and maintenance, your monthly out-of-pocket expenses are $687 ($587 plus $100). The $303 monthly deduction for depreciation, which doesn't cost you any cash, is worth $85 in tax savings (if you're in the 28% tax bracket). So in order to make any money from your rental, you'd have to receive a monthly rent of *more* than $602 a month ($687 less the $85 in tax savings). As a practical matter, you'd better show an even wider margin of profit to make the rental business worth your while. This is because you'll be putting in time and effort. And there may be unexpected expenses, such as a new water heater or an oven replacement, which you'll need to pay for out of your rental income.

If there's a particular property you're interested in, do some leg work before you make a down payment.

Check out rentals in the area you're considering to see whether they'll support the kind of rent you want to charge. Remember to build into the rent figure you're expecting to charge enough leeway to cover not only the expenses you know about (mortgage, insurance, and such) but also the expenses you don't know about that can arise (a period of vacancy or an unexpected repair).

Check out the number of rentals on the market. If there's a glut in that area, you may have trouble finding a tenant. This means having the unit empty and having to pay out-of-pocket the mortgage and other expenses until you find a tenant.

Golden Years Ideas
Because shares of REITs are publicly traded, you can get out of your investment when you want. In contrast, direct ownership of realty is highly illiquid. It may take months or longer to find a buyer and even longer to close a sale.

Investing Through a REIT

You don't have to search around for property if you want to become a landlord. You can share in a pool of properties and get income from them by investing in a real estate investment trust (REIT). REITs are a special type of investment because they must meet certain tax requirements (for example, they must derive a substantial part of their income from rents or mortgages on rental property). Many REITs are sold like stock on the exchange.

Senior Info

There are different types of REITs. *Mortgage REITs* earn income from loans they hold on property. The price of a share of a mortgage REIT is interest sensitive (the price generally goes up when interest rates fall and goes down when interest rates rise). *Equity REITs* own property that produces rental income (and income generated by the sales of such property). The price of a share of an equity REIT is rental sensitive (the price generally goes up when there's high demand for rentals and goes down when there's a glut of rentals on the market). There are also *hybrid REITs* that own both mortgages and rental properties.

REITs offer a number of important advantages to someone interested in investing in real estate:

Golden Years Ideas
As an investor, you're taxed on income from the REIT in much the same way as you're taxed on income from a stock mutual fund. Part of the income paid to you may be ordinary dividends; part may be capital gains.

➤ Diversification. If you buy real estate, your pocketbook will probably limit your holdings to one or only a few properties. By investing in a REIT, you get a share of a larger mix of properties.

➤ Tax law requires the REIT to distribute 95% of its ordinary income each year. So, as an investor, you should be getting an annual income (which may be paid in monthly or other periodic amounts).

➤ Professional real estate management. If you haven't been a landlord before, then you're a novice. By investing in a REIT, you get the benefit of professional management for the properties.

Investing Through a Limited Partnership

Cash Crash
Since the introduction of the passive activity loss rules more than a decade ago, real estate ventures have fallen out of favor with investors because they are no longer able to deduct their real estate losses (part of which are only paper losses resulting in part from depreciation deductions that don't require any cash outlay) against their other income. However, some firms now market investments that are economically profitable to investors, so the passive loss rules aren't a problem for them.

If you want to own real estate but can't afford to go into it big time, another investment option for you is a limited partnership. The real estate partnership, like a REIT, buys different properties in order to provide diversification.

Limited partnership interests in real estate ventures may be organized privately (a few people get together to buy a property with one person acting as the general partner). Because you're a limited partner, you have no personal liability for anything that happens to the venture. This means that creditors of the property can't come after your personal assets to pay their bills. Limited partnership interests are also marketed by brokerage firms on a large scale.

When looking for a limited partnership investment, read the prospectus carefully (or have your financial advisor review it with you). Examine the philosophy of the general partnership (how does the venture hope to make money; when does it plan to wind up things and distribute initial investments, plus profits, to investors?). You don't want to put money in and find you're not getting what you'd hoped or expected.

If you already own interests in real estate limited partnerships, you may be able to sell out to companies that solicit your interests, but usually only for pennies on the dollar.

Other Real Estate Investments May Be for You

There are many other ways to get in on the real estate market and make it pay for you. If you've got some construction skills, like former President Jimmy Carter, you might be able to turn a "fixer-upper" or "handiman special" single-family or multiple-family dwelling into a valuable asset. You can then sell it for a handsome gain or rent it out for a monthly income. All you need is the cash (and/or the ability to get a mortgage) to get into the investment and your own sweat equity (your skills as a tradesman, craftsman, or decorator) to turn it into something quite valuable.

All thumbs? There are still other ways to get into real estate. You can get in on the financing end so that instead of becoming a landlord, you're more like a banker. There are a number of mortgage-backed securities that pass through mortgage interest and principal to investors from a pool of home mortgages. These investments generally offer higher yields than Treasury bonds and they're quite safe (you're pretty well assured that you'll get your principal back). Government agencies and semi-private corporations that offer mortgaged-based securities include:

➤ Government National Mortgage Association (Ginnie Maes)—offer the full faith and credit of the U.S. government that principal and interest on FHA and VA mortgages will be repaid.

➤ Federal National Mortgage Association (Fannie Maes)—issue mortgage-backed securities but they're not under the full faith and credit guarantee.

➤ Federal Home Loan Mortgage Corporation (Freddie Macs)—guarantees timely repaying of interest (principal is guaranteed but may be up to one year late).

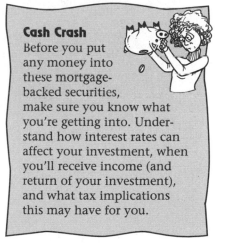

Cash Crash
Getting into a real estate limited partnership is a lot easier than getting out. It's called a highly illiquid asset because there's virtually no market for your limited partnership interest. Be prepared to hold your investment for the long haul or sell out at a big discount (for example, as low as $75 for each $1,000 you've invested). Don't put money in that you expect to need any time in the near future.

Cash Crash
Before you put any money into these mortgage-backed securities, make sure you know what you're getting into. Understand how interest rates can affect your investment, when you'll receive income (and return of your investment), and what tax implications this may have for you.

The plus side to these investments is high liquidity (you can buy and sell them like stocks and bonds, something you can't ordinarily do with more real estate investments). And, they're safer investments than corporate bonds, stocks, and even municipal bonds. But you should understand that the initial yield you're expecting to get may not materialize.

A substantial portion of the mortgages may be paid off earlier than expected. Or you could sell your interest before the mortgages are paid off, getting less than expected if interest rates have risen.

Two other types of real estate–related investments are collateralized mortgage obligations (CMOs) and real estate mortgage investment conduits (REMICs). This alphabet soup of investments offer you the chance to get monthly income (or less frequently if you select) based on mortgage interest. CMOs are simply bundles of Ginnie Maes, Fannie Maes, and Freddie Macs put together by brokerage firms or other private institutions. REMICs are another type of fixed pool of mortgages.

The Least You Need to Know

➤ Owning a two-family home can be a way for you to live "rent free."

➤ Leasing out your vacation home when you're not using it can give you added retirement income.

➤ Leveraging can allow you to own several rental properties without paying the full purchase price for all of them.

➤ REITs allow you to get income from rentals but also give you the liquidity you can't get from owning the properties directly.

➤ Real estate limited partnerships are very difficult to get out of, so invest in them only if you can afford to stay in them.

➤ Mortgage-backed securities allow you to participate in real estate indirectly, with the liquidity of stocks and bonds.

Chapter 13

Getting an Annuity

In This Chapter

➤ Buying commercial annuities

➤ Setting up a private annuity

➤ Giving to charitable remainder trusts and pooled income funds

---

One of the key concerns of any retiree is making sure that income will last for a lifetime. Fear that you'll outlive your retirement savings is a concern of many retirees. One way to make sure that you'll always have an income during your retirement years is with an annuity. An annuity is an arrangement that you can set up to pay a fixed monthly income for life (or if you're married, until the last of you or your spouse dies). There are commercial annuities that you buy from insurance companies. And then there are private affairs that you can set up with family members or with charities.

In this chapter, you'll learn about how annuities work, including their up sides and down. You'll also find out about alternatives to commercial annuities that may provide the income you're looking for while meeting other personal financial or tax objectives. There are several different charitable arrangements you can use to provide you with retirement income.

Commercial Annuities: What They Can Do for You

You may already be getting an annuity, and you don't even know it. If you receive a monthly pension from your employer, you're already getting a type of annuity (an employee annuity). It has many of the features of a commercial annuity:

➤ Fixed monthly income. Some annuities pay at other intervals, such as quarterly, but most pay on a monthly basis.

➤ Payment of income for life. Annuities can be set to run only for a fixed number of years. Joint and survivor annuities run for the joint lives of a husband and wife until the last one dies.

Cash Crash

You don't get something for nothing. There are fees for buying an annuity. So, for example, if you invest $50,000 in a contract with back-end fees, you don't have $50,000 working for you; a portion goes to pay agent's commissions and insurance company fees. Or if you buy an annuity with a surrender charge and cash it in before the end of a certain period (usually 5 to 7 years), you won't get back those fees.

Word to the Wise

The person receiving annuity payments is the *annuitant*. You *annuitize* when you stop investing in the annuity and begin to take your payments.

A commercial annuity is simply a contract you buy from an insurance company. You can buy it with a single payment or by making investments over a period of time. While you're making the investments, income earned by the annuity is tax-deferred. The amount you receive monthly once you annuitize depends on what you put into the contract, your life expectancy (or joint life expectancies), and how well the contract has performed. Once payments begin, they remain the same for the rest of your life (there are no inflation adjustments or other increases). (Instead of payments for life, you can choose to receive payments for a term of years, such as 10 or 20 years.)

Annuities offer certain key advantages over other types of investments. There's no current income tax on income earned by the annuity before you begin to receive payments. So, for example, if you buy a variable annuity and invest in mutual fund–type investments under the annuity's umbrella, the gains realized in those investments aren't currently taxed. Annuities also are an easy way to set up a steady income to meet your current expenses. There's no guesswork about what you'll receive. There's another advantage to commercial annuities that may be important to some people as they get older. People well into their retirement years may be concerned with the possibility of having to go to a nursing home. Unless there's adequate insurance, a nursing home stay can wipe out a lifetime's savings. Many people are forced to turn to Medicaid (a federal/state need-based program) to pay for the nursing home. Buying an annuity isn't considered a "transfer" that could delay or prevent Medicaid eligibility. While the annuity payments must be used for the person's support, should the person die and the contract provide for some guaranteed amount, the person's heirs would benefit accordingly (unless the state goes after that amount).

You buy an annuity through an insurance agent or a stockbroker licensed to sell annuities, but before you go out to buy an annuity, make sure you understand what's involved. You, as the annuitant, are buying the right to receive annuity payments. Payments can begin at any time at your election (generally you *must* annuitize by the time you reach 90, but some allow you to wait up to five years after purchase, so an 89-year-old would not have to take payments until age 94!). Of course, because you're looking for income, this option to delay annuitizing isn't really of concern to you.

Not every dollar you get in annuity income is yours to keep. Uncle Sam has an interest in what you receive. Part of each payment you receive represents a return of your investment plus income earned on that investment. You're taxed on the income part; you don't pay any tax on the return of your own money. So, for example, if you invested $50,000 in a policy and you're expected to receive $100,000 over your lifetime (using your life expectancy to figure your expected return), then half of every monthly payment you receive is income, and the other half is a return of your investment. (In contrast, employer-provided pensions are taxed differently, as you'll see in Chapter 15, "Pension Payout Options for Married Couples.")

When you're in the investment phase and haven't yet annuitized, you can trade your existing contract for another one with a different insurance company to get a better return. This trade is tax free (you don't have to pay any income tax on it) as long as the funds are transferred between the insurance companies and you don't get your hands on the money. Tax-free annuity trades aren't like IRAs that give you a 60-day period in which to take the money and then roll it over.

There are two types of commercial annuities: fixed annuities and variable annuities. A *fixed annuity* is like a bank CD because you know going in exactly what you'll get coming out. (The insurance company tells you what interest rate you're earning on your money and for how long that interest rate applies: one year, five years, or otherwise.) A *variable annuity* is like an investment in the stock market; what you get in the end depends on how well your investment performs. Variable annuities give you the option of choosing

> **Cash Crash**
> A key feature of an annuity is the guaranteed death benefit. If you put $50,000 into a variable annuity and the value of the funds drops to $40,000, your beneficiary will receive $50,000 when you die. But the guarantee only helps your family, not you. If, when you're set to annuitize, the value of the funds is only $40,000, this is the amount on which your monthly benefits will be based (not the $50,000 guaranteed death benefit amount).

> **Golden Years Ideas**
> Check out the insurance company that's selling you the annuity with a reputable rating service, such as A.M. Best and Company (you'll find the rating book at your local library). You're going to be connected with the company for a long time, so make sure it's sound.

from a family of mutual funds (and some even allow you to choose from different mutual fund families). You can be as aggressive or conservative in your choice of funds as you like (or can tolerate depending on how well you can stand the risk).

Today, some tax experts are suggesting that variable annuities aren't the best tax choice because you'll pay ordinary income on the capital gains earned by mutual funds within your annuity (plus you pay insurance charges for the privilege of buying the annuity). However, if you have a long time to invest before you're planning on annuitizing (such as 8 or 10 years), you may still come out ahead with a variable annuity.

Getting the Best of Both Worlds With Private Annuities

You don't have to go through an insurance company to get an annuity. You can arrange one yourself. If you own a business, a building, or other sizable asset or cash that you're willing to part with, you can, in effect, convert it into an annuity. Because you don't use an insurance company, the arrangement is called a private annuity.

Here's how it works: You *sell* your asset to your child (that's usually the person interested in making this arrangement). Instead of paying you cash, your child agrees to provide you with an annuity. You come out a big winner (and your child also benefits from the arrangement).

You're guaranteed a stream of income for your life. In order for the tax benefits to work, the promise to pay you must be unsecured (you're relying on the word of your child, and only you know how good that word really is). To give you an example of what you can expect in terms of income, let's assume you're 65 years old and sell to your child property worth $100,000. If the interest rate factor you agree to use is 10%, you'll receive an annual payment of $14,042 (approximately $1,170 a month for the rest of your life). The amount of the annuity payments are figured using IRS tables (which can't be used if you're terminally ill).

You no longer have to manage the property even though you get to enjoy a benefit from it. You get income; your child gets the headaches of running the business or managing the property.

Tax on the appreciation of your property is spread over your life expectancy. Even though capital gains rates are low now, it still helps to postpone tax whenever possible. With a private annuity, instead of paying capital gains tax in the year you sell your asset, you pay it in small increments while you live (a part of each annuity payment you receive represents some capital gains).

You keep the asset in the family. If it's your business or a building, it may not be so easy to sell even if you wanted to have the asset go to outsiders. Using a private annuity arrangement with your child creates a market for your asset.

Your beneficiaries will realize estate tax savings. Because the obligation to make annuity payments ends at your death, there's nothing to include in your estate (if you spend your annuity payments). If you had simply sold the asset on an installment basis to get the same income over a number of years, your estate would have to include the value of the installment notes you still held at the time of your death.

The key to getting all these benefits is to have the property appraised in order to arrive at an accurate value. If you don't get a correct value and the IRS later challenges it, the tax assumptions you've made can be upset.

Now that you've learned what a private annuity can offer, you may be tempted to run out and set one up. Not so fast. Not everything about a private annuity is positive. There are some drawbacks you should take into account before you go ahead with plans to set one up:

➤ Your income depends on your child. If you transfer an asset that doesn't produce any income (such as a valuable painting), your child has to come up with the money to pay you from somewhere else. Also, remember that the promise to pay you is unsecured. If your child goes bankrupt, you're in trouble. If your child dies before you do, his or her estate is responsible for continuing payment of your annuity. But, again, debts may pose a drain on that estate and put your annuity in jeopardy.

➤ Your child's obligation depends on the time of your death. If you live longer than life expectancy tables say you should, your child will wind up paying you *more* than the value of the asset he or she bought from you.

➤ Your child doesn't get any tax benefit from the arrangement (other than benefiting from the estate tax savings to your estate). There's no deduction for the annuity payments made to you.

Golden Years Ideas

If you think you're in great shape and plan to beat the life expectancy odds, you may want to sell your property and use the proceeds to buy a commercial annuity (the insurance company will be on the hook for larger-than-expected payments if you live as long as you plan to).

Golden Years Ideas

Setting up a private annuity is highly complex and requires the help of a tax professional (your accountant or tax attorney). For example, the annuity must be fixed using IRS valuation tables that professionals should be familiar with. Be sure to factor in the professional fees you'll pay in setting up a private annuity.

'Tis Better to Give, but You'll Also Receive

Donating to charity for many people is reward enough. You know that what you give is going to help a good cause. But you may be able to benefit the charity and yourself at the same time. If you have the right kind of property that you can afford to part with, you'll benefit the charity and be able to enjoy income for the rest of your life.

There are a number of charitable arrangements that serve this purpose quite nicely: charitable remainder trusts, pooled income funds, charitable gifts of your home, and deferred gift annuities. They're not for everyone, but they certainly help those that fit the profile.

Charitable Remainder Trusts

Charitable remainder trusts are trusts you set up to provide you (and your spouse) with income for the rest of your life (or joint lives), with the property passing to the charity when you (or the last of the two of you) die. The charity gets a remainder interest—what remains in the trust when you die. Because you're making a contribution to charity, you're entitled to a charitable deduction that you can use to reduce your income taxes. (The amount of the deduction is the value of the interest passing to charity determined according to IRS tables.) In order to reap the tax benefits that charitable remainder trusts can provide, the trusts must be set up as either unitrusts or annuity trusts.

Charitable remainder trusts can also be set up to run for a term of years instead of your life. CRATs can't exceed 20 years; CRUTs can be any term of years.

Word to the Wise
A trust that gives you (the income beneficiary) an annual income based on a fixed percentage of the value of the assets in the trust each year is referred to as a *charitable remainder unitrust (CRUT)*. For example, if the trust provides an 8% payout, you'll get 8% of the value of the trust each year, which could be more or less, depending on how the assets in the trust perform.

Let's say you like the idea of helping your favorite charity with a charitable remainder trust. Which type of charitable remainder trust is best for you? A charitable remainder annuity trust gives you the security of a fixed income. You know from day one that you'll receive a certain amount of money each month or quarter. (The charity benefits if the trust performs well because the earnings that don't have to be paid to you grow the principal that will go to the charity. If the trust doesn't do as well as expected, some of the principal will have to be used up to pay the income obligation to you.) But if you're in a position to take a little risk, you might want to consider the charitable remainder unitrust. You'll benefit from the investment performance of the trust. If the value of the trust goes up, you'll get more income. Of course, the risk is that the value of the trust will go down, and your income will be reduced.

Charitable remainder trusts, once the secret of the rich and famous but now becoming more widely used, provide several benefits. The following are some of those benefits:

➤ You get an annual income for as long as you (or you and your spouse) live. The certainty of knowing that the money will be paid monthly, quarterly, or however you set it up may be a big comfort, especially as you get into your later years.

➤ You can use a charitable remainder trust to turn an asset that doesn't produce any income into an income-producing asset. One person happened to own a $2 million violin. Obviously, he could have sold it and lived off the proceeds. Instead, he chose to donate it to UJA-Federation through a charitable remainder trust. The trust sold the violin at a Christie's auction and invested the funds to provide him with a handsome income

> **Word to the Wise**
> A trust that gives you an annual income of a fixed amount of not less than 5% of the initial value of the trust is called a *charitable remainder annuity trust (CRAT)*. For example, you'll get 8% of whatever is in the trust when it is set up, and this dollar amount remains constant for as long as you live.

for the rest of his life. Maybe you don't own a $2 million violin, but you might own closely held stock (stock that's not traded on a public exchange) or some other asset that's just lying around and not producing any income for you. These, too, can be used to fund a charitable remainder trust.

➤ You avoid capital gains tax on assets you put into the trust. Suppose that $2 million violin had been bought at a garage sale for $25 (I don't know where that fellow bought the violin or how much he really paid for it)—a fantasy that many of us harbor. By putting it into the trust, he doesn't have to pay the capital gains tax on all that profit. This means that instead of paying Uncle Sam, that money goes to work for him.

➤ You get a one-time charitable deduction. The deduction isn't for the entire value of the assets you've put into the trust. It's limited to the value of the remainder interest passing to charity. The deduction is figured using special IRS tables for this purpose.

Setting up a charitable remainder trust isn't a do-it-yourself affair. You need the help of a professional. The trust must meet certain very specific (and complex) requirements in order to be recognized as a charitable remainder trust. For example, you can't have an annual payout that's more than 50% of the value of the trust, and the value of the remainder interest that will go to charity must be at least 10% of the initial value of the property put into the trust. You have to be careful who acts as trustee to manage the assets held by the trust. The old adage that you have to have money to make money would seem to apply to charitable remainder trusts. It simply doesn't pay to go through the cost of setting it up and managing the trust in order to get an income stream unless you have a sizable amount to put into the trust (say $100,000 or so).

Maybe all these rules sound complicated. Let's take an example to see how a trust can really work for you. Let's say you've got an asset that you bought for $20,000 that's now worth $100,000. When you're 70, you put it into a charitable remainder annuity trust paying you an 8% guaranteed income each year. Each year you'll receive $8,000 in income from the trust (8% of $100,000). You'll get an income tax deduction of $42,248 (the value of the remainder interest that the charity will get when you die, based on IRS tables). You avoid capital gains tax on your $80,000 profit (a savings of $16,000 if that profit were to have been taxed to you at 20%). If you're in the 28% tax bracket and you can use the income tax deduction, you'll save a total of $27,829 in taxes that you would have had to pay ($11,829 [$42,248 × 28%] + $16,000 [$20,000 profit × 20% capital gains tax]).

Which charity do you want to benefit? That's up to you. Most major charities (colleges, hospitals, religious organizations) are very familiar with these arrangements and can tell you how to go about setting them up. To find out more about your pet charity, ask to speak with its office of planned giving or tell them your intentions and ask what you need to do to go forward.

> **Word to the Wise**
> A trust you set up in your lifetime that becomes immediately effective is an *inter vivos trust*. A trust you set up in your will is a *testamentary trust*. This trust takes effect after you die.

For retirement income purposes, you'll be setting up the trust while you're alive. You can set up charitable remainder trusts in your will to take effect after you die (for example, to provide income for your spouse's life, with the property passing to the charity when your spouse dies). However, this won't give you any current income nor any income tax write-offs.

Pooled Income Funds

Don't want the hassle and expense of setting up a charitable remainder trust? There's a simpler way to get the same benefits; just use a pooled income fund. These operate like a charitable remainder trust in that you receive an income for life as a result of your contribution to charity. When you die, the charity gets to keep your property, and it doesn't have any further obligation to your estate.

You contribute property to a charity that pools it with contributions from other people. The funds' managers invest the contributions to produce income (other than tax-exempt income). Your annual income payments depend on how much money the fund earns. So your payments can vary from year to year.

Most major charities have set up pooled income funds. Just ask what you need to do if you're interested in getting an income from a pooled income fund.

Charitable Gifts of Your Home

In Chapter 11, you already learned several ways that you could use your home to get income from it. You can also use your home to produce an annuity for you. You don't have to use a charitable remainder trust to get the same type of benefits. All you need to do is make an agreement with a charity that's in a position to make annuity payments to you. (Only large, well-established charities can afford to make this arrangement with you.) Here's how a gift of a remainder interest in your home works.

Let's say you and your wife are both 70 and own a vacation home you plan to use until you both die. It isn't paying you any money now, so you're thinking about selling it for income. Instead, you donate a remainder interest to the charity, keeping for yourselves the right to live in the home for the rest of your lives. Suppose you bought that home for $75,000 and it's now worth $500,000 (okay, so even if your home didn't appreciate as much, you'll get the idea about how the charitable gift of the remainder interest in your home works from this example). The remainder gift to the charity is initially valued at $163,704 (using IRS tables and certain assumptions). The charity agrees to pay you an annuity of 8% of the gift it's going to receive— $163,704 (which it pays from its own funds). This means you'll get $13,096 each year for as long as you and your spouse live. The income tax deduction for your gift is reduced by the value of the annuity (which is treated as an item of retained value in addition to the vacation home). It's like having your cake and eating it too. You don't have to sell the home to get an income; you can live in the home *and* get an income for life.

Now, you may live many years in retirement and what you plan for now may not be suitable when you get older. You can anticipate your changing needs as long as you put it in writing in the original agreement. If you want to move from the home before you die (when you get really old and need nursing home care), the charity gets the home sooner—and can sell it if it wants—but must continue to pay the annuity based on the proceeds from the sale of the home.

> **Golden Years Ideas**
> If you're hesitant about using a home as charitable gift because you don't want to deprive your children of an inheritance, don't be. You can use the income tax savings you get from your charitable contribution to buy a life insurance policy that will pay them a benefit when you die. This will (depending on your age, health, and other factors) virtually replace the very asset you've given away!

Deferred Gift Annuity

Instead of investing in a commercial annuity to pay you an income down the road, you might want to explore the idea of a deferred gift annuity. This works like a commercial annuity in some ways but has certain advantages. A deferred gift annuity is particularly helpful if you're young now and don't plan to need the money for many years. Here's how it works.

You give money or property to a charity now and, by agreement, the charity will pay you an annuity that will begin at a fixed time in the future. The amount of the annuity you receive depends on your age when the deferred gift is made. You can make your gift all at once or in stages, whichever way you choose. Because you're benefiting a charity, you get an income tax deduction for your gift when you make it. The longer you wait before beginning annuity payments, the larger the tax deduction you receive (it's a portion of what you give, determined by special tables).

Say, for example, that you're 55 and you decide to contribute $5,000 annually to a deferred gift annuity set up with your favorite charity. You plan to take your annuity in 10 years (when you're 65). So you'll invest a total of $50,000 in the arrangement. After 10 years, you'll get an annual annuity of about $5,000. But because you're getting some charitable deduction each year for your contributions, it's not really costing you $50,000 for the annuity (it may be more like $45,000, depending on what assumptions are made). In effect, you may do better with a deferred gift annuity than a commercial annuity because:

➤ You don't have to pay commissions or insurance company fees. Your only cost is professional fees to set up the arrangement (the charity may have these things pre-arranged so it costs you nothing).

➤ You get a charitable deduction that saves you income taxes now (reducing your out-of-pocket costs of funding the annuity).

The Least You Need to Know

➤ A commercial annuity can provide you with a fixed income for life, but there are commissions and fees involved.

➤ A private annuity lets you turn your assets into income with favorable tax returns while keeping those assets all in the family.

➤ A charitable remainder trust lets you benefit both you and your favorite charity.

➤ A pooled income fund gives you an income stream but avoids the steep costs of setting up an individual charitable remainder trust.

➤ Giving a remainder interest in your main residence or vacation home lets you turn a non-income producing asset into income without having to move from the home.

➤ A deferred gift annuity provides similar income to a commercial annuity but lets you benefit your favorite charity at the same time.

Part 4
Pensions Plus

The payoff to your working years is the pension you've built up through contributions by you and/or your employer. For many people, their pension accounts are their largest single asset. You better know what to do with this asset so you don't blow it.

You need to be able to make pension-related decisions whenever they present themselves: at an unexpected early retirement, when a spouse dies, or when you choose to take your pension benefits.

You need to understand the tax impact of pension payouts. After all, taxes affect what you'll have to spend from your pension dollars (after paying taxes). There are many strategies you can use to keep the tax bite as low as possible. These strategies will help you stretch your pension dollars and provide you with financial security.

Quick Thinking When You Get a Pink Slip

In This Chapter

➤ Seeing how good your early retirement package is (or isn't)

➤ Deciding how to treat your retirement plan benefits when you're given early retirement

➤ Planning for medical coverage until you're Medicare-eligible

➤ Using your IRA penalty-free to supplement your retirement income

---

With a few exceptions, there's no such thing as mandatory retirement due to age. Still, your employer may put you into retirement before you had planned to hang up your hat. That's pretty mandatory.

During the past 10 years or so, corporate downsizing has become commonplace, and many talented and experienced workers have been involuntarily retired before their time. If you're like Bob, a 54-year-old who received a pink slip from AT&T after 29 years at that company, you'd better know what to do so you can act quickly.

In this chapter, you'll learn about how to assess an early retirement offer made to you. You'll also find out about your pension options, and which one to take, when you're given early retirement.

Early Retirement: Take It or Leave It

After years with your present employer, you may hear rumors about upcoming layoffs. Take these rumors seriously! They could very well be true. Before you know it, you may become a victim of corporate downsizing, and you'll be forced to make some tough decisions.

Like a friend of mine, you may be given a choice that's really no choice at all: Take the early retirement offer or stay on the job and take your chances on job security in the future. The next round of layoffs might not have as generous an early retirement package. My friend was told that if he chose to stay, he'd be given assignments well below his capabilities (in other words, they'd make it really unpleasant for him to stay). So what choice did he have? Really, none.

But there may be room for you to negotiate the benefits included in your early retirement package. This could make a big difference in your retirement income. It may also help you if you're planning to start your own business following your early retirement.

How Good Is Good?

When the company is pushing you out the door, it may try to ease your pain with a generous retirement package. The package can include a severance payment, pension upgrades, fringe benefits, or a combination of all of these things. Here are some parts of the package to mull over:

Cash Crash
Early retirement can dampen your pension benefits unless you get some upgrades. Tax laws require that those who retire before a pension plan's normal retirement age must get only a percentage of what they'd otherwise receive at normal retirement age. If you're 55, for example, and earning $70,000, a pink slip means you'd receive a pension of only about $14,000 a year compared with over $45,000 a year if you'd stayed on the job another 10 years to the plan's normal retirement age (even if you don't get a single pay increase).

➤ Severance payment. This is usually a cash amount based on how long you've worked for the company. For example, if you've worked at the company for 12 years, you might receive a payment of one month's salary for each of those years, or a full year's salary.

The severance payment might sound like a lot. Don't be impressed. Remember that it's all taxable. And you may find that, as a result of that payment, you fall into a higher tax bracket in the year you retire than you were in your working years. This, then, cuts more deeply into your payment, leaving you less cash to spend after you've paid the taxes.

➤ Pension upgrades. You may be given credit for additional years of service or other credits to build up your benefits under a pension plan (a defined benefit plan that fixes benefits according to your compensation and years of service and then actuarially figures the employer's contributions necessary to meet those projected benefits). The plan may treat you as having already reached its normal retirement age of 65 even though you're only 62. Or it may pay you 30% of the average of your three highest years of earnings instead of the 25% benefit you normally would have received.

Senior Info

If you're given a choice between a cash payment or added pension upgrades, choose wisely. Here's a rule of thumb used to compare apples to apples: Multiply the additional pension credit by 100; then compare this to the severance payment and choose the larger benefit. For example, if you're offered $40,000 cash or an additional pension credit of an added $250 a month, you're probably better off with the cash ($40,000 compared to $25,000 ($250 × 100). In addition, if you're planning to start up a business in retirement, you may just want the cash to get going, even if it means smaller pension payments.

➤ Fringe benefits. These can include continued health insurance and even outplacement job assistance. For example, you may be permitted to pick up your group term life insurance. While you'll have to pay for it now, at least you'll be paying group rates rather than what you'd have to pay if you bought it on your own. You may even be able to convert the term policy to permanent insurance without having to take a physical. But before you make this conversion, shop around and see if you'd get a lower premium for comparable coverage from another company (given your age and health history).

Health Benefits

Health insurance is, perhaps, the single most valued benefit for those under 65 who aren't yet eligible for Medicare because the cost of buying individual coverage can be high. There's no law requiring your employer to pay for your health coverage when you're laid off. If you're lucky, your employer may offer to pay for your coverage for one year following your early retirement.

But you'd better look a gift horse in the mouth if your employer offers to pay for your health coverage indefinitely. This benefit may not last forever. In most cases, the employer can change its mind and end this

Golden Years Ideas

Don't think your employer is doing you any favors by allowing you to pick up your group health insurance at the employer's cost. By law (it's called COBRA), an employer who regularly employs at least 25 workers *must* give you this option for up to 18 months at 102% of the employer's cost. Only if your employer allows you to continue this coverage until you're 65—even though the 18 months has passed—are you really getting a benefit.

coverage at any time (at least that's what the U.S. Supreme Court said where an employer reserved the right to "modify, revoke, suspend, change or terminate" its health coverage program at any time.

Remember that even if you're eligible to collect Social Security benefits because you're already 62, you can't start Medicare coverage until you're 65.

Doing the Math

Add up your early retirement package to see how much you're really getting. Be sure to reduce the size of the package by any taxes you'll have to pay. In figuring the tax bite (see Table 14.1), be sure that you use the tax rates for the tax bracket that the package may put you into (and not just the bracket you're used to).

Table 14.1   Early Retirement Package

1. Items in your package	
Severance payment	$_____
Pension credits (converted to a dollar value)	$_____
Health insurance coverage*	$_____
Outplacement assistance*	$_____
Other benefits	$_____
Total benefits	$_____
2. Less: Tax on benefits	$_____
3. TOTAL (subtract line 2 from line 1)	$_____

*These benefits generally are tax free.

Keep in mind that you may have to pay estimated taxes in the year you retire. Withholding on your wages may not cover the tax liability related to your severance pay (unless there's also withholding on it) or on a pension taken as a lump sum (the automatic 20% withholding on this amount may not be enough). However, if you're over 62, you aren't penalized for underpaying estimated taxes if you can show that there was reasonable cause for the shortfall and you ask the IRS for relief.

Look at the Big Picture

Being forced into retirement before you'd planned can affect your total retirement picture. Maybe you've been saving a certain percentage of your salary toward your retirement. Once you're no longer working, you can't afford this savings. Maybe you expected to have a certain pension when you retired. Now you won't reach that goal (unless you continue working at another place—or your own company—that has a retirement plan).

Make sure you understand the full implications of early retirement. This can help you decide whether you want to try to re-enter the job market or maybe start up your own business. Here are some of the things that probably will change because you've been given early retirement:

➤ Social Security benefits. Unless you're disabled, you can't start to receive benefits until you're 62. And if you take benefits at this age because you're no longer working, you'll receive a smaller monthly benefit than you would have received if you'd waited until 65. (Chapter 3, "Social Security Benefits: Now or Later?" explains whether taking benefits at 62 or waiting until 65 makes sense for you.) If you're under 62 and you don't continue to work until you're eligible for benefits, then early retirement can also affect the benefits you'll eventually receive.

➤ Pension benefits. It's just a fact that if you retire early, your pension benefits will be smaller. You miss out on having those extra years to build up pension credits or to contribute to a retirement plan. And if you tap into your benefits as early as you're allowed, you'll wind up depleting your funds sooner than you might have anticipated.

➤ Health coverage. If you're 65 or older, your health coverage is taken care of under Medicare. You may need to supplement this coverage, but your out-of-pocket costs are certainly smaller than if you're under 65 and have to buy coverage from an insurance company. (See Chapter 4, "Working…The Second Time Around" for more details on Medicare and supplemental health insurance.) If you aren't yet 65, you may still be okay if your employer continues paying for your coverage or if you have a spouse with employer-provided health insurance that can cover you as well. However, if you don't fall in any of these categories, you'll have to pay for the coverage. This can take a big chunk out of your monthly budget.

➤ Other benefits. Once you're out of the door, you may have to pay for benefits that your employer used to cover. For instance, your employer may have paid for a

Cash Crash

If you're not working, then you not only lose out on employer-provided pension benefits, but you also can't contribute to an IRA because you don't have any earned income. However, if your spouse is still working, then your working spouse can contribute up to $2,000 to your IRA in addition to an IRA contribution for himself or herself.

Golden Years Ideas

If you have to find health coverage on your own, try to find it through another group. Trade groups and professional associations typically offer some type of group health insurance. If you don't belong to an association, it may even pay to join one just for this benefit alone. Even AARP (whose membership is open to anyone age 50 and over) offers some health plans. This coverage may be cheaper than what you'd be able to get on your own.

disability policy to provide you with benefits if you become disabled and can't work. If you intend to find a new job or start your own business, you probably want to continue having a disability policy (typically until age 65 when Social Security benefits kick in). You may be able to take over that policy that your employer used to pay. But the premiums are now coming out of your pocket.

Retirement Plan Options

When you're given early retirement, the biggest question generally is what to do with the rest of your life. Should you try to get another job? Should you start your own business? Should you simply put your feet up and relax for the rest of your life?

The *second* biggest question you may face at early retirement is what to do with your pension benefits that you've built up on the job. You may also need to decide what to do with your IRA at this time.

Take 'Em Now or Take 'Em Later

If you're covered by a company retirement plan, you may be given choices when you retire. Generally, you don't have a lot of time to decide what to do; you have to act fast. Here are some options you may have:

> ➤ Begin pension benefits. You may be able to start taking your benefits now (remember that one of the things included in an early retirement package may be that you're treated as if you've reached the normal retirement age under your company's pension plan).

> ➤ Leave funds where they are. You may be able to leave your benefits where they are for the time being. You can then begin your benefit payouts at age 65. This will allow for continued tax deferral of earnings on those benefits. It also continues to protect benefits from the claims of creditors. If you've been on the job only a short time and your benefits are under $5,000, your employer can decide to force you to take the benefits (it's just not administratively sound to keep them in the plan).

> ➤ Take a lump-sum distribution. You can take your benefits now in one lump sum. You'll have to pay tax on it currently, but you may be eligible for

Cash Crash
You're subject to a 10% penalty if you take pension benefits *prematurely*. Usually, this means before age 59½. However, under a special exception, you're permitted to start benefits at age 55 if you're *separated from service* (which means you've been terminated from your job).

Cash Crash
There's an automatic 20% withholding on retirement benefits eligible for a rollover to an IRA or other retirement plan that you've taken as a lump-sum distribution. You can, within 60 days of the distribution, decide *not* to pay tax at this time by rolling it over to an IRA. But because 20% has been withheld, you'll have to come up with that amount to make a 100% rollover and avoid all income tax.

special tax breaks to reduce the taxes if you're at least age 59½. And, if the distribution consists of employer securities, paying tax now will save you taxes later on. The rules for lump-sum distributions are explained in Chapter 16, "Pay Now or Pay Later."

➤ Roll over benefits to your IRA. You can roll over your benefits to an IRA. This way, you'll be able to continue accumulating earnings on a tax-deferred basis. You'll have control of the funds and be able to invest them as you see fit. There is no withholding if funds are transferred directly from your company retirement plan to your IRA. You can take a partial distribution by rolling over some of the benefits to an IRA and keeping some of the cash. However, doing this means you're not eligible for special tax treatment on the portion of the distribution you've kept.

Golden Years Ideas
Use a separate IRA for your rolled-over retirement funds. If you get another job, this will allow you to roll them out of the IRA and into a retirement plan from your new employer (assuming the new employer's plan will accept rollover benefits). Also, depending on what state you live it, the separate IRA may give you added creditor protection.

Each person's situation is different. What might be a good choice for your neighbor might be a bad idea for you. Table 14.2 has some guidelines to help you decide which option to select.

Table 14.2 Deciding on Retirement Plan Options upon Early Retirement

If...	Then...
You need the money now to live on	Begin pension benefits now or take a lump-sum distribution
You need cash to start a business	Take a lump-sum distribution
You plan to continue working for a new employer	Leave the funds where they are or roll them over to your IRA
You're concerned about creditor protection	Leave the funds where they are*
You get a distribution that consists of employer securities	Take a lump-sum distribution to achieve tax advantage
You're under 59½	Begin pension benefits now if you're at least 55, or leave the funds where they are, or roll them over to your IRA

Check on your state's law on creditor protection for IRAs. Some states protect IRAs; others don't. All states, as well as the federal Bankruptcy Code, provide an exemption for qualified plan funds.

Senior Info

Brokerage firms and mutual funds are eager to provide you with free assistance in assessing your retirement plan payout options. They're doing this with a view toward getting your business (having you invest your benefits with them). You might want to discuss your options with a tax professional who has nothing to gain (other than the fee you'll pay him or her) from the choice you make.

IRAs and Early Retirement

IRAs, like company retirement plans, are designed to provide you with retirement income. But what happens if retirement occurs before you'd planned it? Your IRA may be an important source of retirement income during your early retirement years and throughout your life. This may be especially true if you've rolled over company retirement benefits into your IRA and have a lot of money in it.

Golden Years Ideas

As a general rule, you don't want to take money from your IRA any earlier than you need to. The reason: the opportunity for tax-deferred compounding of investment return. If you need money now, it's a good idea to use your personal savings first, before touching your IRA.

You don't have to be retired at the time you take money out of your IRA. You may need funds from your IRA if you are given early retirement and then you take a job paying lower wages.

Congress, in its infinite wisdom, decided that *retirement* doesn't mean your work status; it means being 59$\frac{1}{2}$ years old. Why it chose that particular age isn't really clear. What is clear is that taking money out of your IRA before that age can cost you not only income taxes, but a 10% early distribution penalty as well. This penalty applies even though you've been given early retirement and you aren't working.

You can tap into your IRA before age 59$\frac{1}{2}$ under certain circumstances without penalty if:

➤ You're disabled. You must be so physically or mentally disabled that you're unable to work. Technically, the law defines disability as having a physical or mental condition that can be expected to last indefinitely or result in death and that prevents you from engaging in substantial gainful activity similar to the work you were doing before the disability. Even if you become depressed because of being laid off, you're not necessarily disabled unless you simply can't work.

➤ You use the funds to pay medical expenses. This exception applies only if the medical expenses are more than 7.5% of your adjusted gross income (the amount you're allowed to deduct on your federal income tax return as itemized medical expenses). You don't have to itemize to qualify for this exception.

➤ You're unemployed and use the funds to pay medical insurance. You're considered unemployed if you receive unemployment benefits under federal or state law for at least 12 consecutive weeks. (You can use the funds to pay health insurance in the year of those 12 weeks or in the following year.) If you go back to work, the exception ceases to apply 60 days after you're re-employed.

➤ You pay for higher education costs for yourself, your spouse, and dependents. Suppose you want to be retrained in a new line of work. As long as the program you're in qualifies as *higher education*, you're not subject to the 10% penalty. Higher education costs include tuition, room and board, fees, books, supplies, and equipment (but not transportation to and from school).

➤ You pay first-time homebuying expenses for you, your spouse, child, grandchild, or ancestor of you or your spouse. This includes expenses paid within 120 days of buying, building, or reconstructing a principal residence for one of these people. Costs can include not only the purchase price or construction costs, but also reasonable financing, settlement fees, and other closing costs.

➤ You take distributions in an annuity-type form. You're not subject to the 10% penalty, regardless of your age, if you take distributions in a series of substantially equal periodic payments made not less frequently than annually for your life (or life expectancy) or the joint lives (or joint life expectancies) of you and your spouse.

Does the annuity-type exception sound complicated? It is. The IRS has approved three different methods for figuring penalty-free payouts:

➤ The life expectancy method

➤ The amortization method

➤ The annuity factor method

> **Cash Crash**
> The first-time homebuying exception is limited to $10,000 in a lifetime.

> **Cash Crash**
> You have to make a commitment to take IRA funds under the annuity-type exception. Payments must continue for at least five years or until you turn $59^1/_2$, whichever happens later. So if you start taking distributions at 53, you'll have to continue until you're $59^1/_2$ to avoid the penalty, even if you go back to work when you're 54 and don't need the funds anymore. (If you do stop, you'll owe penalties on what you've already taken.)

> **Cash Crash**
> Make sure you figure annuity-type payouts correctly. If you don't, you'll be subject to penalty on *all* the payments taken to date.

The size of the permitted tax-free payments will vary with the method you select. The easiest method to use is the life expectancy method, which you can probably figure yourself using an income tax guide such as *J.K. Lasser's Your Income Tax*. But to get larger tax-free amounts, use either of the other two methods. You probably need a tax professional to help you figure the amount you can take out each year penalty free.

The Least You Need to Know

➤ While you may not be able to avoid early retirement, you might be able to get a better severance package if you know what to ask for.

➤ As a rule of thumb, take pension credits over a cash severance payment if the monthly credits multiplied by 100 exceed the cash payment.

➤ If you're under 65 when you're laid off, make sure you pick up COBRA health coverage if your employer doesn't give you free coverage.

➤ Early retirement can put a real crimp in your retirement planning by reducing your Social Security benefits and limiting your pension accumulations.

➤ Know your pension options when you're given early retirement.

➤ You can use your IRA funds penalty-free before you're $59^1/_2$ if you take annuity-type payments figured under methods permitted by the IRS.

Chapter 15

Pension Payout Options for Married Couples

In This Chapter

➤ Providing your spouse with your pension benefits

➤ Choosing the most appropriate form of benefits

➤ Waiving a spouse's right to pension protection

➤ Planning for retirement benefits in case of divorce

Years ago, a person could retire and receive a pension for the rest of his life. But when he died, his widow got nothing. Congress thought this was highly unfair, so in 1984, it created pension protection for spouses. As a result of this pension protection, a person who is married won't get any greater benefits from a retirement plan than someone who is single. However, that married person may personally get less because benefit protection afforded to a surviving spouse.

If you're single and plan to stay this way, you can skip this chapter if you want to. The information in this chapter covers married couples.

In this chapter, you'll learn about pension protection for spouses and the different types of pension choices you may be confronted with. You'll also get guidance on when to waive spousal protection and how to do it. Finally, you'll find out what can happen to your pension if you get divorced. In Chapters 16, "Pay Now or Pay Later," and 17, Making Your IRA Last as Long as You Want," you'll see what happens if you inherit someone else's retirement benefits and/or IRAs.

Word to the Wise
Married couples for purposes of spousal protection include only those who have been married for at least one year before the date when retirement benefits begin (or the date the worker dies if this is sooner).

Golden Years Ideas
Protection for your spouse that is explained throughout this chapter applies to most company retirement plans. If you worked for a governmental unit or agency, your spouse may be entitled to special protection. Ask your plan administrator for details.

Word to the Wise
A *pension* is your retirement benefit paid in monthly installments. You may have a choice between monthly payments and a lump sum of everything that's coming to you under your company's retirement plan. Or you may simply receive a pension; a lump-sum payment may not be an alternative.

Protection for Your Spouse

Almost all types of company retirement plans (including Keogh plans set up by self-employed people) are *required* to give some protection to spouses if benefits in the plan are more than $5,000. The worker can't simply cut a spouse out of a share in the pension, and the company can't just end benefits when a worker dies to prevent a widow from collecting something.

Limited protection applies to most profit-sharing and 401(k) plans. They don't have the full extent of spousal protection afforded under pension plans that you'll learn about in a moment, but they automatically treat spouses as beneficiaries. If you die before your benefits have begun, your benefits would automatically be paid to your spouse. If you want to name another beneficiary, your spouse must consent.

This protection for a spouse doesn't apply to IRAs. With an IRA, whatever is in the account is what you get: nothing more, nothing less. You can pass on your IRA funds to anyone you want: your spouse if you want, or your children, or even a charity if you choose. Your spouse can't prevent you from choosing a different beneficiary.

For other retirement plans, there's more to the marriage contract than meets the eye. You, and your retirement plan, have to take your spouse into consideration. Spousal protection applies while the worker is alive as well as after the worker dies.

Joint and Survivor Annuities

If you start to receive a pension from your employer, rest assured that your spouse is protected for life. Your spouse will receive some benefits under the plan (depending on the type you selected when your pension began), *unless* you and your spouse agree otherwise. Federal law requires plans to offer joint and survivor annuities (though plans may choose to offer lump-sum distributions if there's spousal consent). Your spouse will receive these benefits even if he or she remarries.

Just before you're about to start taking your pension, you'll be given a choice on how you want your benefits paid. There's some flexibility, and, as you'll see, whatever choice you make, there's a trade-off: The greater your benefits now, the smaller the protection for your spouse after you die. At one extreme, you can choose up to a 100% survivor annuity so that your spouse continues to receive the same monthly benefit you did when you were alive. Or, at the other extreme, you can choose a 50% survivor annuity, which means that your spouse will get half of the monthly amount you got while you were alive. In this case, you'll get a higher monthly benefit, but your spouse will get less after you die. You might also be given some choices in between, such as a 75% survivor annuity.

To give you an idea of how this could work out in dollars, Table 15.1 is an example of the choices given to a cousin of mine when he retired. Your options may be similar or completely different.

Table 15.1 Monthly Benefits Under Different Joint and Survivor Annuity Options

Pension Option	Your Monthly Benefit	Your Spouse's Benefit After You Die
100% survivor annuity	$1,600	$1,600
50% survivor annuity	$1,950	$975
Survivor annuity waived	$2,300	$0

You must decide which option is best for you. It's your choice. Your spouse's consent is required *only* in the case of waiving more than 50% protection so that you can get the largest monthly benefit possible at this time. Let's assume for the moment that you want to make sure that your spouse will get some part of your pension when you die. Then the choice becomes whether to take it now (with the greater benefit for you) or take it later (with the greater benefit for your spouse). What's the right choice for you may not be the right one for your best friend.

The answer depends on several factors: the ages of you and your spouse, your and your spouse's health, and your personal financial picture now and in the future. While you don't have a crystal ball to tell you how long you'll live and whether your spouse's health will decline, you can make some guesses based on probabilities.

One probability you can use to figure which method will pay the most is to rely on life expectancy statistics. Use your life expectancy and your spouse's life expectancy to see how monthly benefits would total up under different payout scenarios. For example, let's say that at 65, you have a 20-year life expectancy and your spouse, who is 60 at the time, has a 24-year life expectancy. Now just run the numbers to see what the total return under the different options might be. Because your life expectancy is 20 years, you can expect to get paid a total of $384,000 in benefits during your lifetime under the 100% survivor option ($1,600 per month × 12 months × 20 years).

Table 15.2   Total Return Under Different Joint and Survivor Annuity Options

Pension Option	Your Total Benefits	Your Spouse's Total Benefits After You Die	Total Benefits Paid From the Plan
100% survivor annuity	$384,000 ($1,600 × 12 × 20 yrs)	$76,800 ($1,600 × 12 × 4 yrs)	$460,800
50% survivor annuity	$468,000 ($1,950 × 12 × 20 yrs)	$46,800 ($975 × 12 × 4 years)	$514,800

As you can see, if you and your spouse live just as long as the life expectancy tables say you should, you'd collect more, in total, under the 50% option than under the 100% option. But let's say your spouse lives another 10 years beyond what was expected. Under the 100% option, your spouse would collect an additional $192,000—under the 50% option, just $117,000. Now the totals are reversed, and together you've collected more under the 100% option ($652,000) than under the 50% option ($631,800).

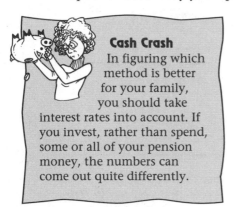

Cash Crash

In figuring which method is better for your family, you should take interest rates into account. If you invest, rather than spend, some or all of your pension money, the numbers can come out quite differently.

Golden Years Ideas

When you're ready to take distributions from a profit-sharing or 401(k) plan, you generally don't need your spouse's consent on the form of benefits you'll receive. But if you choose a life annuity (if that's an option for you), your spouse is then protected under the joint and survivor annuity rules.

Your Financial Situation

There's yet another factor you should weigh: your personal financial situation and how vital these benefits are to your retirement income. If you're highly dependent on these benefits, your choice may be different from the one you'd make if your pension benefits were more or less just gravy.

You should be given your pension options a couple of months before they're set to begin. Have the options explained to you by your plan administrator (the person who runs your pension plan). You may also want to have an accountant review your choices and suggest which one might be best for you given your personal situation.

Remembering Inflation

There's another factor you need to take into account in making your choice besides life expectancy: inflation. Once your benefits start, that dollar amount is fixed forever. There's no such thing as a cost-of-living adjustment as there is with Social Security benefits. So because the buying power of the pension benefits you receive will decline over time due to the impact of inflation, it may be better to use the one-in-the-hand philosophy and take the highest benefits now when they're worth the most.

You can see how the choice affects retirement benefits paid out as a monthly pension. But spousal protection can also apply where a worker has a choice of receiving all of the benefits in a lump-sum distribution. With some exceptions, this type of distribution can't be made unless the spouse consents to it.

Preretirement Survivor Annuities

Maybe you won't retire at 65. If you continue to work, your pension builds up even greater. But just because you didn't start your pension when you were expected to doesn't mean your spouse loses out—quite the contrary. If you die *before* you start to take your pension, your spouse is automatically protected. (This protection also applies if you die *before* you reach the earliest retirement age specified in your plan.)

Your spouse will receive what's called a *preretirement survivor annuity*. The benefit that's paid to your spouse is the same (the actuarial equivalent) of what would have been paid to him or her under a joint and survivor annuity if:

➤ You passed the plan's *early retirement age*. This, for example, could be 50 years old. So if you're 65 when you die and you're still working, benefits to your spouse would be the same as he or she would have received had you begun to take your pension at that time (your age at your death).

➤ You died before reaching the early retirement age. This rule would apply if you died at 49 and your plan's early retirement age is fixed at 50. Here, benefits would be figured as if you reached the early retirement age and began to receive your benefits, having left your employer, and then died on the following day.

In any event, the benefit to your spouse cannot be less than 50% of your account balance as of the date of your death.

Your spouse can start to take benefits from a pension plan on the day that you would have been entitled to take it under the early retirement date. If your spouse doesn't live to this date or elects to defer receipt and dies before the deferred receipt date, then your benefits may simply evaporate (no one will get them).

> **Cash Crash**
> Spousal protection applies only to *vested* benefits (benefits that are yours because you were in the plan for a certain number of years). If you change jobs often and don't vest, your spouse isn't protected.

Waiving Spousal Protection

Just because you're automatically given protection doesn't mean you need it or want it. You're not forced to take spousal protection. You're allowed to waive this right.

There may be several good reasons why you don't want spousal protection, which you'll find out about in just a minute. It has nothing to do with how much you love your spouse; it's a matter of dollars and good sense.

Should You Waive This Protection?

From a personal and money view, there are certain situations in which you may want to waive spousal protection. Remember that waiving this protection means your spouse (the employee) gets the highest monthly benefit possible. Here are some scenarios that favor waiving spousal protection:

➤ You want to benefit your spouse's children. Maybe you're in a second marriage and want the children from your spouse's first marriage to have an interest in your pension. You're allowed to do consent to a waiver of protection.

➤ You don't need protection. Maybe it sounds sexist, but when spousal protection was introduced, it was intended primarily to benefit a stay-at-home wife who didn't have her own retirement plan benefits. Today, many women earn their own pensions and have their own retirement savings. They don't necessarily need pension benefits from a spouse. In fact, receiving these benefits could, for some people, produce unneeded income and complicate estate plans. For example, a couple may, for tax-planning purposes, want to have their respective benefits payable to a couple's children rather than to the spouse.

➤ You are older than your spouse (or in poor health). If you're older than your spouse (or have a medical condition that might lead to a premature death), there may be a statistical likelihood that you will die before your spouse. Not making this waiver means that your spouse will get a smaller monthly benefit, and, in all likelihood, you won't get anything (you'll die before your spouse). You're better off letting your spouse take the larger benefits now because you may not live to collect any benefits.

➤ You're thinking ahead about nursing home care. If there's a likelihood that you'll need this type of care in the future (for example, there's a history of Alzheimer's disease in your family), you won't want the added income afforded by spousal protection if you plan to apply for Medicaid. The income counts against you.

➤ You can earn more on the money. If spousal protection is waived in order to get the highest monthly benefit, your spouse may be able to use that additional income to provide greater protection for you than you would have received under a joint and survivor annuity. Your spouse, for example, can use the added income to pay for life insurance coverage

Golden Years Ideas

If your spouse decides to buy insurance on his or her life to provide you with substitute spousal benefits and you die before your spouse, nothing is really lost. The policy can be canceled (with your spouse recovering the cash value built up within the policy) or a new beneficiary can be named (such as a child or grandchild). Remember that during all this time, your spouse will have received the highest monthly benefit from your retirement plan, and this payment will continue to be made to your spouse after you die.

on his or her life. The proceeds from the life insurance policy would then be payable to you and would, in effect, replace the spousal benefits. Depending on your spouse's age and health, it's possible to get *more* for you through this life insurance approach than you'd have enjoyed under the joint and survivor annuity.

How to Waive This Protection

There's a limited window in which spousal protection can be waived. If a waiver isn't made in this time, you can't change your mind later on.

If you want to waive this protection, you must do so and your spouse must consent within 90 days before the date your pension begins. A waiver to a preretirement survivor annuity can be made any time after you reach 35. A waiver can be revoked as long as the time for making a waiver hasn't passed.

A spouse can give a general consent to allow the worker to change beneficiaries or the form of benefits. If your spouse doesn't give a general consent, he or she must consent to allow you to specify a new beneficiary (such as your child) or the form of benefits chosen (such as the maximum monthly benefits).

> **Cash Crash**
> Consent to a waiver must be in writing and notarized (or witnessed by the plan administrator). The waiver can't be made before you're married, so any language you may have included in a prenuptial agreement doesn't count. Your spouse will have to make an actual waiver *after* the marriage ceremony.

What's the Tax Bite on Your Benefits?

If you receive a monthly pension, you won't know how much income is available for you to spend until you figure out the tax bite on your hard-earned pension. To do this, you'll have to learn some new tax rules. (If you get your benefits paid out in a lump sum, different tax rules apply; these rules are explained in the next chapter.) If you've already started to take your pension, you know from prior years what your tax bite is.

The method for figuring the tax on your monthly pension benefits is simple:

> ➤ If you didn't contribute anything to the pension (it was all your employer's doing), every penny you receive is taxable. There's nothing to figure.
>
> ➤ If both you and your employer contributed to your pension, you'll have to figure what portion of the monthly benefits is taxable. You're not

> **Golden Years Ideas**
> Your company may tell you the taxable part of your pension on Form 1099-R. If it doesn't, this form should include *Total Employee Contributions* (what you put in) to let you figure the taxable portion. You can have the IRS figure the taxable portion for you by paying a $50 fee.

183

taxed on your own contributions; you're taxed on your employer contributions as well as on earnings on your and your employer's contributions.

You figure the taxable portion under a so-called *simplified method*. Let's see how simplified it really is:

1. Start with your *investment* in your plan (what you contributed). This includes your *after-tax* contributions (not 401(k) contributions made under a salary reduction arrangement from your pretax pay) and employer contributions that were treated as additional salary to you. If you don't have your own records on your investments in the plan, you can get this information from your plan administrator or by looking at Form 1099-R, which must be sent to you by the plan.

2. Then divide your total investment by the number of months that apply to you from the following tables. If you're married and waived the spousal annuity, use Table 15.3; if you're getting a joint and survivor annuity, use Table 15.4.

Table 15.3 Single Annuity

Your Age When Annuity Starts	Number of Monthly Payments
55 and under	360
56–60	310
61–65	260
66–70	210
70 and older	160

Table 15.4 Joint and Survivor Annuity

Combined Ages of You and Your Spouse	Number of Monthly Payments
Not more than 110	410
More than 110 but not more than 120	360
More than 120 but not more than 130	310
More than 130 but not more than 140	260
More than 140	210

3. Now that you've divided your investment by the correct number of payments from the table, multiply the result by the number of payments you receive during the year (usually 12, but it may be less in the year your annuity starts).

4. Finally, subtract the results you've gotten so far from the total pension you received during the year. This is the taxable part.

Maybe you didn't follow the steps. Here's an example to help you see what part of your pension may be taxable and what part is tax free.

Let's say that you retire at 65, and your monthly pension of $1,500 starts on January 1. Your pension will be paid out in the form of a joint and survivor annuity to you and your spouse (age 60). Suppose that you made contributions to the plan totaling $36,000 (the first thing you had to figure). Now divide $36,000 by 360 (because the combined age of you, 65, and your spouse, 55, is 120). Your result is $100. Now multiply $100 by 12, the number of months you got your pension during the year, to arrive at the number $1,200 (your tax-free portion). Subtract $1,200 from your monthly pension of $1,500 to find your taxable portion. This means that $300 of each payment, or $3,600 annually, is taxable.

Cash Crash
If you contributed to your pension but don't start receiving it until you're 75, and there's a guaranteed five-year payment, you'll have to figure your taxable pension amount using different, more complicated rules. These rules are explained in IRS Publication 575, Pension and Annuity Income.

What Happens If You Divorce?

No one gets married with the belief that they'll divorce. But the plain fact is that nearly half of all marriages end in divorce (and more than 60% of second marriages end in divorce). If you find that you become one of these statistics, be sure to understand what impact it could have on your retirement benefits or what rights you may have in your spouse's retirement benefits. After all, retirement plan benefits may be a significant asset and a major source of retirement income for you and your ex.

If you're covered by a company retirement plan and you divorce, your spouse may have an interest in benefits earned during the marriage. The extent of that interest depends on the laws of the state in which you live. If you live in one of the nine community property states (Arizona, California, Idaho, Louisiana, Nevada, New Mexico, Texas, Washington, or Wisconsin), your spouse may be entitled automatically to one half of your retirement plan benefits. If you live in any of the other states, retirement plan benefits may be treated as belonging to each spouse according to so-called equitable distribution rules. These rules are supposed to use fairness (the length of the marriage, age of the parties, efforts of the parties in earning the money or acquiring the assets) to divide up property, including retirement benefits.

Just because the law says a spouse has an interest in benefits doesn't mean they'll get paid to that spouse. Negotiations can determine which assets (of which retirement benefits are one asset) get distributed to which spouse. For example, an ex-spouse might be entitled to one half of retirement benefits valued at $100,000. The ex may be willing to take stock, or trade off an interest in the couple's home, instead of actually receiving the retirement benefits.

If your divorce settlement provides that a portion of your benefits will be paid to your ex-spouse, you have to follow certain procedures. If you don't, you'll be taxed on benefits that get paid to your ex (if you follow the procedures, the income tax on benefits paid to your ex are your ex's responsibility).

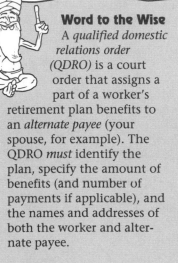

Word to the Wise

A *qualified domestic relations order (QDRO)* is a court order that assigns a part of a worker's retirement plan benefits to an *alternate payee* (your spouse, for example). The QDRO *must* identify the plan, specify the amount of benefits (and number of payments if applicable), and the names and addresses of both the worker and alternate payee.

Golden Years Ideas

The alternate payee is taxed on benefits received. If the benefits are paid in a lump sum, the alternate payee may qualify for special averaging treatment (as explained in the next chapter). However, the tax can be deferred by rolling the benefits over to an IRA set up by the alternate payee.

In order for you, as the participant in the plan, to avoid income tax on benefits paid to your ex, the divorce court must make a qualified domestic relations order (QDRO).

Make sure your attorney knows about the tax rules for property settlements of retirement plan benefits. The IRS has made it easy to ensure that divorce settlement language meets tax law requirements. The IRS has provided sample language for QDROs (in Internal Revenue Notice 97-11) that lawyers and the courts can follow. QDROs aren't required for splitting up IRAs in a divorce.

So you've gotten divorced, and your property settlement includes a QDRO. When will benefits be paid to your ex-spouse? The answer depends on the type of plan you're in. If you're in a profit-sharing plan or other plan that maintains a separate account balance for you, your ex-spouse may be able to get his or her share of benefits immediately following the divorce court's approval of the QDRO. If you're in a pension plan, your ex may have to wait for his or her share until you've reached the earliest retirement date specified in your plan. But benefits can begin to be paid out to your ex even though you're still working and haven't begun to take your share of benefits under the plan.

Let's say your divorce doesn't include a QDRO, so you're not forced to share your benefits with your ex. Make sure you change your beneficiary designation so you don't inadvertently benefit your ex. This can happen when the plan continues to carry the old beneficiary designation specifying that after you die, benefits are to be paid to your wife Sally who's now your former spouse. Your current wife Jean is out of luck, even if your will says she's to get those benefits. The plan must follow the beneficiary designation you made earlier and didn't change, even though it's not what you'd have wanted.

The Least You Need to Know

➤ Spousal protection doesn't apply to IRAs.

➤ Payment of retirement benefits in the form of a joint and survivor annuity is automatic for married people unless they both agree to some other form of payment.

➤ Waiving spousal protection may make sense if you don't think your spouse will live long enough to enjoy it. Consider a supplemental life insurance policy instead.

➤ A spouse's consent to a waiver of spousal protection must be made in writing and notarized (or witnessed by the plan administrator).

➤ If you made after-tax contributions to your pension plan, you figure the taxable portion of your monthly pension by using a simplified method, regardless of whether or not you waive spousal protection.

➤ If you divorce, you could be forced to give some of your retirement plan benefits to your ex-spouse; if you're an ex-spouse, you may be entitled to receive some of your ex's retirement plan benefits.

Pay Now or Pay Later

You're about to retire, and your employer asks you how you want your benefits paid. You may have two choices: as a monthly pension (if you're married, you learned about your pension choices in the previous chapter) or as one lump sum. The choice you make will have an important impact on your tax picture and, ultimately, what you have to spend in retirement. After all, retirement benefits can be very large. My mail carrier has built up one pension working 20 years as a New York city police officer, and in just eight more years, he'll be eligible for a pension from the U.S. Postal Service as well—a double dipper you might say.

In this chapter, you'll learn the rules about retirement plan payout in general: when they must begin and what choices you may have regarding your benefits. You'll find out about paying tax now on lump-sum distributions. You'll also learn whether it makes more sense for you to roll over your distribution into an IRA. And you'll find out what happens when you inherit retirement plan benefits. This chapter doesn't tell you the rules on distributions *from* IRAs; that's covered in the next chapter.

When Your Benefits Begin

It may sound like an obvious statement, but as a general rule, you get your retirement plan benefits when you retire. For many people, this means starting a pension or getting a distribution at age 62 or 65 when they retire from the company they've worked at and start Social Security benefits at the same time.

But this isn't always so. You may start benefits *before* you can take your Social Security benefits if you've been given early retirement from your company. At the other extreme, you may get your benefits much later than 65 if you continue working and opt to postpone receiving them until you retire.

Early Benefits

If you retire early, you may be eligible to start receiving your pension or a distribution from your retirement plan at that time. If, under the terms of the plan, benefits can be paid only in the form of a pension, then payments won't begin until the earliest retirement age spelled out in the plan. This could be age 50, 55, or some other age chosen by the plan. So if you're given early retirement at 49, your pension won't begin right away.

If benefits can be paid out in a lump sum, then regardless of the age at which you retire, you can take those benefits with you. This is sometimes referred to as *portability*. This means that you carry the benefits with you, not literally, but rather that you're entitled to them. So when you leave your job, even though you aren't at retirement age, your 401(k) account can come with you. You might, for example, roll it over to an IRA or directly into a retirement plan with your new employer.

Generally, if you take a distribution of benefits before you're 59$\frac{1}{2}$, there's a 10% early distribution penalty (in addition to regular income tax on the distribution). However, the 10% penalty doesn't apply if you meet any of the following exceptions:

➤ You're separated from service (retire) after age 55.

➤ You take benefits in the form of annuity-type payments (explained in Chapter 14, "Quick Thinking When You Get a Pink Slip").

➤ You're disabled (at any age).

➤ You use the payments to pay medical expenses exceeding 7.5% of your adjusted gross income. But only the portion of the distribution used for this purpose is free from penalty; the balance is still subject to penalty.

➤ You separate or divorce, and payments are made to your spouse (or former spouse) under a qualified domestic relations order (explained in Chapter 15, "Pension Payout Options for Married Couples").

Golden Years Ideas
Even if you don't qualify under any exception, you'll avoid the 10% penalty if, instead of keeping a distribution, you roll it over to an IRA within 60 days (or have it transferred directly into the IRA).

If you get early retirement, you may have the option of leaving your benefits where they are. If you're planning to get another job and don't have a current need for the money, this might not be a bad idea. While the company won't make any further contributions on your behalf, your benefits will continue to grow on a tax-deferred basis. What's more, the funds are fully protected from the claims of creditors. In contrast, only certain states provide similar protection for IRA benefits.

Delayed Benefits

It used to be that, with only a couple of exceptions, you had to start receiving retirement plan benefits when you turned $70^1/_2$ (although the first payment could be postponed until April 1 of the following year), even though you weren't yet retired. However, the rules have changed. Now, if you're still working, you can delay benefits until you actually retire. But if you own more than 5% of the company you're working for, you can't choose to delay benefits; they'll have to begin when you're $70^1/_2$.

If the plan normally pays out benefits starting at age $70^1/_2$ and you're still working and want to postpone benefits, you'll have to sign a statement to this effect. Ask your plan administrator what you have to do to avoid getting benefits until you actually retire.

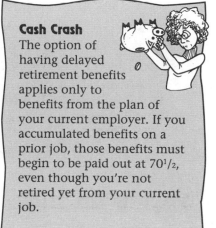

Cash Crash
The option of having delayed retirement benefits applies only to benefits from the plan of your current employer. If you accumulated benefits on a prior job, those benefits must begin to be paid out at $70^1/_2$, even though you're not retired yet from your current job.

If You Get a Lump Sum

Your retirement benefits may be a significant source of retirement income. *How* those benefits are paid to you will affect what you'll receive in total and what taxes you'll have to pay. The tax impact on retirement benefits is important because you can spend only what you have left over after you've paid some of the benefits to the government in the form of taxes.

Senior Info

Some retirement plans don't give you any choice: You're going to be paid in the form of a monthly pension. Figuring the tax bite on a monthly pension was explained in the previous chapter.

What's a lump-sum distribution? The tax law has a very specific meaning. It covers a distribution within one year from a qualified retirement plan of all that's due you on account of your retirement, separation from service, reaching age 59^1/$_2$, or becoming disabled. When a friend of mine retired at age 63 from IBM after 23 years as a secretary, she got a distribution of everything that was in IBM's retirement plan under her name: $270,000. This qualified as a lump-sum distribution.

Why is it important to see if a distribution meets the definition of a lump-sum distribution? The answer is simple. The tax law gives special breaks to lump-sum distributions:

➤ You may qualify for special averaging if you keep the distribution. If my friend uses special averaging, the tax bite on her $270,000 lump-sum distribution in 1998 is $56,770 (this is based on the 10-year averaging option which she is eligible to use).

➤ A portion of the distribution may qualify for special capital gain treatment. (My friend's distribution didn't have any portion eligible for special capital gain treatment because she didn't participate in the plan before 1974.)

➤ You can choose to roll over the distribution to an IRA or to a qualified plan of a new employer (if the plan is willing to accept the distribution). In this case, my friend's distribution will continue to grow. The eventual size of her fund will depend on her rate of return and how long the money stays in the IRA or new qualified plan. But once distributions begin, they're all ordinary income to her.

Paying Tax Now

Those retirement benefits you've been getting credit for all these years could add up to a tidy sum. If you take them all at once, in a lump sum, you're immediately taxable on the funds. But you may be eligible for special tax treatment that greatly reduces the tax bite on the distribution.

Special tax treatment means using a special averaging method to figure the tax on your distribution (instead of just lumping it in with your other income). You may also qualify for special capital gains treatment on a portion of the distribution.

You qualify for special averaging if all of these are true:

➤ You're at least 59^1/$_2$ when you get the distribution.

➤ The distribution is a lump-sum distribution (it meets the preceding definition).

➤ You participated in the plan for at least five years before the distribution.

➤ You didn't use averaging before for any distribution you received after 1986 (such as a distribution from a former employer).

Averaging means that you figure the tax on the distribution paid in a single year. But, because the tax is calculated as if the funds were received over 5 or 10 years (depending on which averaging method is chosen), a lower tax bracket and tax results than if this legal fiction were not applied.

Depending on your age, you may have a choice of averaging:

➤ Five-year averaging is open to anyone who meets the averaging requirements listed earlier.

➤ Ten-year averaging is available only to someone who was born in 1935 or earlier.

If you retire in 1998 at age 65, you can choose between these averaging methods (because you were born in 1933). Beginning in the year 2000, only 10-year averaging will be available to those born before 1936 (five-year averaging will no longer apply to anyone). So, Baby Boomers won't be able to use averaging of any kind after 1999.

If you were born before 1936 and have a choice between the two averaging methods, which one should you choose? The answer depends simply on the size of the distribution. In 1998, if you receive a lump-sum distribution of more than about $340,000 (the threshold is lower in 1999), five-year averaging is better (it gives you the lower tax). If the distribution is under this threshold, 10-year averaging is a better choice for you. Why the difference? With five-year averaging, you use the current tax rates for single taxpayers, regardless of your actual filing status. For 10-year averaging, you use the 1986 tax rates for single taxpayers (these old rates are provided in the official instructions to the IRS form used for averaging).

To give you an idea of how averaging can cut the tax on your lump-sum distribution, you have to run the numbers through the IRS form you use for special averaging, Form 4972. The computation is lengthy, but if you take things line by line, you'll have no difficulty.

There are other ways to assess the pros and cons of averaging. You can use financial software programs such as Quicken and MS Money. You can also consult a financial planner, insurance agent, personal banker, or other financial adviser.

If you've been on the job for more than about 25 years, you might also be able to use special capital gain treatment for a portion of your distribution. A 20% capital gain rate is applied to the portion of the distribution related to the time you were in the plan *before* 1974 (the year that special retirement plan legislation, called ERISA, was enacted). If you weren't in the plan before this date, there's no special capital gain treatment for you. To use capital gain treatment for the pre-1974 portion of the distribution, you must have been born before 1936.

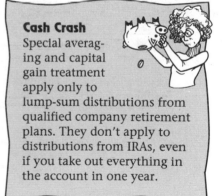

Cash Crash
If you take the distribution (you don't have it transferred directly to an IRA), there's an automatic 20% withholding tax. This means you receive only 80% of your retirement plan account. But you don't lose the 20%. It's a tax payment you get credit for when you file your return. If it turns out that the actual tax on your distribution is less than 20%, you'll get a tax refund. If the tax is more than 20%, you'll owe the government some more money.

Cash Crash
Special averaging and capital gain treatment apply only to lump-sum distributions from qualified company retirement plans. They don't apply to distributions from IRAs, even if you take out everything in the account in one year.

Form **4972**	**Tax on Lump-Sum Distributions**	OMB No. 1545-0193
	From Qualified Retirement Plans	19**97**
Department of the Treasury Internal Revenue Service (99)	▶ **Attach to Form 1040 or Form 1041.** ▶ **See separate instructions.**	Attachment Sequence No. **28**

Name of recipient of distribution	Identifying number

Part I   Complete this part to see if you qualify to use Form 4972

			Yes	No
1	Was this a distribution of a plan participant's entire balance from all of an employer's qualified plans of one kind (pension, profit-sharing, or stock bonus)? If "No," do not use this form	**1**		
2	Did you roll over any part of the distribution? If "Yes," do not use this form	**2**		
3	Was this distribution paid to you as a beneficiary of a plan participant who died after reaching age 59½ (or who had been born before 1936)?	**3**		
4	Were you a plan participant who received this distribution after reaching age 59½ **and** having been in the plan for at least 5 years before the year of the distribution? . . . . If you answered "No" to both questions 3 **and** 4, do not use this form.	**4**		
5a	Did you use Form 4972 after 1986 for a previous distribution from your own plan? If "Yes," do not use this form for a 1997 distribution from your own plan	**5a**		
b	If you are receiving this distribution as a beneficiary of a plan participant who died, did you use Form 4972 for a previous distribution received for that plan participant after 1986? If "Yes," you may not use the form for this distribution	**5b**		

Part II   Complete this part to choose the 20% capital gain election (See instructions.) Do not complete this part unless the participant was born **before** 1936.

6	Capital gain part from box 3 of Form 1099-R	**6**	
7	Multiply line 6 by 20% (.20) . . . . If you also choose to use Part III, go to line 8. Otherwise, include the amount from line 7 in the total on Form 1040, line 39, or Form 1041, Schedule G, line 1b, whichever applies.	**7**	

Part III   Complete this part to choose the 5- or 10-year tax option (See instructions.)

8	Ordinary income from Form 1099-R, box 2a minus box 3. If you did not complete Part II, enter the taxable amount from box 2a of Form 1099-R	**8**	
9	Death benefit exclusion for a beneficiary of a plan participant who died before August 21, 1996	**9**	
10	Total taxable amount. Subtract line 9 from line 8	**10**	
11	Current actuarial value of annuity (from Form 1099-R, box 8)	**11**	
12	Adjusted total taxable amount. Add lines 10 and 11. If this amount is $70,000 or more, **skip** lines 13 through 16, and enter this amount on line 17	**12**	
13	Multiply line 12 by 50% (.50), but **do not** enter more than $10,000 **13**		
14	Subtract $20,000 from line 12. If the result is less than zero, enter -0- **14** **15**		
15	Multiply line 14 by 20% (.20)		
16	Minimum distribution allowance. Subtract line 15 from line 13	**16**	
17	Subtract line 16 from line 12	**17**	
18	Federal estate tax attributable to lump-sum distribution	**18**	
19	Subtract line 18 from line 17	**19**	
	If line 11 is blank, skip lines 20 through 22 and go to line 23.		
20	Divide line 11 by line 12 and enter the result as a decimal	**20**	.
21	Multiply line 16 by the decimal on line 20	**21**	
22	Subtract line 21 from line 11	**22**	

For Paperwork Reduction Act Notice, see separate instructions.   Cat. No. 13187U   Form **4972** (1997)

Form 4972 (1997)   Page **2**

Part III   5- or 10-year tax option–CONTINUED

5-year tax option

23 Multiply line 19 by 20% (.20) . . . . | 23 |

24 Tax on amount on line 23. Use the Tax Rate Schedule for the 5-Year Tax Option in the instructions . . . . | 24 |

25 Multiply line 24 by five (5). If line 11 is blank, skip lines 26 through 28, and enter this amount on line 29 . . . . | 25 |

26 Multiply line 22 by 20% (.20) . . . . | 26 |

27 Tax on amount on line 26. Use the Tax Rate Schedule for the 5-Year Tax Option in the instructions . . . . | 27 |

28 Multiply line 27 by five (5) . . . . | 28 |

29 Subtract line 28 from line 25. (Multiple recipients, see page 2 of the instructions.) . . . | 29 |

Note: *Complete lines 30 through 36 ONLY if the participant was born before 1936. Otherwise, enter the amount from line 29 on line 37.*

10-year tax option

30 Multiply line 19 by 10% (.10) . . . . | 30 |

31 Tax on amount on line 30. Use the Tax Rate Schedule for the 10-Year Tax Option in the instructions . . . . | 31 |

32 Multiply line 31 by ten (10). If line 11 is blank, skip lines 33 through 35, and enter this amount on line 36 . . . . | 32 |

33 Multiply line 22 by 10% (.10) . . . . | 33 |

34 Tax on amount on line 33. Use the Tax Rate Schedule for the 10-Year Tax Option in the instructions . . . . | 34 |

35 Multiply line 34 by ten (10) . . . . | 35 |

36 Subtract line 35 from line 32. (Multiple recipients, see page 2 of the instructions.) . . . | 36 |

37 Compare lines 29 and 36. Generally, you should enter the **smaller** amount here (see instructions) . . . . ▶ | 37 |

38 Tax on lump-sum distribution. Add lines 7 and 37. Also, include in the total on Form 1040, line 39, or Form 1041, Schedule G, line 1b, whichever applies . . . . ▶ | 38 |

IRS Form 4972

Employer Stock Included in Your Distribution

Some employers contribute their own stock to their retirement plans instead of putting in cash. It's cheaper for the company to do it this way, but you may reap a benefit from this action. If your distribution includes employer stock, you may or may not be immediately taxed. You need to know what the company paid for the stock (the stock's value at the time it went into the retirement plan) and the value of the stock when you receive it. It's easy to find out; it's separately reported to you in box 6 of IRS Form 1099-R. It's not included in the taxable amount reported in box 2a.

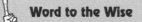

Word to the Wise
Net unrealized appreciation is the increase in the market value of the stock since your employer bought it and put it into the retirement plan (the plan's basis in the stock).

When you get stock as part of a lump-sum distribution, you're not automatically taxed on *net unrealized appreciation.* (You don't even have to meet the five-year participation requirement that otherwise applies to lump-sum distributions.)

You're taxed only on your employer's contribution, which is the cost of the stock going into the plan. Tax on appreciation from the time the stock went into the plan until it was distributed to you is deferred.

If this sounds complicated, it is. Maybe an example will help to clear things up. One long-time retiree got $50,000 worth of employer stock as part of her lump-sum distribution from the company plan. The stock had cost the company only $15,000 when it contributed the stock to the plan. The retiree is taxed on the $15,000. Assuming her tax rate is 28%, the tax is $4,200. Then she sits with the stock and watches it go up. When she sells it, it's worth $80,000. She'll then pay capital gains tax, but there are two parts to the profit. The first is the net unrealized appreciation of $35,000 ($50,000 less $15,000), which is taxed automatically at the most favorable capital gains rate of 20%. Then there's the appreciation on the stock since it was distributed to her of $30,000 ($80,000 less $50,000), which is taxed according to how long the stock was held outside of the plan. If she held it for more than 18 months, this profit is also taxed at 20%; but if it was held for only more than one year but not more than 18 months, a 28% capital gains tax rate applies.

While you can defer tax on the net unrealized appreciation, you can choose to pay tax on it now. You'd include this amount when you figure the tax under the averaging method. There's nothing special to do for making this election to report the net unrealized appreciation currently. You simply take it into account on Form 4972.

Rolling Over Your Benefits to an IRA

Instead of taking your benefits all at once, you can roll them over to an IRA. This is so even though you're 70½ and can no longer make regular IRA contributions. This strategy is good because you postpone taxes, and you'll get to control the funds. Before you opt for the rollover, make sure you understand the full tax implications involved and weigh the benefits against the benefits to be gained from special averaging if you don't make a rollover.

Keep in mind that a rollover applies only to a lump-sum distribution. You can't make a rollover of:

➤ Pension payments to you. You'll have to keep them and pay tax now.

➤ Your after-tax contributions. You can't put these into an IRA, but you're not taxed on these contributions when you get them back. Of the lump-sum distribution, you can rollover everything *but* your own after-tax contributions.

➤ Required distributions after you've reached age $70^1/_2$ or have retired. If the plan is making minimum distributions to you on account of your age (or, if older, when you retire), you have to pay tax now.

Tax Implications of a Rollover

Making a rollover buys you time. You don't pay any tax when you make the rollover. You pay tax only when you take money out of the IRA that the funds were rolled into. In theory, you might find yourself in a lower tax bracket in the years you take the funds out than you are now. In practice, who knows! Your income could increase if your investments perform well or your postretirement job really pays off. The tax rates could always change (they never seem to stay constant for too long).

The decision to make a rollover or to pay tax now is an all-or-nothing decision. You can't roll over part of the distribution and use averaging for the other part. If you roll over *any* part of the distribution to an IRA, you forfeit the opportunity to use averaging, even for the part you keep.

You can make a rollover and preserve the possibility of future averaging if you make a rollover to a special IRA, called a *conduit IRA*. This conduit is nothing more than an IRA in which you segregate your rollover. Then, if you get another job that has a retirement plan, you roll the funds from your conduit IRA into the new plan (assuming the plan will accept the rollover). A conduit IRA is just a regular IRA that's labeled as a conduit. You don't make any IRA contributions to a conduit IRA; you keep your rollover separate.

Cash Crash
If you make a rollover, you can't change your mind. You can't use special averaging, even if you take all of the rolled over funds out of the account all at once. You're stuck with your original decision to make a rollover. If you try to undo the rollover, you're immediately taxed on all the money (and subject to a 10% penalty if you're under $59^1/_2$).

Golden Years Ideas
If you're making a rollover instead of taking the distribution, the plan administrator may insist on rolling over the entire amount into just one IRA. You may prefer multiple accounts—for investment diversification or to make beneficiary designation easier. You can simply make a second transfer from the conduit IRA directly to other newly established IRAs.

Should You Make a Rollover?

This is the $64,000 question. It's really a matter of personal need and tax considerations rather than any hard and fast rule. For most people, a rollover makes more sense than taking a lump-sum distribution. Here are some of the reasons why:

➤ Tax-deferred accumulations. If you make a rollover, the funds continue to earn income that's tax deferred. You're earning interest on interest. Some financial people have called this the *miracle of compounding*. And, since the funds grow without having to pay out tax, there's greater annual growth.

➤ Deferring income tax. By rolling over the funds to an IRA, you delay having to pay the piper. Deferral isn't only a psychological boost; there's a real financial benefit. Delaying taxes always means that your money is working for you, rather than for Uncle Sam.

Golden Years Ideas

If you take a lump-sum distribution but then decide you'd rather have it rolled over to an IRA, you have 60 days to act. Roll over the funds you've received *plus*, from your pocket, the 20% that was withheld, in order to make a complete rollover.

Still, even though there are compelling reasons for making a rollover, according to the Employer Benefit Research Institute, 60% of those leaving the job in 1996 took the money instead of rolling it over. There must be some good reasons why so many people chose this option. Factors favoring the take-it-now approach include:

➤ Need for the funds. If you have a special need for the money now: If you're going to start a postretirement business or you want to buy a retirement home, then taking the cash from the lump-sum distribution makes sense. If you don't need those funds right now and don't anticipate a need within the next few years, think again about paying the tax now and keeping the cash.

➤ Low current tax. Special averaging and capital gain treatment means that you'll probably pay the lowest tax possible on those benefits. Once you make a rollover to an IRA, you lose forever the opportunity to use special averaging and capital gain treatment.

➤ Single hit for Social Security benefits. The receipt of retirement benefits can affect the amount of Social Security benefits that are subject to tax (0%, 50%, 85%). If you take a lump-sum distribution, it will surely cause your Social Security benefits to be taxed to the max (or nearly so, depending on the size of the distribution and the amount of your other income). But that is only for one year. After that, you might more easily control your income (invest the distribution) so that your benefits aren't taxed any higher than they need to be. In contrast, rolling over benefits to an IRA and taking required distributions can mean that Social Security benefits are taxed more highly year after year. You need to decide whether it pays to bite the bullet for one year rather than be bled year after year.

➤ You have tax losses for the year. If you sold property at a loss or you have net operating losses relating to a business you own or used to own, then you might want to report the distribution now. Losses can offset, or partially offset, the tax you'll owe on the distribution.

➤ Receipt of employer securities. If the distribution includes not only cash but also stock in your employer, paying tax now can save you taxes later on should the stock value continue to rise. Tax on the stock is levied only on the value of the shares when they went into your account. You'll pay additional tax—at favorable capital gains rates—when you eventually sell off the shares. In contrast, if you rolled over the stock to your IRA, you'd defer immediate tax. But you'd pay all ordinary income when you later sell the shares.

Inheriting Retirement Benefits

Until now you've learned what happens to *your* benefits when you retire. But what happens if you're lucky enough to inherit someone else's retirement benefits when they die? It's important to know what your options are because this inheritance may prove to be a substantial part of your retirement income. The options for handling an inheritance of retirement benefits may be different depending on whether or not you're the spouse of the person who died.

Cash Crash
After 1999, those born after 1936 will not be able to use special averaging. So even if the funds are needed, it may still pay to defer as much tax as possible by making a rollover.

Golden Years Ideas
Paying tax now if you receive employer securities as part of your distribution can benefit your heirs. If you die and you've already paid tax on the stock, your heirs have no income tax obligation with respect to the stock. They'll get a stepped-up basis for that stock to its value on the date of your death. In contrast, if you rolled over the stock to your IRA and you die, your heirs will owe ordinary income tax on the value of the stock.

You may be asking why retirement benefits aren't like any other inheritance that is free from income tax. The reason is simple: The person who earned the benefits and died never paid any income tax on them (they were tax-deferred throughout his or her life). Now someone must pay the tax and that someone is you, the beneficiary.

Just a word of caution: the tax rules for inherited retirement benefits are extremely complex. It's a good idea to talk your options over with a tax expert.

Inheriting Benefits From a Spouse

When your spouse dies, you may continue to receive benefits under a joint and survivor annuity (as discussed in Chapter 15, "Pension Payout Options for Married Couples"). Alternatively, you may receive a lump-sum distribution of your spouse's benefits. Just like your spouse who participated in the plan, you too can choose to keep the cash by paying the tax now using special averaging as long as your spouse was at least $59^1/_2$ at the time of his or her death.

If you receive a lump-sum distribution, you can roll it over to your own IRA. The decision between using averaging now or rolling over the distribution should be based on the same factors discussed earlier in this chapter.

Inheriting Benefits From Someone Other Than a Spouse

If you inherit qualified retirement plan benefits in a lump-sum distribution, you're eligible to elect special averaging to report the benefits as long as the person who died was at least $59^1/_2$ at the time of his or her death. If benefits are paid to more than one beneficiary, each one of you can decide separately to use averaging for his or her share. Even if other beneficiaries don't use averaging, you may still elect it if you're otherwise eligible. You can't choose to roll over the distribution to an IRA since you're not a surviving spouse.

The Least You Need to Know

➤ When you leave a company that allows benefits to be paid in a lump sum, you can take the benefits with you, regardless of your age.

➤ You don't have to start taking benefits from a company retirement plan until you retire (unless you own more than 5% of the business).

➤ If you receive a lump-sum distribution from your company plan, you qualify for special averaging treatment.

➤ Starting in the year 2000, only those born before 1936 can use special averaging (10-year averaging) to figure the tax on lump-sum distributions.

➤ There's an automatic 20% income tax withholding on lump-sum distributions.

➤ If you receive employer stock as part of a lump-sum distribution, you're not automatically taxed on the increase in the value of the stock from the time it went into the plan and when it was distributed to you.

➤ You can't roll over to an IRA your after-tax contributions to the company plan, nor any required distributions made to you after age $70^1/_2$ (or when you retire if later than that age).

➤ Rolling over retirement plan distributions to an IRA postpones tax until you withdraw the funds from that account.

➤ Special tax rules apply to inherited retirement plan benefits and IRAs.

Chapter 17

Making Your IRA Last As Long As You Want

In This Chapter

➤ Increasing your IRA throughout your retirement years

➤ Taking money out of your IRA: when and how

➤ Saving for yourself and your family through a Roth IRA

➤ Planning for an inherited IRA

Your IRA may be your biggest source of retirement income. This is especially true if you rolled over company pension plan distributions into your IRA. Use your IRA wisely. Make sure you're investing it right. Plan IRA withdrawals so that your money will last as long as you need it to. But in this planning, don't overlook tax rules that require you to take certain minimum amounts.

In this chapter, you'll see how to invest your IRA funds to preserve your capital while still growing it. You'll also find out about tax rules that allow you to tap into your IRA penalty free, regardless of your age and rules that make you start to take money out after you're $70^1/_2$. You'll learn about new Roth IRA rules that allow you to continue building up your retirement funds, regardless of age, as long as you're still working. Finally, you'll see what your options are if you inherit someone else's IRA.

Making Your IRA Grow

Like any investment you have, you want to make sure you're getting the best return possible. This is especially true with IRAs for two reasons. First, like several clients of mine, IRAs may be your single biggest asset (worth more than even your home). While it may not be important that your $1,000 passbook savings account is only earning 2.5% interest, you don't want such meager returns on a $500,000 IRA! Second, you're probably counting on your IRAs to give you a large chunk of your retirement income. In order for your IRA to come through, you have to make sure it produces. There are two sure ways to do this: monitor your accounts regularly to keep investment strategies on track and continue to add money to your IRA if you're eligible to do so.

Re-Examining Your IRA Accounts

You may have one IRA account, or you may have several IRA accounts. There's no limit on the number you can have. As a practical matter, you don't want more accounts than you can comfortably keep watch over since it's important to continually monitor what assets you've got in these accounts. During your working years, you may have taken a more aggressive investment approach. Now, in retirement, you may want to become more conservative.

The rules for asset allocation (you learned about these in Chapter 10, "Asset Allocation After Retirement") apply with equal force to IRAs. Even if you're retired, you want some growth (while some money can be in bonds, you also want some in equities to grow faster than the rate of inflation). Just how much to put into equities depends on several factors:

➤ Your age. As you get older, you usually want to switch gradually from equities into bonds. But no matter how old you get, you still want *some* money in equities.

Cash Crash

You don't want to invest in municipal bonds for your IRA. The reason: You'll get a lower return, and you don't get any added benefit from the fact that interest on the bonds is tax free (the IRA is tax deferred, but you'll pay ordinary income tax on the bonds' interest when you take distributions from your IRA).

➤ Your risk tolerance. If your stomach can stand the ups and downs of the stock market, you may want to put a greater portion of your IRA money into equities. But remember, now that you're in retirement, you may not have a long time frame to wait out serious down turns in the market.

➤ Your other income. If you're very dependent on your IRA for retirement income, you need to be more conservative than someone who can afford to risk the chance of loss.

➤ Your other investments. If you're already heavily invested in equities *outside* of your IRA, you probably want to put your IRA money into fixed income. This asset allocation of having equities *outside* of your IRA and fixed income *inside* your IRA generally makes sense since gains on the equities qualify for low capital gains rates while withdrawals from IRAs (whether related to equities gains or fixed income) are all ordinary income.

As part of the asset allocation process, you also want diversity in your IRAs. For example, after you've decided how much to put into equities, you then must decide what equities to invest in. You don't want *all* your equity money in just one stock or one mutual fund.

Some insurance people may push IRA annuities as an investment vehicle. This may not be the best way to go. The key selling point is a guaranteed death benefit (your beneficiaries won't get less than what you put into the investment). But there's no guarantee for you. So, for example, if you put into the annuity $100,000 and invest it through mutual funds that decline to $90,000, that's all there will be for you to take out when you annuitize. The guarantee doesn't protect you as the owner of the IRA annuity. The downside to this type of IRA investment is the added cost of annuity fees to get the same type of tax deferral you're already enjoying within the IRA.

Golden Years Ideas

Instead of making a rollover, you can transfer the funds *directly* from one IRA account (no matter where it's invested) to another. As long as nothing is distributed to you, there's no limit on the number of direct transfers you can make each year. Plus, this method of transfer means you don't have any day that your money isn't invested and working for you.

So you've looked at your IRA accounts and want to make changes. Go ahead. But do it right. Tax rules say you can make a tax-free IRA rollover once every year. A tax-free rollover means taking money out of your IRA and then, within 60 days, putting it back into another IRA. If you miss the 60-day re-investment deadline, you're taxed on all you took out (and can be liable for penalties if you're under $59^1/_2$).

Building Up Your IRA If You Have a Postretirement Job

If you've followed up retirement from your old job by taking a new job or starting up your own business, you can continue to put money into your IRA. You can do this even if you're collecting a pension from your old job or receiving Social Security benefits. Making IRA contributions will not only provide you with a greater retirement fund when you eventually hang up your spurs for good, but can also give you some current tax benefits.

Golden Years Ideas

If you're over $70^1/_2$ and working and your spouse is younger and not working, you're still able to contribute to your spouse's IRA. The same $2,000 limit applies to a spousal IRA.

You can continue to fund your regular IRA until you turn 70^1/$_2$ if you're still working. You don't have to work full time. As long as you earn $2,000 during the year, you can put this money into an IRA.

This will allow you to create tax-deferred earnings. Table 17.1 is a chart that shows you how your IRA contributions can build up additional funds for retirement, depending on the compounded return you get on your contributions. If you've invested in the stock market and it continues to enjoy stellar performances like we've seen in the past several years, then even higher returns are possible.

Table 17.1 IRA Contributions With Compounding

Number of IRA Contributions*	6%	8%	10%
5 years	$12,015	$12,794	$13,633
10 years	$28,233	$31,879	$36,109
15 years	$50,125	$60,349	$73,164

This assumes you make your annual contributions on January 1 of each year and that your earnings are based on simple interest compounding (daily compounding would produce even greater results).

Whether your IRA contributions are deductible is another question. You can deduct all your contributions if either of the following is true:

➤ You don't participate in a qualified retirement plan on your job.

➤ You do participate in a qualified retirement plan, but your adjusted gross income is below a threshold amount. (Technically you have to modify your adjusted gross income here, but for purposes of our discussion let's keep it simple and call it adjusted gross income.)

The threshold amounts depend on your filing status (single or married filing jointly) and the year of the contribution. You claim a full deduction if your adjusted gross income is *below* the threshold amount; you can't claim any deduction if your adjusted gross income is *above* the phase-out limits.

Table 17.2 IRA Deduction Phase-Outs for Active Participants

Contribution Year	Singles	Joint Returns
1998	$30,000–$40,000	$50,000–$60,000
1999	$31,000–$41,000	$51,000–$61,000
2000	$32,000–$42,000	$52,000–$62,000
2001	$33,000–$43,000	$53,000–$63,000
2002	$34,000–$44,000	$54,000–$64,000

Contribution Year	Singles	Joint Returns
2003	$40,000–$50,000	$60,000–$70,000
2004	$45,000–$55,000	$65,000–$75,000
2005	$50,000–$60,000	$70,000–$80,000
2006	$50,000–$60,000	$75,000–$85,000
2007 and later	$50,000–$60,000	$80,000–$100,000

If you're married, file separate returns and lived with your spouse at any time during the year, your phase-out ranges is from zero to $10,000. In other words, if you're in this category and earn $5,000, your contribution is limited to just $1,000.

What happens if your spouse works for a company that provides retirement plan benefits, but you don't have such coverage on your current job? You're eligible to make a full IRA contribution if the adjusted gross income of you and your spouse *together* is below $150,000 (a partial deduction is allowed if your income is between $150,000 and $160,000).

There's another way to stash retirement cash on a tax-advantaged basis: Roth IRA. This alternative is particularly attractive to seniors, as you'll find out later in this chapter.

Golden Years Ideas

If your income is too high for a deductible IRA, you can still contribute to a nondeductible IRA, regardless of the amount of your income. You might also be able to contribute to a Roth IRA (explained at the end of this chapter).

Taking Money Out of Your IRA

All that money is sitting in your IRA. What if you need it now? What if you don't? When are you allowed to tap into those funds without penalty; when must you start in order to avoid penalty? And how do you take withdrawals so that you'll pay the least amount of tax? All these are great questions that you need to answer so that your IRA money isn't wasted on taxes and penalties.

Remember that taking money from your IRA means paying income tax. If you made *only* deductible contributions to a regular IRA, then *all* money you take out is ordinary income to you. It doesn't matter that the money came from sales of stocks held for a long time. Whatever you take out is considered ordinary income.

If you make both deductible and nondeductible contributions to a regular IRA, then a portion of each withdrawal (that portion representing your nondeductible contributions) is tax free while the balance is taxable. You're not allowed to treat the withdrawals as coming first from your own contributions (so there's no tax); you *must* apportion each withdrawal.

When You Can or Must Take Money From Your IRA

IRAs are meant for retirement. Because the tax law allows you to defer reporting earnings on your IRA until you take withdrawals, that law also has special rules on when you can or must take withdrawals. There are two key ages you need to know about: $59^1/_2$ and $70^1/_2$.

$59^1/_2$

The earliest age at which you can take money from your IRA without any tax penalty is $59^1/_2$. Once you cross this age barrier, it doesn't matter what you use the money for. But regardless of age, you'll still pay income tax on your withdrawals.

Cash Crash

Tax penalties aren't the only things you should be concerned about. There may be investment penalties to taking money out early. For example, there may be sales charges or bank CD penalties.

Cash Crash

Even if you qualify under an exception, remember that you're still going to pay regular income taxes on the withdrawals. The only way to avoid the tax is to rollover the funds within 60 days of receiving them, that is, put them back in the original IRA account or another IRA account.

There are, however, a number of exceptions to the tax penalty that allow earlier withdrawals penalty-free:

➤ You take benefits in the form of annuity-type payments (explained in Chapter 14, "Quick Thinking When You Get a Pink Slip").

➤ You're disabled (at any age).

➤ You use the withdrawals to pay medical expenses exceeding 7.5% of your adjusted gross income. But only the portion of the distribution used for this purpose is free from penalty; the balance is still subject to penalty.

➤ Transfers to your spouse (or former spouse) incident to a divorce. You don't need the formalities of a qualified domestic relations order (QDRO) that you need for such distributions from a company pension plan. The rules for QDROs are explained in Chapter 15, "Pension Payout Options for Married Couples."

➤ You're unemployed and use the withdrawals to pay medical insurance. You're treated as being unemployed for this purpose only if you've received unemployment compensation for 12 consecutive weeks (or, if you're self-employed, you would have been eligible for benefits had you instead been an employee). This exception stops once you've been re-employed for 60 days.

➤ You use the payments to pay first-time home buying expenses for yourself, spouse, child, grandchild, or ancestor of you or your spouse. There's a lifetime cap on this exception of $10,000. Funds from the IRA must be used with 120 days of withdrawal to buy, build, or improve a first home (including reasonable finance and settlement costs). A home is treated as a first home if you haven't owned a home within the past two years.

70¹/₂

The age that you have to start taking distributions from your regular IRAs (there's no required distributions from Roth IRAs) is 70¹/₂. If you don't, you're subject to a whopping 50% penalty on amounts you should have taken but didn't. You'll see in a minute how to figure *minimum* distributions.

Between 59¹/₂, when you're *permitted* to take money out penalty free, and 70¹/₂, when you *must* take some money out to avoid a penalty, you're in no man's land. You're allowed, but not required, to take money out during these years. Again, there's no penalty but you're taxed on the distributions.

Effective Withdrawal Strategies You Can Follow

You're allowed to take out as much from your IRA as you want at any time (keeping in mind the possible 10% penalty for early withdrawals). But once you're 70¹/₂, you'll have to start taking *required minimum distributions* from your regular IRA in order to avoid a 50% penalty.

Forget what you took out so far. Your required minimum distributions are based only on what's in the account as of now (more exactly, on December 31 of the year before you turn 70¹/₂). You don't get any credit for earlier withdrawals.

Let's say you want to take out as little as possible but avoid the penalty. In theory, you're supposed to exhaust your IRA over your lifetime. In practice, depending on how you figure your distributions, you'll never run out of money in your IRA no matter how

Golden Years Ideas

If you're approaching 70¹/₂, you'd better start thinking about minimum distribution rules. If you want to, you should name a beneficiary by your birthday (which will reduce the size of the annual distributions you have to take). You should also decide on the method you'll use to figure your distributions (these methods are explained later in this chapter).

Golden Years Ideas

If you need retirement income, use up your savings *outside* your IRA first. The reason: You'll continue tax-deferred compounding inside the IRA. So if you own shares in a mutual fund outside your IRA and shares inside your IRA, sell the outside shares first. Also, the sale of those shares will probably be at favorable capital gains rates, while a sale of inside shares, the proceeds of which are then withdrawn will produce ordinary income for you.

Golden Years Ideas

You can get out of the 50% penalty if you've made an honest mistake. The penalty can be waived if there's reasonable cause for not taking the full amount you should have (for example, you got bad advice from someone at the bank where you keep your IRA). But you have to ask the IRS for this waiver.

long you live. This is because no matter how old you get, you'll always have some life expectancy.

Whether you're married or single, you can name a beneficiary. The beneficiary is someone who will inherit your IRA (what's left in it) when you die. But a beneficiary is also important while you're alive. Naming a beneficiary can reduce the amount of your required minimum distributions, as you'll see in a minute.

If you don't name any beneficiary (or your beneficiary is your estate or a charity, neither of which can have a life expectancy), then figuring the required distribution is easy. You just divide your account balance by your life expectancy for the year. You find your life expectancy factor from Table 17.3, an IRS table.

Table 17.3 Single Life Expectancy

Age	Life Expectancy Factor	Age	Life Expectancy Factor	Age	Life Expectancy Factor
70	16.0	86	6.5	101	2.5
71	15.3	87	6.1	102	2.3
72	14.6	88	5.7	103	2.1
73	13.9	89	5.3	104	1.9
74	13.2	90	5.0	105	1.8
75	12.5	91	4.7	106	1.6
76	11.9	92	4.4	107	1.4
77	11.2	93	4.1	108	1.3
78	10.6	94	3.9	109	1.1
79	10.0	95	3.7	110	1.0
80	9.5	96	3.4	111	0.9
81	8.9	97	3.2	112	0.8
82	8.4	98	3.0	113	0.7
83	7.9	99	2.8	114	0.6
84	7.4	100	2.7	115	0.5
85	6.9				

*Source: IRS

So, for example, when you're 70$^1/_2$, find the life expectancy from the table, which is 15.3 for age 71. Then, assuming you have $100,000 in your IRA, your required minimum distribution is $6,536 ($100,000 ÷ 15.3). You can see that it's only a small amount you *must* take out (though you can always take out more).

Senior Info

As you're taking out required minimum distributions each year, you may find your IRA is *increasing*, not shrinking. This is because you'll continue to earn money on funds remaining in the account. If you can grow your account at, for example, 10% annually, you'll enjoy many more years of an expanding IRA. Your IRA won't start to decrease for nine years (in year eight, you'll break even with your required withdrawal equaling your earnings). If your IRA earns more than 10%, there are more years of continued growth in the account.

You can keep your required distributions even smaller if you name a beneficiary (other than your estate or a charity).

If you've named a beneficiary, there are two ways to figure distributions: term certain method and recalculation method. Both methods are acceptable to the IRS for beating the penalty. But each method is better in certain situations. Here's how to figure distributions under each method. Yes, the computations are complicated, but if you don't get it into your head how the methods work, you won't be able to get the most mileage from your IRA:

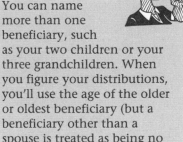

Golden Years Ideas

You can name more than one beneficiary, such as your two children or your three grandchildren. When you figure your distributions, you'll use the age of the older or oldest beneficiary (but a beneficiary other than a spouse is treated as being no younger than you by more than 10 years, regardless of actual age.) For example, if you're 70$^1/_2$ and your beneficiary is 17, your beneficiary is treated as being 60$^1/_2$ (ten years younger than you).

➤ Term certain method. This method is easier to figure than the other method. You just find your joint life expectancies in the joint life expectancy tables contained in IRS Publication 590 by looking across the top for your age and down the side for your beneficiary's age (or assumed age). Then you use that as a divisor to find your required minimum distribution just as those without beneficiaries do. But each year you reduce that joint life expectancy by one.

Cash Crash
Make sure the bank, brokerage firm, or mutual fund that's acting as the custodian of your IRA knows your choice of methods. If you don't make one, the custodian may *automatically* use one method or the other. Look over your IRA documents you signed when you set up the account (if you still have them) and see if there's any default method (the method that will be used if you don't say otherwise). Make sure the custodian will honor your choice if you don't want the method it chose for you automatically.

➤ Recalculation method. Instead of simply reducing your joint life expectancy each year by one, you're allowed under this method to re-figure it. Since life expectancy tables actually add *more* than one year of expected life span for each year you survive, you'll get a larger divisor for figuring your required minimum distribution. The result: a smaller required minimum distribution each year than under the term certain method.

Which method is better? The answer depends on your personal situation. You're better off using the term certain method in most cases. This is so even though the recalculation method produces the smaller required distributions. The recalculation method can spell disaster if your spouse dies first. In this case, because your spouse has no more life expectancy, you're forced to continue figuring your distributions using just your single life expectancy. With the term certain method, you can still use joint life expectancy (minus one each year) even if your spouse dies.

Still, there are some situations that make it wiser to choose the recalculation method. Here are just three scenarios that could apply to you:

Scenario 1   You're concerned about outliving your IRA. If you think you're going to beat the life expectancy odds, then the recalculation method will ensure that there's always something left in the IRA (the term certain method eventually taps out the entire fund).

Scenario 2   Your beneficiary is a charity. In this case, you'd take out *less* under the recalculation method, leaving more in your IRA to pass on to the charity.

Scenario 3   You have a spouse who is much younger than you. It's reasonable to assume that your spouse will outlive you (although anything can happen). If you want to take as little as possible, the recalculation method is the ticket. When you die, your spouse can simply roll over what's left in your IRA into his or her IRA, name a new beneficiary, and start to figure required minimum distributions all over again.

Now you know *how* much you have to take out. The question remains: *When?* Withdrawals must be made no later than December 31 each year. You may not want to wait until the last minute. Go ahead and take the distribution on November 30 if you wish. But taking the funds out too early means you're losing the opportunity for getting earnings on those funds.

But in the year you turn 70$\frac{1}{2}$, you have additional time to take your first distribution. You have until April 1 of the following year.

Roth IRAs: Retirement Saver for Any Age

Most people don't think of retirement as a time to be saving more money. Still, if you've taken a job (even part-time) or started up your own business, you're in a position to salt money away even though you're retired and collecting Social Security benefits and a company pension plan from your old job. You can use a Roth IRA.

A Roth IRA is a type of IRA that has the same $2,000 annual contribution limit. You're eligible to make contributions if you have earnings and your adjusted gross income is no more than $95,000 if you're single or $150,000 on a joint return. (The $2,000 contribution limit phases out for income between $95,000 and $110,000 for singles and $150,000 to $160,000 for married people.) The key features of the Roth IRA include:

➤ Opportunity to make contributions as long as you're still working. There's no age 70$\frac{1}{2}$ cutoff like the regular IRA.

➤ No required minimum distribution. You don't have to start taking money out of your Roth IRA at any particular time. You can leave money in the Roth IRA to build up on a tax-advantaged basis. If you want to take out money, the amount is up to you.

➤ Distributions may be fully tax free. You're allowed to withdraw your own contributions at any time without income tax or penalties (there's no apportionment requirement as in the case of withdrawals from a nondeductible IRA). And, if you leave the money in your Roth IRA for at least five years and don't take distributions until after age 59$\frac{1}{2}$ (or on account of disability or to pay first-time home buying expenses as explained earlier in this chapter), there's no income tax on the earnings. And there are no tax penalties to be concerned with.

Cash Crash

It's generally not a good idea to delay the distribution until April 1 of the year after you turn 70$\frac{1}{2}$. The reason: It will mean you have to take *two* required distributions in the same year—one on April 1 and the second year's distribution by December 31.

Golden Years Ideas

If you don't take money out of your Roth IRA, it means there's more for your beneficiaries. And they'll inherit your IRA without any income tax to worry about (beneficiaries of regular IRAs are responsible for income taxes on their inheritance when they take distributions, as required by law).

Golden Years Ideas

If you make the conversion in 1998, you can spread out evenly over four years the income you have to take into account. This four-year option applies only to 1998 conversions. And if you take money out of the Roth IRA before the end of five years after the conversion, there may be additional penalties.

You're allowed to convert your regular IRA into a Roth IRA. This will keep you from having to take money out at age 70$\frac{1}{2}$. But there's an immediate tax cost to doing so. You'll have to pay income tax on everything in the regular IRA (other than any nondeductible IRA contributions you may have made). You're eligible to make the conversion if your adjusted gross income is no more than $100,000 for the year (if you file jointly, it's your combined income that counts).

Inheriting an IRA

Like qualified retirement plan benefits, you can face an income tax liability by inheriting someone else's deductible or regular nondeductible IRA. Anyone who inherits this IRA can take the money out and pay income tax whenever desired. There's no 10% early distribution penalty imposed on you even if you're under 59$\frac{1}{2}$ since the benefits are payable on account of death. However, you can't leave the funds in the IRA indefinitely; you *must* satisfy required minimum distribution rules. The tax rules differ depending on whether or not you're the spouse of the IRA owner.

If you're the spouse of the IRA owner and you inherit his or her IRA, you have two choices to satisfy required minimum distribution rules:

➤ You can rollover the IRA to your own IRA. This option applies whether or not your spouse had already begun to take required minimum distributions. Making a rollover lets you plan for withdrawals as you would for your retirement savings. In other words, you can spread out withdrawals if you want to according to the rules explained earlier in this chapter.

➤ If required minimum distributions have not yet begun for your spouse, you can begin them by the later of December 31 of the year your spouse would have reached age 70$\frac{1}{2}$, or December 31 of the year following the year of your spouse's death. Alternatively, you can take everything by December 31 of the fifth year following the year of your spouse's death. If required distributions have begun, you can continue to receive distributions under the method selected by your spouse.

If you inherit an IRA from someone who isn't your spouse, here are your choices for satisfying required minimum distributions:

➤ If required minimum distributions had not yet begun because the owner died before age 70$\frac{1}{2}$, you must take out everything in the IRA either by December 31 of the fifth year following the owner's death or over your life expectancy, whichever you choose (or whichever was chosen for you by the terms of the IRA). If no choice is made by you or the plan, you must take all by December 31 of the fifth year following the owner's death.

➤ If required minimum distributions had begun before the owner's death (he or she was over $70^1/_2$), you must continue to take distributions at least as rapidly as under the method being used at the owner's death.

If you inherit a Roth IRA, your relationship to the IRA owner is irrelevant. There's no income tax to report; the account passes to you tax free. However, you're still required to take funds out of the Roth IRA (you can't continue tax deferral indefinitely). Generally, withdrawals must be taken over your life expectancy based on IRS tables.

The Least You Need to Know

➤ You should check on your IRA investments to see that they're invested in vehicles that allow for continued growth and that meet your other needs.

➤ You can continue to make regular IRA contributions up to age $70^1/_2$ if you're still working.

➤ Taking money from your IRA too early can result not only in tax penalties but also investment charges and other penalties.

➤ After you're $59^1/_2$, you can take money out of your regular IRA without the 10% early distribution penalty, regardless of what you use the money for.

➤ You have to start required distributions from regular IRAs at $70^1/_2$.

➤ Naming a beneficiary who is younger than you means smaller required minimum distributions.

➤ Generally, you'll want to use the term certain method to figure required minimum distributions, but there are exceptions.

➤ You can put money into a Roth IRA, regardless of your age, as long as you're still working (and your income isn't over the eligibility limit).

➤ If you inherit someone else's IRA, you must follow special tax rules on withdrawals.

Part 5
Avoiding Catastrophe

Earthquakes, tornadoes, and ice storms can wreak havoc with your property. These are natural disasters that, except for having adequate insurance, you can't do much about. But there are other catastrophes you need to think about: health emergencies, crooks trying to part you from your money, and even death. You can do something should these events strike you or your family.

You don't want to go on wild spending sprees and blow your nest egg too quickly. You don't want to fall victim to telemarketing schemes and other frauds directed mainly at seniors. You want to avoid having all your assets wiped out in no time if you need to go into a nursing home. You want to be able to protect your spouse and family with adequate insurance when you die. And, most of all, you want to make plans now for someone to handle your money if you become too sick or too old to do it on your own.

Avoiding catastrophe, wherever it might arise, is a big job. You've got to become savvy about many things you may not have given any thought to before retirement, such as budgeting, long-term care insurance, and durable powers of attorney. But a little information now can help you to take steps that will avoid catastrophe for you and your family.

Chapter 18

Keeping Spending in Line

In This Chapter

➤ Making a budget you can live with

➤ Living within your budget

➤ Avoiding scams that can take your cash

You've often heard it repeated that retirees live on fixed incomes. Now you know as well as I do that income isn't really fixed. You saw in the early chapters how your investment returns can fluctuate greatly from month to month, let alone year to year. Still, a part of your income is relatively fixed. Social Security benefits are constant from month to month and only go up by the cost of living each year. And you may also be locked into a pension that never increases. So, unless you're working in your retirement years or you're a Rockefeller, you need to keep a vigilant watch over how you spend your limited dollars.

In this chapter, you'll learn about making a budget that's workable. After all, you want to be able to travel, take a course, indulge in your hobby, and otherwise pursue your retirement dreams. You'll also learn about scams—many of which are targeted at the elderly—that can quickly separate you from your hard-earned lifetime savings.

Budgeting So You Won't Go Broke

Many people live their whole lives without ever having to make and keep to a budget. They're the fortunate ones whose income can support their lifestyle without any checks and balances. But not everyone can afford to take such a casual approach to spending. If you're primarily dependent on your pension and Social Security benefits for the bulk of your retirement income, then you need to keep a vigilant watch on how you spend your limited income. If you don't, you'll wind up eating into your savings, which will put you in a downward spiral from which you may never recover. Here's how the spiral works: By eating into your savings, you'll reduce your income because there will be less capital to generate income, which will mean you'll again have to dip into savings, further reducing your income.

The solution for the person on a more or less fixed income is to set up a budget that's in line with your income. (Remember that you figured out your monthly income in Chapter 2, "Richer Than You Think.") And then, after making the budget, you have to stick to it.

Golden Years Ideas

Married people should confer on the budget so that each spouse's needs and wants are addressed. During working years, it may have been left up to one spouse to handle home finances (with or without a budget). In retirement, it's a good idea for the chore to be shared to avoid problems.

Crafting Your Budget

It's not hard to make a budget. Use the following chart (see Table 18.1) to make your own budget. It's a rather detailed budget to take into account most of the types of expenses you may encounter.

To make your own budget, just fill in the numbers for each *month*. If you pay a bill once a year (such as homeowner's insurance), then divide by 12. If you pay a bill twice a year, divide by 6. If you pay a bill quarterly, divide by 3. Not every item in this chart may apply to you. You may have other expenses, like alimony payments, not itemized in the chart (just enter your figures in the spaces marked Other).

Table 18.1 Your Monthly Budget

Type of Expense	*Monthly Amount*
Housing	
Rent/mortgage	$_____
Tenant's/homeowner's insurance	$_____
Real estate taxes (town and school)	$_____
Homeowner's association fees	$_____
Cleaning/gardening	$_____
Other property maintenance (for example, septic, gutter, or chimney cleaning)	$_____
Utilities	
Electricity	$_____
Oil	$_____
Gas	$_____
Water	$_____
Garbage	$_____

Type of Expense	Monthly Amount
Telephone	$_____
Cable TV	$_____
Medical Expenses	
Medicare Part B	$_____
Medigap insurance	$_____
Long-term care insurance	$_____
Drugs and vitamins	$_____
Glasses, hearing aids, other health aids	$_____
Transportation Expenses	
Finance payments or lease payments	$_____
Insurance	$_____
Gas and oil	$_____
Maintenance	$_____
Parking and tolls	$_____
Bus and/or Train	$_____
Personal Expenses	
Food and household items	$_____
Clothing	$_____
Haircuts, hair and nail salon	$_____
Toiletries and cosmetics	$_____
Dry cleaning	$_____
Travel and Entertainment	
Eating out	$_____
Vacations	$_____
Movies and theater	$_____
Other	$_____
Income Taxes	
Federal	$_____
State	$_____
Local	$_____
Tax preparation fees	$_____
Gifts	
Family members	$_____
Charities	$_____
Other	
Life insurance	$_____
Subscriptions	$_____
Education	$_____
Organization dues	$_____
TOTAL	$_____

The budget chart you've just completed, long as it is, doesn't include certain expenses that some people may be paying and need to include in their own chart:

➤ Debt repayment. Maybe you've had some unexpected expenses like a broken refrigerator that had to be replaced, or a friend's death that caused you to incur expensive airline tickets so you could attend the funeral. These events made you charge heavily and may have put you into debt. If you carry credit card debt, you'll have to repay your debt each month. If you pay only the monthly minimum that the credit card company requires, you'll be in debt almost forever. Make sure your payments are large enough to pay down the principal amount of your debt. This may require you to give up a dinner out each month or make some other financial sacrifice temporarily until the debt is paid off.

Golden Years Ideas

Your initial monthly budget may have to be changed over time as expenses increase or your needs change. For example, you may want to add a long-term care policy to cover nursing home expenses. Or you might join a Medicare HMO and be able to drop your Medigap coverage, freeing up income for other purposes.

➤ Help for children. Some retirees are still helping their children—supporting them entirely or just giving them a little extra each month. If you're helping out your son, the struggling actor, you need to factor this into your budget.

➤ Help for your parents. Some retirees are providing financial assistance to elderly parents. It may be a fixed amount or some extra funds from time to time. You can list it in your budget under Gifts or enter it as an Other expense.

Senior Info

According to demographic projections, it's estimated that within 50 years, nearly one-third of those between 60 and 74 will have at least one living parent. (Right now there is already a large percentage of retirees with living parents.) Many of these retirees will be giving help to that parent—financial or otherwise.

➤ Emergency fund. In making a budget, it may be a good idea to build in a cushion to take care of the unexpected. You can do this by setting up an emergency fund account that you contribute to monthly. It's just a form of forced savings. You won't find a dedicated space for this expense in your budgeting chart, but you can enter it as an Other expense.

Stick to Your Budget

What good is going through the exercise of making a budget if you don't follow it? None. So you have to find a system that you can use to stick to your budget.

One way to follow a budget is to keep track of your expenses. Use an account book (even a blank spiral notebook) or a software program (like Quicken) into which you'll enter expenses as they occur. You don't have to be a slave to the system and enter every penny. The idea is to know where your dollars are going.

Then, each month, total up your spending to see how well you've kept to the budget. You may have to rethink the budget if you're constantly going over the limits in each category you've set up. This might mean increasing the limits if your income permits or changing your spending habits.

Keeping Your Spending in Line

It seems that every day you go to the supermarket, the price of lettuce or orange juice keeps going up. And when you go to the pharmacy, constant price increases in prescription drugs are even more dramatic. That's what inflation does to you: In plain terms, it causes prices to rise.

You have two simple choices: increase your income or cut your expenses. It may be possible to increase your income in several ways as you've seen in the earlier chapters in this book (including depleting your savings in a controlled way). But cutting your expenses is even more savvy than increasing spending. The reason: You have to increase your income more than you have to cut your spending.

You have to increase your income to cover not only the expenses you need to pay for but also the taxes on that income. For example, let's say you want an extra $50 a month to pay for a nice dinner out. You can *save* $50 by not spending it on other things (for example, cutting $50 out of your monthly food bill). Or you must increase your income by $69 (the money you'd have to earn to pay the $50 expense plus taxes on the $69 at a 28% income tax rate).

Once you have a budget, you have to stick to it. This is easier said than done. The following pages contain some useful ideas for cutting your expenses and paying your bills.

Money Saving Ideas

If you're watching your pennies, then every expense counts. And you'd be surprised at how fast those pennies turn into thousands of dollars. Fortunately, there is a limitless number of ways to save on your expenses. If you use your imagination, you'll certainly come up with a few of your own. To get you started, here are some ideas that may be useful for keeping your spending in line or finding extra income within your budget to splurge with. (Numerous discounts especially for seniors will help you keep your spending down; these discounts are listed in Chapter 22, "Discounts for Seniors.")

Insurance Costs

There are several ways you can cut your premiums, maybe even significantly. You can increase the deductibles on your insurance policies. You buy insurance—whether it's collision on your car or theft for your possessions—to cover the event you hope will never happen. Odds are it won't. So why pay high premiums year after year. You can *self-insure* for the amount of the deductible in case the worst happens. This simply means putting in a savings fund the amount of the deductible (the most you'd have to pay out-of-pocket if you put in a claim). In the meantime, your regular insurance costs will drop. For example, doubling the deductible on a car insurance policy from $250 to $500 can cut your premiums by as much as 15%.

Cut your car insurance costs even more by dropping collision coverage if your car is more than five years old. The cost of this coverage is steep, and the amount you'd collect in the event of an accident may be modest.

Take advantage of car insurance discount possibilities. You can get a discount for taking a defensive driving course, for having a good driving record, for regularly wearing seat belts, and for having certain types of equipment in your car (air bags or car alarms). Ask your agent what may qualify you for additional discounts off your car insurance.

Get multiple policy discounts by having your different insurance policies with the same company. Allstate carries not only my homeowner's insurance but also my car insurance and umbrella policy. Of course, it's still a good idea to shop each policy carefully. It may be that you'd pay less in total premiums by having separate policies with different insurers than having all of your policies with the same company.

Most of all, don't take insurance you don't need or that isn't cost effective. When you rent a car on vacation, you may not need the rental company's collision or other insurance coverage. It may be covered under your personal car insurance or as part of your credit card. Don't buy flight insurance if you've got enough life insurance already (as you'll see in Chapter 20, "Using Life Insurance for Protection"). Don't buy specialized medical policies to cover only cancer or other named conditions. It's better to have good comprehensive coverage.

Food

We're not machines that run on batteries. We need daily nutrition. A key way to keep your food budget under control is planning. Make a list of needed items so you won't spend frivolously on impulse purchases when you're at the store. You'll also be able to take advantage of sale items, stocking up on discounted items you know you'll use.

Use coupons wisely. Nearly three-quarters of households with more than one person in it use coupons weekly. Annual coupon redemption is around eight billion. Just clip, present, and save. Even better, look for in-store discounts in weekly circulars. Most stores in my area now have plastic cards for regular shoppers that can be used in place of store coupons for maximum savings (you can't overlook a coupon if you buy the right stuff).

There may also be offers to get rebates (send in a certain label, cash register receipt, and rebate offer coupon to get money back or discounts on future purchases). Remember: Refund/rebate money is free (you're not taxed on it).

Grow your own food. If you live in the suburbs, you don't have to be a farmer to grow enough vegetables to reduce your monthly food bill. And you'll get the added benefit of exercise and a sense of accomplishment. Of course, you must have a green thumb. I estimate that one year it cost me about $8 in garden supplies for each tomato I harvested (it would have been cheaper to buy the most expensive organic tomatoes at the market).

Buy generic brands, like A&P's America's Choice. Some store brands are superb (like A&P's coffee); others are at least on a par with name brands. Of course, you can't use national brand coupons for generic purchases, so there's some trade-off.

Supermarkets aren't the only place to buy food. Shop at stores that offer you the best value. These might include buyers clubs (like Sam's and B.J.'s), farmer's markets, food outlets (for example, Pepperidge Farm's Thrift Shops offer discounts up to 50% off day-old bread) and food co-ops.

> **Cash Crash**
> Don't buy in such bulk that you'll wind up wasting what you bought. Canned goods do go bad after a while.

> **Golden Years Ideas**
> Look for stores that offer senior discounts of as much as 5% or 10% of your bill. Some stores have a *senior day* (for example, 10% off every Wednesday for seniors).

Credit Card Smarts

It's possible to make money by spending money! Certain companies offer credit cards that give you money back, based on the amount of your purchases. Of course, don't make purchases just to get the money back (you won't come out ahead in the long run). But if you'd have to make the purchases anyway, then using these special credit cards can certainly pay off.

> **Senior Info**
>
> Cash back credit cards that may be useful to you:
>
> Discover (800-DISCOVER)—1% back on annual purchases (though not every purchase counts); Gateway Mastercard (800-847-7378)—1% credit toward the purchase of Gateway computer equipment; Shell Mastercard (800-993-8111)—10% discount on Shell gas purchases.

Save more money with credit cards by only having those with no annual fees. If you have just two cards that each has annual fees of $20, you'd save $40 each year. In just five years, you'd have $200 more in your pocket.

Don't charge more than you can afford to pay off each month. Once you get into paying credit card finance charges, you're really sunk. Those charges can be as much as $1^1/_2$% each month (18% annually). It may even make sense to dip into your savings to pay off the bill instead of paying that interest charge. After all, what savings account do you know of that pays 18%? So by paying off your debt, you're really making money. Then, you can then pay yourself back in installments to rebuild your savings.

Entertainment

Being on a budget doesn't mean you can't eat out once in a while, go to the movies, or otherwise enjoy yourself. You just have to do it in a money-smart way. You can take advantage of discount opportunities. Many restaurants run early bird specials that retirees have gotten a notorious reputation for taking advantage of. There's good reason. Only those who aren't on a job until 5 p.m. or later can take advantage of the 4–6 p.m. offer at restaurants to buy full-course meals at reduced prices.

Some restaurants offer special menus for seniors (limited choices, or smaller portions, at reduced prices). You can also spend your entertainment dollars most effectively if you use discount books. Many areas have regional guides that offer restaurant discounts and other entertainment savings. Discounts might be two-for-one entrée offers, a percentage off the total bill, or other savings plans. The cost of the guide in my area is $35 for the year. You can usually make back the cost with one or two meals. The discount guides are usually sold by PTAs and other local groups as fund-raisers, or they're on sale at your local pharmacies or other stores.

Strategies to Help With Monthly Spending

If you're finding it hard to pay your bills because some months they're large and outstrip your income (even though other months they're small and well within your income), take heart. There are various ways you can pay your bills at a more even rate so that you don't run short in any one month.

You can become your own banker, socking away a little each month to cover the spikes in your monthly bills. For example, say your telephone bills average $75 a month. You might want to put $5 or $10 dollars aside each month so that if one month your bill runs $100, you'll have the extra $25 on hand.

Here are some types of expenses that can put on a monthly basis so that making payments is easier:

➤ Car insurance. Instead of paying your bill all at once, take advantage of the insurance company's offer to pay your bill over several months. For example, on my six-month policy, I can pay all at once, or in up to four equal installments. There's a modest charge (usually just a dollar or so per payment) to pay the bill in installments.

➤ Other insurance. Like car insurance, you may be able to pay other types of insurance, such as your homeowner's policy or an umbrella policy, in monthly installments. Ask your insurance agent whether you can arrange for monthly payments and what it will cost you in service charges to do so.

➤ Electric bill. Generally, you're billed each month for your actual use. However, most utility companies can put you on a payment plan. They take your estimated annual bill and divide it by 12 to find your monthly obligation. At the end of the year, they compare the estimate to your actual usage and bill you for the difference. Of course, this strategy can backfire if the estimation is based on low usage and, for some reason (an extremely hot summer that boosts your air conditioning usage), your actual usage is much greater.

Hanging Up on Telemarketing Frauds and Other Scams

When the phone rings, it may be your granddaughter inviting you to her dance recital. It may be your neighbor asking about whether rumors of the town widening the road in front of your house are true. Or it just could be a telemarketing scam or a phony telegram trying to part you from your money. A loss to your savings due to fraud can put a big dent not only in your pride, but also in your income.

According to Congress, there are about 140,000 telemarketing companies operating today. Of these, it's estimated that 10% (or 14,000) are fraudulent. And 80% of telemarketers investigated by the FBI geared their sales pitch to older Americans. The Justice Department says that every year, one in six Americans is a victim of consumer fraud and nearly $40 billion is lost in telemarketing scams.

Telemarketers aren't the only ones preying on seniors. You may receive mail solicitations promising you bargains, prizes, and great discounts on such services as home repairs.

Of course, not every telemarketer or other sales promoter is illegitimate. Many have worthwhile products or services to sell. The trick is to tell the difference between the good and bad ones and keep your money safe.

Spotting the Scam Before It Gets You

Before you turn over your life's savings, as some elderly people unfortunately have done, learn to recognize when you're being preyed upon. Here are some of the offers you might be enticed by phone or junk mail to put your money into:

➤ Contests. The caller or letter says you've won a trip or other prizes, even though you never entered any contest. The catch: You have to pay money to find out what you won and cover handling charges. It's illegal to require any payment to enter a contest. It's not illegal to charge you prize collection costs, but the costs can be so high that the value of what you won isn't worth those costs. If, indeed, you've already won something, you have to be told exactly what it is and what it would cost you to collect. You can then make the decision whether it's worth proceeding.

➤ Charities. You're asked to donate money to a fake charity. One of the most popular of these scams is an organization that claims to benefit children of police or fire fighters. While there are legitimate charities doing this type of work, there are many others that only claim to do it so that they can line their pockets with your generous gifts.

➤ Home repairs. You've been selected as a showcase for your neighborhood. You're to receive vinyl siding or a new roof at a "bargain" price just for letting the company feature your home in its neighborhood sales effort. While this approach is sometimes legitimate, you may, in fact, be paying *more* than the going rate for the home repairs you receive or be convinced to make unnecessary repairs.

➤ Help. If you've already been scammed, you may be preyed on again. You may be offered help in collecting what you've already lost if you'll just pay a fee for this service. Before you know it, you've lost twice: the initial loss and the fee that doesn't bring any action.

You can also spot a fraud by the sales pitch used to entice you. You'll hear phrases like "you must act right now" or "you alone have been selected." These are tip-offs that something isn't right. Stay cool and don't be pressured into anything. Remember that the old adage that you don't get something for nothing became an adage because it's true.

Dealing With Suspected Fraud

You can protect yourself from losing money in unscrupulous transactions if you know what questions to ask. Here's the information you want:

Golden Years Ideas

If you've been a victim of fraud, or have successfully dodged a scam, report it to the National Fraud Information Center (NFIC) so that others don't become victims.

➤ The telemarketing company's name and address

➤ A clear explanation of the offer and refund policy

➤ Materials sent to you *before* you agree to anything

Under no circumstances should you *ever* give out your credit card number or authorize any bank withdrawals from your account unless you've made the phone call to ask for the goods or services. The same caution applies to sending in money without first getting the information and materials you requested.

If you're going to take a loan to make home repairs, understand that Truth in Lending law requires you to get full disclosure on the interest rates you'll pay and gives you a three-day window to rescind the transaction.

If you suspect there's something fishy, you can check whether the company has already been reported. This information will be with the Better Business Bureau in your area, your state's Attorney General's office, or the National Fraud Information Center (800-876-7060).

The Least You Need to Know

➤ Making a budget will protect your retirement savings.

➤ A budget should include monthly contributions to an emergency fund.

➤ Using an account book or software program can help you track your monthly expenses and avoid going over budget.

➤ Reducing your expenses through various savings mechanisms can help you stick to your budget.

➤ Converting an annual expense into a monthly payment, such as with car insurance, can help to make monthly payments easier.

➤ Avoiding telemarketing and mail scams is easy if you know the right questions to ask and you aren't pressured into quick answers.

Chapter 19

Planning for Long-Term Health Care Needs

In This Chapter

➤ Facing the need for long-term care planning

➤ Buying long-term care insurance

➤ Moving to a continuing care facility

➤ Planning for Medicaid eligibility

➤ Making medical decisions in advance

Ask any retiree what the one thing is he or she fears most, and you'll probably hear that it's having to go into a nursing home and spending every last penny of savings in the blink of an eye. This fear isn't totally misplaced. If you're over 65, you have about a 40% chance that you'll spend some time during your life in a nursing home. And the cost of nursing home care can run on average $40,000 annually, with the bill topping $100,000 per year in certain parts of the country. (Long-term care in your own home doesn't cost much less than nursing home care.) But the truth is that most nursing home residents are very old—over 85. So unless you're already in this age category, you probably have many years before you need to worry in earnest. This also means you have plenty of years in which to plan so you won't have to worry.

In this chapter, you'll learn about insurance to cover you if you go into a nursing home or require round-the-clock nursing care in your home. This insurance is called long-term care insurance. You'll also find out about a housing arrangement that eliminates the need for long-term care insurance; it's provided as part of the housing package. You'll learn a little about Medicaid and other government programs that many people rely on to pay their nursing home bills. Finally, you'll learn about some steps you can take now to see that your medical care in the future meets your personal objectives.

Why You'd Better Plan for Long-Term Care

Just because you've got Medicare coverage and carry a supplemental Medicare policy doesn't mean you're protected if you suffer a stroke or some other debilitating condition that requires a certain level of care. (This care is called *custodial care* and is different from a doctor's care or skilled nursing care.) Medicare covers the costs (doctor's care and skilled nursing care) associated with acute diseases, like heart attacks and cancer. Medicare isn't meant to cover the long-term care required for chronic conditions and diseases like Alzheimer's disease or just plain growing old. This long-term care includes assistance with daily living activities, like bathing, getting in and out of bed, and preparing meals. And because Medicare doesn't cover this level of care, your Medigap policy won't cover it either (Medigap only *supplements* Medicare). You'll have to figure out some other way to pay for the costs of nursing home care.

Now, if you're very well heeled, you don't have to worry about how you'll pay for long-term care. You'll just pay for it out of your income. But most retirees don't have such a high level of income and using up their assets to pay for this care will wipe out their life's savings in no time. Fortunately, you have several alternatives for paying the high cost of long-term care if your income and assets just aren't enough:

Golden Years Ideas

You can find an elder law attorney (someone who specializes in issues like Medicaid, estate planning, and other legal aspects of growing older) in your area by calling the National Academy of Elder Attorneys for a referral (520-881-4005). The Academy also awards a Certified Elder Law Attorney designation to those who've passed an exam and established a certain level of expertise in the field.

➤ Buy a long-term care insurance policy.

➤ Use your life insurance while you're alive to pay for long-term care under certain circumstances (this alternative is discussed in Chapter 20, "Using Life Insurance for Protection").

➤ Move to a continuing care facility before the need for nursing home care arises.

➤ Plan your assets so you'll qualify for government benefits under Medicaid.

Long-term care planning is a complex matter. Your choice of which methods to use in paying for long-term care, should you need it, depends on a variety of factors. These factors can include your overall financial picture, how quickly you start to plan, and how suddenly your need for long-term care arises. You may want to talk to an expert, such as an elder law attorney.

Insuring for Nursing Home (or In-Home) Care

You insure your car against the possibility of an accident you may never have. You insure your home against the hurricane damage you may never have. So why not also insure yourself for the possibility that you may someday need nursing home care?

You can buy a special type of insurance to cover this contingency. It's called a long-term care policy (or sometimes a nursing home policy). These policies are relatively new (they've been around for only a little over 10 years). But interest in them has jumped dramatically as retirees become aware of their potential financial exposure should they need to go into a nursing home.

The policy generally pays a dollar amount per day if you require the kind of care covered by the policy. This might be $100 a day or $150 a day (whatever coverage you select). Policies that cover both nursing home and in-home care may only pay the top benefit for nursing home care; the benefit for in-home care may be limited to 50% of that benefit. So, for example, if the policies has a $150 per day benefit, this means it will pay $150 per day for a nursing home stay and $75 per day for in-home care. Some policies pay the actual cost of care, up to the per day dollar limit. Some insurers are now treating the benefit as a "pot of money" that can be applied to later care days if less than the daily limit is expended on a particular care day.

The premium for the policy is fixed according to your age when you take it out: The younger you are, the lower the premium (which stays the same for as long as you have the policy).

Senior Info

One study showed that most retirees can't afford the high cost of long-term care insurance (84% of those between 65 and 79 couldn't afford even the most basic of policies). For example, a 67-year-old in Oregon can buy a policy costing as little as $350 a year (depending on the insurance company) for a $60 per day benefit with no inflation protection. That same person can pay more than of $3,000 a year for a $100 per day benefit with inflation protection. Of course, tax deductions may make the premiums more affordable for some people.

Before you opt for long-term care insurance, be sure to consider your other options. It's worth mentioning that people who buy long-term care insurance generally are wealthier than most. For example, about 42% of those buying this coverage have liquid assets (stocks, bonds, and bank accounts) over $100,000. These are people with money they want to protect for their children; they don't want to use up every last penny on a nursing home. Long-term care insurance, then, is designed to protect those assets by paying all or most of the nursing home costs.

Choosing a Policy

Let's say you like the idea of buying a long-term care policy. There's a lot to consider. Many major insurers offer this kind of coverage, but choosing one isn't easy. Unlike supplemental Medicare policies, long-term care policies aren't entirely standardized, so it's hard to compare apples to apples. In 1996, Congress created certain consumer protection requirements for long-term care policies (although many states had already put such protections or even greater protections in place). If policies contain these requirements, then policy holders may be able to deduct their premiums and benefits can be received tax free (within limits).

One important requirement is *renewability*. Like Medigap policies, long-term care policies must be automatically renewable. This means that if you want to continue coverage and you pay the premium, you can't be dropped. Another requirement is a ban on *post-claims underwriting*. This means that if a company sells you a policy and you have a condition that it was aware of, the company can't later refuse to cover that condition after you've passed the period fixed in the policy for noncoverage of pre-existing conditions.

Despite some standardization, there's still a wide variety among policies. Here are some of the features that a good policy should contain:

➤ Benefit amount. You select what you'd want to receive each day you were in a nursing home: $100 (that's only $36,500 a year, below the national average for nursing home costs); $150 (that's $54,750, just about the national average); or more. You'll see this amount also called the *indemnity amount* in the policy.

A policy that covers both nursing home and in-home care generally doesn't pay the same for both types of coverage; in-home coverage is usually less. Make sure that the benefit amount for in-home care is at least 50% of the daily nursing home benefit. Even better, look for a policy that pays the *same* benefit for in-home care or add a rider to the policy providing for this benefit level. In view of the high cost of round-the-clock in-home care, it may not cost any less than a nursing home stay.

Golden Years Ideas
The amount of coverage you should take depends on where you live (nursing home costs may only run $80 a day in your area). Also, you might want to take a minimum amount, say $100 per day, if you think you can swing the rest of the costs out of your savings.

Because the policy pays off in dollars and it may be many years before you need them, you might want an "inflation rider." Policies *must* offer this option; you're not required to take it. An inflation rider will adjust the dollars you actually get to reflect increases in inflation since you first bought the policy. For younger retirees, this feature is very important because medical costs increase each year (usually more than the general rate of inflation), and it may be many years before coverage is used. For those 75 and older, it may not be worth the added cost to take an inflation rider. After all, inflation protection can increase the premium by 30% to 50%.

➤ Length of coverage. No one can know how long they'll be in a nursing home, if at all. The average stay runs about 30 months (about 2¹/₂ years). You can buy coverage that will run for your lifetime or only for a limited number of years. Lifetime coverage, the most expensive kind, is a good idea for those who have a lot of personal savings and can afford the premiums. If you can't afford this deluxe coverage, then consider coverage for at least three years. This will protect you for more than the average stay and also will give you enough time to plan for Medicaid, as you'll see later in this chapter.

➤ Elimination period. Like a deductible, you generally have to cover a certain amount of care before the insurance company takes over. You can fix the length of time you'll pay out of pocket. Once this time is up, the policy kicks in. So, for example, you might take a 30-day, 60-day, 90-day, or longer elimination period. The longer the period, the smaller your premiums. But you don't get something for nothing: The longer the period, the greater your financial exposure. You can buy a first-day policy that has no elimination period, but the premiums are, of course, higher.

➤ Care that's covered. Some people need the type of care they can only get in a nursing home; others may be helped in their own homes. Make sure the policy you buy has the type of coverage you want (in-home care, nursing home care, or both). Some policies are now covering things like specialized housing, respite care, and adult day care.

Cash Crash
Some people have chronic conditions that just deteriorate over time, without ever having to go into a hospital for doctor's or skilled nursing care. Today's policies don't require any prior hospitalization or prior skilled nursing care before coverage begins. But people holding policies that are more than 10 years old may still have this feature.

Word to the Wise
Activities of daily living (ADLs) include eating, dressing, toileting, transferring (getting in and out of bed), bathing, and continence. Needing assistance with some of these activities may be all that's needed to start collecting benefits even though there's no specific condition other than old age.

Also read the fine print on what is needed for you to start collecting benefits. Benefits kick in when you need assistance with at least two daily living activities or there's cognitive impairment that requires you having supervision for your own or other people's safety.

If care must be *medically necessary*, who decides on this state of events? A letter from your doctor may be enough; a review by the insurance company may be required.

➤ Pre-existing conditions. If you've already been diagnosed with Alzheimer's disease or are suffering from another condition that you received treatment for within six months of the time you bought the policy, you may have to wait six months (or some other waiting period) before the policy will cover you. New York, like most states, has a maximum six-month limit on pre-existing conditions for policies sold within the state. Make sure you understand what's covered and what's not. If you don't see it spelled out in the policy, ask the agent to put it in writing.

Word to the Wise
Exclusions are conditions that won't be covered by a policy. Some policies, for example, used to exclude *organically based mental conditions* (a fancy term that covers Alzheimer's disease) but states may no longer have this particular exclusion.

➤ Insurance company. Because you're going to be with the company for a long time, you want to make sure it will be there when you need it. If you're considering any company other than a well-known insurer, like Travelers or American Express, check out the company's rating with a rating service, such as A.M. Best.

Senior Info

In California, Connecticut, Indiana, Iowa, and New York, there is a special program that combines private insurance with Medicaid coverage (the law prevents other states from now adopting this special program). While the rules differ in these states, the upshot is that you'll qualify for Medicaid regardless of your assets if you buy a special policy under this program to cover you for three years in a nursing home. You won't need to spend down your own assets to become eligible for Medicaid. The catch: You must continue to be a resident in the state, so buying the policy won't help you if you relocate to another state later on.

Now that you know what to look for in a policy, you can use the following chart to shop around before you settle on a particular insurance company (see Table 19.1). Fill in the features offered by each company in the space provided so that you can make an informed decision on which policy is best for you.

Table 19.1 What to Look for in a Policy

Feature	Policy 1	Policy 2	Policy 3
Benefit amount	_____	_____	_____
Length of coverage	_____	_____	_____
Elimination period	_____	_____	_____
Care that's covered	_____	_____	_____
Pre-existing conditions	_____	_____	_____
Insurance company	_____	_____	_____

If you already have a policy, you may also want to convert it to a newer one that has better features. What's more, the newer policies have lower premiums because the rates are based on a broader base of policy holders and more actuarial information. But if you've owned the policy for a long time, your current age may mean higher premiums (remember premiums become fixed at the age you take out the policy).

Golden Years Ideas

Check out the tax rules in your state on deducting the cost of long-term care insurance. Some states, like New York, allow a deduction against state income taxes in the same amount as under federal law.

Deducting Your Costs

Depending on how old you are when you take out the policy, you could pay several hundred or several thousand dollars a year, year in and year out, and maybe never have to put in a claim. This could add up to a pretty penny over time. Fortunately, you can ease the pain of paying, somewhat, by deducting your costs on your federal income tax return.

The deduction you can take on your federal income tax return depends on your age for the year of the return. Table 19.2 shows the limits for 1998 (they're adjusted each year for inflation).

Table 19.2 Limit on Deduction for Long-Term Care Premiums

Your Age on December 31	Your Dollar Limit
40 or less	$210
More than 40 but not more than 50	$380
More than 50 but not more than 60	$770
More than 60 but not more than 70	$2,050
More than 70	$2,520

Source: Internal Revenue Service

Golden Years Ideas

While insurance is available to those who are middle-aged and the premiums are dirt cheap at that time, most financial people suggest that you don't buy a long-term care policy before you're about 65. You'll pay a higher premium than you would if you'd taken out the policy at 50, but you'll pay those premiums for many years less.

You can't simply deduct the dollar limit for your age. Instead, the dollar amount you're allowed to take is treated just like any other medical expense. Your total medical expenses are deductible only to the extent they're more than 7.5% of your adjusted gross income and you itemize your deductions (instead of taking the standard deduction). So if you take the standard deduction, you won't get any tax benefit for paying long-term care insurance premiums. However, if you've started a postretirement business and are self-employed or you've set up an S corporation, you may be able to deduct your costs directly from your income (even if you take the standard deduction). Each year, medical insurance of self-employed people and shareholders who own more than 2% of their S corporations can deduct a percentage of the cost as an adjustment to gross income (in the same way that IRA deductions are taken). The percentage limit is set to increase as in Table 19.3.

Table 19.3 Percentage of Medical Insurance Deductible—From Gross Income by Self-Employed People

Year	Percentage
1998 and 1999	45%
2000 and 2001	50%
2002	60%
2003 through 2005	80%
2006	90%
2007 and later	100%

Source: Internal Revenue Code

Choosing a Living Arrangement for the Long Term

Maybe you (or a loved one) have reached the stage where living independently is no longer possible. You can't move the vacuum cleaner or get to the supermarket alone. Nursing home care isn't really necessary yet, but extensive assistance is required. There's a growing alternative housing arrangement that provides this level of care: It's called a *continuing care facility* (sometimes called a *lifetime care facility* or a *continuing care retirement community*). (This was also explained in Chapter 11, "Turn Your Home Into Retirement Income.")

A continuing care facility is a place where you get your own room or apartment that's furnished with your belongings, group meals, cleaning services, some recreation, and, most importantly, medical services and the promise of long-term care. Someone I know in Florida moved into just such a place. One side of the building houses those seniors who still have a certain measure of independence. When their health or abilities fail, they move to the other side of the place where nursing home care is provided. Overall, the place is more upbeat and less hospital-like than a nursing home.

Continuing care facilities are springing up everywhere as the demand for this type of arrangement mushrooms. Some facilities are run by nonprofit organizations, but the vast majority are businesses that run them to make a profit.

If you move to a continuing care facility, you don't have to carry long-term care insurance. Your entry into the facility assures you that you'll receive nursing home care if and when you need it.

The cost of staying in a continuing care facility isn't cheap. First, there may or may not be a one-time entrance fee. This could run as much as $50,000 or more.

Whether or not there's an entrance fee, there's a monthly maintenance fee: a single fee that covers the rent on your unit, meals, and all other services.

Cash Crash
The entrance fee may be partially or fully refundable if you die or decide to move within a certain period of time. Understand that if the fee *is* partially or fully refundable, the federal tax law creates a legal fiction that you've loaned money to the facility and you'll have to pick up interest on you're your phantom loan (the interest that could have been earned on the money). However, if the facility is qualified, then there's no imputed interest on a certain amount that adjusts annually for inflation ($134,800 in 1998).

Understanding When Uncle Sam Will Pay for Nursing Home Bills

The way things stand now in this country, people who are poor (or become so by spending down their assets on long-term care) can get just about the same nursing home care as the rich. The difference is that the rich pay out of pocket; the bill for others is paid by the taxpayers.

There are two types of programs that poorer individuals can rely on to cover their long-term care needs: Medicaid (Medi-Cal in California) and Veteran's benefits.

Medicaid

Medicare, Medicaid, they're all the same, right? No, they're not! Medicare is a federal program you're entitled to because you've worked a certain number of years and paid into the system. You collect regardless of your income or your assets. In contrast, Medicaid is a need-based joint federal/state program. You're only entitled to benefits if you're poor (as the program defines it).

Some people become eligible for Medicaid coverage because they've spent most of their money; others try to impoverish themselves by giving their assets away to their family so they'll become eligible. Before this goes any further, understand that the rules are very complex and are changing all the time. To make matters worse, it's a crime for someone (like a lawyer) to counsel an individual on how to beat Medicaid, so it may be hard to find guidance. With that said, here are the rules as they now stand. You make the decisions on what you're going to do about them.

You qualify for Medicaid coverage if you're over 65 (or disabled or blind) and your income and assets are below certain levels. These vary from state to state. Some states are more generous than others in extending Medicaid coverage to their residents.

Medicaid is supposed to be for poor people. So, limits are imposed on the extent to which people (and their spouses) can give away their assets and still claim Medicaid benefits within 36 months of going into a nursing home (60 months in the case of transfers to a trust). This is called the *look-back period.* Transfers to spouses or to someone else for the benefit of a spouse or minor or disabled child don't count. Transfers before the look-back period, regardless of amount, don't count.

You may lose coverage entirely or just have to wait a certain number of months before Medicaid will take over for you. If there have been transfers within the look-back period, then you have to figure a "penalty period." This is the number of months during which Medicaid benefits won't be provided. The number of months depends on the size of the transfers, divided by the amount that the state considers to represent the cost of paying privately for nursing home care. For example, if there's been a $50,000 transfer within the look-back period and the state says the cost of paying privately is $5,000 a month, then the penalty period is 10 months following the transfer.

If you have more assets than the law allows for Medicaid coverage, you're not out of luck. You can always spend down (use up) your assets until you reach the eligibility level (using up your assets for medical isn't a transfer giving rise to a penalty period). But in some states, if your income is above certain limits (regardless of your assets), there may be little you can do to qualify for Medicaid. You can't just spend what you have to qualify. After all, you can't simply refuse to accept Social Security benefits, pensions, or interest income you're entitled to. You're just out of luck. These states are called *income cap states*, and there are 20 of them at present. However, in so-called medically needy states, Medicaid will pay for your care, regardless of your income, if you spend down the excess on your care.

Special rules apply for married couples to protect the healthy spouse (called the *community spouse* because he or she stays within the community) when the other spouse goes into a nursing home.

To learn more about Medicaid rules in your state you can talk with an elder law attorney.

Veteran's Benefits

Medicaid isn't the only government program that can be used to pay for long-term care. If you're a veteran, you may be eligible for care in a nursing home at a Veteran's Administration

(VA) facility. Today, there are more than a million and a half veterans over the age of 75 (of a total of about seven million over the age of 65). Most of these veterans are men.

As long as you're a veteran and at least 65 years old, you're entitled to treatment in a VA nursing home whether or not your condition is service related. But who *pays* for the treatment is another question.

Treatment is *free* if you qualify. There are two key ways of qualifying: having a service-related condition or having a non-service-related disability and being unable to pay for required care. If you have a non–service-related condition, you're considered unable to pay (and eligible for free care) if you meet *any* of the following tests:

➤ You're eligible for Medicaid.

➤ You receive a VA pension.

➤ You're single, and your income in 1997 was $21,001 (this number increases each year along with inflation). If you have a dependent, the income cap in 1997 was $25,204 (plus $1,404 for every additional dependent).

Even if your income is too high (by just a little) for automatic eligibility, you may still be able to get free care if there are facilities available. Ask at your local VA office. Also ask at your town or city hall because many localities also can advise on veteran's programs.

To find out about VA benefits, call your local VA office.

> **Golden Years Ideas**
> Where the level of care needed is less than that given in a nursing home, a veteran who is needy may be able to go into a domicilary. There are also community residential care facilities for veterans who don't need hospitalization or nursing home care but can no longer live independently.

Living Wills and Other Advance Medical Directives

You have the right as a competent adult to decide on the type of care you want and don't want. We're not talking assisted suicide here. We're talking about withholding life supports and other extraordinary means to sustain life when there may be no reasonable hope of recovery or other criteria are met. You can make an advance medical directive to say what you want and don't want. You can also appoint someone—your spouse, your child, your friend—to speak on your behalf if you can't speak for yourself.

Why take this step and make an advance medical directive? If you don't, your loved ones may be forced to incur unbelievable anguish and enormous expense watching you languish in a near-death state for days or possibly even years.

The highest court in the land has recognized that you have a constitutional right to state in unequivocal terms that you do or do not want to be kept alive on life support systems in certain situations. Almost every state has enacted living will statutes.

Even in states without statutes, living wills are recognized as an expression of your rights regarding your own treatment. You may also be able to have notations made on your medical records that you don't want CPR performed on you (this is called a do-not-resuscitate order or DNR).

> **Word to the Wise**
>
> A *living will* is a written document in which you state your wishes on the use of life support systems and other measures in the event you're in a medical state where there's no hope of recovery and you can't speak for yourself.

Most states also allow you to name someone to make medical decisions on your behalf if you can't speak for yourself. Say you're in a coma and can't consent to some drastic procedure designed to try to save your life. Someone you've named—hopefully someone who's fully aware of your wishes—can speak for you. The document you use to name someone is called different things in different states: medical durable power of attorney, health care proxy, or some other similar term. It allows the person you designate to consent to any medical treatment if you're unconscious, medically incapacitated or otherwise unable to consent to treatment personally.

Make sure you've discussed your wishes with the person you name. If you don't want to be kept alive by means of artificial nutrition and hydration (tubes through which food and water are passed), make this very clear to your stand-in. If you don't communicate your desires, it will be hard (legally and emotionally) for your stand-in to act should the need ever arise. Make sure that if a separate part of the form and a separate signature are required for the power to terminate nutrition and hydration that the t's have been crossed and the i's dotted.

You can have an attorney draw up the documents that meet your state's requirements. The cost is usually minimal (some attorneys draw them up for free when they're doing a will or a trust). These documents can be tailored to your wishes. For example, Jehovah's Witness has tailored a living will to make sure that the signer isn't given a blood transfusion in violation of his or her religious beliefs. You can also use preprinted forms available free of charge from Choice in Dying, Inc. (800-989-WILL). And, whenever you're admitted to a health care facility that gets Medicare funding, the facility is required to discuss advance medical directives with you and should be able provide blank forms for you to sign on the spot.

Signing on the dotted line isn't the end of your work on advance medical directives. See that copies of the forms are given to your family and get put in your medical records.

The Least You Need to Know

➤ Odds are about 40% that you'll spend some time in your life in a nursing home, so planning for this contingency is important.

➤ Medicare and Medigap policies generally don't cover the costs of nursing home care.

➤ Long-term care insurance can be used to pay a set dollar amount for nursing home or in-home care for chronic conditions or just old age.

➤ You may be able to deduct a portion of long-term care insurance premiums from your federal income tax return.

➤ Moving into a continuing care facility means you don't need long-term care insurance because this level of care comes with the package.

➤ Medicaid will pay for nursing home care only if your income and assets are below set amounts (though in medically needy states, Medicaid will pay, regardless of income, if you spend down the excess).

➤ Veterans may be able to get free care in VA facilities.

➤ You can sign a document—a living will or a health care proxy—now that will affect medical decisions for you in the future.

Chapter 20

Using Life Insurance for Protection

In This Chapter

➤ Understanding your life insurance options

➤ Reducing your life insurance coverage as your needs diminish

➤ Taking on more coverage to protect your family

➤ Using life insurance while you're still alive

➤ Finding the best policy for you

You may think of life insurance as something used by a young breadwinner to protect his or her family in case of an early death. Well, just because you've passed this phase doesn't mean you don't still need life insurance. You may need it to protect your spouse. You may want it to help your heirs pay estate taxes. Whatever your reasons, you're never too old for life insurance.

In this chapter, you'll learn what life insurance options you have and how life insurance can help your family avoid catastrophe when you die. You'll also learn about some interesting ways you can use life insurance—for you during your life and for your family after your death—that you might not have thought about. And you'll find out about getting insurance, even if you're over 65.

Life Insurance Primer

Before you start to decide how much life insurance you need, it's important to know what it's all about. Life insurance is a contract you make with an insurance company to pay your beneficiary a fixed amount when you die. There are different types of life insurance policies:

➤ Term insurance. This policy provides only a death benefit, proceeds that will be paid to your beneficiary. (The death benefit is also called an *insurance* element.) There is no investment element involved, so no matter how long you pay the premiums, you never build up any cash surrender value.

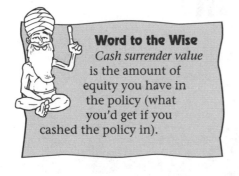

Word to the Wise

Cash surrender value is the amount of equity you have in the policy (what you'd get if you cashed the policy in).

With term insurance, premiums go up as you age (although you can get a policy where the premiums are fixed for a certain number of years: three, five, ten, or more years). Level term insurance provides fixed premiums for a set period (with premium increases at each renewal). Decreasing term insurance provides constant premiums with ever-decreasing coverage. Decreasing term insurance typically is used for a specific use (such as to cover the outstanding balance of the mortgage if your family is relying on you to pay for it).

➤ Whole life policy. This type of life insurance combines a death benefit with an investment element. The longer you have the policy, the more you build up your cash surrender value. Whole life is also called *permanent* insurance because it becomes, in effect, an asset you can benefit from during your life (as you'll see later in this chapter in "Using Life Insurance While You're Alive") as well as providing money to your heirs.

➤ Universal life (UL) policy. This is a type of whole life policy in which you're allowed to adjust the premiums after the first year. You can reduce or increase them (as long as there is enough money in the policy to maintain the insurance element). Like a whole life policy, there is a cash surrender value to a UL policy. But the main feature of the UL policy is that it functions like a savings account, earning market rate interest (after paying the insurance element and fees). This interest is not taxed.

➤ Endowment policy. This is a type of life insurance that's more like a savings plan. You pay into the policy for a set number of years, with insurance running only for that period of time. At the end of the savings period, the insurance ends, and you can take the face value of the policy in a lump sum or annuitize it to get monthly payments. Endowment policies aren't bought primarily for their insurance element (especially because it's only for a limited time), but will provide that benefit if you die before you've completed the pay-in period.

Senior Info

Because the premiums are based on life expectancy, here's one place where it pays to be sexist. Women pay lower premiums for the same coverage at the same age because they have longer life expectancies.

Shopping for Life Insurance

Like buying anything else, it's important to comparison shop before you put your money down. There's a big variation between companies and the fees they charge for the same amount of insurance.

The best way to shop is to decide *what* you want. Here are some features to look for in a policy:

➤ Conversion option. If you buy term insurance, make sure you're able to convert the policy to whole life *without* a medical exam. This way, you can lock into the fixed premiums of whole life when you want to. For example, say you took out a $500,000 term policy to protect your family until your children were out of college and on their own. Now that happy day has arrived. You don't need so much insurance, so you convert that policy to a $100,000 whole life and don't have to worry about premium increases any more.

➤ Inflation adjustment. If you're still young so that actuarially speaking you're not expected to die for many years, you may want to see that the money you've esti- mated as your insurance needs will, in fact, have the same buying power. The way to do this is with an inflation adjustment. You pay for this added benefit, but the face of your policy increases each year.

➤ Disability rider. If you're still working, this feature will take over premium payments if you become disabled and can't work. Again, you'll pay extra for this feature, and it may be more important to a younger person.

You can buy life insurance from a life insurance agent. An agent represents a particular company (New York Life, Metropolitan Life). But an insurance broker can write coverage from a number of different companies. You may also be able to buy insurance directly from the company (for example, through the Internet).

You can get an idea of what term insurance will cost you at your age by asking an agent, broker, or the company itself to price a policy. You can also get an idea for coverage between $2,500 and $25 million from Quotesmith (800-431-1147). You can even get a quote from them on-line at http://www.quotesmith.com. Another source for insurance quotes by phone is the Wholesale Insurance Network (800-808-5810). For older people buying life insurance, it's not necessarily the initial quote that you'll wind up paying. The quote is usually for someone in perfect health. As we age, most people have some condition or another—high cholesterol, high blood pressure, a prior bout with cancer—that can raise the cost of insurance. This is called *rating*, and it can increase the premiums significantly. Find out what the insurance will cost *you* given your health history.

Before buying a policy, check on the rating of the insurance company. There are several independent rating services you can check out: A.M. Best Company, Standard & Poor's Corp., Moody's Investors Service, Duff & Phelps Credit Rating Co., and Weiss Research. You may be able to find this information at your local library.

Paying for Life Insurance

When you buy a house, you know that after paying the mortgage for 25 or 30 years, you've paid it off and you're done making mortgage payments. Not so with life insurance. As a general rule, you pay the premiums for as long as you live. But there are exceptions to the general rule.

You may be able to buy certain insurance that only requires a limited number of payments. For example, the old government life insurance for veterans that my father bought after World War II was a 20-year paid-up policy; after 20 years, you were finished making payments.

Golden Years Ideas
Instead of writing a check monthly, quarterly, semi-annually, or annually for your premiums, you can arrange to have the money debited from your checking account. All you do is sign an authorization letter, which the insurance company can provide you, telling the bank to take the money from your account on a certain date. This will prevent your policy from lapsing for nonpayment if the premium notice gets lost in the mail or you're away on a long vacation when it arrives.

Today, depending on the type of policy you have, you can arrange to have a paid-up plan. This is also called a *vanishing premium.* You pay premiums long enough to build up enough cash value in the policy that can be used to continue paying the insurance element for as long as you live. The premium payment depends on the performance of the policy. I have one that projected an 8-year period, but with the low interest rates, it's more like 12 years before the policy becomes self-sustaining. And even after you're in a position to stop paying premiums, you may have to ante up again if the policy doesn't make enough to continue carrying the death benefit.

It's critical that you *not* overlook or delay premium payments. If you do, your policy could lapse. Most companies give you a 30-day grace period (if your premium is late by say 10 days, you're still insured). They will notify you (or someone you designate to receive such notice) that the premium is late. However, once the grace period passes and policy lapses, it's not a simple matter to reinstate it; you basically have to start from scratch.

Reviewing Your Insurance Needs

Now that you know how to go about getting insurance, let's see what you need. While you were raising a family, you probably took on life insurance to protect your family by providing a fund to replace the wages you'd never be able to earn if you died early. Many people, maybe you, too, never look at their coverage once they've put it in place. They simply pay the premiums forever. At your stage in life, this could be a big mistake. If you're *over* insured, you're missing the chance to earn more on your money. If you're *under* insured, you're exposing your family to potential disaster.

It's important to look again at why you're carrying life insurance and whether the kind and amount you have are right.

➤ Replacing income. Proceeds from life insurance (and the income that can be earned on them) can be used to provide income for your family. If you're still working and dependent on your earnings, your spouse may need the insurance proceeds to replace your lost wages when you die.

➤ Financing estate costs. Whether or not you're working, you may have sizable assets that will cause your estate to owe taxes—federal and possibly state estate taxes (see Table 20.1). There's no federal estate tax if the size of your estate (other than property passing to your spouse or to charity) is under the exemption amount in effect for the year you die.

Cash Crash

If you own your life insurance when you die, are treated as owning it (because you possess "incidents of ownership" like the right to borrow against the policy or change beneficiaries), or have gifted the policy within three years of your death, it's an asset in your estate and adds to your estate tax costs. You can *remove* this asset by giving it away to your children directly or through a trust and living at least three years after the gift. Better still, have the trust take out the policy so that it's immediately out of your estate.

Table 20.1 Estate That Can Pass Federal Estate Tax-Free

Year of Death	Applicable Exemption Amount
1998	$625,000
1999	$650,000
2000 and 2001	$675,000
2002 and 2003	$700,000
2004	$850,000
2005	$950,000
2006 and later	$1,000,000

Source: Internal Revenue Code

Of course, even if you're under the federal limit, your estate may still owe death taxes to your state.

Trusts that are used to own insurance on your life are *irrevocable* trusts (you can't change your mind once they're created). Since the trusts, and not you, own the policy, your estate doesn't include the policy. Typically, these trusts are used to own second-to-die insurance (explained later in this chapter). Using life insurance trusts in estate planning is discussed more thoroughly later in this chapter as well as in Chapter 26, "Estate Planning for the Rich and Not-So-Rich."

There may also be administrative costs (attorney's fees and selling costs) to settle your estate. Life insurance can be used to provide the necessary cash to meet this contingency.

Use the chart in Table 20.2 to map out what you need in the way of life insurance.

Table 20.2 Estimating Your Life Insurance Needs

Your Financial Needs	Amount of Insurance
Estate taxes (37% to 55% of your assets over your exemption amount)	$_____
Administrative fees (probate costs, attorney's fees—estimate 5% of your assets)	$_____
Funeral expenses (estimate between $5,000 and $15,000)	$_____
Family's living expenses (assume $100,000 in life insurance for each $8,000 of income needed)	$_____
TOTAL	$_____

Downsizing Your Insurance Coverage

After reviewing your needs, you may find that you're carrying too much insurance. You have many alternative strategies that you can now adopt to reduce your coverage and make those years of paying insurance premiums pay off for you.

➤ Cash in the policy. If you own term life insurance, cashing in the policy won't bring you any cash. It will, however, end your obligation to continue paying premiums. The money you would have used to pay the premiums can now be used for other purposes. If you own permanent life insurance (a whole life policy or a universal life policy), you can end your premium payment obligation *and* get cash. You can simply surrender the policy to the insurance company and get a check for the cash surrender value of the policy. This is the value of the policy you've built up over the years. It may be quite a lot, depending on how long you've owned the policy and how well the policy performed. The money you get is tax free (for the most part, it's really just a return of your own premiums) *except* if that amount is greater than what you paid. The excess amount is then taxable.

➤ Decrease your coverage. If you're carrying a $500,000 policy but don't need so much, just reduce the face amount to $250,000, or even $100,000 if that's all you need. Your premiums will be reduced, so you'll have more retirement income to spend on other things. You can even convert your coverage to a paid up policy (with a smaller death benefit) and eliminate entirely the need to ever make another premium payment. If you don't opt for a paid up policy and have cash value built up, you can pocket some money as well.

➤ Trade your policy for another. You can exchange your life insurance policy for an annuity contract. Doing this means you'll convert the cash surrender value of the life insurance policy into an annuity that can pay you income for life (or for the joint lives of you and your spouse).

➤ Give your policy away. If you don't need the added income that an annuity could bring, instead of just cashing it in, you can benefit you and your family by simply giving the policy away. You can donate it to charity and get a current income tax deduction. (Generally, the deduction is the amount of what you put into the policy.) A client of mine donated an old life insurance policy to his alma mater and, because of the size of the policy, was able to fund a chair in memory of his father (and get a tax deduction to boot). He continued to donate the premiums to the college each year to keep the policy in force. Or instead of giving the policy to a charity, you can give it to your children or grandchildren. They'll own an asset that they can borrow against, cash in, or simply wait to collect. By changing ownership of the policy to them, you'll remove the policy from your estate and avoid estate taxes (assuming you live at least three years after the transfer).

Golden Years Ideas
Be sure that you swap the life insurance policy for the annuity without first having the cash value paid out to you. A swap is a tax-free exchange; a payout is taxable even if you then buy the annuity.

Cash Crash
Giving the policy to your children or grandchildren can result in gift tax if the value of the policy (essentially its cash surrender value) is more than your annual gift tax exclusion (currently $10,000 for each recipient, or $20,000 if your spouse consents to your making the gift). So if you're married and give a $50,000 policy that's worth $20,000 or less to your grandchild, you won't have any gift tax to worry about. But if the value is more, you'll eat into the amount you can pass tax free when you die.

You may want to explore the option of reducing your life insurance to free up money to pay for a long-term care insurance policy. The long-term care coverage will protect you if you need this type of care and ensure that your assets remain for your family (and aren't used up on your care). You may even be able to convert an existing whole life policy into

a long-term care policy. Long-term care insurance is explained in Chapter 19, "Planning for Long-Term Health Care Needs."

Increasing Your Coverage

After your insurance analysis, you may find that you still need to keep your coverage, or even *increase* it. Maybe that business you started in retirement has really taken off, and your interest in it has boosted your projected estate taxes. Or maybe your collection of fine silver has grown so large that your heirs will need some ready cash to pay off your estate tax bill. Just because you're no spring chicken doesn't mean you can't still get new insurance.

If you're married and need more insurance to cover your estate needs, you might consider a second-to-die policy.

There are two key reasons why a second-to-die policy may fit your insurance requirements nicely. First, it pays off when needed most. As a married person, there's no estate tax on property left to your spouse. But when your spouse dies, estate tax will be due if your spouse owns more than the estate tax exemption amount in effect at that time. Second, it costs less than insuring both spouses under two separate policies. It's only one policy.

There's a third important advantage to second-to-die insurance, especially for retirees. Even if one spouse already has diabetes, a heart condition, or other health problems, the couple can probably still easily get a policy. After all, the insurance company needs only one healthy spouse to live long enough for the insurance company to come out ahead.

Using Life Insurance While You're Alive

Most people never see a penny of their life insurance. The policy generally doesn't pay off until they're dead. The money goes to the beneficiaries. But today, there are some ways that life insurance can be used to provide the insured with a lifetime benefit.

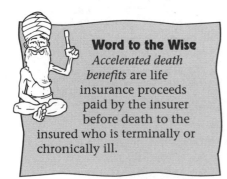

You can borrow against your life insurance for quick cash. You can get the proceeds paid out as accelerated death benefits from the insurance company or as a viatical settlement (explained below).

You can also get the proceeds paid to you under a viatical settlement. The arrangement is similar to accelerated death benefits in that you must be terminally or chronically ill. The difference is that a third party is paying you proceeds. Since the third party expects to make a profit on the arrangement, you may receive less from it than directly from the insurance company via accelerated death benefits.

Borrowing on Your Life Insurance

To borrow on your life insurance, all you need is to make a phone call to the insurer. Ask for the amount you want (up to the cash value in your policy). The check is usually in the mail to you within 24 to 48 hours.

The interest rate on the loan is usually lower than the rate your local bank is charging on a personal loan. The interest rate fluctuates from time to time, so just because it's low when you first borrow doesn't mean it will stay that way.

There are no time limits on repaying the loan. Repayment is entirely up to you. You can pay it back all at once whenever you want or in monthly amounts as you arrange. Just remember that while the loan is outstanding, interest will continue to build up.

If you die before you've paid back the loan, your beneficiaries will receive the proceeds *reduced* by the loan outstanding, including any interest remaining. This may be *less* than you estimated for their needs.

If you've taken out a loan against your life insurance policy and you decide you want to give your policy to your child, don't (at least until you've paid back the loan). A transfer of a policy subject to a loan is treated, for tax purposes, as a transfer *for value* (the new owner is taking a policy subject to a loan). So when you die and your child collects the proceeds (less the loan), your child is taxed on anything over the amount of the loan (the amount treated as the child's purchase price for the policy). So, for example, if you have a $100,000 policy with a $20,000 cash surrender value, it's not a good idea to borrow $10,000 just to bring the value of the policy to the gift-tax-free level. If you do, when your child collects the $100,000, $80,000 of the proceeds will be taxable.

Cash Crash

If you borrow against the policy and don't pay the interest (you just charge it against the policy), you might have the situation where the loan equals the policy's value. If this happens, you face a double whammy: The policy terminates *and*, even though you don't get any cash, you have taxable income to the extent that the unpaid loan exceeds the amount of premiums you put into the policy.

Word to the Wise

A *viatical settlement* is an arrangement in which a third party pays a terminally or chronically ill insured a portion of the proceeds that would otherwise be payable on death (there's a discount, based on current interest rates and expected time of death, sufficient to generate a profit for the third party). Generally, the third party assumes responsibility for paying future premiums. On the death of the insured, the third party collects the proceeds.

Accelerating Death Benefits

In most states, insurance companies are allowed to pay out some or all of the proceeds of a life insurance policy to the insured while he or she is alive. Similarly, certain companies are allowed to buy your life insurance from you in what's called a *viatical settlement*. In a viatical settlement, you're getting a discounted benefit (the company becomes the owner of your policy and has to wait until you die to collect the full proceeds from the insurer).

But these lifetime payouts can happen only under very limited circumstances. You have to be certified by a medical professional that you're either terminally ill or chronically ill. The circumstances are listed as follows:

➤ *Terminally ill* means you have an illness or condition that is reasonably expected to result in death within 24 months of certification. Certification must be made by a doctor.

➤ *Chronically ill* means you can't perform at least two activities of daily living (eating, toileting, transferring, bathing, dressing, and continence) for a period of at least 90 days due to a functional loss of capacity, or you require substantial supervision to protect you from threats to your health or safety because of severe cognitive impairment. (Regulations yet to be issued by the IRS may also expand the definition of chronically ill.) Certification must be made by a licensed health care practitioner (doctor, registered nurse, or licensed social worker) within the 12 months of taking the benefits.

Golden Years Ideas

Life insurance paid as accelerated death benefits or a *viatical settlement* started as a way for those afflicted with AIDs to find extra cash for their lifetime care. But it wasn't until 1996 when Congress agreed to allow the insured to treat the payments as tax free (the same way that beneficiaries of proceeds paid on the death of the insured are treated) that the idea really became mainstream.

If you're terminally ill, then *all* benefits you receive are tax free. If you're chronically ill, then only a limited amount of benefits are tax free. *All* amounts used to pay for long-term care are tax free. Any additional amounts are tax free up to a cap of $180 per day ($65,700 annually) in 1998 (these figures are adjusted annually for inflation).

If you're able to take accelerated death benefits, should you? This is a good question, and the answer is similar to the one that applies to borrowing from your policy. Taking benefits now means they won't be there later (after you die) for your beneficiaries. If you had planned specific uses for that money (such as paying your estate taxes), then it simply won't be there for the purpose intended.

Instead of relying on accelerated death benefits to pay for your long-term care, it may be smarter to plan for this expense. Paying for long-term care is explained in Chapter 19, "Planning for Long-Term Health Care Needs."

The Least You Need to Know

➤ Cash surrender value builds up only in permanent insurance and not in term insurance.

➤ Arranging for vanishing premiums means you can stop making payments once the policy becomes self-sustaining.

➤ Keep enough life insurance to cover your estate taxes, funeral expenses, and other costs that will arise upon your death.

➤ If you don't need all of your existing coverage, you can cancel your policy, decrease your coverage, trade it in for an annuity, or give the policy away.

➤ Borrowing on your life insurance is easy to arrange, but there are traps you want to avoid.

➤ If you become terminally or chronically ill, you may be able to tap into your policy while you're still alive to provide you with needed tax-free cash.

Chapter 21

Money Management: Keeping Things Out of Court

In This Chapter

➤ Preplanning for money management if you become disabled

➤ Using joint bank and brokerage accounts

➤ Naming an agent to manage your money when you can't

➤ Setting up a living trust

Did you ever think who would write out your rent check or deposit your dividends into your bank account if you became incapacitated because an auto accident left you in a coma or your arthritis was so bad you couldn't sign checks? You should think about this possibility. If you don't, then the courts may have to get involved. The cost of resolving who should handle your financial affairs may be high if you don't take action while you're able to.

In this chapter, you'll find out about what steps you should take now (if you haven't already done so) to make it possible for your loved ones to manage your financial affairs if you become mentally incapable of doing it. These steps run from the simple to the complex. The one or ones you should use, as you'll see, depend on the size and kinds of assets you have.

Letting Someone Else Manage Your Assets

No one likes to think about being so ill or out of it that he or she can't get to the bank to make a deposit or withdrawal, balance a checkbook, or decide to buy or sell IBM stock. Still, the possibility that such a thing could happen one day shouldn't be ignored. Of course, as long as you have your mental faculties, you can always take steps to let someone else do the legwork if you can't. But if you develop Alzheimer's disease or are otherwise mentally incompetent, you want to know now that things will be handled for you.

If you don't do anything now and you become mentally incapacitated, your family or friends will be forced to go to court in order to pay your rent and telephone bill with your funds. They'll have to put you through a costly (because you need to be represented by a lawyer) and embarrassing proceeding (because your health becomes a matter of public record) called *guardianship*.

The rules for the process are different in each state, but the idea is the same. Someone, called a guardian, conservator, committee, fiduciary, tutor, or curator (depending on which state you live in), is named as a *fiduciary* to make money decisions and act on your behalf. You become a ward of that person. About half a million Americans already are wards or subject to another form of supervision by a fiduciary. Some states require a showing of full-blown incapacity to order a guardianship. Some states, like New York, grant limited authority to the fiduciary to the extent needed by the individual. So if someone still has all of his or her marbles and is fully capable of making investment decisions but just physically can't get to the bank, the fiduciary would be authorized only in banking matters (investment decisions would be left to the individual). (The individual could name someone to do the banking, but the limited guardianship includes court supervision on how money is being spent.)

Word to the Wise
A *fiduciary* is someone who acts in a position of trust on behalf of another person. The fiduciary in a guardianship situation is accountable to the court on how your money is spent.

Even if you get Alzheimer's disease like former President Reagan and can no longer handle money, you don't have to face court action to have you labeled *incompetent*. You take the necessary steps now to avoid this problem and give your loved ones a simple way in which to take care of your money if you can't. There are a number good ways you can arrange for money management that may be needed if you become incapacitated: joint accounts, durable powers of attorney, living trusts, and other arrangements.

Joint Accounts

The simplest way to allow someone access to your money is to put their name on your account as co-owner. Doing so gives that joint owner as much *legal* right to the money as you have (even though the money may be entirely yours). So, for example, if you name your daughter as joint owner of your accounts, she can withdraw cash from your account to pay your bills. She can sell your stock to invest in another company's stock. She can switch your mutual funds and redeem shares. When funds are sold and a check is issued, it's payable to both owners (so you need both signatures to cash it).

Setting up a joint account is simple. All you do is ask the bank, brokerage firm, or mutual fund to retitle the account to include the name of a joint owner. It doesn't cost you any fees to do it. Then, either you or your co-tenant can access the money in the account.

You can use joint accounts as a mere convenience. These accounts don't have automatic rights of survivorship; they merely allow the co-tenant to write checks and spend your money, presumably for your benefit. If you want the money to pass automatically to your co-tenant when you die, make sure the account is properly titled (look at the signature card or other paperwork used to set up the account).

Putting your money in joint name may result in gift taxes. Changing title to your home usually is treated as a gift. Putting someone's name on your bank accounts isn't a gift until that person withdraws funds for his or her own benefit. Check with your accountant or tax attorney before taking any steps.

> **Word to the Wise**
> *Joint tenancy with rights of survivorship* means each co-owner is treated as owning the whole. When one owner dies, the other automatically becomes the owner of the entire account. This type of ownership is different from tenancy in common where owners are like partners, with each owning a certain share (for example, one half). This type of ownership is often used with real estate. However, with this type of ownership, the surviving tenant doesn't automatically get the property when the co-tenant dies. The share can be sold, given away, or bequeathed to heirs.

Also, putting money in a joint name can have implications for Medicaid eligibility. Setting up the joint account may be considered a transfer that gives rise to a penalty period. Again, an elder law attorney should advise you on whether the joint account is the best solution for handling your money.

But before you rush across the street to your savings bank, make sure you understand the down side to this action:

➤ Your funds can be tapped by the joint owner. Now presumably, the joint owner is your spouse, child, or trusted friend who wouldn't think of using a penny of your money for himself or herself. Of course, there's no court looking over the joint owner's shoulder on how your money is being spent. And if your co-owner has financial difficulties, creditors can get at your funds. This is exactly what happened to a mother in California whose daughter, her co-owner, suffered financial reverses. The daughter's creditors were able to clean out the mother's accounts, all perfectly legal.

➤ You may still have financial issues that your co-owner can't handle. Just because you name someone as a joint owner on your accounts doesn't give that person the right to sell a house in your name. Also, your joint owner may not be savvy in financial matters, and there's no guarantee he or she will make good investment choices for you.

➤ You can ruin your estate planning. Let's say you have three sons who you love equally and plan to leave equal shares of your property when you die. One son lives in your apartment building; the other two live in different cities. You put the name of your son who lives near you on all your accounts. When you die, he automatically inherits all the money in your accounts; your other sons are cut out entirely. There can also be unintended estate tax consequences. If you put your spouse's name on all your accounts and, together, you and your spouse have more than the amount that can pass free from federal estate taxes ($625,000 in 1998, increasing to $1 million by 2006), you'll pay more estate tax than you'd have to if you'd done things differently. True, there'll be no federal estate tax when the first of you dies. But when the second spouse dies, that estate will pay a higher estate tax. By using joint accounts, you wasted the opportunity to pass—tax free—up to the applicable exemption amount.

Durable Powers of Attorney

Instead of putting someone else's name on your accounts or retitling your property, you can keep everything in your own name but give someone financial authority. You do this with a simple legal document called a durable power of attorney. It's called *durable* because it continues to be effective even though you become incapacitated. (Every state recognizes this document, though the rules on signing and other requirements may vary depending on where you live.)

> **Word to the Wise**
> A *principal* is the person who signs the document to give someone else the power to handle his or her money. An *agent (attorney in fact)* is the person named by the person to act in a fiduciary capacity on behalf of the principal.

The durable power of attorney is a *financial* document; it relates to money matters. In most states, a durable power of attorney for health care (or a health care proxy) must be created with a separate form, even if the same person is both your agent under the durable power of attorney and your health care agent.

You, as principal, name someone to be your agent (or attorney in fact) to act on your behalf. You can name two agents to act for you. Their power can be *joint* (both must act together) or *several* (each can act alone without consent from the other agent). However, as a practical matter it's simpler to allow each agent to act separately. (An exception might be when the agent is making gifts to him/herself; joint action may be better.)

Once the durable power of attorney is signed and notarized according to your state law, it's official even though you're still perfectly capable of doing for yourself. You can, in most states, choose to use a *springing* power of attorney. This is a type of durable power of attorney that doesn't take effect *until* you become incapacitated (which you define in your document if state law doesn't do it for you). It *springs* into effect at that time.

If you're psychologically uncomfortable with the idea of giving complete authority over your money, you may want to make a regular durable power of attorney but let your lawyer hold onto it until you become incapacitated. At that time, it can be given to your agent and put into use.

Naming an Agent

Who should be your agent? Even though the agent is called an attorney in fact, it doesn't have to be someone who's licensed to practice law in your state. You can appoint anyone of legal age: your spouse, your child, your best friend, or your accountant. (Some states require that the agent be in-state, so if your child lives in another state, you'll have to find a different agent.)

On the theory that two heads are better than one, you can name two agents. You have to decide whether you want them to act together on everything or whether each can act alone on your behalf. Requiring joint action is called acting jointly. Both agents must agree before anything can be done. This alternative is usually chosen when there's *any* concern about how each agent will act. Joint action is a checks and balances strategy. Allowing for separate or individual action is called acting severally. This alternative is usually chosen to make it easier for the agents. Two signatures aren't required; each can act alone. As mentioned earlier, it's generally better to allow for separate action when joint agents are named.

You want to name someone who's good with money. After all, it's *your* money. If you have several children, make sure there are no hurt feelings on the part of those not named. Just explain you named the child who is in the best position to act (the one who lives nearest you or who's the best at handling money).

Cash Crash

Some people think they'll protect their money by using a springing power of attorney. The agent can't act unless and until you're incapacitated. I think this is foolish logic. If you're worried about the trustworthiness or ability of the agent, why postpone action until you're in no position to change it? Don't name anyone you have any reservations about. What's more, there may be confusion about whether the triggering event has been satisfied, which can prevent brokerage firms and other third parties from recognizing your agent's authority.

Golden Years Ideas

Make sure the person you've named as agent knows about what you've done. Also make sure this person knows where you keep the durable power of attorney as well as your other financial records.

Generally, you don't pay the agent to act on your behalf. But if you have no family willing to do the job for free and you name a nonrelative (like your accountant or attorney), you should discuss what it will cost you and put the agreement in writing. Usually the professional agent will bill you for the time spent each month on writing out your checks, disputing a bill that's in error, and reviewing your portfolio if necessary.

Powers Under a Durable Power of Attorney

Golden Years Ideas
While in theory your agent has full authority under the document you've signed, in practice, banks, brokerage firms, and mutual funds get a little stuffy about accepting someone else's forms. Save your agent hassles down the road by also signing a power of attorney form of the company with each account you have.

Golden Years Ideas
You don't have to name one agent to handle your personal and business matters. You can use different agents for different purposes (with one document or two, depending on what's involved). For example, you might want your son, the artist, to handle your personal banking and brokerage transactions while your daughter, the lawyer, might be able to run your business.

An agent acting under a durable power of attorney can do much more than just a joint owner. For example, your agent can handle the investments in your retirement accounts; you can't just put someone else's name on your IRA to allow that person to make investment decisions for you. All states have statutory forms that contain a laundry list of powers that you can limit if you prefer or add to. Here's a list of the powers your agent can have:

➤ Conduct real estate transactions. If you run short of money, your agent can mortgage your home or even sell it.

➤ Make transactions for goods and services. If your washing machine is beyond repair, your agent can buy you a new one, even on credit.

➤ Buy and sell your stocks, bonds, and other securities. The investment decisions of buying, selling, and trading are left completely up to your agent.

➤ Handle your banking transactions. Your agent may not only make deposits and sign your checks, but can also take out loans or repay the ones you've taken.

➤ Handle your business affairs. If you own a business, who's going to run things if you become incapacitated? Your agent can (if he or she knows how). For example, if you're a partner in a partnership, your agent can enter into a buy-sell agreement so that your interest can be bought out in view of your incapacity.

➤ Other powers: In addition to the powers you're automatically given under your state's law, there's almost no limit to the power you can grant to your agent. The following are other powers for your agent:

➤ Act in estate matters (contest a will, make a disclaimer)

➤ Collect military benefits

➤ Gain access to safe deposit boxes

➤ Deal with retirement accounts (decide on how distributions should be made)

➤ Complete charitable pledges

➤ Fund trusts already set up

➤ Handle claims and litigation (start a lawsuit, settle a claim, file an appeal)

➤ Get records and reports (collect information from Social Security and Medicare)

➤ Handle tax matters (talk to the IRS, file returns, endorse refund checks, settle tax disputes, file for refunds)

➤ Forgive and collect debts

➤ Make gifts

➤ Other powers (a so-called umbrella clause)

In addition to the broad powers you can give an agent, a durable power of attorney has another advantage over joint ownership: You don't have the same estate and gift tax issues with a durable power of attorney that you have with joint ownership. Because the money and property is still in your name, your estate plans aren't affected at all by the durable power of attorney.

But there's one big negative to remember: There's no check on the power of your agent. The agent doesn't account to the court or anyone else on how your money is being spent. Presumably you'd name someone in whom you have complete trust. And beyond the question of trust, you hope that the agent knows what he or she is doing with the money. But if you don't have a relative who lives near you who wants to take on the role of helping you out, you may need to name a relative stranger (your accountant, attorney, or neighbor). Make sure that person knows your money philosophies. After all, if you've always been a conservative investor,

Golden Years Ideas
Even if you have a durable power of attorney, it's a good idea to execute the IRS version, Form 2848 in addition. This will save time and hassle for your agent. You can get this form by calling the IRS at 800-829-1040 or off the web site at http://www.irs.ustreas.gov.

Cash Crash
Giving the power to make gifts can raise problems. While it may be helpful for your estate or Medicaid planning to permit them, an unrestricted power could cause tax problems for your agent if the agent dies before you (the IRS may say the power is a general power of appointment so that the agent's estate is taxable on the value of all of your property!). You can limit this power to the annual gift tax exclusion or to the gifts you usually make each year if you're in the habit of doing so. If you want to permit larger gifts, you could require a third party's consent.

you don't want your agent to suddenly start investing in a highly speculative thing like pork belly futures.

It's a good idea to have a lawyer draft a durable power of attorney for you (and I'm not just saying this because I'm an attorney). The reason: The basic form can be tailored to meet your needs. For instance, it can be amended to give your agent the power to make gifts on your behalf to meet your estate planning objectives or to fund a trust set up by you (things that might not be included in your state's basic form). The lawyer's fee should be modest because it's a routine matter.

Instead of having a lawyer draft a durable power of attorney, you can use a preprinted form you can pick up at your local stationery or office supply store. Just make sure the form you've bought is the current one in use in your state (and not an older version on the shelf).

If you own property in more than one state (for example, you own a home in New Jersey and a condo in Arizona), it's a good idea to have a durable power of attorney for each state. Make sure you sign the form in accordance with the requirements of each state.

Living Trusts

If you have sizable assets, you may want a more sophisticated arrangement for handling your financial affairs if you become incapacitated. You can use a living trust (also called an *inter vivos trust* because you set it up when you're alive). A living trust is a trust you set up now but keep the power to cancel or change it (it's also called a *revocable trust* in view of the power to revoke it). The trust becomes irrevocable (and can't be changed) once you become incapacitated or die. (You can set up a trust that's irrevocable from the start to serve certain estate planning and Medicaid planning goals, but they're generally not called living trusts and aren't discussed here.)

> **Word to the Wise**
> A separate legal entity that you can create is called a *trust*. It generally has its own tax identification number. It can sue or be sued just like a living, breathing person. A trust is set up by a *grantor (or settlor)*. Title to property is held by a *trustee* (the person who manages the trust) for the benefit of the *beneficiary*. In some states, the grantor, trustee, and beneficiary can be the same person.

You may see living trusts referred to as *grantor trusts*. This is because the income earned in the trust is taxed to a grantor who is also the beneficiary of the trust.

Like an agent acting under a durable power of attorney, a trustee is a fiduciary acting in a position of trust on your behalf. The trustee has the *duty* to take possession of the property you've placed in the trust and to use reasonable care and skill in managing it. The trustee has the *powers* granted by state law and your trust document.

While it may be years before you need someone to manage your money for you, be sure you've named a trustee who will act in your best interests when you no longer can. You can name someone to act along with you as a co-trustee (in some states, this is required because a grantor in those states can't be the only trustee and beneficiary). Or, if you can and want to act alone if there are other beneficiaries of the trust beside you such as your spouse, you can name a *successor* trustee to take over when you're no longer able to fulfill your role as trustee. A trustee can be a relative, friend, or any other person you have confidence in. A trustee can also be an institution such as a bank's trust department.

> **Cash Crash**
> Trust departments may charge sizable trustee's fees for managing a trust. Before you name a trust department as your trustee, discuss the fee schedule. You may be able to negotiate lower fees if the investments held by your trust are uncomplicated.

What Living Trusts Can and Can't Do for You

Today living trusts are extremely popular estate planning devices. The main attraction of living trusts is that they're effective in avoiding *probate*. Probate is a court process of transferring the property of someone who dies when that property doesn't pass to someone else automatically (such as with joint tenancies, life insurance, and designated beneficiaries on retirement accounts). In California, Florida, and certain other states, probate can be costly and lengthy, so living trusts are often used in those places. (The estate planning benefits to living trusts are discussed more fully in Chapter 26, "Estate Planning for the Rich and Not-So-Rich.")

Living trusts benefit the living because they:

➤ Consolidate your assets in one place. You change the title to your accounts and other property into the trust's name. For example, if I were to set up a living trust for myself and name my daughter as trustee, my mutual funds would changed from Barbara Weltman to the Barbara Weltman Revocable Trust dated 2/1/98, Emily Weltman, trustee. That's a mouthful, but banks, brokerage firms, and mutual funds are used to this type of account designation. Consolidating your assets takes some time, but in the long run, it simplifies record keeping for you and your family.

➤ Allow your trustee to decide how to use your money on your behalf. You generally can act as trustee for as long as you're able to do so. (In some states, you must have a trustee who's not a beneficiary working with you; in other states, you can act alone.) This allows you maximum control over your property for as long as you're able. Then, when you become incapacitated, the person you name in the trust document to be your successor trustee (or the trustee who's been acting as your co-trustee all along) can take over.

But a living trust doesn't do everything you may want or expect. Living trusts don't save any estate taxes (other than those that could be saved if you used a will). For estate tax purposes, the assets in a living trust are considered part of your estate because you owned and controlled them at the time of your death. So, if your objective is to get assets out of your estate, a living trust won't do this. But there's no gift tax cost for using a living trust because you don't make a gift of the property to anyone (you continue to enjoy it as long as you live and have the right to take it out of the trust and put it in your pocket whenever you want).

Cash Crash
Beware of non-attorney companies or unscrupulous lawyers who pitch living trusts at estate planning seminars and sell at high fees boilerplate trusts that may not serve your particular needs. These people may be more than willing to sell you a trust even if your assets are below the recommended $50,000 minimum.

Living trusts won't help you in Medicaid planning. Assets in these trusts are available for Medicaid purposes. For this purpose you may want to explore the use of an irrevocable income-only trust.

There's no magic dollar amount you need to have before you embark on a living trust. But, as a practical matter, it doesn't pay for a few thousand dollars (you're better off using joint ownership or a durable power of attorney in this case). The reason: You pay to set up the trust (maybe as much as several thousand dollars, depending on the trust's complexity). And if the trustee other than you is a bank's trust department or nonrelative, you may also pay the trustee to manage your money. Some advisers suggest having at *least* $50,000 before going forward with a living trust.

How Living Trusts Stack Up

In some places, there are companies aggressively marketing to seniors the idea of living trusts. Now, these trusts may make sense for some people, but they're not for everyone. Before you rush out and spend thousands of dollars setting up a living trust, make sure you weigh your options. Use Table 21.1 to decide which money management tool is right for you. Understand that you're not limited to one tool over the other. You can certainly combine them if it works for your situation. For example, you might want to have your daughter as joint owner of your bank account, but put rental real estate you own into a trust and have your accountant act as trustee to manage those properties.

Table 21.1 Comparison of Money Management Tools

Factors	Joint Ownership	Durable Power of Attorney	Living Trust
Setting it up	Easy	Slightly more complicated	Most complicated (need formalities)
Cost of setting up	None	Minimal	Up to several thousand dollars

Factors	Joint Ownership	Durable Power of Attorney	Living Trust
Range of financial control	Limited to property that person is joint owner of	As broad as the document allows	Broadest range of activities permitted
Fees of money manager	No fees to joint owner or attorney	Generally no fees to agent (may pay fees if agent is accountant or attorney)	Generally no fees to family member acting as trustee; substantial fees to bank acting as trustee
Accountability of person handling your money	None	None	Trustee is accountable to the beneficiaries who inherit your money when you die

Other Arrangements for Handling Your Money in Different Circumstances

Depending on your finances, you may be able to use less formal arrangements to see that your money is managed for you should you lack the mental capacity to do it yourself.

You might consider an advance written designation of a guardian in case a future need should arise. You simply put your choice of guardian in writing (you can even incorporate this choice in a durable power of attorney). The court will honor it unless there's some compelling reason not to carry out your wishes.

You may be able to use "daily money management" (DMM). A private service bureau takes care of your financial paperwork while you retain complete legal control over your funds. The service bureau receives a fee for its services. This type of arrangement works best when you're mentally competent but physically unable to get to the bank or handle the other physical tasks of money management.

Another arrangement that can be helpful in handling your money is designation of a "representative payee" for Social Security. With this arrangement, your Social Security benefits are paid to the representative payee to be used for your benefit. The Social Security Administration can appoint one if it determines that it's in your best interests. Or you can ask that benefits be paid to a representative payee you select. Typically, a spouse or other relative is chosen, but you can tell SSA your preference. The representative payee each year must tell SSA how your benefits have been spent and SSA has the power to replace the representative payee if necessary.

The Least You Need to Know

➤ If you become incapacitated and have not set up ways for someone else to handle your money, then a lengthy and expensive court process may be necessary.

➤ The simplest way to have someone manage your money when you can't is to put your accounts in joint name so that the joint owner can use those assets for you if you can't act for yourself.

➤ Sign a durable power of attorney now to see that someone's there to handle your financial affairs if you can't.

➤ Wealthy individuals may want to use living trusts to provide lifetime asset management.

➤ Other arrangements may be helpful in money management under certain circumstances.

Part 6
It Pays to Be Old

Age has its rewards. We're not talking about wisdom. We're not even talking about a seat on the bus. We're talking financial rewards. There are savings to be had just because of your age; savings on everything from property taxes to your car insurance to travel expenses. All you need to know is where to look.

On top of money-saving opportunities, there are also tax breaks you may be entitled to just because of your age. Again, it's only a question of knowing that the savings are out there for the taking. You don't have to become a tax maven to find out what tax rules can be helpful to you during your retirement years.

Chapter 22

Discounts for Seniors

In This Chapter

➤ Getting property tax reductions

➤ Finding discounts on goods and services

➤ Getting breaks on banking

While aging may bring physical aches and pains, financially speaking it pays to be old. Almost everywhere you turn, you can get a special break just because of your age. You don't have to be retired; you only have to be of retirement age. The breaks you can find will save you pennies in some cases, but dollars in others on expenses you have to pay for anyway. You'll also find many discounts available for your discretionary and luxury purchases.

In this chapter, you'll find out about getting breaks on your property tax bill and other housing-related costs. You'll also see where to look to find senior citizen discounts for things you want and use, such as insurance, credit cards, travel, banking, and more.

Saving on Housing Costs

As you reviewed your monthly bills in Chapter 18, "Keeping Spending in Line," when you prepared a budget, you probably noticed that housing took up a very sizable portion of that budget. If you want to stay in your home (instead of moving to a less costly housing arrangement), there are many ways to bring down your monthly costs.

The first place to look is your local tax assessor's office. You may be entitled to a cut in your property taxes. The cuts don't come automatically; you have to apply for them. There may also be savings on fuel, home improvements, and other home-related expenses through various federal, state, or local programs.

Bringing Down Your Real Estate Tax Bill

One of the largest bills any homeowner faces each year is the one for property taxes. Typically, property taxes are made up of town or city taxes plus school taxes. There may also be special assessments for fire districts, sewer districts, garbage collection, and water use. These tax elements may be billed separately, even at different times of the year, or as one bill.

Homeowners who itemize their tax deductions on their federal income tax return realize *some* income tax savings as a result of this write-off. But the value of the tax deduction is only as great as the tax bracket you're in. So, for example, if you're in the 28% tax bracket and your property taxes are $3,000 a year, your tax savings for claiming this deduction is $840.

Better than tax savings is the opportunity for seniors to get some sort of a reduction of their property tax bill. Different localities provide property tax breaks in different ways. You may find specific dollar exemptions from taxes. You may see a *refund* paid to seniors. You may see a percentage reduction. At present, 22 states provide senior citizen real estate tax relief.

Some states now allow seniors to *defer* paying property taxes (with interest accruing on the amount deferred). The taxes are then paid when the home is sold or the owner dies. Property tax deferral to older homeowners is available in some form in the following states:

➤ California

➤ Colorado

➤ Connecticut

➤ District of Columbia

➤ Florida

➤ Georgia

➤ Illinois

➤ Iowa

➤ Maine

➤ Massachusetts

➤ New Hampshire

➤ Oregon

➤ Texas

➤ Utah

➤ Virginia

➤ Washington

➤ Wisconsin

However it works in your area, there are sure to be some property tax breaks you might qualify for.

There are usually two ways of qualifying for property tax breaks:

➤ Age-based. Many localities offer property tax relief for those who are 65 and older. Where a home is owned jointly by a husband and wife, usually only one spouse has to meet the age requirement. There may be a lower age requirement for surviving spouses in some localities. A property tax reduction may or may not be available without regard to the owner's income or financial status. There may also be certain residency requirements, such as having owned the home for a certain length of time or that the owner currently uses the home as a primary residence.

➤ Income-based. Many localities offer property tax relief for seniors, but only those with lower incomes. For example, under New York state's new school tax relief exemption (called the "STAR" program that will first apply to the 1999-2000 school taxes), those age 65 and over with a total income of no more than $60,000 can receive a special school tax reduction. (All homeowners, regardless of age or income, can get some relief if they show that the home is their primary residence.)

Even if you don't own your home, you may be entitled to some rent relief if your income is below certain levels. This, for example, may be the opportunity to claim a certain percentage of the rent as a tax deduction on a state income tax return or to avoid scheduled rent increases.

There may also be special property tax reductions for veterans (with or without income requirements).

To find out about property tax relief in your area, contact your city or town assessor's office. Be prepared to present proof of your age (such as a birth certificate) and, if claiming an income-based break, proof of your income (usually a state or federal income tax return).

Special Assistance With Fuel and Home Improvements

If you want to stay in your home but your income isn't enough to support the upkeep, you may be entitled to some federal, state, or local assistance because of your age and your income. The assistance can take several forms:

➤ Fuel payments. You may be entitled to help with your heating bills under the federal Low-Income Home Energy Assistance Act. If you're already receiving VA pension benefits, food stamps, or certain other assistance, you're probably eligible for fuel assistance.

➤ Home improvements. You may qualify for special help in weatherizing your home, a step that will save you money on your fuel bills. Generally, help is available to those age 60 and older even if

Golden Years Ideas
Utility companies generally can't automatically shut off your heat and electricity for nonpayment of bills. They're required to give certain notice to customers who are seniors before they can take any action.

you're not a low-income person receiving other types of assistance. Generally, the dollar amount of grants you can get to add insulation, weather-stripping, storm doors, and other energy-saving improvements is limited. Ask your local Social Services department what's available in your area and how you can get an application.

➤ Home protection. Delaware has a program for low-income homeowners 60 and older that provides free deadbolts and installation of them to burglar-proof your home.

Cashing in on Your Age

A person's age used to be a highly personal matter. Women, especially, were reluctant to divulge their birthdays. Today, however, age is a badge of honor in many cases, particularly when you get a price reduction or other break because of it.

Depending on the benefit involved, you have to meet different age requirements. "Senior citizen" can mean anything from 50 and up. In most cases, you don't have to be retired, just considered to be of retirement age. You may qualify for some benefits but not for others, depending on your age.

There are many ways to locate free and discounted goods and services nationwide that you may be entitled to. Many of these are listed in Michael Lesko's books for seniors: *Discounts for Seniors*, *Senior Yellow Pages*, and *Free Stuff For Seniors*. You can find these books in your local libraries, bookstores, and even portions of them are on the Internet at http://www.thirdage.com.

Be sure to check out what's available in your area. While taking an informal survey of senior discounts in my area, I was able to turn up in less than five minutes some interesting savings opportunities. For example, there is a 10% discount every Wednesday at Caldor's (a local retail chain); a 10% discount every Tuesday by participating stores at a local mall; special senior menus at Friendly's (a sandwich and ice cream restaurant in the New England area); matinee movie ticket prices at evening showings other than Fridays and Saturdays at the local multiplex; discounts on haircuts and other beauty salon services every Tuesday and Wednesday; and reduced tuition at the local community college.

Senior Info

"Seniors" for purposes of local discounts generally are people who've obtained senior ID cards from the county Office of the Aging. (In Westchester County, NY, you can get a senior ID card at 60 years old.) Most other places have similar senior ID programs. To find out what's in your area, contact your local Office of the Aging (State Offices of the Aging are listed in the Appendix A, "Retiree Resources." These offices can refer you to your local offices.)

Calendar of Discounts for Seniors

Whether it's travel, insurance, or state car registration and your driver's license, there may be a break here for you. Here's a small sampling of what you may be able to get at each birthday you attain:

➤ Age 50. You're considered a "senior" and eligible at many colleges and universities for reduced tuition and special educational programs. You're also eligible to become a member of AARP. Membership is just $8 a year. (Your spouse can then become a member even though he or she is under 50.) This small price entitles you to big savings on many types of expenses. You can get reduced hotel/motel room rates at such national chains as Best Western International, Clarion, Comfort, Courtyard, Crowne Plaza Hotels, Days Inn, Econo Lodge, Holiday Inns, Howard Johnson, ITT Sheraton, Ramada, Super 8 Motels, Travelodge, and many others. AARP membership also entitles you to discounts of between 10% and 15% on car rentals from Avis, Hertz, and National. Cruise discounts can be found at Carnival and Holland America for AARP members. Also FTD Florists offer AARP member discounts. There are medical insurance plans that are also available through AARP.

➤ Age 54. You can join the Hostelling International—American Youth Hostels (202-783-6161) for a modest annual fee. This entitles you to stay at various youth hostels worldwide.

➤ Age 55. You may be entitled to insurance rate reductions. For example, Allstate offers both homeowners and car insurance discounts (about 10%) to those age 55 who are *retired*. Retired for this purpose means working no more than 26 hours a week. Senior discounts for homeowners and car insurance with other insurance companies range from 5% to 15%. Pennsylvania mandates auto insurance discounts for anyone 55 and older who completes a mature drivers improvement course.

You can also join SeniorNet, an organization to promote learning and computer use among those 55 and older. The cost: $35 a year ($40 per couple). This entitles you to such discounts as computer books from Macmillan Publishing (800-882-8583) and 40% discounts on CDs and videos on computer learning from Gartner Group Learning (800-925-2665).

Golden Years Ideas
Just because you're entitled to the AARP room rate doesn't mean it's the best price you can get. Hotels and motels may offer lower rates for certain conditions. Always ask for the lowest rate that you may be entitled to.

➤ Age 62. This is not just the age you can start to collect your Social Security benefits if you're eligible to collect. It's also the age you can get a $20 annual discount off an American Express green card or gold card. Besides the membership discount, you also receive a quarterly newsletter with special purchases and services opportunities for seniors.

Being 62 is also the age at which you can buy a Golden Age Passport to gain free admission to the national parks (including federal monuments and recreation areas). The cost: only $10. You can buy the pass at the entrance to any federal park that charges admission.

You can also qualify for a 15% discount on AMTRAK (800-872-7245) fares (other than the Autotrain).

Continental Airlines (800-441-1135) has Freedom Certificate Booklets: eight one-way trips anywhere in the continental U.S. for about $1,000 (or $125 a trip). The only catch: You have to use them all within a year.

New Jersey offers discounts on bus and rail travel if you're at least 62.

➤ Age 65. Federal Medicare and Social Security benefits aren't the only benefits you get at 65. Many states offer a variety of breaks for 65-year-olds. Your car registration fees are waived in Alaska; your driver's license is free in Oklahoma (it's free in Illinois, but only when you turn 87!). You're entitled to free transit service in Pennsylvania and transit discounts in the District of Columbia, Maryland, and in New York City.

You never know when you'll run into a discount opportunity, so always carry proof of age with you. Your driver's license is perfect for this. If you don't drive, you can get an identification card at your state department of motor vehicles (it looks just like a driver's license, photo and all).

Banking on Your Age

Tired of getting nickeled and dimed by your local bank every time your write a check or use the ATM? Well, you might be paying fees you don't have to pay anymore. If you've reached a certain age, your bank may reduce or waive entirely those pesky fees. You may also be entitled to other bank-related benefits, like free safety deposit box rental, travel discounts, or special seminars.

The age at which these benefits can begin vary greatly from bank to bank. Some start as early as 50. Others have a 55 or 60 age requirement. Here's a listing of some of the larger banks that provide special breaks for senior customers; your local bank may have its own list of discounts for seniors.

Table 22.1 Banks With Discounts for Seniors

Bank	Age for Discounts	Benefits	Phone Number of Main Branch
Bank of New York	60	Unlimited check writing; no per check charge; no monthly fee; free ATM (minimum balance of $1,000 required)	212-475-1784
Barnett Banks	55	No fee credit cards; free checking (minimum balance of $2,500 required)	800-545-2811
First Citizens Bank	60	Unlimited check writing; no per check charge; free safe deposit box; free travelers checks; special rates on CDs	919-755-7000
Fleet Bank	60	No minimum balance; unlimited check writing; no monthly fee	617-346-0197
Key Bank	62	Discount Prime Checking (no minimum balance; no monthly fee; unlimited check writing; no per check charge)	216-689-5580
Michigan National Bank	50	Unlimited check writing; free standard checks; free ATM (minimum daily balance of $500)	810-473-3000
Nations Bank	55	Senior Economy Checking ($6/month; no minimum balance; 1 free check order/year; no per check charge)	404-581-2121
NBD Bank	50	No monthly fee; no per check charge; no minimum balance (with $5,000 balance—no fee MasterCard or Visa; free ATM; free travelers checks)	313-225-1000
NBD National Bank Indiana	60	Lifetime Checking (interest bearing checking with $5,000 balance; free ATM or debit card; free seminars)	317-266-6000

continues

Table 22.1 Continued

Bank	Age for Discounts	Benefits	Phone Number of Main Branch
Southern Bank Concord NC	50	Silver Service Account (free checking; no minimum balance; free safe deposit box; travel discounts)	704-788-3193
Wachovia Bank	50	Free order of checks annually; discount on safe deposit box; unlimited check writing; no monthly fee; no per check charge	704-255-2211

The best way to find out what discounts or freebies you may be entitled to is to ask at your local bank. (Remember that the programs change all the time, and what may be listed earlier can always be amended or dropped.) If there's nothing at your current bank, then shop around. You're bound to find some breaks.

The Least You Need to Know

➤ As a senior, you may be entitled to a reduction of your property taxes (or be able to defer payment until you sell your home).

➤ Low-income seniors may be able to get fuel assistance to help with heating costs.

➤ Discounts (and freebies) for "seniors" can apply at various ages starting as young as 50.

➤ Getting a senior ID card may entitle you to numerous discounts in your area if this program is available in your state.

➤ Membership in AARP and other senior organizations can give you discounts on a number of goods and services you want to buy.

➤ Banks across the country offer discounts and free services to seniors, but ages and the amount of savings vary widely from bank to bank.

Chapter 23

Special Income Tax Breaks for Seniors

In This Chapter

➤ Taking a higher standard deduction

➤ Claiming a special tax credit

➤ Deducting your medical expenses

➤ Escaping estimated tax penalties

➤ Using other tax rules in your retirement years

Taxes. The annual ritual in which you settle up with Uncle Sam. It's not a pleasant chore. But there's no getting around it. Fortunately, the federal tax law has some key breaks for you just because of your age.

In this chapter, you'll learn about the tax breaks designed just for seniors. You'll see whether you qualify to take advantage of them and lower your federal income tax bill. And you'll also find out about other tax rules that may be of particular interest to seniors in retirement, whether or not these rules are keyed to a particular age.

Taking a Higher Standard Deduction

Once you turn 65, the tax law gives you a birthday present of sorts. You can claim an additional standard deduction amount. This deduction is on top of the standard deduction you're allowed to take because of your filing status. You claim the standard deduction *plus* the additional amount only if you don't itemize your deductions. So if your medical expenses, real estate taxes, mortgage interest, and charitable contributions are more than the combination of your standard deduction and additional amount, you'll wind up itemizing your deductions. In this case, you won't get any benefit from the additional standard deduction amount.

In 1998, the *regular* standard deduction is $7,100 on a joint return and for certain widow(er)s with dependent children, $4,250 for single taxpayers, $6,250 for heads of households, and $3,550 for married persons filing separate returns.

In 1998, the *additional standard deduction amount* is $850 for each married person who is 65 and older or $1,050 for an unmarried person. If you and your spouse are both 68, for example, you'll claim $1,700 as an additional standard deduction amount on a joint return ($850 × 2).

The standard deduction amount and the additional amount are indexed for inflation each year. This means that the deductible amounts may be higher in 1999 and later years.

The additional standard deduction amount also applies for those who are legally blind, regardless of age (although the additional standard deduction amount for blindness doesn't raise your filing threshold).

If you're 65 or older *and* blind, you can deduct double the additional amount.

You're treated as being 65 for the year if your 65th birthday is January 1st of the following year or any earlier date (for example, you're considered 65 for 1998 taxes if your 65th birthday is January 1, 1999). The same rule applies to being blind: You're treated as being blind for the year if you're legally blind by January 1st of the following year.

The standard deduction isn't available to everyone. If you're claimed as a dependent on someone else's return (for example, your child provides more than half of your support and claims you as a dependent on his/her return), your standard deduction is a limited one. You can only

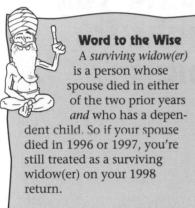

Word to the Wise
A *surviving widow(er)* is a person whose spouse died in either of the two prior years *and* who has a dependent child. So if your spouse died in 1996 or 1997, you're still treated as a surviving widow(er) on your 1998 return.

Golden Years Ideas
The additional standard deduction amount means that seniors have higher thresholds for filing income tax returns. You don't have to file a federal income tax return if your income is below a threshold amount that depends on your filing status. For those 65 and older, the threshold amounts are higher than the threshold amounts for younger taxpayers by the additional standard deduction amount. Of course, these amounts rise every year.

deduct a dependent's standard deduction ($700 in 1998). Also, if you're married and your spouse itemizes deductions instead of claiming the standard deduction, then you're forced to itemize as well; you can't claim the standard deduction in this case.

Take Credit for Being Older

If you're 65, you may be able to take a special tax credit, called the *credit for the elderly or disabled*. Even if you're under 65, you can still qualify if you retired before the end of the year because of a permanent and total disability and you're receiving disability income from your former employer. You're treated as being permanently and totally disabled only if you're unable to engage in any substantial gainful activity because of a medically determinable physical or mental impairment. This condition must be expected to result in death or to last for a continuous period of not less than 12 months.

Word to the Wise
Blind for tax purposes is having a field of vision 20 degrees or less, or your sight with glasses or contacts isn't any better than 20/200. You have to prove that you're blind with a statement from your doctor or registered optometrist (you send in the copy with your return and keep the original in your files). After the first year of being blind, you simply write in your own statement about your condition.

The credit is 15% of a base amount that depends on your filing status. The base amount, as you'll see in a minute, is then reduced by certain items.

A credit is even better than a deduction. The reason: A credit reduces your taxes dollar-for-dollar while a deduction provides a benefit only as great as your tax bracket. For example, if you're entitled to a $1,000 credit, it cuts your tax bill by $1,000. If you're entitled to a $1,000 deduction and you're in the 28% tax bracket, it cuts your tax bill by $280 ($1,000 × 28%).

The credit for the elderly can't be taken by *everyone* this age, only those with limited incomes who don't receive Social Security benefits (or only very small benefits). The same goes for federal pensions such as pensions from the Veteran's Administration.

Save yourself the trouble of trying to figure the credit if you're single (or married with one spouse 65 or older) and your Social Security benefits are more than $417 a month (or you're married, both spouses are 65 or older, and your monthly benefits are more than $625). Also, you can't take the credit if your adjusted gross income is $20,000 or more on a joint return where one spouse is eligible (or $25,000 if both spouses are eligible), or $17,500 if you're single, head of household, or a qualifying widow(er). But if you're below these levels, it's as easy as one, two, three. (Maybe you're not eligible, but you have an elderly parent who is.) Go ahead and see how much of a credit you can take by following these three steps.

Step 1: Find Your Base Amount

Your base amount is:

➤ $5,000 if you're single, head of household, qualifying widow(er), or you file a joint return, but only one spouse is eligible (65 or older or disabled).

➤ $7,500 if you're married, file a joint return, and both spouses are eligible.

➤ $3,750 if you're married and file separate returns. You're eligible to claim the credit on a separate return *only* if you lived apart from your spouse at all times during the year.

If you're disabled, your base amount is limited to the *lower* of the base amount dependent on your filing status or your disability income. If you file a joint return and your spouse is 65 and older, your base amount is the lower of $7,500 or $5,000 plus your disability income. If both you and your spouse are under 65 and disabled, your base amount is your total disability income not exceeding $7,500.

Step 2: Reduce the Base Amount by Certain Income

Your base amount in step 1 is reduced by nontaxable Social Security benefits and pensions and *excess adjusted gross income*. Subtract from your base amount any *nontaxable* Social Security benefits, Railroad Retirement benefits, tax-free pensions, annuities, or disability income administered under federal law (such as the Veteran's Administration). You don't have to reduce the base amount by military disability pensions for active service, certain disability annuities paid under the Foreign Service Act of 1980, and workers' compensation benefits.

You also subtract from the base amount one half of excess adjusted gross income. Excess adjusted gross income is income over $10,000 if you file a joint return; $7,500 if you're single, head of household, or a qualifying widow(er); or $5,000 if you're married but file separate returns. As you can see, even if your Social Security benefits don't disqualify you, your other income may be too high to allow you to claim any credit.

Golden Years Ideas
You don't even have to figure the credit; the IRS will do it for you. All you have to do is fill in the first page of Schedule R to show you're entitled to the credit and write "CFE" on the line on your Form 1040 for claiming the credit for the elderly or the disabled.

Step 3: Apply the 15% Credit to Your Final Base Amount

All this may sound complicated. It's really easy if you follow the line-by-line instructions to Schedule R, Credit for the Elderly or the Disabled, which you file along with your Form 1040. As you can see from the form that follows, the questions walk you through eligibility *and* how to figure the credit if you're eligible. (This form is the one used for 1997 income tax returns. Don't file it with your 1998 or later-year return; get the current form from the IRS.)

Schedule R **(Form 1040)**	**Credit for the Elderly or the Disabled**	OMB No. 1545-0074 **1997**
Department of the Treasury Internal Revenue Service (99)	▶ **Attach to Form 1040.** ▶ **See separate instructions for Schedule R.**	Attachment Sequence No. **16**
Name(s) shown on Form 1040		**Your social security number**

You may be able to take this credit and reduce your tax if by the end of 1997:

- You were age 65 or older,   **OR**   • You were under age 65, you retired on **permanent and total** disability, and you received taxable disability income.

But you must also meet other tests. See the separate instructions for Schedule R.

TIP: In most cases, the IRS can figure the credit for you. See the instructions.

Part I   **Check the Box for Your Filing Status and Age**

If your filing status is:		And by the end of 1997:	Check only one box:
Single, Head of household, or Qualifying widow(er) with dependent child	**1**	You were 65 or older **1**	☐
	2	You were under 65 and you retired on permanent and total disability . . . **2**	☐
	3	Both spouses were 65 or older **3**	☐
	4	Both spouses were under 65, but only one spouse retired on permanent and total disability **4**	☐
Married filing a joint return	**5**	Both spouses were under 65, and both retired on permanent and total disability **5**	☐
	6	One spouse was 65 or older, and the other spouse was under 65 and retired on permanent and total disability **6**	☐
	7	One spouse was 65 or older, and the other spouse was under 65 and **NOT** retired on permanent and total disability **7**	☐
Married filing a separate return	**8**	You were 65 or older and you lived apart from your spouse for all of 1997 . . **8**	☐
	9	You were under 65, you retired on permanent and total disability, and you lived apart from your spouse for all of 1997 . . . . **9**	☐

Did you check **box 1, 3, 7,** **or 8?**	— Yes ——▶	Skip Part II and complete Part III on back.
	— No ——▶	Complete Parts II and III.

Part II   **Statement of Permanent and Total Disability** (Complete **only** if you checked box 2, 4, 5, 6, or 9 above.)

IF: 1 You filed a physician's statement for this disability for 1983 or an earlier year, or you filed a statement for tax years after 1983 and your physician signed line B on the statement, **AND**

  2 Due to your continued disabled condition, you were unable to engage in any substantial gainful activity in 1997, check this box . . . . ▶ ☐

- If you checked this box, you do not have to file another statement for 1997.
- If you **did not** check this box, have your physician complete the statement below.

Physician's Statement (See instructions on back.)

I certify that _____
                                           Name of disabled person

was permanently and totally disabled on January 1, 1976, or January 1, 1977, **OR** was permanently and totally disabled on the date he or she retired. If retired after 1976, enter the date retired. ▶ _____

Physician: Sign your name on **either** line A or B below.

A The disability has lasted or can be expected to last continuously for at least a year		
	Physician's signature	Date
B There is no reasonable probability that the disabled condition will ever improve		
	Physician's signature	Date
Physician's name	Physician's address	

For Paperwork Reduction Act Notice, see Form 1040 instructions.   Cat. No. 11359K   **Schedule R (Form 1040) 1997**

Schedule R (Form 1040) 1997   Page **2**

Part III   Figure Your Credit

10   **If you checked (in Part I):**   **Enter:**

     Box 1, 2, 4, or 7 . . . . $5,000

     Box 3, 5, or 6 . . . . $7,500 . . . . **10**

     Box 8 or 9 . . . . $3,750

Did you check	Yes ➤ You **must** complete line 11.
box 2, 4, 5, 6,	
or 9 in Part I?	No ➤ Enter the amount from line 10 on line 12 and go to line 13.

11   **If you checked:**

- Box 6 in Part I, add $5,000 to the taxable disability income of the spouse who was under age 65. Enter the total.
- Box 2, 4, or 9 in Part I, enter your taxable disability income. **11**
- Box 5 in Part I, add your taxable disability income to your spouse's taxable disability income. Enter the total.

     TIP: For more details on what to include on line 11, see the instructions.

12   If you completed line 11, enter the **smaller** of line 10 or line 11; **all others,** enter the amount from line 10 . . . . **12**

13   Enter the following pensions, annuities, or disability income that you (and your spouse if filing a joint return) received in 1997:

   a Nontaxable part of social security benefits, and

     Nontaxable part of railroad retirement benefits treated as   . . . **13a**

     social security. See instructions.

   b Nontaxable veterans' pensions, and

     Any other pension, annuity, or disability benefit that is   . . . **13b**

     excluded from income under any other provision of law.

     See instructions.

   c Add lines 13a and 13b. (Even though these income items are not taxable, they **must** be included here to figure your credit.) If you did not receive any of the types of nontaxable income listed on line 13a or 13b, enter -0- on line 13c **13c**

14   Enter the amount from Form 1040, line 33   **14**

15   **If you checked (in Part I):**   **Enter:**

     Box 1 or 2 . . . . $7,500

     Box 3, 4, 5, 6, or 7 . . . . $10,000   **15**

     Box 8 or 9 . . . . $5,000

16   Subtract line 15 from line 14. If zero or less, enter -0- **16**

17   Enter one-half of line 16 . . . . **17**

18   Add lines 13c and 17 . . . . **18**

19   Subtract line 18 from line 12. If zero or less, **stop;** you **cannot** take the credit. Otherwise, go to line 20 . . . . **19**

20   Multiply line 19 by 15% (.15). Enter the result here and on Form 1040, line 41. **Caution:** *If you file Schedule C, C-EZ, D, E, or F (Form 1040), your credit may be limited. See the instructions for line 20 for the amount of credit you can claim* **20**

Instructions for Physician's Statement

Taxpayer

If you retired after 1976, enter the date you retired in the space provided in Part II.

Physician

A person is permanently and totally disabled if **both** of the following apply:

   1. He or she cannot engage in any substantial gainful activity because of a physical or mental condition, and

2. A physician determines that the disability has lasted or can be expected to last continuously for at least a year or can lead to death.

✳

Schedule R for Claiming the Credit for the Elderly

Writing Off Your Doctor's Bills and Other Medical Expenses

Of course, a deduction for medical expenses isn't limited to seniors; it's available to all taxpayers. But it's been estimated that seniors pay about 15% to 20% of their incomes on medical bills. So even if you have medical insurance, you may be out-of-pocket for various medical expenses that your policy doesn't cover. And if you don't have medical insurance, you may be paying a lot more. Fortunately, you may be able to get Uncle Sam to kick in for some of the cost by providing you with tax savings.

If you itemize your deductions, you can write off medical expenses not covered by insurance that are more than 7.5% of your adjusted gross income. You must absorb the first 7.5% of your adjusted gross income. Every dollar of medical expenses over that is deductible.

You deduct your medical expenses on Schedule A, which you attach to your Form 1040. The following portion of Schedule A is used to claim your medical expense deduction. As you can see, it incorporates the 7.5% income limit right on the form.

SCHEDULES A&B (Form 1040) Department of the Treasury Internal Revenue Service (99)	Schedule A—Itemized Deductions (Schedule B is on back) ▶ Attach to Form 1040. ▶ See Instructions for Schedules A and B (Form 1040).	OMB No. 1545-0074 1997 Attachment Sequence No. 07
Name(s) shown on Form 1040		Your social security number

Medical and Dental Expenses		**Caution:** *Do not include expenses reimbursed or paid by others.*		
	1	Medical and dental expenses (see page A-1)	1	
	2	Enter amount from Form 1040, line 33 . 2		
	3	Multiply line 2 above by 7.5% (.075)	3	
	4	Subtract line 3 from line 1. If line 3 is more than line 1, enter -0-		4

Itemizing Your Medical Expenses

What's Deductible

Here's a list of the types of medical expenses you may pay that are deductible:

➤ Health insurance. This includes major medical, premiums to HMOs, Medicare Part B (even if it's subtracted from your Social Security benefits and not paid directly by you), Medicare Part A if you're not automatically covered and choose to pay for this coverage, Medigap coverage, and long-term care insurance (up to a dollar limit that's geared to your age, as explained in Chapter 19, "Planning for Long-Term Health Care Needs").

Golden Years Ideas

If you're self-employed and neither you nor your spouse has any employer-paid health coverage, instead of writing off your health insurance as an itemized deduction, you can deduct it directly from your income (even if you don't itemize other deductions). The percentage of the health insurance deductible depends on the year (45% in 1998, increasing to 100% by 2007).

➤ Doctor's bills. Whatever your insurance doesn't cover, you can deduct. This includes not only physician's or dentist's bills, but also those of a chiropractor, a Christian Science practitioner, an optometrist or an optician, a registered nurse, and a practical or other nonprofessional nurse providing medical services.

➤ Hospital costs. Room charges (including meals) and lab fees are deductible. Nursing home costs for medically necessary long-term care are also deductible.

➤ Drugs and equipment. Prescription medicine and insulin are deductible. Eyeglasses, contacts, hearing aids, canes, walkers, and other similar medical equipment is deductible.

➤ Transportation for medical purposes. If you use your car for getting to or from the doctor or for other medical purposes, you can deduct 10¢ a mile (this rate could be increased by the IRS in future years). Ambulance and ambulette services are also deductible. You can also deduct the cost of cab fare, bus fare, train, or even plane fare that you have to pay to get medical treatment.

➤ Home improvements. You can deduct capital improvements to your home. For example, chair rails or grab bars in bathrooms, widening doorways and hallways, and installing ramps for wheelchair access. To accommodate a physical condition, you may be able to deduct the cost as a medical expense. The deductible expense is the cost of the improvement *except* to the extent it adds to the value of your home. So, for example, if your doctor directs you to put in a pool so you can exercise daily to help your arthritis, you can't deduct anything if the $30,000 cost of the pool adds to the value of your home by at least $30,000. However, if you put in a chair lift so you can get up and down your two-story home, the cost is probably fully deductible because it doesn't add anything to the value of your home. Be sure to get appraisals of your home so you can know whether the medical improvements have added to your home's value.

What's Not Deductible

While most medical expenses are deductible, some types of expenses that may seem perfectly reasonable to you are just not allowed. Here are some of them:

➤ Other insurance. You can't deduct as a medical expense premiums for life insurance, prepaid funeral contracts, or policies that guarantee to provide you with a dollar amount per day if you're hospitalized. If you're still working, you can't deduct the Medicare portion of FICA or self-employment tax that you pay on your earnings (for example, amounts withheld from your salary).

➤ Doctors' bills. You can't deduct the cost of cosmetic surgery *unless* it's done to correct a congenital abnormality, disfiguring disease, or an accidental injury.

➤ Drugs and equipment. You can't deduct over-the-counter drugs. Also, the cost of marijuana, even though it may be legal in your state when prescribed by a doctor.

> **Golden Years Ideas**
>
> For a complete listing of what's deductible and what's not, look at IRS Publication 502, Medical and Dental Expenses. You can get a free copy of this publication by downloading it from the IRS Web site at http://www.irs.ustreas.gov or by calling 800-829-FORMS.

You can't deduct the cost of health clubs, weight loss programs, stop smoking programs *unless* your doctor orders you to exercise, lose weight, or stop smoking to alleviate a specific medical condition. Improving your general health isn't good enough.

Ideas for Getting the Most Tax Mileage from Your Medical Expenses

Because medical expenses may represent a large portion of your monthly expenses, you want to be able to deduct as much as you're allowed. There are several strategies you can use to minimize your nondeductible costs:

➤ Bunch your deductions. If your itemized deductions annually run around the standard deduction amount for your filing status, try to bunch your deductions so you'll be able to itemize every other year (and claim the standard deduction in off years). You can do this by making sure you schedule voluntary medical procedures only in those years you'll itemize. For example, if you're planning on extensive dental work that's not covered by your insurance, do it in the year your total itemized deductions are high enough to allow you to get a benefit from your deductible medical expenses.

➤ Pay by credit card. Medical expenses paid by credit card are deductible in the year you charge the expense, even if you pay the credit card bill in the following year. So if you expect that your itemized deductions for the year are high enough to allow you to deduct your medical expenses, go ahead and have those medical procedures done before the end of the year even if you're short of cash. You just charge the expense now and pay for it later.

➤ Take advantage of flexible spending arrangements. If you're still working and your employer offers you the opportunity to join a flexible spending plan for medical costs, jump at it. With this type of arrangement, you agree to reduce your salary by a set dollar amount, such as $200 a month. This gives you $2,400 worth of medical expenses that can be reimbursed from the plan. The advantage to you is that you've shifted your medical expenses to pretax dollars. Your annual W-2 shows a reduced salary that you pay income tax on, and the medical expenses (up to the dollar limit in your plan) are paid with money you didn't have to first pay income tax on. The only caution is that flexible spending arrangements are use-it-or-lose-it plans. If you don't have medical expenses of at least the amount you've committed to the plan, you'll just lose that income and won't ever get it back.

Cash Crash

Don't file separately, even if it allows a greater medical expense deduction, if it prevents you from taking advantage of other tax benefits. Many benefits are conditioned on married people filing joint returns. For example, an IRA for a nonworking spouse can be claimed only if the couple files jointly. Check out the options thoroughly before deciding on a separate return.

➤ File separate returns. If one spouse has high, unreimbursed medical expenses and the other does not, consider filing separate tax returns. This will lower the adjusted gross income threshold for the spouse with the medical expenses. Each spouse can deduct expenses he or she paid separately, plus 50% of expenses paid with joint funds. The couple may save on total taxes if they follow this approach. Of course, the only way to be sure that filing separately will save taxes is to figure the tax both ways (jointly and separately) and to use the method that results in the lower *total* tax.

Estimated Tax Penalty Relief for Retirees

The law says you have to pay most of your taxes through withholding or quarterly estimated taxes or pay penalties. In your working years, this may not have been any problem because you adjusted your withholding from your wages to cover your tax liability (and maybe even build in a refund each year). However, in the year you retire, you may find that you're betwixt and between. You may have unexpected income, such as severance payments or distributions from retirement plans, but you didn't plan for it in your withholding.

The IRS may waive any estimated penalty if you retired after age 62 or became disabled this year or last year. The underpayment must be because of reasonable cause and not due to willful neglect.

The waiver isn't automatic. You have to ask the IRS for it. You make this request by attaching to your return a statement that you prepare explaining your reason for under-paying your taxes. Attach to the statement any documentation you may have to prove your case.

If you're receiving a pension or IRA distributions, you avoid having to pay estimated taxes by having adequate amounts withheld from your pension or IRA distributions. Taxes are *automatically* withheld from these amounts unless you request otherwise. However, you can also ask that *additional* amounts be withheld from pension and IRA distributions to cover your tax liability that may result from your interest, dividends, and other income. You make the request to increase withholding (or to opt out entirely) on IRS Form W-4P, Withholding Certificate for Pension or Annuity Payments.

If you're receiving Social Security benefits, you may be able to request to have withholding taken out. At the time this book was written, the tax rules permitted withholding, but the Social Security rules hadn't been amended to allow for withholding. If you're interested in withholding, ask your local Social Security office if it's available yet and what you must do to get it going (you can find your local office listing in Appendix A).

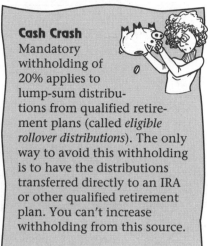

Cash Crash
Mandatory withholding of 20% applies to lump-sum distributions from qualified retirement plans (called *eligible rollover distributions*). The only way to avoid this withholding is to have the distributions transferred directly to an IRA or other qualified retirement plan. You can't increase withholding from this source.

Tax Rules You Can (or Must) Use

Certain tax rules are geared only for those who are seniors, as you've seen earlier in this chapter. Other rules, like the medical deduction you've also seen in this chapter, can be claimed by anyone, regardless of age. However, like the medical deduction, seniors may be more likely to take advantage of certain tax rules than younger individuals. Many of these rules have been covered in more detail in other chapters throughout this book. Here's a roundup of tax rules that you may run into in retirement:

➤ Home sale exclusion. If you sell your home, you may be able to avoid paying any tax on up to $250,000 of gain ($500,000 on a joint return). In the past, the home sale exclusion was limited to those age 55 and older. Today, it's open to homeowners of any age. The requirements for the new exclusion are simple: You have to own and use your principal residence (your main home) for at least two out of five years before the sale. However, the two-year rule drops to one year of use if you're forced to move to a nursing home because of a physical or mental condition.

Golden Years Ideas
Even if you've already used the old $125,000 exclusion for those age 55 and older, you can still qualify for the new home sale exclusion. All you have to do is meet the new ownership and use tests.

➤ Social Securitybenefits. Some of your benefits (50% or 85%) may be taxable, or they may be entirely tax free. The answer depends on the amount of your benefits and other income. Remember where the breakpoints fall (see Table 23.1).

Table 23.1   How Much of Your Social Security Benefits Are Taxable

Your Income* Is	You're Single	You're Married Filing Jointly
Under $25,000	0	
Under $32,000		0
$25,000 but under $34,000	50%	
$32,000 but under $44,000		50%
$34,000 and over	85%	
$44,000 and over		85%

Income means your taxable income (interest, dividends, stock gain, and so on), all of your tax-exempt interest, plus one-half of Social Security benefits.

Golden Years Ideas
If you're disabled and receiving Social Security benefits because of the disability, you figure your tax in the same way as those receiving old age and survivor benefits.

If you're married, filed a separate return, and lived apart from your spouse for the entire year, you're treated the same as a single person. But if you're married and filed a separate return but didn't live apart for the whole year, 85% of your benefits is treated as taxable regardless of the amount of your income.

➤ **IRAs, pensions, and annuities.** If you receive a distribution from these sources, you'll get a report showing the amount for the year on IRS Form 1099-R. This amount is also reported to the IRS. None, some, or all of the amount reported may be taxable.

➤ **Income in respect of a decedent.** In many cases, at the time a person dies, he or she is owed money from various sources (for example, a plumber who died may still be owed accounts receivable that had not been collected at the time of his death). If these funds are paid after the person's death but are not included in his or her last tax return, they're known as *income in respect of a decedent* and become part of the person's estate. If the estate is large enough to be subject to federal estate tax, the person who inherits this income can treat the extra estate tax as an itemized deduction when he or she collects it and reports the income. The portion of the estate tax related to the income is treated as an itemized deduction, but it's not subject to the 2% of adjusted gross income limit that applies to other miscellaneous itemized deductions.

➤ **Reimbursements for certain volunteer services.** If you participate in the Retired Senior Volunteer Program (RSVP), the Foster Grandparent Program, the Senior Companion Program, the Service Corps of Retired Executives (SCORE), or the Active Corps of Executives (ACE) and you receive amounts for supportive services or reimbursements for your out-of-pocket expenses, you're not taxed on these amounts.

➤ Executor's fees. If you serve as an executor, administrator, or personal representative of your spouse's or anyone else's estate and you receive executor's fees, they're taxable to you. You report them as *other income* on your federal tax return. You don't have to pay self-employment tax on them unless you're in the business of being an executor (you're an attorney who regularly acts as executor of clients' estates).

Not every tax rule is a tax break for you. As you retire, you may lose out on some tax breaks. For example, if you retire in New York and move to the Sun Belt, you can't deduct your moving expenses. The moving expense deduction is limited to those who relocate for work opportunities. You don't have to get a job; you can start your own business and be self-employed.

If you move, however, it's important to let the IRS know your new address. You do this by filing IRS Form 8822, Change of Address, with the IRS. Don't file it with your tax return. Don't wait until you file your tax return to send in the form. As soon as you move, send in the form to the IRS service center where you've been filing your returns up to now (they're listed in the instructions to Form 8822).

Senior Info

Need help with your federal income taxes? There's free help available. You can get some help directly from the IRS (800-829-1040). You can also get help through Tax Counseling for the Elderly (TCE). This is a volunteer organization operating in most communities that provides help in preparing basic income tax returns. There's also the American Association of Retired Persons (AARP) Tax-Aide, another help group for low- and middle-income seniors that visits 10,000 sites nationwide each year (888-227-7669).

The Least You Need to Know

➤ Seniors who've reached their 65th birthday can claim an additional standard deduction amount.

➤ Seniors who have limited Social Security benefits and other income may be entitled to a special tax credit.

➤ Deducting medical expenses is an important way for retirees to minimize the high cost of medical treatment (the government's paying for part via your tax savings).

➤ You may be able to get estimated tax penalties waived in the year you retire (if you're over 62 when you retire).

➤ If you're reimbursed for your out-of-pocket expenses while acting as a volunteer in various federally sponsored programs, you're not taxed on these amounts.

➤ If you relocate when you retire, tell the IRS your new address.

Part 7
Leaving Something to Your Heirs

If things work out as planned, you'll have enough money to live out a comfortable retirement. To do so, you'll have to maintain a nice nest egg to feed off of. This means that when you die, there'll be something let over to pass along.

If you don't do some advance legwork, your money will pass along according to the dictates of your state law, which may not coincide with your wishes. Also, a good part of your money could be eaten up by taxes.

With planning, you can ensure that your money will end up in the hands of the people you want. And you'll be able to reduce the taxes that will eventually be paid on your estate. This will give you peace of mind that you've done everything you could not only to take care of yourself through your retirement years, but also to protect your family after you die.

Chapter 24

Where There's a Will...

In This Chapter

➤ Making a will to avoid involuntary estate planning by your state

➤ Learning the will lingo

➤ Deciding what you want to do with your stuff

➤ Organizing things for your family

You may be thinking that retirement is about living, and a will is about dying. You're right. But during your retirement years, you should be doing more than just *thinking* about your own mortality. You should be *planning* what happens to your home and other things when you die. The simplest way to handle directions on what to do with your property when you die is to make a will.

In this chapter, you'll learn what happens to everything you've accumulated, why it's important to have a will, and what happens if you don't. You'll find out how to help with your final instructions and organize things to make it easier for your loved ones.

In Chapter 25, "Beyond Wills," you'll learn about alternative ways of disposing of your property without using a will. In Chapter 26, "Estate Planning for the Rich and Not-So-Rich," you'll learn about estate taxes and how making a will can fit into your estate plan.

Why You Need a Will

When you die, certain things happen to some of your property automatically. For example, if you've named a beneficiary of your retirement plan benefits or IRAs, that person gets your benefits by what's called *operation of law*. The person automatically becomes the owner. (Generally, the only thing that person has to do is present a death certificate.) Property that passes by operation of law is discussed in Chapter 26, "Estate Planning for the Rich and Not-So-Rich."

But not everything you own is handled so neatly. If you own a car when you die, who gets it? Who is responsible for filing your last tax return? Who pays your last cable TV bill? If you die because of malpractice or an accident, who brings a lawsuit?

Property that doesn't pass by operation of law and the responsibility of overseeing that property is handled through a process called *probate*. A court, called a probate court or, in some states, a surrogate's court, oversees the settling of an estate (transferring assets to heirs, paying off debts and taxes, and accounting for all of these transactions).

Cash Crash

If you own real estate in another state, your family will have to go through two probate processes: one in the state where you have your main home and a second one, called *ancillary probate*, in the state where your real estate is situated. You can avoid the need for ancillary probate in certain ways as discussed in Chapter 25.

If you don't take any steps, your state decides for you. Your state has an automatic estate plan in store for you. It's called *intestacy*, meaning that the law spells out what happens to your things when there's no will. The rules vary from state to state. In New York, for example, if you die leaving your spouse but no children or grandchildren surviving you, then everything goes to your spouse. If there are also children, then $50,000 plus one half of the property goes to the spouse with the rest to the children. The laws of intestacy also say who gets the property when there are no children or spouse surviving.

There's another important reason for making a will besides having a distribution plan for your property. It's estate tax savings, as you see in Chapter 26.

Senior Info

For help with your overall estate planning, try these helpful resources on the Internet:

Estate Planning Services	http://www.estateplanningresources.com
Martin Shenkman, Esq.	http://www.laweasy.com
National Association of Financial and Estate Planning	http://www.nafep.com
Nolo Press' Encyclopedia (wills and estate planning)	http://www.nolo.com/ChuckEP/EP.index.html
Senior Law	http://www.seniorlaw.com
The Estate Preservation Alliance	http://www.tepa.com

Will Speak

The language of wills and estate planning may seem strange to you and full of legalese. Don't be put off. It's just a matter of learning the terminology. The more you learn what's involved, the better equipped you'll be to discuss things with an attorney. You'll also save money because you won't waste the attorney's time to explain the basics; you'll already be up to speed and ready to focus on your particular needs and wishes.

Here are some of the terms you need to be familiar with:

➤ *Will* (also called a last will and testament). This is a legal document that should cover certain basic things: Who gets your property, who manages your estate, and (if you have minor children or grandchildren that you're raising) who will be the minors' guardian. A will can do more, such as provide estate tax saving mechanisms (as discussed in Chapter 26). A will must be signed with certain formalities. You need witnesses (generally two witnesses, but the number required varies with state law). This signing is called *executing* the will.

Golden Years Ideas
When signing a will, the witnesses should also sign a *self-proving affidavit*. This says that they've witnessed the will signing and can say you appear to have been competent to sign. Having this affidavit avoids the need for witnesses to later come to court to say the same thing. By that time, the witnesses may have moved or could themselves be dead.

➤ *Codicil.* This is a document used to make an amendment to a will. A codicil can, for example, be used to change the name of an executor or add a special bequest for an heir. A codicil must be signed with the same formalities as the will itself. As a practical matter, if you already have a will and you want to make a change, it's just as easy today to redo the will (it's already in your attorney's computer). The only time it's advisable to use a codicil is when there's a question about the competency of the person signing the will. If, for example, that person has already shown the early stages of Alzheimer's disease, it's safer to make changes to a will using a codicil. If the person is proved to have been incompetent when the codicil was made, at least the original will can stand up in court.

➤ *Estate.* This is the extent of a person's property holdings. It covers property that a person has title to or an interest in. There are two types of estates that shouldn't be confused. The first is a *probate* estate. This is composed only of property subject to probate (property that doesn't pass automatically to someone else). Then there's the *gross estate* for estate tax purposes. This encompasses much more than the probate estate. It covers *all* property that the decedent had an interest in, including property passing outside of a will, such as life insurance proceeds. You don't have to be concerned with a gross estate if the value of all the assets is under the federal estate tax threshold ($625,000 in 1998, increasing to $1 million by 2006) or the state death tax threshold for your state.

➤ *Bequest.* When you die, this is the gift you make of your property (other than real estate) to someone. In common terms, it's an inheritance. If you're making a gift of real estate, it's called a *devise.*

➤ *Heir.* This is the person who inherits your property. An heir is sometimes called a beneficiary.

➤ *Testator.* This is you, the person who makes out a will. That's why a person who dies with a will is called being testate (having a will) as opposed to dying intestate (without a will).

➤ *Executor.* This is the person named in your will (and approved by the probate court) to quarterback your estate. He (or an *executrix* if it's a she) gathers the assets, brings the will to probate court, pays off the decedent's debts, files estate tax returns and pays any estate taxes, distributes the assets and then accounts to the probate court for everything he's done. In some states, this person is simply called a *personal representative.* If there's no will, the person who does just about the same thing is called an *administrator* (or *administratrix*) (or personal representative).

➤ *Trustee.* This is the person who manages a trust, whether it's set up during life or under the terms of a will. A trustee of a trust set up under a will (a testamentary trust) can be the same person as the executor. A trustee is a type of fiduciary who holds a position of trust.

➤ *Guardian.* This is the person named in a will to care for a decedent's children (if there's no other living parent) and to manage the children's inheritance. The choice of guardian must be approved by the probate court, and the guardian is answerable to that court. (You already saw in Chapter 21, "Money Management: Keeping Things Out of Court" how a guardian can be appointed for an incapacitated adult.)

➤ *Testamentary trust.* This is a trust you set up in your will. It doesn't come into existence until you die; it gets funded during the probate process. There are different types of testamentary trusts (which are discussed in Chapter 26).

What You Want Your Will to Do

You will should reflect your overall estate plan. Your estate plan is a plan to dispose of your assets to implement your personal wishes and tax-saving objectives.

When you write a will (probably you won't literally write it; your attorney will), there are certain things you want to cover:

➤ You want to say who gets your property. It's one thing if you leave everything to one person—that's easy. But if you have more than one person you want to provide for, things get more complicated. You have to be careful how to create the gifts for your heirs.

➤ You also have to name the people who will act in special roles in your estate: your executor, trustee (if you're setting up a trust), and guardian (if you have minor children or grandchildren you need to protect).

You can write a will yourself (today there are many software programs that help you to do it by using a computer). However, most people use an attorney. There's a good reason for not doing it yourself (and I'm not just saying this because I'm an attorney): Because your entire wealth and your family's well-being are at stake, it's just too important to make a mistake. What's more, the cost of making a will is usually only a modest fee of under $100 to only several hundred dollars (but the cost gets higher when there's extensive estate planning involved).

It's common practice to leave the will with the attorney who prepared it (with you keeping a copy on hand carrying a notation that the original is on file with your attorney). It's also common to deposit your will with the probate court while you're alive (you can always substitute a newer will for one on file with the court). Whichever storage method you select, make sure your executor knows that you've appointed him or her and where to find your will.

Cash Crash
While your will is an important document, don't store it in a safe deposit box. This can lead to delay in getting it when needed (especially in states that seal the boxes when the owner dies).

A word of caution: Writing a will isn't the only thing there is to an estate plan. Depending on the size of your estate, you'll probably need to do some estate tax planning. You'll also want to coordinate your will with other estate planning measures, such as trusts you may set up and gifts you may make. Living trusts are discussed in Chapter 25; gift giving is discussed in Chapter 26.

Passing Property Properly

When you make a will, you're trying to forecast what property you'll have and who'll be there to inherit it on some unknown date in the future. Because you're not a seer, you can only make a best case guess.

Some people may be under the impression that a will is a detailed inventory of your assets that you then assign piece by piece to your sisters, brothers, nieces, nephews, and friends. There's nothing preventing you from doing this, but, as a practical matter, it's just not done this way. The reason: Your property holdings aren't static. You're constantly buying and selling, even if you don't realize it. You may own stock now that could be merged with another company in the future, getting a totally new name. Or you may have a vacation home that you're going to sell in a few years.

You can choose to give *specific* bequests by giving a set dollar amount or certain property to your relative or friend. For example, if you have a favorite painting, you might leave it to your best friend, who has always admired it, if you know your children don't care for it. Or you could give $20,000 to each of your children and leave the rest of your property, however much that may be, to your spouse.

Golden Years Ideas
Instead of specifying which daughter gets your diamond pin and which one gets your china, you might use a *letter of instruction*. This is just a note you write to your executor spelling out who gets what. It's not legally binding on your executor, but it gives him or her a clear indication of your wishes, and they're usually followed. What's more, you can easily write a new one as you acquire new items or give others away.

In disposing of your personal property, you can give your executor discretion to distribute items to your children or other individuals. Alternatively, you can allow the executor to divide classes of your personal property (house contents, china, silver, and paintings) into a certain number of lots of roughly equal value and then distribute one lot to each person. Your heirs can always swap items among themselves. It's generally *not* a good idea to leave specific items, such as your diamond brooch, to someone because you might sell or give it away before you die, leaving nothing for that person to inherit.

A will generally gives to the people you name a share (or percentage) of your total holdings. For example, if you have two children surviving you, each may get half of your estate. They're sharing what's called your *residuary* estate (the estate that remains after all other bequests and expenses have been paid out). Unfortunately, there may be little or nothing left in your residuary estate if your estate is solely responsible for estate taxes and there's been a great number of other bequests made from your estate.

Most people provide for their spouses, but some just don't want to for whatever reason. You can disinherit your spouse only so much. The laws in each state provide some protection by allowing a spouse to *elect* a certain share allowed by state law. This right of election to inherit a certain part of the estate applies even if the will says otherwise. The only way to prevent this right of election is with a prenuptial or postnuptial agreement in which the spouse waives this right of election.

Many people also provide for their children. But you don't have to. There's nothing in the law *requiring* you to leave anything to your children. And there's nothing requiring you to give equal amounts to each child. If you still have business interests and one of your children works in the business, you may want to give that property to that child and give something else, even if it's of lesser value, to your other child. Or you may want to use your estate to provide for one child where the other has received gifts from you over the years. As a practical matter (to avoid a will challenge), it's a good idea to specify in your will that you've decided for personal reasons not to leave anything to one child or the other.

You can give your property to charity. The same rules that applied to bequests to individuals apply to charitable bequests. You can give a specific dollar amount, or certain shares of stock, or just a portion of your total estate.

How can you provide for the dog or cat you love so much? It's not a good idea to leave them anything in your will. (In all states except California and Tennessee, pets are just property, and property can't own other property.) The best way is to leave your pet and adequate funds for the pet's care to someone you know is willing to take on the responsibility. In some states, such as New York, you can use so-called honorary trusts to provide money for the care of a pet. Don't leave your cat to your son who's allergic to cats or to your daughter currently living in an ashram in India. Alternatively, there may be certain charitable organizations that will, in return for a bequest, care for your pet.

Golden Years Ideas
When naming a charity in your will, provide the organization's name and current address. It's also a good idea to provide some alternate charities to take this inheritance if the first charity is no longer in existence or loses its tax-exempt status.

In most families, there's no thought that needs to be given to a challenge to your will. But some families may not get along very well. How can you protect your plans and avoid the possibility that someone will contest your will? There's no iron-clad way to do it. Relatives can get funny after a person dies and think they're entitled to certain things, regardless of how the decedent saw it. The multi-million dollar estate of Harry Winston, the famous jeweler, has been decimated by a will contest between his two sons, each claiming that he is entitled to something other than what the will said.

You're allowed to include a clause in your will, called a noncontestability clause. It provides that anyone who brings an action to contest the will forfeits any inheritance.

Naming Names

Who should be your executor? Who should serve in other capacities? These are important decisions that you want to make carefully. All of these positions are ones requiring your utmost trust.

Legally, an executor can be anyone who is of adult age and mentally competent. It doesn't have to be a relative, although state law may require that non-relatives live in state to act as executors.

Your executor should be someone who's capable of handling the job. This is a person who's savvy with financial matters and willing to take on the job. An executor also needs to be a diplomat, able to handle with finesse the squabbles that may break out between relatives over who gets your totally worthless but sentimentally priceless souvenir from the war or your old picture album.

Typically, a married person names his or her spouse to act as executor. This may not be a good idea if the spouse is aging and may not be fully up to the job.

Sometimes there isn't a clear choice for the job. A spouse may be sick, or there may be no spouse or children to name.

Often, people name co-executors, two executors to act together. For example, people may name their spouse and one adult child to act as co-executors. Depending on how the family gets along, this may or may not be a good idea. In most cases, this works fine; but if your spouse and child continually butt heads, it can hamper the settling of your estate.

Cash Crash
If you have more than one child and you want to name only one to act as executor, make sure this won't cause hard feelings among the family. Talk to your children and explain the reasons for your choice. Maybe the child you've named is a financial whiz in your home town while the other one's an artist living in Prague. Proximity to your property, knowledge of money matters, and a strong sense of responsibility should be guiding factors in your choice.

If you're not naming your spouse or children, then consider naming an executor who's younger than you are. This way, at least you can assume that person will outlive you and will be available to act.

You should also think about successor executors. These are people who will act if the first ones you've named can't or won't act for any reason (death, disability, simply declining the position, or resigning later on).

An executor is entitled by law to certain fees for performing his or her job. However, you can require your executor to waive the fees by putting it as a condition in your will. Or you can leave this condition out and simply let your executor decide whether or not to take fees (typically family members don't take fees unless it produces a favorable tax result).

The same care you used to choose an executor should apply to your choice of trustee if you're setting up a trust under your will. The trustee can be the same person as your executor (for example, your spouse can be both your executor and a trustee of your testamentary trust). However, if your trustee is also a beneficiary of the trust, you'll need a co-trustee whose interests are not the same as that trustee-beneficiary. Some people choose trust departments at banks to act as trustees. This makes sense only for larger trusts that can afford to pay the fees charged by these trust departments. Using a trust department is helpful where there's no clear choice among your relatives or friends to act as trustee. After all, the trust will go on for many years and outlive those you appoint to manage it (other than a trust department that theoretically goes on forever).

If you still have minor children or you're raising your grandchildren, be sure to suggest a guardian for them in your will (if there's no other living parent or guardian surviving you). The guardian will raise them, so it should be someone who has the same values and beliefs you hope to instill in the children. The guardian will also oversee the minors' inheritance unless you appoint a separate guardian for the children's property (something you might consider doing if the person you'd like to raise them just isn't good with money).

Other Clauses You Might Include in Your Will

In addition to property dispositions and appointment of fiduciaries, you may want to include other things in your will. Here are some clauses to ponder:

➤ Statement of domicile. If you live in one state, there's no question about your domicile. But if you have two homes, which state is your domicile? The answer to that is critical because it controls the state in which your will can be probated.

➤ Final instructions. You can include directions on where you want to be buried or that you want to be cremated and have your ashes scattered over the Atlantic Ocean. Now that you know you can say it in your will, don't. It's much better to simply inform your family, tell them directly, or leave a letter of final instruction. This is because they have to make funeral arrangements quickly, and it could be days or even longer before your will is located.

> **Word to the Wise**
> *Domicile* is the state in which you live, or if you have more than one home, the state in which you have the most attachment—physical and emotional. It's usually the place where you're registered to vote, have a driver's license, and membership in a church or synagogue.

> **Cash Crash**
> If you want to make organ donations (called *anatomical gifts*) or leave your body to science, don't use your will for this purpose. It's better to tell your family about your wishes and/or use a notation on your driver's license or other written document that can be easily accessed at the moment of your death. By the time your will is found, your body may have already been disposed of.

➤ Debts, funeral expenses, estate expenses, and taxes. Who's going to pay your last phone bill or the cost of your mausoleum? Your estate covers these costs before everything gets distributed to heirs. But the question of who pays estate taxes is another matter. It can be the estate or everyone who gets something whether it's under your will or outside your will (such as your life insurance or IRA beneficiary). The answer depends on how your estate is arranged and how large you expect your estate tax bill will be. The simplest way is to have the estate pay it. This is called *without apportionment.* But if your estate is composed of many will substitutes and there's only a little money in your probate estate, you may want to *apportion* the tax liability so that each beneficiary's share is reduced by a share of the taxes. In deciding how to handle this issue, consider the impact your decision will have on your estate plans. Let's say you have an IRA and a house of equal value. If you give your IRA to one child and your house (that passes under your will) to your other child, the one inheriting the house will have to ante up the tax money if your will provides that payment of taxes be made *without apportionment.*

➤ Simultaneous death clause. If you and your spouse (or other beneficiary) die under circumstances where it's impossible to determine which one died first (you both die in a plane crash or other common disaster), what happens to the bequests you've made? If you don't do anything, your state law may say what happens. For example, in New York the person passing on the property is deemed to have survived the other person so that the property goes to whomever is next in line. But for tax planning and to avoid family fights, it may be better to spell out what happens (it may be the same as under state law or a different result).

Making Things Easier When You Die

When you die, your family and friends have to go through an emotional process of grieving for you. The emotional trauma is magnified if your personal affairs have not been put in order. You can minimize problems for your loved ones if you leave things organized.

There are two key areas you need to address:

➤ Your wishes regarding your funeral. This is something your family has to organize under extreme time pressure at a moment when they're emotionally distraught. You can help them out by telling them *beforehand* what you have in mind about your final resting place.

➤ Your financial affairs. If you're like my friend down the street, you (and only you) know where your last stock statements are kept among the piles of paper strewn around the house. But when you're dead, how is anyone going to find them? And will anyone know who your accountant is? Where you've put your will? It's vital for your family to put things in order.

Instructions for Your Family About Your Funeral

Funerals are never joyous occasions. But they can be *less* unpleasant for your family and friends if you've taken a hand in guiding them on your wishes about your final farewell and last resting place. It's more than just a matter of whether you want to be buried next to your first wife or cremated. It's also about dollars and cents. After all, the average cost of a funeral today tops $10,000 (according to the National Funeral Directors Association, the average cost of a casket alone in 1995 was $4,624). You wouldn't spend $1,000 on a new refrigerator without shopping around, yet your family might easily pay 10 times that amount for your funeral without question.

Some people make their funeral arrangements well before they die. They buy what's called a prepaid funeral contract. Generally, for just one large payment, everything from coffin to service to burial and continued care of the grave site is covered.

The funeral industry is big business. Watch out so you and your family won't get ripped off. The Federal Trade Commission has adopted rules to protect against misrepresentation of funeral pricing and unwanted purchases. You can get price information over the phone, and you're entitled to an itemized price list for the goods and services you're buying.

State law varies on funeral requirements, and it's a good idea to know beforehand what rules apply in your state. For instance, New York doesn't require embalming or that you have a casket or other container if you're being cremated; a funeral home that says otherwise is just trying to rip you off. If you or your family suspect that they've been illegally taken advantage of, contact the office in your state that handles consumer fraud (they're listed in Appendix A).

Getting Things in Order

Maybe you know that the guy named Harry Corwin in your little black book is your insurance agent, but your family may not. It's important for them that you make

Golden Years Ideas
You can't avoid dying, but there are two ways you can keep your funeral costs down. One is to be cremated, an increasingly popular choice among many people. Another way is to donate your body to a medical school or other research facility. Of course, these choices should be made in the context of your religious and personal preferences.

Cash Crash
Before you agree to a prepaid funeral contract, understand the drawbacks. Unfortunately, there's a chance for fraud. But even with reputable funeral homes, you could lose money if you want out at any time (you move out of state and decide you'd rather be buried near your new home, or you just decide you don't like the funeral director anymore). The prepaid contract may also allow the funeral home to keep any earnings on your investment over and above the costs of the services you've contracted for.

up a list of the people you rely on for various types of advice and assistance. You also want to help your family find your important papers after you die. Obviously, if you can keep them all in one place, it's the best way to go. But if not, at least leave some clues. Use Tables 24.1 and 24.2 to provide a road map of sorts for your family when you die.

Table 24.1 Advisers and Other Important Information

Names	Phone Numbers
Lawyer:	
Stockbroker:	
Stockbroker:	
Insurance agent:	
Accountant:	
Trustee of any trust you've set up:	
Executor named in your will:	
Guardian named in your will:	

Table 24.2 Location of Important Papers and Other Things

Papers or Things	Location
Will	
Trusts	
Tax returns	
Bank books	
Financial statements (from brokerage firms, mutual funds)	

Papers or Things	Location
Safe deposit box	
Box located at:	_____
Keys located at:	_____
Insurance policies/annuity contracts	_____
Retirement accounts	_____

The Least You Need to Know

➤ If you don't have a will, your state law will say who inherits your property.

➤ Learning the terminology of wills can help you decide what you want in yours and can save you money at the lawyer's office.

➤ Don't store your will in your safe deposit box; keep the original on hand (or a copy with instructions on where the original can be found).

➤ Use a letter of instruction to tell your family who should get which pieces of jewelry or other personal property.

➤ Generally you *must* give your spouse a certain share of your estate; you don't have to leave your children anything if you don't want to.

➤ In choosing an executor, pick someone in whom you have complete trust, who is knowledgeable about money matters, and who is willing to take the job.

➤ You can make life easier for your family if you tell them what you want in the way of a funeral and where they can find your important papers and phone numbers of your advisers.

Beyond Wills

Many people have become phobic about probate. They've heard horror stories about long delays and high costs in settling estates. They've seen newspaper stories reporting in detail what famous people have left in their wills. These stories have been publicized by lawyers and companies in the business of selling expensive living trusts. As a result, people are anxious to find any mechanism that will prevent them from having to step into a probate court. Well, there are ways to arrange your property so that it will pass automatically on your death, without any probate.

In this chapter, you'll learn about using other devices, called *will substitutes*, to dispose of your property when you die. You'll learn when it's a good idea to use them and when it's not.

Will Alternatives

Not everything you've accumulated in life needs to be disposed of under the terms of your will. You can use what are called *will substitutes* because they are arrangements that also pass property to your heirs. Will substitutes pass property automatically by operation of law so no probate is needed to confer title or ownership.

There are several different will alternatives; these can be used together. Using one mechanism doesn't mean you can't use other ones as well. You can use will alternatives in conjunction with having a will. Will alternatives include:

➤ Joint bank accounts

➤ Joint brokerage accounts

➤ Jointly owned stocks, bonds, and mutual fund shares

➤ Jointly owned real estate

➤ Life insurance

➤ Annuities

➤ Retirement accounts with designated beneficiaries

➤ Trusts

Before you re-arrange your holdings to remove property from your probate estate, ask yourself whether you need to avoid probate in the first place. The answer depends on the state you live in. In many states, probate isn't a costly and lengthy process. In New York, for example, the highest probate fee is $1,000 and applies to estates valued at $500,000 or more. This means that multi-million dollar estates pay only a $1,000 probate fee. You don't have to aggressively try to avoid probate in the following states because the process and cost isn't onerous:

➤ Alabama

➤ Alaska

➤ Colorado

➤ Connecticut

➤ District of Columbia

➤ Georgia

➤ Idaho

➤ Iowa

➤ Kansas

➤ Kentucky

➤ Louisiana

➤ Maine

➤ Maryland

➤ Mississippi

➤ Montana

➤ New Jersey

➤ New Mexico

➤ New York

➤ North Carolina

➤ North Dakota

➤ Pennsylvania

➤ South Carolina

➤ Tennessee

➤ Texas

➤ Washington

➤ West Virginia

Even where a will is appropriate, it's still a good idea to have certain will substitutes as a means of providing *liquidity* for your estate. Liquidity means cash or assets readily convertible into cash (like stocks and bonds). Your estate (and your heirs) need a certain amount of liquidity just to pay bills as they come due. And, most importantly, to pay estate taxes (generally nine months from the date of death but it can be earlier in certain states). For example, a joint bank account can be handy to give a surviving spouse the necessary cash to pay the regular household bills; a life insurance policy can be used to pay the estate taxes. But be aware that joint bank accounts and other property passing outside the will over a certain size can be frozen until state tax authorities grant waivers.

Joint Ownership

Joint ownership, as you've already seen, can be used effectively as a financial management tool during your lifetime if you become disabled or incompetent. Your joint owner can use the property for your benefit, relieving you of having to make deposits, write checks, make investment decisions, and other chores you may no longer be able to do. But joint ownership doesn't have to be only a convenience account for your benefit. It can also serve as an important estate planning purpose. It passes the property automatically to the surviving joint owner *without* the need for probate.

Any two or more people or entities (like corporations) can become joint tenants. You don't have to be related, and you don't even need the knowledge and consent of the other tenant to set it up. You can set up a joint tenancy with your property by just putting the name of someone else on the account or title. There are no special costs charged by the banks or brokerage firms to set up joint tenancies.

Before you rush out to change the title to all your property, there are certain drawbacks to joint ownership that you should consider:

> ➤ During your life, there's nothing preventing the joint tenant from wiping out your account. This can happen involuntarily, for example, if your joint tenant suffers financial difficulties and creditors look to your joint bank account for satisfaction. And even if your joint owner is trying to act in your best interest, he or she may not do the best job in managing the money in a joint name (for example, your joint tenant may invest the money in a losing stock).

Cash Crash
Even if you think you've arranged for all your property to pass automatically when you die, it's still a good idea to make a will. You may have overlooked some item, like your car. And you never know when you'll acquire new assets that you didn't get time to put into a trust or make other provisions for.

Cash Crash
While ownership automatically transfers to someone else for property that passes by operation of law, that person may not get the funds immediately when you die. Depending on who the person is (a spouse or someone else), how much is involved, and in what state the owner lived, the state may have to issue what's called *tax waivers* to allow distribution before estate taxes are paid.

➤ When you set up the joint tenancy, you may create gift tax problems for yourself. If you own real estate in your name and change the title to joint name, you've created a gift for gift tax purposes. Depending on the value of the property involved, you could owe gift taxes. Or you could just wind up using part of the exemption amount, which will cause your estate to go into a higher tax bracket. (Gift tax issues are discussed more fully in the next chapter.)

➤ At death, your estate planning goals can be defeated by using joint ownership. If your will provides certain bequests, the money in the joint account isn't available to pay those bequests. You may inadvertently disinherit some people or short change others. Your will provides that each of your three children get one third of your estate. You make your daughter who lives in your city a joint owner of your bank account and brokerage account. When you die, that daughter will get a much greater share of your property than your other two children.

➤ You could cause higher estate taxes for your spouse's estate. If your spouse and you own property valued at more than twice the applicable exclusion ($1,250,000 in 1998 [$625,000 × 2 = $1,250,000]), and you leave everything to your spouse, joint ownership will prevent your being able to use your exclusion. True, your estate won't pay any estate tax because of the marital deduction. But when your spouse dies, his or her estate could wind up paying more than a quarter of a million dollars it didn't have to if other arrangements had been made.

Joint Bank Accounts

With the drawbacks of joint ownership in mind, you may still want to put some or even all of your money into joint name. Joint bank accounts are easy to arrange. You simply put the account in the name of both you and someone else as joint owners with right of survivorship. The money left in the account on the day of your death belongs entirely to your joint owner.

Some people use accounts titled "in trust for." (In New York, these are referred to as *Totten trusts*.) An "in trust for" account works the same as a joint account in terms of passing on the funds automatically at death. The difference between the joint account and the "in trust for" account is simple: With the joint account, the other owner can access the money while you're alive (which can be a good or a bad thing, depending on your situation). With an "in trust for" account, the money is yours completely until the day you die.

Joint Brokerage Accounts

Like joint bank accounts, joint brokerage accounts are easy to arrange. Firms like Merrill Lynch or Charles Schwab will give you the paperwork to set up a joint account. Just title the account as a joint account with right of survivorship. The right of survivorship means that whichever joint owner survives the other, he or she takes all. You may see "ROS" after your names on your monthly account statements to indicate "right of survivorship."

In some states, you don't have to use joint ownership to pass your brokerage account on to someone automatically. There's an arrangement called a *pay-on-death* designation. You simply specify that at death, the account is to be retitled in the name of Sam or Betty or whomever you choose. This keeps maximum control of the property in your hands while you're alive but avoids probate on it when you die. The only drawback: Brokerage firms may charge a fee ($75 per transfer with one firm); there's no cost for a joint account. And it's not available in every state.

> **Cash Crash**
> While the account belongs automatically to the surviving owner, that person still has to take some steps to get the title of the account changed to the survivor. Generally this means presenting a death certificate and signing a document that's called an affidavit of domicile.

Joint Stocks, Bonds, and Mutual Fund Shares

Like a brokerage account, you can title these securities jointly so that they'll pass automatically to the joint owner when you die. For stocks and bonds, ask the transfer agent to re-register the securities in joint name (you'll find the transfer agent, usually a bank, listed on the back of the securities or on the quarterly statement you receive from the company in which you've invested). For mutual fund shares, you must ask the fund to send you the necessary papers to sign so that title can be changed.

Real Estate Held Jointly

If you have title to real estate as joint tenants with right of survivorship (or if you're married and your state provides for tenancy by the entirety), then the surviving joint owner inherits the entire property. But if you're only a co-tenant in a co-tenancy, the other co-tenant doesn't inherit your share automatically. You can say in your will who should become the new owner (your interest in a co-tenancy is an asset of your probate estate).

Changing title to real estate so that the new deed is recorded in the public records generally involves an attorney's fee. In some states, title companies will handle the paperwork to change title.

> **Cash Crash**
> Before changing title to real estate, check with the title insurance company to see if there's any effect on the title insurance. If there's a mortgage on the property, you may need permission from the bank or mortgage company to change the title (permission generally isn't necessary if you're only adding your spouse as joint owner).

Beneficiary Designation

You may already have used a will alternative and not even known it. If you own a life insurance policy, you've probably named a beneficiary to get the proceeds when you die. This is called a beneficiary designation. The insurance company will automatically pay the proceeds to the named beneficiary upon proof of death (and after any state death tax waivers if applicable).

Cash Crash

You don't want to name a beneficiary who's already receiving Medicaid (or may need to receive it in the future). In this case, unless you're talking about large sums, your property will just supplement the benefits already available with Medicaid without adding appreciably to the welfare of that beneficiary. So, if your parent is very elderly, think twice before naming or keeping that parent as your beneficiary.

While beneficiary designation will keep the property out of your probate estate, there's one instance when you can trip up and reroute the property right back into your probate estate. This can happen if you name your estate (or your executor in his or her capacity as executor) as the beneficiary.

Making a beneficiary designation is easy. You just write in the name of the person you want to inherit the property on the form provided by the company that sold you your life insurance or IRA. You can usually change the beneficiary designation at any time up to your death. There's no cost involved for making a change. You don't even have to notify the beneficiary of your action. (There are situations where you may make an irrevocable designation, in which case the beneficiary must consent to any change.)

And there's no gift tax cost in making a beneficiary designation. The reason: It's not considered a completed gift because you're free to change the beneficiary designation at any time.

Life Insurance

Proceeds are payable automatically to the person named as beneficiary in the insurance contract you bought. You make the designation when you buy the policy. If you want to change that designation later on, just ask for a *change of beneficiary* form from the insurance company. There's no cost or other consequences for making the change.

Annuities

If you had a joint and survivor annuity or an annuity with a guaranteed payment (and you died before you received this guaranteed amount), then the person you named in the annuity contract as your beneficiary will receive benefits. This may be a continued monthly payment of benefits under a joint and survivor annuity, or a lump sum payment to a beneficiary for the unpaid balance of a guaranteed amount.

Retirement Accounts

Your company benefits and IRAs pass automatically to beneficiaries if you've named them. If you haven't designated anyone (or you've named your estate), then they are merely assets of your estate (and pass through probate).

Who should be your beneficiaries? First decide who you want to pass the money on to. But in making this decision, keep income tax in mind. This is because, unlike just about any other asset you pass on, retirement accounts (other than Roth IRAs and retirement benefits derived from your own after-tax contributions) don't pass income-tax free to the beneficiary. Because you never paid income tax on the money, your beneficiary will.

Here are the consequences of naming different types of beneficiaries:

➤ Spouse. If you name your spouse as beneficiary of your IRA, your spouse will be able to roll over your account into his or her own name. This will allow your spouse to figure required minimum distributions based on his or her own age and choice of beneficiaries, rather than on yours.

➤ Your children or other people. These beneficiaries will have to start reporting income from their inheritance within set times. (The exact time depends on whether or not you've already started your required minimum distributions.) Depending on the overall size of your estate and your beneficiaries' income tax bracket, the combined tax bite on your retirement accounts can be about 70%.

➤ Charity. If you leave your retirement accounts to charity, there won't be any income tax to deplete your gift (because charities are exempt from income tax). So, if you're planning to make a gift to charity anyway, it may be a good idea to use this asset over any other one to satisfy the gift.

Put Your Trust in Trusts

You may have seen advertisements for lawyers or companies selling living trusts as the best way to beat probate and provide all kinds of other benefits. The ads aren't entirely off base. This is because trusts of any type can be used to pass on property to a beneficiary named in the trust instrument. But don't jump in and set up a living trust until you know what it's all about.

Here's how a trust works. You (or more likely your lawyer) write a trust document (called an instrument or a deed of trust) spelling out the rules on how the trust will operate. You say in that document who's to be the beneficiary and who's to be the trustee to manage the property. Then you change the title of your property to read "The *YOUR NAME* Trust" (or any variation on this theme). For personal items, such as

> **Word to the Wise**
> *Trust fund* is the property transferred into the trust. It's also called *principal* or *corpus*.

jewelry, you'll have to list them in the trust document or leave a letter stating that the property is owned by the trust. Then the trustee you've named in the trust (which may or may not be you) runs the trust in accordance with the trust document.

There are two types of trusts: irrevocable trusts and revocable trusts. Both avoid probate. The difference is that once you've set up and transferred property to an irrevocable trust, you can't change your mind and get your property back. With a revocable trust, you can, as the name implies, revoke it at any time up until your death. If you and your spouse are beneficiaries, you can revoke provisions that become irrevocable on the first spouse's death (these are various tax-saving clauses) only until that spouse's death. Living trusts are revocable trusts (discussed next). (Certain types of irrevocable trusts are discussed in the next chapter.)

What a Living Trust Can Do for You

To find out what a living trust can do for you, you have to understand what a trust is all about. This is a trust you set up now to hold your property. You keep the right to revoke or amend it at any time. You name yourself the income beneficiary (the current beneficiary) to get the income from the trust for as long as you live. You can name your spouse as another income beneficiary. While you're both alive, you share the income; when one of you dies, the other gets all the income for the rest of his or her life. (You're allowed to have an income interest for just a number of years, called a term interest, but it's not usually done in living trusts.) You can also have trust property distributed to you or used for your benefit. This is called *invading* the principal.

You specify a beneficiary who will receive the remainder interest (this person is called a remainderman) to inherit whatever's left in the trust at the time when you die. The remainderman can be your child or anyone else (including a charity). You can have multiple beneficiaries, such as all your children.

Your trustee has certain duties and powers with respect to your trust. Your trustee has a duty to take possession of the property you've given to the trust. The trustee must also exercise reasonable care and skill in managing the trust. The trustee may be required to make a periodic accounting of the trust's activities (obviously you won't make an accounting to yourself if you're acting as trustee, but you may want this done if a bank trust department is your trustee). The trustee must keep the trust's property separate from his or her own. And finally, the trustee can't delegate these fiduciary duties.

Golden Years Ideas

You can set up a trust now but wait to transfer property until later on. This is called a *standby trust* or an *unfunded trust*. Usually people take this step to ensure that there will be a vehicle for money management in the event of disability (a durable power of attorney can give the agent power to transfer property into the trust and fund it). If you fail to fund the trust before you die, you won't get the probate-avoidance you'd hoped for because everything is still in your name.

The trustee has certain powers to act. These powers are given by state law and are expanded on or contracted in the trust instrument. For example, a trustee has the power to buy and sell property, vote securities, make repairs, and contest, compromise, or settle claims relating to trust property. The trust instrument can add powers such as the power to borrow or lend trust funds, employ agents, run a business, or keep assets that aren't productive (something that otherwise wouldn't be allowed).

Who should be your trustee? Depending on your state's law, you can act as trustee of your own trust even though you're also the beneficiary. Some states require independent trustees, although you can act as a co-trustee. You can have an institution such as a bank trust department act as your trustee.

In addition to a trustee (and co-trustee if you want or need one), you should also provide for a successor trustee: someone to act once the original trustee can't because of any reason (death, disability, resignation, or removal by a court for doing a bad job). This can be your child or anyone else who was eligible to be a trustee in the first place. Alternatively, you may want to put in place a procedure for getting a new trustee when an old one resigns (such as unanimous consent by all beneficiaries).

Golden Years Ideas

A bank trust department may charge high fees for being the trustee. As a practical matter, it doesn't pay to get involved with this arrangement unless your trust is large and can afford the fee. What's more, the bank trust department may not even accept appointment as trustee unless the trust is large enough to produce certain revenue for the company. If you want a bank trust department and your trust is rather simple (you don't have any business interests), try to negotiate for lower fees.

As you've learned, a living trust can avoid probate. This can save you money and even time in getting your property into the proper hands after your death. Of course, it's not necessary in many states. And a living trust can serve your lifetime financial management needs (as you saw in Chapter 21, "Money Management: Keeping Things Out of Court"). But here are some special estate-related reasons why it may be a good idea to use a living trust:

➤ Avoid ancillary probate. If you own real estate in more than one state, remember that your estate will have to go through an ancillary probate proceeding for the property located in the state you weren't domiciled in. Without it, you can't change title to the property. Even in states where probate isn't a big deal, this can still be timely and costly. With a living trust, the title is automatically transferred via the trust; no additional probate is required.

➤ Provide for outsiders. Your family may have a claim on your assets; non-relatives do not. If you want to provide for someone who's not related to you, especially where there's any chance of family friction, use a living trust to pass along the property. It's much more difficult to contest a trust than it is to contest a will.

➤ Keep things private. Probate is a matter of public record. Anyone can go to the courthouse and look up a will that's been probated. In contrast, a living trust isn't a public matter; it's entirely private.

What a Living Trust Won't Do for You

A living trust can do many things for you as you have seen. But it can't do *everything*. The following is a list of what a living trust won't do for you:

➤ Save estate taxes. A living trust won't save any more estate taxes than you could have saved with a will. This is because you're treated as owning whatever's in the trust at your death because you could have revoked the trust and reclaimed the property at that time. You can, however, include certain tax-saving provisions in trust to ensure that the estate's tax picture will be optimized.

➤ Speed up distribution. A living trust says who owns what automatically. But, as a practical matter, if the estate is large enough, there'll be estate taxes to pay. They're due nine months after the date of death (or sooner in some states). Typically, a living trust contributes its proportionate share of taxes. So the trust isn't distributed until the taxes have been settled.

➤ Save attorney's fees. It's a question of now or later. With a will, attorney's fees to draft it are low, but there'll be more fees later to settle the estate. With a living trust, the setup fee may be high (from several hundred dollars for simple trusts to several thousand dollars for complicated trusts), but there'll be smaller attorney's fees to settle the estate later on. It's almost a wash either way you go.

➤ Handle everything. It's virtually impossible to put everything you own into a trust. Your car, for example, may stay in your own name. You may not be able to transfer shares in cooperative apartments into the name of the trust; it would violate your co-op agreement. You may have a pending lawsuit that's not settled until after your death; you need a will to say who gets your award. And you can't use a trust to name a guardian for minor children; you need a will for this purpose.

➤ Simplify your life. Having a trust adds complexity rather than simplicity to your financial life. You need to keep separate books for trust transactions. If you're the trustee and beneficiary, then, for income tax purposes, you're treated as the owner of the trust. This means that the trust doesn't have to file its own tax return; you just report all the income and other transactions from the trust on your personal income tax return. But if there are other beneficiaries or other circumstances, the trust must get its own tax identification number and file its own return; you then pick up your share of trust income.

➤ Protect your assets from creditors. Unlike irrevocable trusts, living trusts, which are revocable, remain subject to the claims of your creditors in the same way as any property in your own name.

With these shortcomings in mind, you can decide whether using a living trust will meet your estate planning needs. If you decide you want a living trust, make sure it is coordinated with the terms of your will.

The Least You Need to Know

➤ Using will substitutes such as life insurance and beneficiary designations of retirement accounts avoids the need to provide in your will which beneficiary should inherit these interests.

➤ Probate need not be aggressively avoided in many states because the process there isn't costly or lengthy.

➤ Joint ownership has some down sides that need to be considered before transferring assets into joint name.

➤ Pay-on-death designation of securities and brokerage accounts can be used in some states instead of joint ownership.

➤ There are no fees for changing bank accounts, stocks, bonds, mutual funds shares, and brokerage accounts into joint name.

➤ Life insurance, annuities, and retirement accounts with beneficiary designations (other than your estate) pass outside of probate.

➤ Living trusts, which can be revoked or amended while you're alive, pass outside of probate.

➤ Living trusts don't solve all of your estate planning issues, and you may still need to make a will and undertake other estate planning measures.

Chapter 26

Estate Planning for the Rich and Not-So-Rich

People say the two things you can't avoid are death and taxes. Well, when you die, your family may have to deal with death taxes. Depending on how much you own when you die, the government's final tax bite may be a hefty one. During your retirement, while you may be focusing on making more money, you shouldn't overlook the need to think about what will happen to that money when you die.

In this chapter, you'll learn the basics of estate taxes and various estate planning strategies to minimize taxes. You'll find out why you may want to make gifts to your family or charity and how to use trusts for a tax-saving advantage.

Everything You Need to Know About Estate Taxes

When you hear the word *estate*, you may picture a mansion situated on several acres—the home of a wealthy individual. In tax parlance, the word *estate* isn't limited to a home. It includes *all* property that you have an interest in. You need to know how large your estate really is so that you can begin to get an idea about the estate taxes that could be involved when you die.

You also need to know how estate taxes work. They're not at all like income taxes, so your experience with years of paying income taxes won't help you.

Sizing Up Your Estate

If you were asked, "How large is your estate?" would you know the answer off hand? Probably not. Most people are surprised to find out just how wealthy the government thinks they are. It's not your standard of living that determines the size of your estate. It's just a matter of adding things up.

Use the following chart to map out what you have, called your *gross estate*. It's important to estimate what things are worth today so you can move ahead with your estate planning. Obviously, you can't know what they'll be worth when you die or even if you'll still own the same assets. The purpose of adding up what you've got is to know whether you need to undertake any estate planning strategies and what they might include (see Table 26.1). (There's an added benefit to making this list: It will help your family know what you've got when you die and you're not there to tell them.)

Table 26.1 Inventory of Your Assets

Item	Current Value
Bank accounts	$_____
Bonds	$_____
Business interests (for example, partnership or limited liability company interests)	$_____
Car/boat	$_____
Cash	$_____
CDs	$_____
Collections (for example, stamps, art)	$_____
Commercial annuities	$_____
IRAs	$_____
Jewelry	$_____
Life insurance*	$_____
Mortgages you hold (and other debts owed to you)	$_____
Mutual funds	$_____
Pensions	$_____
Personal things (for example, books, clothing)	$_____
Real estate	$_____
Stocks	$_____
Other	$_____

Include the face value of any policy you own (less outstanding loans) or are treated as owning because you have the right to change beneficiaries, take loans, or cancel the policy. If you've transferred any policies within the past three years, also include them in your list.

You don't have to include property interests that will end with your death. So, for example, if you have a life income interest in a trust (perhaps one created by your late spouse or your parent) and that interest ceases the moment you die, you don't own an asset here that can be included in your estate. You can't say where the rest of the trust property goes or pass anything on.

If you've set up a living trust in which you keep the right to revoke it as long as you live, *all* assets in the trust are treated as belonging to you and part of your estate. The fact that title to the property is in the name of the trust doesn't change this result. (Tax-saving measures you can take for your living trust are discussed later in this chapter in the section called "Tax Saving Ideas You Can Use.")

Projecting Your Tax Liability

The estate of every person gets an exemption amount. This exemption amount is the value of property you can pass federal estate tax-free (see Table 26.2). (The rules for your state death taxes aren't covered in this book. It's a good idea to check them out with your state tax authority or with an estate planning lawyer in your area.)

Table 26.2 Estate That Can Pass Federal Estate Tax-Free

Year of Death	Applicable Exemption Amount
1998	$625,000
1999	$650,000
2000 and 2001	$675,000
2002 and 2003	$700,000
2004	$850,000
2005	$950,000
2006 and later	$1,000,000

Source: Internal Revenue Code

As a practical matter, the exemption isn't just a subtraction from your estate. It's converted into a tax credit (called a *unified credit*) that's used to offset the tax on your estate. Telling you what the credit is wouldn't mean much because you don't really know how much that credit would effectively shield from tax. Just keep the exemption amount in mind when you're doing your estate planning.

If the value of your assets on the date of your death are below the applicable exemption amount, you can forget about estate planning; your estate won't have to file a federal estate tax return (IRS Form 706) or pay any federal estate taxes. (It may choose to file one just as a precaution in case the value of your assets are in dispute and ultimately turn out to be worth more than originally projected.) So if your estate today is worth $400,000, even with moderate growth in your investments, you probably will stay below the estate tax threshold (especially if you plan on spending some of that money before you die). If you're already at the current threshold, you should be concerned about taxes. While you could spend your money and reduce the size of your estate, your assets could very well appreciate and push you over the exemption amount.

Let's say your estate is already over the threshold amount. Does that mean your estate will owe any federal estate taxes? Not necessarily. There are several ways you're allowed to reduce the size of your estate. Here are some common reductions you may be entitled to:

➤ Funeral expenses. The thousands of dollars paid for your funeral and burial are a deductible item.

➤ Expenses of a last illness. While Medicare and other insurance may pick up most of the costs, they may still be some amounts that aren't covered. Your estate may pay these sums and claim a deduction. Alternatively, your estate can waive the deduction to allow it to be claimed on your final income tax return (a waiver would be made if it produces greater tax savings on your income tax return).

➤ Executor's fees. If your spouse or children serve, they probably won't take any fees. But if an outsider serves as executor, he or she is entitled to fees (state law may specify maximum executor fees, which vary with the size of your estate).

➤ Attorney's fees. Typically, an attorney charges fees to probate the estate. Fees may be based on an hourly rate. However, it's more common for attorneys to base fees on a percentage of the estate.

➤ Accounting fees to prepare the estate tax return.

➤ Debts you owe at the time of your death (including mortgages on your home or other property, telephone bills, credit card charges, and other outstanding bills).

➤ Administration expenses. Your estate may have to spend money to preserve or insure your property until it can be distributed to heirs. These costs are deductible.

Cash Crash

Unless your spouse is a U.S. citizen, you don't automatically get an unlimited marital deduction (being a resident alien isn't good enough for the marital deduction rule). You can maximize your marital deduction by passing property to your non-U.S. citizen spouse in a special way—by using a *qualified domestic trust* (QDOT).

➤ Marital deduction. Your estate also gets an unlimited deduction for anything your spouse inherits. The deduction doesn't cover life income interests you give your spouse unless he or she has a power of appointment over the property or the life income interest is in a special type of trust, called a QTIP trust (discussed later in this chapter in the section called "Tax Saving Ideas You Can Use").

➤ Charitable deduction. Your estate can deduct *everything* you leave to charity. There's no dollar limit or any limit based on the size of your estate.

➤ Exclusion for family-owned businesses. If your estate is made up in part of an interest in a family-owned business, it may be eligible for a special exclusion.

The exclusion is set at about $675,000 in 1998. The exclusion, combined with the increased applicable exemption amount available to every estate of $625,000, means that a total of $1.3 million can be passed tax free in 1998. Each year, as the applicable exemption amount increases, the exclusion for family-owned businesses decreases (though they don't increase and decrease dollar for dollar, because the exemption amount is really a tax credit while the exclusion is a before-tax reduction).

After you add up all these deductible items, subtract them from your *gross estate* to get an idea of your *taxable estate* (the dollar amount to which the tax is applied). Table 26.3 is a chart of the federal estate tax rates on taxable estates. The tax, however, is only a tentative tax; the exemption amount in the form of the unified credit must still be applied (and there may be other applicable credits). In view of the exemption amount, if your estate is taxable, it will be paying tax at rates ranging from 37% to 55%.

Cash Crash
The exclusion for family-owned businesses is highly complex, and many estate planning experts believe it will be usable only in limited situations. Don't automatically assume that because you own a business, your estate will be entitled to this special tax break. Check it out with an estate attorney.

Table 26.3 Federal Estate Tax Rates on Taxable Estates

If the taxable estate is this...	The tentative tax is this ...
Not over $10,000	18% of such amount
Over $10,000 but not over $20,000	$1,800, plus 20% of amount over $10,000
Over $20,000 but not over $40,000	$3,800, plus 22% of amount over $20,000
Over $40,000 but not over $60,000	$8,200, plus 24% of amount over $40,000
Over $60,000 but not over $80,000	$13,000, plus 26% of amount over $60,000
Over $80,000 but not over $100,000	$18,200, plus 28% of amount over $80,000
Over $100,000 but not over $150,000	$23,800, plus 30% of amount over $100,000
Over $150,000 but not over $250,000	$38,800, plus 32% of amount over $150,000
Over $250,000 but not over $500,000	$70,800, plus 34% of amount over $250,000
Over $500,000 but not over $750,000	$155,800, plus 37% of amount over $500,000
Over $750,000 but not over $1,000,000	$248,300, plus 39% of amount over $750,000
Over $1,000,000 but not over $1,250,000	$345,800, plus 41% of amount over $1,000,000
Over $1,250,000 but not over $1,500,000	$448,300, plus 43% of amount over $1,250,000
Over $1,500,000 but not over $2,000,000	$555,800, plus 45% of amount over $1,500,000
Over $2,000,000 but not over $2,500,000	$780,800, plus 49% of amount over $2,000,000
Over $2,500,000 but not over $3,000,000	$1,025,800, plus 53% of amount over $2,500,000
Over $3,000,000	$1,290,800, plus 55% of amount over $3,000,000*

Source: Internal Revenue Code

*Note: Estates over $10 million lose the benefit of the graduated estate tax rates and effectively pay a flat 55% tax rate.

There are several tax credits that can be used to reduce the tentative tax to the final estate tax liability. Here are the most common ones:

➤ Unified credit. This is the exemption amount taken from Table 26.2.

➤ State death tax credit. Every state can claim a tax credit (a dollar-for-dollar reduction of the tax) for any state death taxes that have been paid up to a certain limit. Most states use what's called a *pick up* tax as their state estate tax amount. The estate pays the tax equal to what is claimed as a credit on the federal tax return. Some states have estate taxes exceeding this credit amount. A few states don't have any death taxes, so no credit can be claimed.

➤ Credit for prior transfers. If you've inherited property from someone and you die within 10 years of the inheritance, your estate can claim a credit for all or part of the federal estate tax that had been paid on that inheritance. In other words, Uncle Sam says he'll only take an estate tax once every 10 years on property. The full credit for your estate applies only if you die within two years of the inheritance; it's reduced by 20% for each two years thereafter.

Give Now, Save Later

Unlike the pharaohs who were buried with their worldly goods, we pass on and leave our property behind. Recognizing that you can't take it with you, you might want to give some of your property away while you're alive. Doing this makes good sense for a number of reasons. You can help your family when they need it and can see them enjoying that help. Also, there may be significant tax savings for you and your estate.

Every person can give away each year up to $10,000 per person to as many people as desired. This is called the annual *gift tax exclusion*. So, for example, if you have six grandchildren, you can give them each up to $10,000 every year, for a total of $60,000 annually. Making this type of transfer year after year for a decade would remove $600,000 from your estate. By making the gift, you've not only helped your family now, you've also saved your estate between $222,000 and $330,000 in taxes (depending on the amount of your other assets). But the exclusion applies only to gifts in which the person gets an immediate interest in the property; it doesn't apply to certain transfers in trust since these are considered *future* interests (although there are exceptions).

Golden Years Ideas
The annual gift tax exclusion will be indexed for inflation beginning after 1998. However, under the mechanism for making the inflation adjustment, it's not expected that the exclusion will increase until the year 2002 if inflation stays at about 3%.

If you think about it, you're really giving away more than $10,000 each year. You're really transferring all the income that can be earned on that gift and any possible future appreciation on that gift. That's why if you decide to make gifts other than cash, it's important to choose your property carefully.

There are pros and cons to giving stocks and other property expected to appreciate. On the one hand, you remove the asset *and* the appreciation from your estate. But on the other hand, you may be costing your family unnecessary taxes. This is because your heirs get what's called a *stepped up basis* for inherited property. Instead of taking over your basis, as is required for lifetime gifts, they get to use as their basis the value of the property on your death (or other value used for estate tax purposes). In effect, this wipes out all of the appreciation so that if they sell the property shortly thereafter, there's no (or very little) gain to them. Of course, with the reduction of the capital gains rates, the desire to avoid giving your family a potential tax bill is certainly reduced.

For property that has declined in value, it's generally better for you to sell the property, take your loss (if it's allowable), and then give away the proceeds. This is because the person getting your property as a gift can use the property's value as its basis (the person's basis is limited to your cost or other basis). Holding this type of property until you die means your heirs can use the decreased value as their basis but, unless the value continues to decline, no one claims a write-off for the loss you've suffered.

There's no formality required in making a gift. You simply give the property to whomever you choose; it doesn't have to be a relative of yours. You don't have to tell the government about your gift on any tax return.

Giving away a piece of jewelry you rarely wear or a painting that's collecting dust is one thing. Before you rush out and give all your property away so that there'll be nothing to tax in your estate, make sure you can afford to make the gift. Don't give away property you're using to live on. For example, if you're spending the dividends you get from your mutual funds, don't give those shares away; you still need the income. You can't give the shares away and keep the right to the dividends. As they say in the tax law, the apple goes with the tree. So make gifts only from money or property you're sure you won't need.

Double Your Pleasure

If you're married, you can double your annual gift tax exclusion by having your spouse join in the gift. So, for example, if you give your child $20,000 cash from your separate bank account, it's not taxable if your spouse agrees that the gift is a joint one and consents to it. It's called a *split gift*. The only catch: You have to file a gift tax return (Form 709) to sign consent for the split gift. The portion of the form used for this purpose follows:

Form **709** (Rev. December 1996) Department of the Treasury Internal Revenue Service	**United States Gift (and Generation-Skipping Transfer) Tax Return** (Section 6019 of the Internal Revenue Code) (For gifts made after December 31, 1991) **Calendar year 19** .... ▶ **See separate instructions. For Privacy Act Notice, see the instructions for Form 1040.**	OMB No. 1545-0020

			Yes	No
1 Donor's first name and middle initial	2 Donor's last name	3 Donor's social security number		
4 Address (number, street, and apartment number)		5 Legal residence (domicile) (county and state)		
6 City, state, and ZIP code		7 Citizenship		
8 If the donor died during the year, check here ▶ ☐ and enter date of death......................... , ...				
9 If you received an extension of time to file this Form 709, check here ▶ ☐ and attach the Form 4868, 2688, 2350, or extension letter				
10 Enter the total number of separate donees listed on Schedule A—count each person only once. ▶				
11a Have you (the donor) previously filed a Form 709 (or 709-A) for any other year? If the answer is "No," do not complete line 11b .				
11b If the answer to line 11a is "Yes," has your address changed since you last filed Form 709 (or 709-A)?				
12 Gifts by husband or wife to third parties.–Do you consent to have the gifts (including generation-skipping transfers) made by you and by your spouse to third parties during the calendar year considered as made one-half by each of you? (See instructions.) (If the answer is "Yes," the following information must be furnished and your spouse must sign the consent shown below. **If the answer is "No," skip lines 13-18 and go to Schedule A.**).				
13 Name of consenting spouse	14 SSN			
15 Were you married to one another during the entire calendar year? (see instructions)				
16 If the answer to 15 is "No," check whether ☐ married ☐ divorced or ☐ widowed, and give date (see instructions) ▶				
17 Will a gift tax return for this calendar year be filed by your spouse?				
18 **Consent of Spouse–** I consent to have the gifts (and generation-skipping transfers) made by me and by my spouse to third parties during the calendar year considered as made one-half by each of us. We are both aware of the joint and several liability for tax created by the execution of this consent.				

Part 1–General Information

Consenting spouse's signature ▶   Date ▶

Consenting to a Split Gift

The gift tax return is an annual return due on April 15th of the year following the year in which you make the gift, the same day as your federal income tax return. If you get an automatic filing extension for your income tax return, you have an additional four months to file the gift tax return. But don't send the returns together.

Special Gift Giving Ideas

These aren't suggestions for perfume and roses. These are special ways to pass along your property while you're alive and achieve gift tax savings at the same time. One way is to make certain *direct* gifts that don't count toward your annual gift tax limit. You can pay the higher education costs or medical expenses *directly* to the school or medical provider. There's no dollar limit on this type of gift. You can make these direct gifts for the benefit of someone and still give that person $10,000 each year.

You can also help your children or grandchildren fund their college education by contributing on their behalf to a qualified state tuition program (a state-sponsored program guaranteeing that tuition is covered if the child attends a state school or giving credit or repayment if the child goes elsewhere or doesn't attend any school). From a gift tax perspective, this isn't considered a direct payment to the school, so you can't rely on the unlimited direct payment exemption from gift tax. The gift to the qualified state tuition program qualifies for the annual gift tax exclusion. If you should contribute more, you're allowed to elect to have your gift treated as if it were made ratably over five years. So if you give $25,000 to a qualified state tuition program on behalf of your granddaughter, you can treat the gift as being $5,000 a year for five years. There's no gift tax, but you have to make the election. The election is made by filing a gift tax return for the year of the gift.

Family limited partnerships (FLPs) are another way you can make gifts now to save taxes later. FLPs are partnerships you set up to own and manage your business and/or investments. You act as a general partner while you're alive. You make gifts to your children or others of limited partnership interests. (Because they're limited partners, they can't tell you, the general partner, what to do.) Because the limited partnership interests don't have a say in management and can be tied up in restrictions on transferability, they're valued for gift tax purposes at deep discounts (as much as 50%). Because the limited partners own their interests now, it keeps much of the future appreciation on assets in the partnership out of your estate.

Tax Saving Ideas You Can Use

Almost every day, you'll find some estate planning seminar inviting you to learn how you can save on your estate taxes. Everyone wants to save taxes. Fortunately, there are several well-used techniques that you may be able to use.

Certain techniques apply only to married people. Others can be used by anyone. You've already seen how giving your property away in small amounts year after year can amount to big estate tax savings.

Cash Crash

If you elect to treat a gift to a qualified state tuition program as having been made over five years and you die before the end of that period, any portion of the gift that hasn't yet been allocated is included in your gross estate. So if you make a gift of $25,000 and die after year two, $5,000 is allocated to the two prior years, $5,000 is allocated to the year of death, and $10,000 (the unallocated portion) is included in your gross estate.

Cash Crash

Family limited partnerships are tricky. Don't do anything without talking to a tax expert in this area. Also, because they provide such potential tax savings, Congress may in the future look more closely at them and close this loophole.

Married People Have Special Planning Options

By and large, the income tax rules penalize married people. But the estate tax rules reward the institution of marriage. This is because of the unlimited marital deduction. The government figures that it will get its due; it's only postponing the inevitable until the surviving spouse dies. This is true to some extent. Of course, there's nothing preventing a surviving spouse from spending all of the inheritance or giving it away tax free before his or her death. Still, married couples should think not only what happens when the first spouse dies (the first estate) but also what the estate tax consequences will be when the second spouse dies (the second estate).

Every couple whose combined estate exceeds twice the applicable exemption amount ($1,250,000 in 1998, which is $625,000 applicable exemption amount × 2) should think about how to maximize that exemption. You don't want to waste it in the first estate by indiscriminately using the unlimited marital deduction. Doing so will mean there's no estate tax when the first spouse dies because of the unlimited marital deduction. But when the second spouse dies, the combined estates will be taxed to the hilt. The first estate won't have used its applicable exemption amount.

To avoid this problem and make sure that the first estate makes use of the applicable exemption amount, a special trust, called a *credit shelter trust* (also called a by-pass trust), is used. Basically, when you die a trust created in accordance with the terms of your will is funded with the amount of the applicable exemption amount. Income on this money can be used for the benefit of your spouse or any other person you select. Principal can be tapped if necessary for this person's benefit. When the spouse or other income beneficiary dies, the property passes to someone else, such as your child, free of any estate tax (your exemption amount shielded this trust in the first place). There's nothing to include in the estate of your spouse or other income beneficiary.

Because the applicable exemption amount is increasing over the next several years, it's important that the language of the trust allows for the maximum amount applicable for the year of your death. Don't use a dollar amount because it will be outdated very shortly if you want the maximum amount. Another reason not to use a dollar amount is that you may lose capacity to make a new will and wouldn't be able to change a specific dollar amount.

Golden Years Ideas

It's important to use a credit shelter trust arrangement within a living trust. Remember that a living trust, by itself, doesn't automatically save any estate taxes. However, when the first spouse dies, the living trust can be divided into a credit shelter amount in the same way that a credit shelter trust can be set up under the terms of a will.

Another type of trust that can be used for estate tax savings by married couples is a qualified terminable interest trust (QTIP). This is a trust in which your surviving spouse is given an income interest, but you decide where the property will go when your spouse dies. Property going into the trust qualifies for the unlimited marital deduction; the trust becomes taxable when the surviving spouse dies.

QTIPs are particularly useful for people with second marriages who want to provide both for their current spouse and the children of their prior marriage. You're giving your spouse the income (and usually the right to principal if necessary), but you're ultimately leaving your property to your children.

Getting Life Insurance Out of Your State

Married people have the unlimited marital deduction to postpone tax on the death of the first spouse. Single people do not. But both married and single people can make one important estate tax saving step. They can get life insurance out of their estates and save taxes that would otherwise have been due on those policies. (Remember that while life insurance isn't part of your probate estate, it's still in your estate for tax purposes.)

The easiest way is just to give the policy to your child or someone else. If you're no longer the owner (or treated as the owner for tax purposes), it's not an asset of your estate even though you're the insured.

You're treated as the owner if you keep the right to change beneficiaries, borrow against the policy, or cancel it. So before you give away a policy, think about what you're giving up. You lose the ability to take accelerated death benefits should you be in need of cash if you become terminally or chronically ill. You won't be able to borrow against the policy as a ready source of cash.

Generally, it's not a great idea to give the policy to your spouse. This just postpones the day of reckoning to your spouse's death when the proceeds (or what's left of them) will be taxed in your spouse's estate.

Instead of simply transferring the policy to someone, you can put it into a trust, called a life insurance trust. This is an *irrevocable trust*, so you can't get the policy back once you've made the transfer. The trust holds the policy, pays the premiums, and collects the proceeds when you die, distributing them according to the terms of the trust. (You can gift additional sums each year to cover premiums or simply transfer enough into the trust to pay for future premiums.)

Giving away a policy can entail gift tax consequences, depending on the insurance involved. With term insurance, there's no problem because the policy has no value. But with permanent insurance, the gift is essentially the cash surrender value, which could easily exceed the annual gift tax exclusion.

The proceeds can still be used for the same purposes you bought the policy for: providing for your family and paying estate taxes and expenses. The only caution is that the trust can't *require* that funds be used to pay estate taxes or else the policy will be right back in your estate. What's more, the trust can provide additional benefits for your family: Proceeds held in the trust can be protected from the claims of the beneficiaries' creditors. And like any trust, management of trust assets can be overseen by professional managers if you name an institution to serve as trustee.

Cash Crash
To remove life insurance from your estate, you must live at least three years after you've made the transfer. If you die within three years, the insurance is included in your estate.

Golden Years Ideas
You can continue paying the premiums. To do so without any gift tax cost, you need to include in the trust a special provision, called a *Crummey power*, that gives the beneficiaries the right to withdraw contributions to the trust (your contributions that you intend will be used for premium payments) for a set time (typically 30 or 60 days of notice to the beneficiary of the contribution). Without a Crummey power, your gifts to the trust don't qualify for the annual gift tax exclusion.

An even better way to keep life insurance out of your estate is to have someone else buy it in the first place. In this case, there's no three-year waiting period; it's immediately considered someone else's property.

Skipping Generations

The Rockefellers and Astors had a way to pass on their property with estate tax savings along the way. They figured that they could leave their wealth to their grandchildren, skipping a generation, because their children were already well provided for. This meant estate taxes were levied only on them, not on their children. Congress didn't like this strategy and imposed a generation-skipping transfer tax. This is a tax that's due when property is transferred from one generation to another, skipping one or more generations in the middle.

Fortunately, this tax applies only to the very wealthy. Most families can't afford to skip a generation in the first place. And even if they can afford it, there's a $1 million exemption, so only generation-skipping transfers exceeding this amount are subject to this special tax.

Wealthy individuals who've already provided for their children (or who have children who don't need their money) might consider leaving up to $1 million to their grandchildren and save their children considerable estate taxes.

The Least You Need to Know

➤ You need to add up your assets to know whether you should plan for federal estate taxes.

➤ Living trusts are part of your gross estate.

➤ Your estate doesn't have to file a federal estate tax return or pay any tax if it's less than the applicable exemption amount.

➤ Your taxable estate is figured by subtracting certain allowable deductions such as bequests to your spouse or to charity.

➤ Making tax-free gifts is an easy way to reduce your estate for estate tax purposes.

➤ There's no gift on transfers up to $10,000 each year per recipient.

➤ Family limited partnerships can be used to transfer business and investment property at greatly discounted values.

➤ Married couples with combined estates exceeding twice the applicable exemption amount should use a credit shelter trust to maximize use of the applicable exemption in the estate of the first spouse to die.

➤ A QTIP can be used to provide for your spouse and protect your children from a prior marriage.

➤ An irrevocable life insurance trust can remove the proceeds of the policy from your estate.

Retiree Resources

Two key resources for retirees are the Office (or Department) for the Aging in your state and the place to complain if you've been (or have come close to being) the victim of a consumer fraud. (This is usually a division of the Office of the Attorney General for each state.) Use the following numbers to locate the office that can help you. Usually there are county or local offices you can find from calling the state number.

State	Office of the Aging	Place for Consumer Complaints
Alabama	800-243-5463	800-392-5658 (in AL)
	334-242-5743	205-242-7334
Alaska	907-465-3250	
Arizona	602-542-4446	800-352-8431 (in AZ)
		602-542-3702
Arkansas	501-682-8491	800-482-8982 (in AR)
		501-682-2341
California	800-321-2362 (northern CA)	800-952-5210
	800-400-4664 (southern CA)	916-445-0660
	916-322-5630	800-952-5210 (in CA for auto repair complaints)
		916-366-5100 (for auto repair complaints)
Colorado	303-620-4146	800-332-2071
		303-866-5189
Connecticut	203-424-5025	860-566-4999
		800-538-CARS (for auto repair complaints)
Delaware	800-223-9074	800-220-5424
	302-577-4791	302-577-3250
District of Columbia	202-724-5622	
Florida	904-488-2881	800-HELP-FLA (in FL)
		904-488-2226
Georgia	404-657-5258	800-869-1123 (in GA)
	404-656-3790	

continues

continued

State	Office of the Aging	Place for Consumer Complaints
Hawaii	808-586-0100	808-587-3222
Idaho	208-334-3833	800-432-3545
		208-334-2400
Illinois	800-252-2904	800-642-3112 (in IL)
		217-782-0244
Indiana	317-232-1147	800-382-5516 (in IN)
		317-232-6330
Iowa	515-281-5188	800-426-6283 (in IA)
		515-281-3592
Kansas	800-432-3535	800-432-2310 (in KA)
		913-296-2751
Kentucky	502-564-6930	502-573-2200
Louisiana	504-925-1700	800-351-4889
		504-342-9638
Maine	207-624-5335	207-626-8849
Maryland	410-225-1102	401-528-8662
Massachusetts	800-882-2003	617-727-8400
	617-727-7750	
Michigan	517-373-8230	517-373-1140
Minnesota	800-333-2433	800-657-3787
	612-296-2770	
Mississippi	800-948-3090	800-281-4418
	601-359-4929	601-359-4230
Missouri	800-235-5503	800-392-8222 (in MO)
	573-751-3082	314-751-3321
Montana	406-444-5900	406-444-4312
Nebraska	402-471-2308	402-471-2682
Nevada	800-243-3638	800-992-0900 (in NV)
		702-688-1800
New Hampshire	800-852-3345 (ext. 4680)	603-271-3641
	603-271-4384	
New Jersey	800-792-8820	201-504-6200
	609-292-4833	
New Mexico	800-432-2080	800-678-1508 (in NM)
	505-827-7640	505-827-6060

State	Office of the Aging	Place for Consumer Complaints
New York	800-342-9871	800-771-7755
	518-474-4425	518-474-7121
		212-416-8345
North Carolina	919-733-3983	919-733-7741
North Dakota	800-755-8521	800-472-2600 (in ND)
	701-328-8910	701-328-3404
Ohio	614-466-7246	614-466-3376
Oklahoma	800-211-2116	405-521-4274
	405-521-2327	
Oregon	800-232-3020	503-378-4320
	503-945-5811	
Pennsylvania	717-783-1550	800-441-2555 (in PA)
		717-787-9707
Rhode Island	800-322-2880	800-852-7776
	401-277-2858	401-277-2104
South Carolina	803-737-7500	800-922-1594 (in SC)
		803-734-9452
South Dakota	605-773-3656	800-300-1986
		605-773-4400
Tennessee	615-741-2056	800-342-8385 (in TN)
		615-741-4737
Texas	512-424-6840	800-621-0508
		512-463-2070
Utah	801-487-3465	800-874-0904
		801-530-6645
Vermont	802-479-0531	802-828-3171
Virginia	800-552-4464	800-552-9963
	804-225-2271	804-786-2042
Washington	360-493-2500	800-551-4636 (in WA)
		206-464-6684
West Virginia	800-642-3671	800-368-8808 (in WV)
	304-558-3317	304-558-8986
Wisconsin	800-242-1060	800-422-7128
	608-266-2536	608-224-4952
		608-266-1852
Wyoming	800-442-2766	800-428-5799
	307-777-7986	307-777-7874

Glossary

Accelerated death benefits   Proceeds of life insurance paid to the insured by the insurance company on account of terminal or chronic illness.

Activities of daily living (ADLs)   Eating, toileting, dressing, transferring, bathing, and continence. ADLs are used to determine the level of a person's competence and need for assistance or nursing home care.

Administrator   The person who quarterbacks an estate in much the same way as an executor if a person dies without a will. An administrator is someone appointed by the probate court to handle this role.

Advance medical directive   Do-not-resuscitate order. See *Living will*.

Age Discrimination in Employment Act (ADEA)   A federal law that protects workers over 40 from age discrimination in the work place.

Agent   Person who acts in a fiduciary capacity on behalf of a principal. For purposes of a power of attorney, also called attorney-in-fact.

Alternate payee   Person who is assigned part of a worker's retirement benefits by a court order called a QDRO.

Americans with Disabilities Act (ADA)   A federal law requiring employers (other than small employers) to reasonably accommodate a worker's disabilities (like providing wheel chair access).

Anatomical gifts   Organ donations.

Ancillary probate   A second probate to handle real property located in a state other than the decedent's home state.

Annuitant   Person receiving annuity payments.

Annuitize   Time when you stop investment and start taking monthly payments under an annuity.

Annuity   Income payments generally for life (or joint lives of you and your spouse), but can be for a term of years. Commercial annuity is bought from an insurance company. Employee annuity is a pension from a company pension plan. Private annuity is an arrangement you make with family members (you sell property in exchange for a monthly income for life).

Annuity trust   Type of charitable remainder trust where income is a percentage (not less than 5%) of the value of the property placed in the trust.

Applicable exemption amount   The amount that every person can pass free of federal estate or gift taxes.

Attorney-in-fact   The agent acting under a power of attorney.

Averaging   Method used to figure the tax on a lump-sum distribution from a qualified retirement plan (5-year or 10-year averaging). Also called special averaging.

Basis   Tax term meaning your investment in an asset (cash, property, improvements) or other value fixed by the tax law.

Bear market   A period when the stock market is declining.

Beneficiary   Person who inherits property; person who has an interest in a trust.

Bequest   This is a gift of personal property made when someone dies. It's also called an inheritance.

Blind   For tax purposes, having a field of vision 20 degrees or less, or your sight with glasses or contacts isn't any better than 20/200.

Bull market   A period when the stock market is rising.

Business opportunity   Non-franchise arrangement in which you buy a concept for a product or service (but aren't restricted in the area in which you can operate).

Business plan   Report that says what your business is all about, how you intend to cover your expenses and make a profit, where you see the business in three to five years, and how you expect to get there.

Cafeteria plan   A plan that lets an employee choose between cash and at least one tax-free fringe benefit.

Capital   Money needed to start a business or make an investment.

Cash surrender value   The amount of equity you have in a life insurance policy (what you'd get if you cashed the policy in).

Charitable remainder trust   Gift of property via a trust where you keep the right to receive income (income interest) for your life and the charity gets the right to the property remaining in the trust when you die (remainder interest).

COBRA Continued medical insurance through your employer's group plan that must be offered when a person retires or terminates for reasons other than gross misconduct, although you pay 102% of the premium that the company would otherwise pay.

Codicil A document used to make an amendment or change to a will.

Consumer price index (CPI) The measurement figured by the federal government of an increase in the price of certain items.

Continuing care facility Senior retirement community that provides a housing unit, meals, cleaning, social activities, and some medical services (including long-term care); also called lifetime care facility.

Credit shelter trust Trust used by married couples to ensure that the estate of the first spouse to die makes full use of its applicable exemption amount. Also called a by-pass trust.

Debt Borrowing. Debt may be evidenced by a note or a bond (such as a Treasury bill showing the government is a debtor).

Deferred gift annuity Arrangement in which you donate property to a charity; charity agrees to pay you an income for life beginning at some specified future date.

Delayed retirement credit (DRC) Increased Social Security benefits for delaying the start of collecting benefits past normal retirement age (but not past 70).

Depreciation Tax deduction for the cost of property you own taken over its life (as set by the tax law).

Domicile The state in which you live, or if you have more than one home, the state to which you have the most attachment.

Do-not-resuscitate order (DNR) Notation in your medical records that you don't want CPR performed on you if your heart stops beating.

Dow Jones Industrial Average (DJIA) Group of 30 blue chip stocks (also called "the DOW").

Durable power of attorney Document authorizing one person (the agent) to handle the financial affairs of another person (the principal) even when the principal becomes incapacitated.

Early distribution penalty 10% tax penalty for taking money out of a retirement plan or IRA before age $59\frac{1}{2}$ (and no exception to the penalty applies). Also called a premature distribution penalty.

Early retirement Early termination of employment; also earliest age at which you can start taking benefits from a qualified retirement plan.

Elder law attorney   Lawyer specializing in legal issues of concern to seniors.

Equal Employment Opportunity Commission (EEOC)   A federal agency that handles charges of age discrimination and other work-related discriminatory practices.

Equity   Investment in a company that gives you an ownership interest. Equity can be evidenced by shares of stock (or shares in mutual funds). In the context of your home, what you'd pocket (after paying off the mortgage) if you sold your home today.

Errors and omissions insurance (E&O)   Insurance to pay claims resulting from your errors, omissions, and wrongful acts in the performance of your services.

Escrow   Arrangement in which a third party (usually a lawyer) holds money until certain conditions are met, at which time funds are paid out.

Estate   The extent of a person's property holdings (things a person has title to or an interest in). A *probate* estate is made up of assets subject to probate. A *gross* estate is a tax term meaning everything that a person has an interest in at the moment of death (whether the property passes under a will or via a will substitute).

Exclusions   For tax purposes, income that's not taxed. For insurance purposes, conditions that aren't covered by a policy.

Executor   A person named in a will (and approved by a probate court) to serve as quarterback of an estate (called a personal representative in some states).

Family limited partnerships (FLPs)   Partnership you set up to hold your investments and/or business; you keep a general partnership interest and give away limited partnership interests to your children or others at deep discounts for gift tax purposes.

Fiduciary   Person who acts in a position of trust on behalf of another person.

First-time home buying expenses   Exception to the 10% early distribution penalty for IRAs (including Roth IRAs). Expenses are those for you, your spouse, child, grandchild, or ancestor of you or your spouse paid within 120 days of buying, building, or reconstructing a principal residence (where such person hasn't owned a home within two years).

Flex time   Setting your own hours as long as you work a minimum number per week.

Franchise   Business arrangement that gives you the right to sell a product/service in a particular area. The company selling the concept is the franchisor; you are the franchisee.

Fringe benefits   Employer paid or subsidized benefits, such as health insurance, group term life insurance, and outplacement services; benefits that may be partially or wholly tax free.

Gain   Tax term meaning profit.

Gift tax Tax paid by the person making a gift if the value of the gift is over a certain amount.

Gift tax exclusion $10,000 each year per recipient ($20,000 if your spouse consents to the gift). Note: Exclusion amount is indexed for inflation beginning after 1998.

Grantor Person who sets up a trust. Also called the settlor.

Guardian A person who cares for a minor child (and his or her property) if there's no living parent.

Health care proxy Someone whom you appoint to make your medical decisions if you can't speak for yourself.

Heir This is a person who inherits property (also called a beneficiary).

Home equity conversion Arrangement for a homeowner to extract cash from a home while continuing to live in it. See *Reverse mortgage*; *Sale-leaseback*.

Income Wages, dividends, interest, and gains from the sale of stocks and other assets. For purposes of figuring the taxable portion of Social Security benefits, it includes tax-free interest and one half of Social Security benefits.

Independent contractor A self-employed person who contracts to provide work according to his or her own methods and who isn't under the control of the person/ business for whom the work is being performed.

Inflation A rise in the cost of goods and services that reduces the purchasing power of a dollar.

Internet Worldwide collection of computer networks that you can access with a computer, modem, telephone line, and an on-line service provider or Internet service provider (also called "the Net" and the "information superhighway").

Inter vivos trust A trust you set up during your lifetime (it can be revocable or irrevocable) as opposed to a trust you set up under the terms of a will.

Intestacy When a person dies without a will. In this case, his property will pass to relatives according to state law on intestate succession.

Job sharing Two or more workers splitting the responsibilities of one job.

Joint and survivor annuity Benefits are paid over the lives of a husband and wife (though benefits to a surviving spouse may be reduced when the first spouse dies). Preretirement joint and survivor annuity pays an amount to the spouse of a worker who dies before benefits commenced.

Joint tenancy with rights of survivorship   A joint ownership arrangement where the surviving joint tenant automatically inherits the entire property on the death of the other tenant.

Letter of instruction   A nonbinding statement to tell those you leave behind how you want certain items of property distributed (instead of specifically listing them in a will) and how you want your funeral handled.

Leveraging   Paying only part of the cost of property and financing the rest to be able to own the whole thing (example: making a down payment and using a mortgage to pay the rest of the property's cost).

Life expectancy   This is the average age that someone is expected to reach (not to be confused with life span, the top age a human being usually can live).

Living trust   Trust you set up while you're alive in which you keep the right to revoke or amend the trust. Also called a revocable inter vivos trust.

Living will   Written statement expressing a person's wishes regarding use of extraordinary medical procedures to prolong life.

Long-term care   Care for chronic conditions or old age provided in a nursing home or in home. Also called custodial care.

Long-term care policy   Insurance to pay for nursing home and/or in-home care for someone requiring assistance with ADLs or cognitive disability.

Margin   A means of borrowing against the value of your portfolio (generally referred to as "on margin").

Marital deduction   Unlimited deduction for federal estate and gift tax purposes for property passing to a surviving spouse.

Marketing   The overall process to get people to buy your product is called *marketing* (including market research to find out if there's any interest in what you're selling, advertising to inform the public about you, promotions to induce sales, and, finally, clinching the sale).

Married couple   For pension and Social Security benefit purposes, it means spouses married at least one year.

Medicaid A federal/state program providing health benefits to people who fit a definition of "indigency" that involves factors such as income, resources, and transfers of assets.

Medical durable power of attorney   See *Health care proxy*.

Medicare   A federal program primarily providing health benefits to people over 65.

Medicare+Choice   Beginning in 1999, a managed care alternative to traditional Medicare.

Medigap insurance   Private health insurance to supplement Medicare coverage.

Minimum distribution   The smallest amount required to be taken from a qualified plan or IRA generally starting at age 70$^1/_2$ to avoid a 50% tax penalty. Also called a required minimum distribution.

Net unrealized appreciation   The appreciation on employer securities (increase in value since their purchase) paid to you as part of a lump-sum distribution from a qualified plan.

Networking   Word-of-mouth communication about you, your work, or your company to promote something and to find out about other things.

Network marketing   Direct sales to consumers with distributors getting money from both direct sales and a percentage of the direct sales of other distributors they bring into the network (also called multi-level marketing).

Normal retirement age   For Social Security purposes, it's 65 (increasing gradually to 67). For company retirement plans, it's the age fixed in the plan (typically 65 but often lower).

Part-time   Working a job for fewer than a full number of hours per week (typically fewer than 35 hours per week).

Pay-on-death designation   Method to transfer ownership of securities and brokerage accounts by means of written instructions without going through probate.

Pension   Benefits from a company retirement plan paid in monthly amounts.

Pension upgrades   Credit given on early retirement for additional years of service to build up pension benefits of the retiree.

Pooled income fund   Like a charitable remainder trust, but instead of setting up a separate trust, your gift is "pooled" with property donated by other people, and your income interest is based on how well the fund performs each year.

Primary insurance amount (PIA)   Your full Social Security benefits taken at the normal retirement age (currently 65 but increasing to 67).

Principal   Capital investment. Also, trust fund (corpus). Also, person who signs a power of attorney giving authority for someone to act on his or her behalf in money matters.

Principal residence   Tax term meaning your main home (and not just a vacation home).

Probate   The process of settling a decedent's estate. The court that oversees the process is called a probate court or surrogate's court.

Qualified domestic relations order (QDRO)   Court order calling itself a QDRO that assigns part of a worker's retirement plan benefit to someone else (called an alternate payee).

Qualified domestic trust (QDOT)   Trust for the benefit of a spouse who isn't a U.S. citizen that allows a marital deduction to be taken for trust property.

Qualified terminable interest trust (QTIP)   Trust in which a surviving spouse gets a life interest, and value of trust is taxed on the surviving spouse's death; trust for which a marital deduction is allowed.

Real estate investment trust (REIT)   Like a mutual fund holding real estate instead of stocks. Mortgage REITs earn income from loans they hold on property; equity REITs produce rental income.

Recalculation method   Method of figuring required distributions from IRAs.

Required minimum distribution   See *Minimum distribution*.

Reverse mortgage   Type of mortgage in which a homeowner over 62 receives cash (all at once, monthly or on demand) based on a percent of the value of an unmortgaged home.

Revocable trust   Trust you set up while you're alive in which you keep the right to modify the terms of the trust or cancel it and get the property back.

Rider   Additional clause to an existing contract or insurance policy to cover a special item or event (usually an upgrade to an insurance policy); sometimes referred to as an endorsement.

Right of election   A spouse's right under state law to inherit a certain portion of a decedent's estate instead of taking what's given under the terms of the decedent's will.

Rollover   Transfer of retirement benefits or IRAs to other qualified plans or IRAs. May be a direct transfer (from plan to plan) or a distribution to you followed by a transfer to an IRA within 60 days of the distribution.

Sale-leaseback   Arrangement in which you sell your home (usually to your child) and immediately rent the home on a long-term basis; type of home equity conversion.

Seasonal work   Working full-time for part of the year (such as holiday time).

Second-to-die insurance   Life insurance that covers the lives of both spouses but pays off only when both spouses have died.

Self-proving affidavit   A document signed by witnesses to a will at the same time as they're doing the witnessing to attest to the fact that the person signing the will appears competent to make a will.

Simultaneous death clause   A clause in a will stipulating that if the testator dies in a common disaster with a beneficiary, one (or the other) is presumed to have outlived the other.

Small Business Administration (SBA)   A federal agency to help small business get started and grow; agency that sponsors loan programs.

Specific bequest   A gift under a will of a dollar amount or certain item to a particular person or charity.

Split gift   A gift during life by a married person in which the other spouse agrees to make the gift a joint one even though only one spouse's property is used.

Springing power of attorney   Power of attorney that becomes effective when a certain event happens (typically when the principal becomes incompetent).

Surviving widow(er)   A person whose spouse died in either of the two prior years *and* who has a dependent child.

Tax deferral   Postponement of income tax until some future time.

Tax waivers   Permission by state taxing authorities that title to property passing by operation of law can be changed before the state's death taxes have been paid.

Telecommuting   Working for a company full time from home.

Temporary work   Working on a nonpermanent basis; working through a temporary agency that places you on job assignments at different companies.

Tenancy in common   Ownership arrangement where each owner owns a percentage of the whole and can give away or bequeath that share at death.

Term certain method   Method of figuring minimum distributions from IRAs.

Testamentary trust   A trust created by a will that comes into effect after a person's death.

Testator   A person who makes a will.

Transfer at death   An arrangement available in some states to pass your brokerage account or securities automatically on your death to someone you designate and avoid probate.

Trust   A legal entity you set up by writing a trust agreement and transferring property to the name of the trust.

Trustee   A person (individual or institution) who manages a trust; a type of fiduciary.

Trust fund   Property transferred into a trust. Also called principal or corpus.

Turnkey business   Business that's ready to go into operation, with all materials, processes, and equity in place to produce a product or a service.

Undercapitalization   Not having enough cash to pay business expenses before the business becomes self-supporting.

Unified credit   A tax credit against the federal estate tax that operates to exempt a certain estate ($625,000 in 1998, increasing to $1 million by 2006).

Uniform Franchise Offering (UFO) Circular   A document that, under federal law, must be given to you if you're required to pay at least $500 within six months. The UFO discloses certain franchise and other business information.

Unitrust   Type of charitable remainder trust where income is based on a fixed percentage of the trust's value each year.

Vacation home   Second home used for less than an entire year.

Variance   A change or alteration of a zoning rule granted specifically for one person.

Vested benefits   Retirement benefits that, because you've worked for a certain length of time, cannot be taken away.

Veterans benefits   Federal benefits for persons who served in the military.

Viatical settlement   Arrangement where a third party buys a life insurance policy from a terminally or chronically ill person.

Web site   Address on the Internet; a home page is part of a Web site.

Will   A legal document used to distribute your property and appoint various fiduciaries.

Will alternatives (or substitutes)   Ways to pass your property without the need for a will (such as beneficiary designations in life insurance and retirement accounts, joint property ownership, and trusts).

Index

D

G - H

U - V

W